BUDGET BRITAIN

CW00363217

BY ANTONIA HEBBERT

Antonia Hebbert is an adventurous traveller around Britain, and having been the editor of many AA travel guides, including *Secret Britain*, is well qualified to write this Guide, which not only helps you to stretch your budget, but also introduces you to many unexpected facets of town and country.

PUBLISHED BY THE AUTOMOBILE ASSOCIATION
FANUM HOUSE, BASINGSTOKE, HAMPSHIRE RG21 2EA

WRITTEN BY ANTONIA HEBBERT

ADDITIONAL RESEARCH BY CHARLES HEBBERT, NIA WILLIAMS AND JANE BAINBRIDGE

EDITED, DESIGNED AND PRODUCED BY THE PUBLISHING DIVISION OF THE AUTOMOBILE ASSOCIATION. MAPS PREPARED BY THE CARTOGRAPHIC DEPARTMENT OF THE AUTOMOBILE ASSOCIATION

MAPS © THE AUTOMOBILE ASSOCIATION 1991

ILLUSTRATIONS: ALAN ROE

ILLUSTRATION PAGES 6 AND 7: GORDON LAWSON

COVER DESIGN: THE PAUL HAMPSON PARTNERSHIP

EVERY EFFORT IS MADE TO ENSURE ACCURACY, BUT THE PUBLISHERS DO NOT HOLD THEMSELVES RESPONSIBLE FOR ANY CONSEQUENCES THAT MAY ARISE FROM ERRORS OR OMISSIONS. WHILST THE CONTENTS ARE BELIEVED CORRECT AT THE TIME OF GOING TO PRESS, CHANGES MAY HAVE OCCURRED SINCE THAT TIME OR WILL OCCUR DURING THE CURRENCY OF THIS BOOK.

© THE AUTOMOBILE ASSOCIATION JANUARY 1992

ALL RIGHTS RESERVED. NO PART OF THE PUBLICATION MAY BE REPRODUCED, STORED IN A RETRIEVAL SYSTEM, OR TRANSMITTED IN ANY FORM OR BY ANY MEANS - ELECTRONIC, PHOTOCOPYING, RECORDING, OR OTHERWISE - UNLESS THE WRITTEN PERMISSION OF THE PUBLISHERS HAS BEEN OBTAINED BEFOREHAND.

PRINTED AND BOUND IN GREAT BRITAIN BY: BENHAM AND CO LTD, COLCHESTER.

A CIP CATALOGUE RECORD FOR THIS BOOK IS AVAILABLE FROM THE BRITISH LIBRARY.

PUBLISHED BY THE AUTOMOBILE ASSOCIATION, FANUM HOUSE, BASINGSTOKE, HAMPSHIRE RG21 2EA

CONTENTS

Our Budget Guide aims to help you enjoy your holiday in Britain without spending your money either wastefully or unsuspectingly. First read the Introduction thoroughly because the information given there is essential to your budgeting success, from travel and accommodation to shopping and moneysavers.

Each of the eight chapters that follow will help you plan a grand tour of the region, with a variety of outings both to well-known architectural and tourist attractions and also to relatively undiscovered places. Each chapter contains moneysaving tips appropriate to the region and comprehensive orientation sections containing accommodation addresses, places to eat, transport etc relating to the major

centres. In addition, each chapter has a map of the region and several outings maps highlighting places mentioned in the book.

For visitors from across the Atlantic we explain a selection of words and phrases which may cause confusion in spite of our common language.

Finally, at the end of the book you will find a comprehensive index of places, people and general subjects to help you find your way around the guide.

Please note all of the prices, opening times, travel information, etc was correct at the time of going to print, but this kind of information is always subject to change. We strongly advise that you double-check details before setting off for a day out.

Local flavour

Inland from Sidmouth, Ottery St Mary celebrates 5 November (Bonfire Night) with a huge bonfire followed by a wild race (the competitors carry burning barrels of tar). At any time of year it's an interesting unspoilt town.

BUDGET FOR A DAY

Train fare
Guided Walk   Free
Cathedral
Pallant House
Bus to Fishbourne
Roman Palace
Lunch
Afternoon tea

plus accommodation   £ 19.60

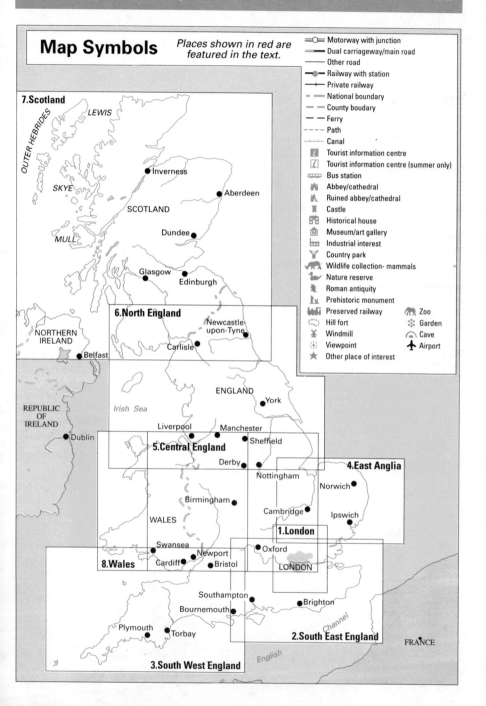

Map Symbols

Places shown in red are featured in the text.

- ═○═ Motorway with junction
- ══ Dual carriageway/main road
- ── Other road
- ─●─ Railway with station
- ─┼─ Private railway
- ─ ─ National boundary
- ── County boudary
- ── Ferry
- ─ ─ ─ Path
- ┴┴ Canal
- ⑂ Tourist information centre
- ⑂ Tourist information centre (summer only)
- Bus station
- Abbey/cathedral
- Ruined abbey/cathedral
- Castle
- Historical house
- Museum/art gallery
- Industrial interest
- Country park
- Wildlife collection- mammals
- Nature reserve
- Roman antiquity
- Prehistoric monument
- Preserved railway
- Hill fort
- Windmill
- Viewpoint
- Other place of interest
- Zoo
- Garden
- Cave
- Airport

7.Scotland

OUTER HEBRIDES

LEWIS

SKYE

MULL

SCOTLAND

Inverness

Aberdeen

Dundee

Glasgow

Edinburgh

6.North England

NORTHERN IRELAND

Belfast

Newcastle-upon-Tyne

Carlisle

ENGLAND

York

Irish Sea

REPUBLIC OF IRELAND

Dublin

Liverpool

Manchester

Sheffield

5.Central England

Derby

Nottingham

4.East Anglia

Norwich

Birmingham

Cambridge

Ipswich

WALES

Swansea

Newport

Cardiff

Bristol

8.Wales

Oxford

1.London

LONDON

Southampton

Bournemouth

Brighton

Plymouth

Torbay

2.South East England

FRANCE

English Channel

3.South West England

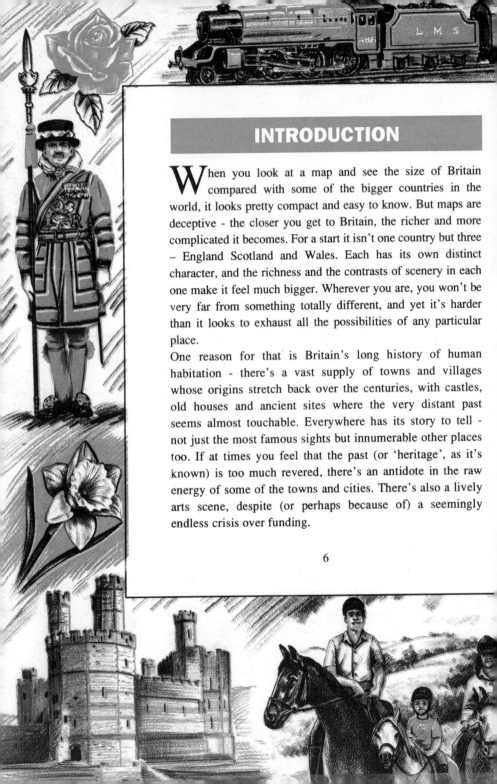

INTRODUCTION

When you look at a map and see the size of Britain compared with some of the bigger countries in the world, it looks pretty compact and easy to know. But maps are deceptive - the closer you get to Britain, the richer and more complicated it becomes. For a start it isn't one country but three – England Scotland and Wales. Each has its own distinct character, and the richness and the contrasts of scenery in each one make it feel much bigger. Wherever you are, you won't be very far from something totally different, and yet it's harder than it looks to exhaust all the possibilities of any particular place.

One reason for that is Britain's long history of human habitation - there's a vast supply of towns and villages whose origins stretch back over the centuries, with castles, old houses and ancient sites where the very distant past seems almost touchable. Everywhere has its story to tell - not just the most famous sights but innumerable other places too. If at times you feel that the past (or 'heritage', as it's known) is too much revered, there's an antidote in the raw energy of some of the towns and cities. There's also a lively arts scene, despite (or perhaps because of) a seemingly endless crisis over funding.

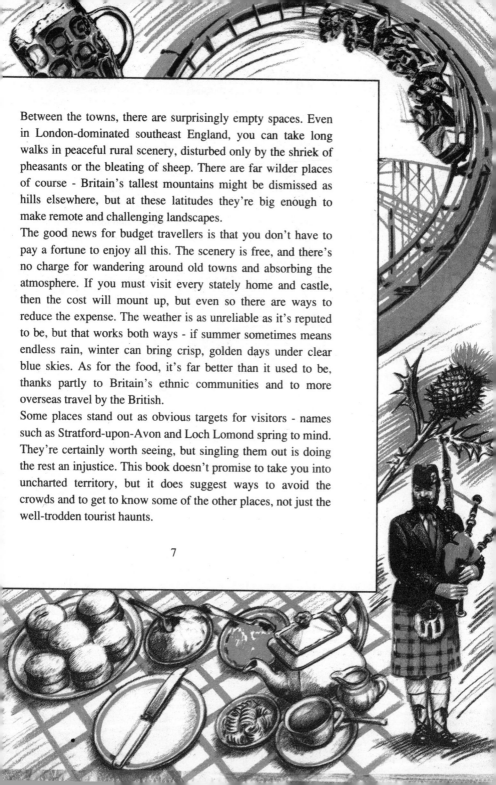

Between the towns, there are surprisingly empty spaces. Even in London-dominated southeast England, you can take long walks in peaceful rural scenery, disturbed only by the shriek of pheasants or the bleating of sheep. There are far wilder places of course - Britain's tallest mountains might be dismissed as hills elsewhere, but at these latitudes they're big enough to make remote and challenging landscapes.

The good news for budget travellers is that you don't have to pay a fortune to enjoy all this. The scenery is free, and there's no charge for wandering around old towns and absorbing the atmosphere. If you must visit every stately home and castle, then the cost will mount up, but even so there are ways to reduce the expense. The weather is as unreliable as it's reputed to be, but that works both ways - if summer sometimes means endless rain, winter can bring crisp, golden days under clear blue skies. As for the food, it's far better than it used to be, thanks partly to Britain's ethnic communities and to more overseas travel by the British.

Some places stand out as obvious targets for visitors - names such as Stratford-upon-Avon and Loch Lomond spring to mind. They're certainly worth seeing, but singling them out is doing the rest an injustice. This book doesn't promise to take you into uncharted territory, but it does suggest ways to avoid the crowds and to get to know some of the other places, not just the well-trodden tourist haunts.

7

GETTING TO BRITAIN

VISAS AND CUSTOMS

Citizens of the United States and Canada need valid passports to enter Britain, but not visas (except US citizens who intend to stay for more than six months). Right of entry does not include a right to work, so be prepared to prove that you are financially independent.

For further information about passports, contact: US – Washington Passport Agency, Department of State, 1425 K St NW, Washington DC 20522-1705; Canada – Bureau of Passports, External Affairs, Ottawa K1A 0G3.

BY AIR

Air services to Britain are good. Most flights arrive at London's Heathrow and Gatwick airports. The greatest choice of carriers and fares is on the London routes, so even if your final destination is outside the southeast of England, compare the prices you can get with air fares to London.

Fares and flight availability vary significantly, especially in the busy summer period. As a rule, the cheaper the ticket, the less flexibility you have. Fare prices vary widely, depending on factors such as season, the day of the week on which you travel, world oil prices, etc. It's also worthwhile asking several different travel agents – you will often be given different prices for the same or similar services.

Major carriers also offer less expensive APEX (Advanced Purchase Excursion) fares which have to be bought two to four weeks in advance and the length of stay is restricted to between seven days and three months.

Most major carriers also offer standby tickets which are good value, but you can't reserve a seat, and your flight is only confirmed (or not) a short time before the plane leaves. Some airlines issue predictions of seat availability on flights.

Charter flights are very competitively priced, but this has to be balanced against the likelihood of cancellation and delays. Check carefully on the regulations about changing travel arrangements and cancellation refunds.

Consolidators, fare-brokers and travel clubs (which you may have to join for an annual membership fee) offer discounted tickets for transatlantic flights. But don't be blinded by the knock-down prices: make sure you are equipped with full information.

Gatwick　(telephone 0293 28822 or 081 668 4211) is south of London with an excellent rail link to London's Victoria train station, which is connected to the other major London railway stations by the underground railway (tube) system. During the day the service operates every 15 minutes and takes 30 minutes; at night the service is hourly and takes 35 to 45 minutes. Coach services also connect the airport to Victoria coach station (a short distance from the railway station), and connecting coach services run to destinations throughout the country. The airport is connected to the London/Brighton road (M23) and is close to the M25 London orbital motorway, which is linked into the national motorway network.

Heathrow　(telephone 081-759 4321) is Britain's busiest airport. It's located on the western edge of London just off the M4 motorway (which links London to Wales and the west), close to the M4/M25 junction. The London Underground connects the airport to the city centre and the major London railway stations – it takes about 50 minutes to Piccadilly Circus. Heathrow does not have an overground railway station but it is connected to main line British Rail stations at Reading and Woking by rail-air coach links. There is an express coach link to central London, and National Express coaches run from the airport to destinations all over Britain.

Heathrow and Gatwick are connected by the non-stop Speedlink coach service – a journey time of about 60 minutes.

Manchester　(telephone 061-489 3000) is about 10 miles south of the city. There is an express coach (number 757) to the city centre, which takes about 20 minutes. Heald Green and Wilmslow railway stations are two and four miles away respectively. They are connected to the airport by local bus services. National Express coaches run from the airport throughout the country, and motorists have direct access to the M56 for Manchester city centre and the national motorway system.

Glasgow (telephone 041-887 1111) is 10 miles from the city centre. An express coach service runs to the city every half hour and takes 20 minutes. The nearest British Rail station is Paisley Gilmour Street, which is two miles from the airport. The airport is close to the M8 motorway, which can be joined at junction 29.

Prestwick (telephone 0292 79822) is 30 miles south of Glasgow. There is direct access from Prestwick railway station, a mile from the airport. A coach service (Glasgow to Ayr) also connects the airport to the city; the journey takes about 45 minutes and coaches run every half hour at busy periods.

BY FERRY

There is a huge range of ferry services coming to Britain from the rest of Europe.

The shortest crossings are from France: Calais and Boulogne to Dover and Folkestone (under two hours). There are also crossings from Dunkirk to Ramsgate, Dieppe to Newhaven, Le Havre, Caen, Cherbourg and St Malo to Portsmouth and Roscoff to Plymouth (6½ hours).

From Belgium, ferry services run from Oostende and Zeebrugge to Dover, Felixstowe and Hull. Services from the Netherlands run from Hoek van Holland to Harwich, from Rotterdam to Hull and from Vlissingen to Sheerness.

There are direct ferry services from Denmark, Spain, Scandinavia and Ireland.

WEATHER AND WHEN TO GO

As a rule Britain's weather is mild and damp, but there are occasional extremes. In 1988 and 1989 hurricane force winds tore through the south of the country, and in 1990 summer temperatures rivalled the Mediterranean.

Under the influence of the Atlantic Gulf Stream, the west of the country tends to be wetter and milder than the east. The south tends to be sunnier, but the higher latitudes of the north, especially Scotland, give longer summer days (though less daylight in winter). In the high hills and mountains of Wales, northern England and Scotland conditions can differ radically from those at lower levels. These exposed uplands have extremely high rainfall, and are prone to mist, fog and gales.

Not surprisingly, the changing weather is closely reported. Weather bulletins frequently follow news slots on radio and television and newspapers publish detailed forecasts. There is also a national telephone information service, Weather Call (071-975 9000).

Britain is geared up for visitors during the six months from April to October, outside which attractions, accommodation and transport are likely to be restricted in their opening hours and availability. The busiest period is July and August, when the British take their holidays.

On the eight statutory holidays – called bank holidays – banks, offices, factories and shops close and some services are restricted. On Christmas Day and Boxing Day (the day after Christmas), practically everything shuts down. There are plenty of local festivals and countless carnivals and celebrations enliven the scene throughout the year.

GETTING ABOUT

BY TRAIN

Britain's extensive rail network can provide one of the best ways to see the country. Train journeys can be much more than a means of getting to a destination; they can also provide an opportunity to marvel at the feats of the Victorian railway engineers, besides giving some of the best views.

The rail network is run by British Rail, called Scotrail in Scotland and Network South East in southeast England. The fastest long-distance journeys are the InterCity services. Be aware that the InterCity network is closed on Christmas Day and there is a restricted service on other bank holidays. Trains usually pull two classes of carriage. Standard class ranges from tatty to very comfortable on main-line trains and major InterCity services. First class travel is more expensive, but on Saturday, Sunday and bank holidays you can get your standard Inter City ticket upgraded to first class by paying a £3 supplement, provided first class seats are available. The supplement can be paid when you buy your ticket or on the train.

The fares schedule seems at first to be incredibly complicated, but provided you don't travel in peak hours or on busy days you can use the fares system to travel comfortably and save money too. (Also see *Moneysavers*). Broadly speaking, the expensive times to travel are early mornings from Monday to Thursday, all day Friday, and in the periods leading up to major public holidays.

Ticket prices are in three colour bands: red (open returns) for expensive peak hour services; white (saver) for busy service times; and blue (super saver), when the cheapest travel is available. For return journeys (that is, out and back), only open returns can be used on all services; the ticket office will provide details of restrictions on saver and super saver tickets.

Children between the ages of five and 15 travel at half the adult fare, and under fives travel free.

Railcard holders get further discounts on

saver and super saver tickets, usually a quarter or a third off. Different railcards are available for people with disabilities, young people (16- to 23-year-olds), certain UK students over 23, families and senior citizens (over 60). Railcards can be obtained from major railway stations and British Rail appointed travel agents.

If you have to travel at a busy time, your best move is to reserve a seat. Seat reservations usually cost £1 for up to four people travelling together; on certain services where reservations are compulsory they are free. Reservations can be made until two hours before departure or, for some early morning trains, the evening before, either when you buy your ticket, or by telephone.

Some overnight services have sleeper berths for long-distance routes, for which a sleeper supplement is payable on top of the rail fare. Sleepers can be booked at British Rail stations and Travel Centres and at appointed travel agents; book as far ahead as possible.

Most InterCity trains have a buffet or restaurant car. Smaller trains, especially on long provincial routes, may have a trolley serving snacks and drinks. Check the train timetable or announcement panel for details. Most large stations also have refreshment facilities – look out for 'Travellers Fare' – but look out for the prices too.

BY COACH AND BUS

National Express, Scottish City Link and Caledonian Express together provide the country's most comprehensive coach network. Coaches don't usually have personal facilities on board; they make two-hourly refreshment and lavatory stops. However, some major routes offer a faster and more comfortable service with reclining seats, on-board lavatory and washrooms and usually light refreshments.

Coach tickets can be bought on the day of travel but it's a good idea to buy them in advance from National Express/Caledonian Express agencies (telephone 021-456 1122), most bus company offices, and some travel agents and local shops.

If you want to guarantee yourself a place on a particular coach – especially at busy times and

The coach network links Britain's major towns.

on overnight services – get an 'Assured Reservation', which must be made ahead of your day of travel and costs £1.20 per ticket (several people may travel on the same ticket).

Fares depend on when and where you want to travel. The cheaper the ticket, the more restrictions are likely to apply. Singles, day returns and economy return fares (for travel on any day, except Fridays and Saturdays in July and August), are usually the same price; return fares for a specific length of time usually cost one third more.

From October to April 'Boomerang' fares are offered. They are 10 per cent cheaper than the economy returns but are only available on outward and return journeys made on Tuesday, Wednesday or Saturday.

Discounts are available for children aged five to 15 and for people over 60. Children under five not occupying a seat travel free. There are also discount cards for young people and visitors to Britain (see information on the Britexpress card in *Moneysavers*).

Further information about National Express/Caledonian Express services can be obtained from the companies' local agents – details are in local telephone directories. There is also a main London enquiry number, telephone 071-730 0202.

Local buses offer useful routes and can give a rich taste of local life, but finding out about them may be a struggle. Timetables and routes can be changed at a few weeks notice, bus stops may be hard to find, and several poorly co-ordinated bus companies may serve the same town. There *may* be a bus office or a local authority information office with details of all companies, but the most useful first sources of help are tourist information centres.

Important The bus travel details in this book are as up to date as possible, but they are liable to change at short notice. Always check locally, and check that the information you are given is up to date.

BY CAR

When driving in Britain you must hold a current driving licence. United States and Canadian driver's licences are valid, but it's a good idea to get an International Driving Permit as well before coming to Britain.

All traffic travels on the left side of the road, and all direction and speed signs are in miles. The national speed limit for passenger cars is 60mph, except on dual carriageways and motorways, where it is 70mph. In built-up areas such as towns and villages the speed limit usually falls to 30mph, but watch out for any signs which override the usual limits.

Seat belts are compulsory for the driver and front seat passengers. It is against the law to drive with more than the 80 milligrams of alcohol in 100 millilitres of blood – *the best possible advice is don't drink and drive.*

If you haven't driven in Britain before the best guide to the rules of the road, road signs and people's driving habits is the *Highway Code*, published by Her Majesty's Stationery Office (HMSO), which you can get from any good newsagent or bookshop.

With the exception of a few major bridges and tunnels there are no toll roads on the national road network. Motorways – 'M' roads – are fast roads (dual or triple carriageways) for fast traffic. 'A' roads – trunk roads – cover most of the country, and vary from motorway-type dual carriageways to narrow winding country roads. 'B' roads are minor roads. National and local radio stations have regular travel bulletins which give up to the minute traffic and weather reports. The AA provides a recorded telephone information service, Roadwatch, which can advise you about possible delays. This information is also available on the televised information pages of 'Oracle'.

Unleaded as well as leaded petrol is widely available, and an environmental petrol tax means that unleaded is always cheaper. Petrol is usually sold by the gallon, but petrol stations are increasingly displaying the price in litres. Unleaded petrol has a minimum octane rating of 95, with super octane available from some stations with a rating of around 98. The most widely available leaded petrol is 'four-star', which has a minimum octane rating of 97. Petrol stations are usually self-service and tend to be situated in and around towns and on the motorways and major roads. Motorway service stations and some service stations on busy major roads and in large towns open round the clock, or at least late into the night.

CAR HIRE

Hiring a car is usually quite straightforward, but you'll need a valid driver's licence, enough money for a deposit and, in some cases, you must be 21 or over. Hire conditions are broadly similar, whichever company you use. Be sure, though, before signing any agreements to check the hire conditions carefully and determine what your own responsibilities are. Hire charges usually include insurance cover, breakdown service membership and free mileage.

It's useful to remember that many national companies offer a discounted tourist hire rate to anyone booking a hire car in the United States before coming to Britain. For periods of more than 21 days, it could be more economical to lease a car. Three companies in the USA which can advise you on leasing a British car are: Kemwell, 106 Calvert Street, Harrison, New York, telephone 800 678 0678; Europe by Car, 1 Rockerfeller Plaza, New York, telephone 212 245 1713 and Auto Europe, PO Box 1097, Camden, Maine, telephone 800 223 5555.

BY BICYCLE

Cycling is a great way to explore the scenery, and bicycles can be hired throughout Britain. Some cycle hire shops just supply a bicycle and lock; others supply routes, helmets and other accessories. The firms listed in this book have not been checked for quality. It is up to you to check the state of the bicycle. You should also check the terms of the hire agreement. A typical shop will ask for a deposit of £50, and perhaps some security such as a passport or credit card.

If the hire fee includes insurance, it will be for the bicycle rather than for you. Check that your own insurance gives adequate third-party and injury cover. Long-term visitors and residents might consider one of the special insurance schemes for cyclists. The Cyclists' Touring Club offers insurance schemes to members, plus cycle hire lists, maps and general advice; contact them at Cotterell House, 69 Meadrow, Godalming, Surrey GU7 3HS, telephone 0486 87217.

Cyclists as road users have to follow the rules of the road. If you must cycle at night, make yourself as visible as possible with luminous gear and reflectors. Front and rear lighting is required by law. Protective cycle helmets are always a good idea, especially if you intend to cycle in London. Britain has an increasing number of cycle routes, in towns and outside them. Some are mentioned in this book, but tourist information centres and cycle shops may have details of others.

Never leave lights or other easily removable things on your bicycle. Always leave your bike locked to something immoveable, but park it neatly — bicycles carelessly attached to street furniture are a major problem for blind people and others.

A popular touring combination is rail and bicycle (coaches don't take cycles). Bicycles can be carried free of charge on many trains, but some routes have restrictions and charges. For full details see the British Rail leaflet, *The Rail Traveller's Guide to Biking by Train*

ACCOMMODATION

There is no official system of classification of accommodation in Britain, but the star rating system devised by the motoring organisations is the most widely recognised. The AA classifies hotels from one to five stars to give an indication of the facilities they offer, with a percentage score for quality within that classification. Those with the highest levels of accommodation, food and service are awarded Red Stars. In 1987 the tourist boards in England, Wales and Scotland established a grading system of one to five crowns and these are awarded to many different kinds of accommodation, from hotels to holiday homes. All of the schemes you may come across are very complex if looked at in detail, but the general principal is the greater the number of symbols, the higher the level of facilities and/or quality. The schemes are all voluntary, so the absence of rating does not necessarily mean low standards.

Hotels are different from guesthouses because they provide more facilities, such as a full meal service and a bar. If possible, when you want a room, ask to look at it before you agree to take it. The terms on which you take a room vary: bed and breakfast is just what it says (usually a full 'British' breakfast, but sometimes a light Continental breakfast of coffee and rolls); 'half board' adds one main meal to the bed and breakfast – usually dinner, but on Sundays a traditional lunch might be the main meal; 'full board' includes the accommodation plus breakfast, lunch and dinner.

Bed and breakfast places (look out for B&B signs)are the mainstay of holiday accommodation in Britain. Mainly family homes and farmhouses, they offer a good insight

Bed and breakfast is a popular budget option.

into the way of life of the area you are visiting. Don't expect en suite bathrooms – although some have them – but they are usually excellent value (especially outside London) and have a personal touch usually missing in hotels.

Self catering holiday homes are available throughout the country. They are usually available for weekly periods, although some will do weekends in the low season. The tourist boards produce lists, and there are a number of companies which act as agents for large numbers of properties – look out for advertisements in national newspapers and magazines.

Many British universities provide rooms in halls of residence to paying guests outside term time: The British Universities Accommodation Consortium, University Park, Nottingham, telephone 0602 504571. The other possibility is the network of youth hostels – despite the name, there is no age limit – and they are run by the Youth Hostel Association, Trevelyan House, 8 St Stephen's Hill, St Albans, Hertfordshire, telephone 0727 55215. Hostels are inexpensive and of a good, if basic, general standard, usually with facilities to cook for yourself.

Another option to save money is to do a holiday house exchange. There are plenty of house exchange agencies which offer services ranging from assessing your personal requirements to including your details in a directory. In the USA contact Global Home Exchange, PO Box 2015, South Burlington, Vermont 05401 2015, telephone 802 985 3825 or Worldwide Home Exchange, 6609 Quincy Street, Philadelphia, Pensylvania 19119.

EATING OUT

For years Britain has suffered from a reputation for indifferent cuisine. Nowadays a reasonable standard can be found in most places, but the true glories of traditional British food are breakfast, afternoon tea and Sunday lunch.

A full breakfast is a three course meal: fruit juice or cereal, fried bacon, eggs, sausages, mushrooms and tomatoes, followed by toast and marmalade, all washed down with plenty of tea or coffee. This is one of the joys of bed and

breakfast (see *Accommodation*), and there are plenty of variations on the theme. Porridge (served with salt in Scotland and sugar in Wales and England) often replaces the cereal in the winter months, and kippers (smoked fish) can also be on the menu; most places offer some degree of choice.

Afternoon tea is as much a social event, as a refreshment, and is very much a design-it-yourself affair: it can be a small snack or something approaching an evening meal. In the best tea shops you might find a choice of sandwiches, toast, crumpets, savoury scones or bread and butter, plus cakes, tea breads and fruit loaves – look out for *bara brith* (currant bread) in Wales and lardy cake in Wiltshire – or scones, plain or fruit, served with butter and jam. A regional variation of tea-time fare is the cream tea. The West Country is the home of this indulgence: scones, jam and lashings of thick clotted cream, but it is served in teashops all over the country.

High tea is really a full meal – mainly found in northern parts and Wales – and consists of substantial savoury dishes plus the cakes and trimmings of an afternoon tea.

Sunday lunch epitomises the traditional British approach to a main meal: 'roast meat and two veg'. Roast beef is traditionally served with Yorkshire pudding, a savoury batter pudding which soaks up the meat stock or gravy. Many restaurants and pubs offer full Sunday lunches at reasonable prices and 'carvery' restaurants offer similar fare on any day of the week, sometimes on a lavish scale.

Seaside towns and suburbs are good places to find traditional fish and chip shops, which range from cramped takeaway counters to full-scale restaurants. The range of quality is broad, too – those that get their fish straight from the quay are the ones to seek out. If you pick a good 'chippy', this can be one of the most nutritious budget meals around.

Despite the growth of chain restaurants with standardised menus, British food benefits from a wide variety of regional and international influences. Scottish specialities such as haggis are well known; in Wales look out for the *Blas ar Gymru* (A Taste of Wales) sign in restaurants. Yorkshire pudding, Cornish pasties and Lancashire hotpot are available throughout the country, but local restaurants, frequently with justification, claim to make the most authentic versions.

European food is a long-established option, but in the last few decades there has been an explosion in choice. The real bargain in exotic eating is Indian food. Outside the Indian sub-continent, Britain probably has some of the finest Indian restaurants in the world, particularly in Asian areas of large cities such as Bradford, Birmingham, Leicester and London.

Another trend has been the demand for organically grown food and meat-free menus. Wholefood and vegetarian restaurants have flourished throughout Britain. Over half the listings in the Vegetarian Society's worldwide guide are in Britain, and most restaurants and cafés now offer vegetarian alternatives to their meat dishes.

RESTAURANTS

Restaurants usually have a choice of menus. The table d'hôte or set menu offers a restricted choice of popular dishes making up a three-course meal, including a starter and a pudding. If you want a full meal set menus are generally the best value, especially for Sunday lunch. The à la carte menu offers the full range of dishes, individually priced. For a full meal à la carte tends to be more expensive, but if you only want one or two courses it could be your best buy.

Menus are usually posted outside restaurants, which are required by law to show their prices inclusive of tax (Value Added Tax at 17½ per cent). Before ordering, check for any extras that will be added to the bill such as a cover charge. If you are satisfied with the service you have received it is the usual practice to leave a tip of 10 to 15 per cent of the total bill, but before tipping check the bill and make sure that service hasn't already been added.

PUBS

The pub (public house) is a focus of British social life. In Scotland, hotels sometimes serve the same purpose. People go there to eat, meet friends, compete in quiz matches and listen to live music while they have a drink. Most pubs have two or more bars; a no-nonsense, no-frills service is found in the 'public bars'; 'lounge bars' are quieter and plusher, but what is gained in comfort is often lost in atmosphere.

Pubs are indelibly linked with beer, though in reality many pub-goers drink spirits, wines,

The ploughman's lunch is a traditional pub meal.

Some pubs have a sideline in hot lunches and/or evening meals and sometimes provide first-class home-made food although you may find that the food is limited to sandwiches and salads. Many pubs have now taken to selling coffee, too. The buildings themselves can be a prime attraction: half-timbered old inns are still familiar features in country towns and villages.

No one under 18 can be served alcoholic drinks. Children under the age of 14 are not allowed in pub bars, but more and more pubs are introducing family rooms where children are allowed in, and many have gardens with tables for the whole family to enjoy.

Pubs can be open from 11am to 11pm Monday to Saturday, and lunchtime and evening on Sunday. Many pubs close on weekday afternoons, though – much depends on the amount of trade they might expect – and those that stay open may serve teas. Ten minutes before closing, 'time' is called to give patrons a chance to drink up.

and soft drinks. Some pubs also offer cocktails. The beer is significant because it divides pubs into two types. Tied houses are tied to a specific brewery; free houses are privately owned and offer a wider range of brands – usually a better bet for 'real ales', made in the traditional way.

Beer is served in pints and half-pints. No one asks for 'beer' – it's usually 'lager' or 'bitter'. Lager is generally the lightest in colour, fizzy and cold. It's available on draught (drawn from a cask or keg), but imported bottled lagers are widely sold. 'Bitter' is sold on draught. It's darker with less froth, and gets its bitter flavour from hops. It may be called 'special', 'export' or 'best', but ask for 'half a bitter, please,' and you'll be understood. Pale ale and light ale are bottled bitters. 'Mild' (not always available) is sold on draught, and is sweeter. 'Stout' is very dark and rich – most people know it as Guinness, because that's by far the commonest brand.

Local flavour

Pub etiquette requires you to always go to the bar to buy your drinks, and always pay straight away. Never tip bar staff. If you want to show your appreciation offer your barmaid or barman a drink. If someone buys you a drink, be sure to reciprocate.

SIGHTSEEING

Treasures from all over the world are collected in Britain's museums and galleries. But Britain's own treasures – prehistoric monuments, Roman remains, medieval castles and cathedrals, superb stately homes and engaging town and city architecture – are also world class. The most humble-looking parish churches can be fascinating buildings, with histories stretching back over 1,000 years.

The national museums in London, Edinburgh and Cardiff are musts for any visitor. But there are some excellent collections beyond the well trodden routes that deserve close investigation:

the Burrell collection in Glasgow, Liverpool's Walker Art Gallery, the Northern Tate, and the Lady Lever Gallery (in Port Sunlight, near Liverpool), Birmingham's City Museum and Art Gallery, Cambridge's Fitzwilliam Museum and Oxford's Ashmolian Museum.

The national collections in London and elsewhere are run by public authorities and are generally open 9.30am to 5.30pm Monday to Saturday and Sunday afternoon. They usually open on bank holidays, but not on the major holidays – Christmas Day, Boxing Day and New Year's Day.

Other museums and galleries are run by local councils, independent bodies, private companies and individuals. The range and eccentricities of these collections are frequently reflected in opening days and times. If you want to see a particular collection, it's always a good idea to telephone and check the opening times.

Prehistoric monuments are scattered throughout Britain. A few of them, most notably Stonehenge, near Salisbury in Wiltshire, have restricted access and opening hours and charge for admission. Most monuments – standing stones, hill forts, ancient villages and paths – are open at all reasonable times and entrance is free.

The most spectacular remnant of Roman Britain is Hadrian's Wall, which runs across the north of England. Other sites you can visit include towns and garrisons (as at Caerleon and Wroxeter), the remains of villas (such as Fishbourne and Chedworth) and some excellent museums, like the Corinium Museum in Cirencester. Most sites charge an entrance fee; opening times vary greatly.

Britain's castles range from grassed over mounds and moats to spectacular ruins and fortresses converted over the centuries into rambling family homes. Admission charges and opening times vary.

There's usually a charge for visiting the ruins of medieval abbeys of Britain. Cathedrals don't usually charge visitors – but most suggest a 'voluntary donation' of about £2 towards the upkeep of the building. They may also charge a fee for the use of a camera and there may be special exhibitions for which admission is charged. These buildings are still places of worship, and you should heed notices asking visitors to respect the peace and calm of the building. There is rarely any charge for visiting parish churches, but you're invited to put a contribution in the donations box. Vandalism and theft means that some churches are kept locked when there is no service, but churches of special interest usually have a notice telling you where to get the key.

Stately homes attract people for their architecture and contents, associations with famous people or simply for a glimpse into the life of another age. Many houses also have magnificent gardens, which may be more of an attraction than the house (Stourhead and Sissinghurst for instance). A lot of houses are still family homes, so don't expect to be able to wander around the whole of the property. Again, opening times vary.

The National Trust is Britain's premier conservation organisation, and it has over 200 buildings and 100 gardens open to the public. Trust members enjoy free entry to properties; non-members pay an admission charge (half price for children under 17 with an adult, free for under fives), but see *Moneysavers*. Check with properties for specific opening times. Some are only open half the week; most close in winter. The National Trust for Scotland is a separate organisation (both bodies, though, allow the other's members free entry to their properties).

The National Trust is also Britain's largest private landowner, protecting wild landscapes and beauty spots for public enjoyment. Subject to the needs of farming and forestry, countryside owned by the National Trust is open all year round. There are no admission charges, although there may be a parking charge.

There are 10 national parks in Britain: Dartmoor, Exmoor, Brecon Beacons, Pembroke Coast, Snowdonia, Peak District, Yorkshire Dales, North Yorkshire Moors and the Lake District (other areas recently suggested for park status include the Cambrian Mountains in Wales and the New Forest in southern England). The parks cover hundreds of square miles of areas of spectacular natural beauty, including towns and villages, and are protected from development by National Park Authorities. Detailed information about the parks can be found within the following chapters.

There are thousands of beaches along Britain's 7,000-mile coastline. As well as the popular holiday resorts – Blackpool, Bournemouth and Great Yarmouth are among the best known – lovely beaches can be found in hidden coves and along broad stretches of shoreline.

Britain's premier beaches are those which are accepted into the European Blue Flag scheme, run by the Foundation for Environmental Education in Europe. Among the requirements which enable resorts to fly the distinctive blue flag, beaches must have a high standard of water cleanliness, there must be good facilities (toilets, first aid, life-saving equipment, etc) and the beaches must be cleaned daily during the busy season.

Be sure to take care when swimming from any beach – tidal and estuary currents can be very strong and would cause difficulties for even the most experienced swimmer.

MAPS

Britain is reputedly the best-mapped country in the world. This is largely the result of the country's official mapping organisation – the Ordnance Survey (OS). Good maps giving a scale of about four miles to one inch are fairly widely available from several sources (including the AA's annually updated *Big Road Atlas of Britain*).

But for walking or more detailed exploration of an area, the OS Landranger series maps (scale: one mile to 1¼ inches) are ideal. Each Landranger map covers an area of 25 square miles, and 204 Landranger maps cover Britain and its islands. They include information such

as camp sites, picnic areas, etc, as well as public footpaths and bridleways. These maps are available from bookshops and newsagents – especially within the areas they cover, price £3.70 each. The Ordnance Survey also publishes a series of Outdoor Leisure maps, produced to the same scale as the Landranger series, for some of the more popular leisure and recreation areas in the country. Each covers an area of about 195 square miles.

For more information or details of the OS mail order service, contact the Ordnance Survey, Romsey Road, Southampton SO9 4DH; telephone 0703 792763.

SHOPPING

Napoleon called Britain a nation of shopkeepers. Today it's certainly a nation of shoppers. Shopping precincts and shopping malls are everywhere, with the result that many British town centres look the same. You can still find the individual and eccentric shop alongside the large chain stores though. Oxford Street in London, the Bull Ring in Birmingham and Sauchiehall Street in Glasgow are shopping honeypots. These three cities are the largest shopping centres in Britain, and they're also typical of the country's high streets – busy at the best of times, they're particularly congested in the month before Christmas and during the January sales.

Each region has its traditional department stores – now largely owned by major companies, but they still pride themselves on their origins as family stores.

Fashion shops are everywhere. Second-hand clothes and bric-a-brac are sold at high street charity shops. They're worth a browse and are especially popular with young people looking for budget or eccentric clothing. Oxfam is the most prominent – as well as second-hand goods

Markets are good for fresh produce and bargains.

it sells handicrafts produced all over the world.

Markets are best for local colour, and they offer some terrific bargains. But keep in mind the legal phrase 'caveat emptor' – buyer beware. If you know what you're looking for you can find plenty of good buys, but the unsuspecting customer may end up with shoddy goods.

Each town has its own market day or days. In country towns and villages especially, the market is more than just somewhere to shop: it's also a place to meet friends and catch up on the local news.

Shopping hours are generally 9am to 5.30pm Monday to Saturday (newsagents usually open much earlier). As as a rule supermarkets and corner grocery shops open earlier and close later than other shops. Many large shopping towns operate late-night shopping on at least one evening a week – usually until 7.30pm or 8pm. Outside the cities and larger towns, many places have a half-day closing during the week, when the shops shut for the day at noon.

Sunday shopping laws are complicated and controversial. Their enforcement depends on the attitude of the local government council, so while in one area you may only find the newsagent and corner shop selling groceries open, a high street two or three miles away may be as busy as any other shopping day.

Traditionally there are two seasons for sales – New Year, running from the end of December to February, and summer, any time in June, July or August. Look out for the last few days of a sale when many stores reduce the prices even further. Stores have begun to break ranks over these sales periods – there's always a sale on somewhere. Sales goods should be of the shop's usual quality, but sold at a discount. 'Seconds' are different – they don't meet the required standard but can still be very good buys.

Tax-free shopping   Practically all goods and services sold in Britain are subject to Value Added Tax – a sales tax of 17½ per cent. The major exceptions are groceries, books and newspapers, and children's clothes. In ordinary retail shops, the price marked will always include the VAT. Visitors from overseas can claim back the Value Added Tax paid for some items bought in Britain through the the Retail Export Scheme. This moneysaver only covers goods bought in certain shops – usually expensive ones – but is useful if you want to make any large purchases. Shops usually advertise the fact that they run the scheme, but it may be as well to check. There's no refund of VAT paid for services such as accommodation, eating out, entertainment and fares.

When you pay for the goods tell the shopkeeper that you want to claim a refund. You may be asked to show your passport. You pay the full price, but will be given a form – VAT 407 – to claim back the tax. Keep the form safe: you have to fill it in and then get it endorsed by Customs before you leave the country, or by a public official at home. The endorsed form should be sent back to the shop from which the items were bought. Refunds are usually made quite quickly, but keep a note of the name and address of the shop in case you need to chase up the payment. British Customs and Excise publish a detailed leaflet explaining the scheme.

Food shopping   In the main shopping streets of large towns you will be hard pressed to find many food shops. A department store or Marks and Spencer store might have a food hall, but they tend to be expensive; other options may include a supermarket or self-service grocery. If there's a covered market, make a bee-line for it, as many of the stalls can offer good value and tasty food ideas. The easiest place to find food shops is in neighbourhood shopping areas and in large supermarkets on the outskirts of towns. In smaller towns you'll find traditional butchers, bakers, fruiterers and greengrocers giving a plainer but more personal service.

Complaints   If you have any complaints about the service you've received or anything you've bought, the first step is to go back to the shop and discuss the problem with the manager. If you are not satisfied, seek advice on your consumer rights from one of the Citizen's Advice Bureaux (CAB). There are Bureaux throughout the country – contact address and telephone numbers are listed in local telephone books.

ENTERTAINMENT

THEATRE

London is Britain's entertainment capital, with a superb range of year-round shows and concerts. That said, the quality and variety of entertainment in regional centres can be

The Albert Hall is one of London's major venues.

excellent, equalling the best that London has to offer. Outside London, major venues include Glasgow's Citizens Theatre; the Manchester Royal Exchange; the Theatre Royal in Newcastle (where the Royal Shakespeare Company, RSC, have an annual season); the Crucible in Sheffield; the Leicester Haymarket; Bristol's Old Vic; Theatr Clwyd in North Wales and the RSC theatres in Stratford upon Avon. Far from being in London's shadow, many of the regional theatres feature shows which end up in the capital – so canny theatregoers who spot a future smash-hit early in its run can enjoy their evening for a fraction of London's West End price.

If you haven't got time to queue for tickets or you can't get to the box office, your best bet is to use a ticket agency. It can, however, prove an expensive option, with some agencies charging a commission of 20, or even 25 per cent.

Major agencies include: Keith Prowse and Co Ltd, Banda House, Cambridge Grove, Hammersmith, London W6 0LE, telephone 081-741 7441; Edwards and Edwards, 156 Shaftesbury Avenue, London SC2H 8PP, telephone 071-379 5822; Premier Box Office, 188 Shaftesbury Avenue, London WC2H 8JB, telephone 071-240 2245; Ticket Masters, telephone 071-379 4444; also at branches of WH Smith Travel.

OPERA

Only two of Britain's six major opera companies are based in London: the Royal Opera Company and the English National Opera. Glyndebourne, near Lewes in Sussex, hosts the prestigious Glyndebourne Opera every summer (May to August). Tickets are expensive and are sold well in advance, but you may catch the company on tour in one of the major cities.

The other three companies tour extensively. The excellent Welsh National Opera tours the west of England and the Midlands as well as Wales, from its base in Cardiff. Opera North is based in Leeds and offers an annual season at the city's stunning Grand Theatre. And Scottish Opera has its home in Glasgow.

Opera ticket prices range from a few pounds to £90 (for the best seats at the Royal Opera House). For popular performances by major companies you will have to book ahead to guarantee seats.

DANCE

Traditionally London has dominated British dance, though things are now changing. The Royal Ballet, London Festival Ballet, Ballet Rambert and London Contemporary Dance are all based in the city. But in 1990 the Saddlers Wells Ballet left for a new home to become the Birmingham Royal Ballet, and Glasgow's Scottish Ballet has an impressive reputation. If your taste lies in more contemporary dance, there are plenty of innovative dancers and companies to be found on tour at arts centres and smaller theatres throughout the country.

MUSIC

Orchestral concerts are held throughout the year, all over Britain, at venues which range from the top international halls to country churches. Many of the professional orchestras are to be found in London. Elsewhere there are other excellent orchestras and performers: the BBC has a number of regional orchestras, and others include the City of Birmingham Symphony Orchestra, the Halle, Scottish National Orchestra, Royal Liverpool Philharmonic, and the Bournemouth Symphony Orchestra. All the orchestras and performers tour extensively to major towns and cities.

Britain's choral tradition originated and still exists in church music. Cathedrals throughout the country, and the Oxford and Cambridge colleges, have world-renowned choirs. There are also mixed choirs and male voice choirs in virtually every town in the country. Look out for details in local papers.

Musical festivals and concerts bring together the best of national and international talent; Leeds hosts a well known piano competition, and the Cardiff Singer of the World contest is held every year at St David's Centre (see *Festivals*, below).

NIGHTSPOTS

If your interest is in clubbing or discos, larger towns and cities tend to have a greater number and choice of nightspots. Many clubs have theme nights (such as Singles Nights, or '60s Nights) and some have dress requirements (often 'smart casual' – meaning no denim). Some clubs offer free entry up to a certain time in the evenings, others offer free entry on certain nights to women – check the listing section of local newspapers and magazines for information. There may also be budget nights, which are worth investigation. However, be prepared for a shock at the bar – most clubs charge extortionate prices for drinks and some of the major clubs – particularly in London's West End – charge a small fortune for admission.

FESTIVALS

February Jorvik Viking Festival – a celebration of York's Viking history. Contact: Rosalind Bowden, CRM Ltd, 37 Micklegate, York YO1 1JH, telephone 0904 611944.

May Mayfest – Glasgow's annual arts extravaganza. Contact: Festival Director, 18 Albion Street, Glasgow GL1 1LH, telephone 031-552 8000.

May Chelsea Flower Show – Britain's major flower show, held at the the Royal Hospital, Chelsea. Contact: Royal Horticultural Society, Vincent Square, London SW1 2PE, telephone 071-834 4333.

May–June Bath International Festival – arts and music festival. Contact: Phillip Walker, Bath Festival Office, Linley House, 1 Pierrepoint Place, Bath, Avon BA1 1JY, telephone 0225 462231.

May–August Glyndebourne Festival Opera season – world class opera in a Sussex country house. For booking details see *Opera* section.

May–September Chichester Festival Theatre season – classical and contemporary theatre festival. Contact: Box Office, Chichester Festival Theatre, Oaklands Park, Chichester, West Sussex PO19 4AP, telephone 0243 781312.

June Aldeburgh Festival of Music and the Arts – arts festival founded by Benjamin Britten. Contact: Aldeburgh Foundation, High Street, Aldeburgh, Suffolk IP15 5AX, telephone 0728 452935.

July Llangollen International Music Eisteddfod – international festival of music and dance. Contact: Llangollen International Festival Office, Llangollen, Clwyd LL20 8NG, telephone 0978 860236.

July–September Henry Wood Promenade Concerts – world-famous concert season at the Royal Albert Hall, London. Contact: Nicola Goold, Room 425, 16 Langham Street, London W1A 1AA, telephone 071-927 4296.

August Eisteddfod Genedlaithol Frenhinol Cymru (Royal National Eisteddfod of Wales) – premier cultural event in Wales covering all the arts. Proceedings are conducted in the Welsh language, there are free simultaneous translation facilities. Contact: Eisteddfod Office, 40 Parc Ty Glas, Llanishen, Cardiff, South Glamorgan, telephone 0222 763777.

August–October Blackpool Illuminations – spectacular light show along five miles of seafront. Contact: Tourism and Attractions Department, 1 Clifton Street, Blackpool, Lancashire FY1 1LY, telephone 0253 25212.

September Braemar Royal Highland Gathering – celebrated meeting of kilted Scotsmen. Contact: Booking Secretary, Balcrieth, Ballater, Aberdeenshire, tel 03397 55377.

September–October Swansea Music Festival – professional music, dance and arts festival. Contact: Sophie Black, Swansea

Festival Office, The Guildhall, Swansea, West Glamorgan SA1 4PA, telephone 0792 31301.
October Cheltenham Festival of Literature – a celebration of all aspects of literature. Contact: Mr Kim Sargeant, Festival Organiser, Cheltenham Borough Council, Town Hall, Imperial Square, Cheltenham, Gloucestershire GL50 1QA, telephone 0242 521621.
November–December Cambridge Mozart Festival – a series of concerts to mark the bicentenary of the composer's death. Contact: Mrs Gillian Perkins, 10 Gurney Way, Cambridge, Cambridgeshire CB4 2ED, telephone 0223 350544.

MONEYSAVERS

TRAVEL

If you want to see Britain by train, a BritRail Pass gives unlimited travel on scheduled services. BritRail Passes are only available to overseas visitors to Britain. They cannot be bought in Britain; visitors from the USA and Canada must get one before leaving home. British Rail have the following offices in North America:

Los Angeles, telephone 213 624 8787
Dallas, telephone 214 748 0860
New York, telephone 212 599 5400
Vancouver, telephone 604 683 6896
Toronto, telephone 416 929 3333

The passes are available for first class (Gold Pass) and standard/economy class (Silver Pass) travel and for periods of eight days, 15 days and 22 days or one month.

If you're planning to travel at a relaxed pace with breaks to explore the local area, you might prefer to buy the BritRail Flexi Pass, which restricts the number of days you travel within a certain period: four days' travel in an eight day period, eight days in 15 days, and 15 days in one month.

Passes for children (five to 15) cost half the adult fare. Discounts are offered to young people (age 16-25) on standard class travel (Silver Passes) and to senior citizens (60 plus) on first-class travel (Gold Passes). Children under five travel free.

Rail Rover passes can be bought at principal railway stations in Britain. The All-Line Rail Rover gives you the freedom to travel throughout the country by train, and is available for seven or 14 days, first or standard class. Regional Rail Rovers are good value for anyone wanting to concentrate on a region rather than tour the whole country.

Children and Railcard (except Family Railcard) holders are entitled to one third off the adult price of most Regional passes.

For coach travel anyone can buy a Tourist Trail Pass to get unlimited travel on the National Express and Scottish Citylink network throughout England, Wales and Scotland. Passes are available throughout the year and can be bought for periods of five, eight, 12, 22 or 30 days. Anyone over 60 and children between the ages of five and 15 can get discounts of around one third on the adult price of passes.

Another moneysaver on coaches is the Britexpress card, which entitles the holder to a one-third discount on standard adult fares. The card is only available to overseas visitors between the ages of 16 and 59 (senior citizens and children are entitled to one third off the adult fare).

Tourist Trail Passes and Britexpress cards are available in Britain, or visitors from the USA and Canada can obtain them before leaving home. For further information in Britain contact a major coach station or National Express, 4 Vicarage Road, Edgbaston, Birmingham B15 3ES, telephone 021-456 1122. In Canada contact UTL Holiday Tours, Ontario, telephone 416 593 6777 and in the United States, Worldwide Marketing Associates, Vista, California, telephone 619 696 7184.

PLACES OF INTEREST

Overseas visitors who want to do a lot of sightseeing should buy a 'Great British Heritage

Pass', which entitles you to unlimited entry to 600 properties and historic sites throughout England, Wales and Scotland. Full details are supplied when you buy the pass. It is only available to overseas visitors, and can be bought in North America from British Airways travel agents, and at the British Travel Shop, Box 1224, Clifton, New Jersey, telephone 212 765 0898. They're also sold in Britain at the British Travel Centre, 12 Regents Street, London and at major tourist information centres. Remember to take your passport as proof of your status.

A number of organisations offer annual membership which entitles members to free entry to their properties – and sometimes to the properties of other associated organisations too. With National Trust membership you can visit National Trust and National Trust for Scotland properties. Children, family groups and senior citizens are often offered discounts on the membership fee. For details of annual membership write to:

English Heritage Membership, PO Box 1BB, London W1A 1BB

Heritage in Wales, PO Box 38, Swansea, West Glamorgan, Wales

Friends of Scottish Monuments, PO Box 157, Edinburgh EH3 5RD, Scotland

National Trust, Membership Department, PO Box 39, Bromley, Kent

National Trust for Scotland, Membership Department, 5 Charlotte Square, Edinburgh, EH2 4DU

Historic Houses Association, PO Box 21, Letchworth, Hertfordshire.

THEATRE

Theatres are increasingly making it their practice to sell left over tickets at knockdown prices immediately before the performance. These 'standby' tickets are usually only available to students, but check at the ticket box office – individual theatres may have their own schemes. Matinées and Monday to Thursday evening shows may cost less than Friday and Saturday evenings.

ACCOMMODATION

Single rooms for a single night are the most expensive per person. Double or twin rooms are often cheaper, and prices are often reduced for a longer stay. Travel out of season for reduced rates. Addresses of regional tourist boards are given at the start of *Orientation* sections. Contact these in advance for details of special offer breaks in their region. Many hotels offer cut-price weekend packages. Self-catering is often the cheapest option for families and groups.

LOCAL CUSTOMS

To the outside world there may be such a thing as a typical Britisher, but to the British themselves, the country is a patchwork of different local identities that are often proudly maintained. Call a Scot or a Welsh person English and you may well cause offence.

Stereotypes are never reliable. In London you may come across bowler-hatted commuters with rolled-up umbrellas and copies of *The Times*, but you'll also come across a dizzying mixture of styles, races, ages and religions. You may encounter plenty of 'British reserve', especially in the southeast of England (don't expect people to chat to you on the Underground), but you will also find exuberance, friendliness and warmth (and a few hot tempers) all over the country. The Scottish don't all play the bagpipes; and the Welsh don't all burst into song at the drop of a hat. But the traditions and customs which give rise to these generalisations are valued and respected, as are the customs of a multitude of other communities which make up the United Kingdom.

One of the customs which does seem to apply to the whole country, though, is the queue. Be prepared to stand in line for anything from a stamp to a stately home.

The British attitude to dress is relaxed. Special dress requirements in public places are rare. At some expensive restaurants men are expected to wear a jacket and tie, and women should not wear trousers (unless they are very glamorous); and many nightclubs ask patrons not to wear jeans, but to be 'smart casual'. If you are invited to a private party or function the invitation will usually tell you what standard of dress is required: if in doubt, ask.

Some bemoan the fact the people no longer get 'dressed up' to go to the theatre, or to the ballet or opera. People are more inclined to wear their best in the stalls and dress circles, but any outfit which is clean and tidy is usually acceptable.

If there is a dress rule, it's to wear what's appropriate for the place and the weather. What goes down well in London's trendy Kings Road is likely to elicit a few comments in a small town; and city heels are not the most sensible footwear for the country.

Britain's untrustworthy climate means that it's always a good idea to have a raincoat or umbrella close at hand, whatever time of the year. In winter you'll need a warm coat and woollens, and even in the summer a light jacket or coat is a sensible precaution. And make sure you bring a pair of comfortable waterproof shoes.

STREETWISE

The first rule for being streetwise is not to look like a tourist. As soon as you unfold a map or whip out a camera you're liable to be marked down as fair game for all the touts and street traders in the area. Ticket touts hang around popular theatres and major sporting events selling ridiculously over-priced tickets. Even if you feel you can afford the high asking price, be very careful: it's not unusual to find that the ticket is in fact a forgery and won't get you in.

Along shopping streets throughout the country, you'll see street traders selling goods from suitcases and keeping an eye out for the police. At best they're selling tacky forgeries and goods that will fall apart as soon as you get them home; at worst they are selling sub-standard and dangerous goods which fail to meet proper safety standards.

When you look at some of the tourist services take a close look beneath the glossy packaging. Guided tours are a good example: some are worth every penny, but with a one day local travel pass you could often do the job for yourself at a fraction of the tour cost.

Streetwise Britishers shop around for fuel to save money; a general rule for finding the best value petrol is to look for an out-of-town supermarket. New supermarkets usually have a filling station selling at a discounted price.

Crime rates in Britain are quite low, although there are periodic scare stories about the rising level of offences. The vast majority of crime is against property rather than people, and tends to involve petty theft by opportunists. About one quarter of all crime involves car thefts or thefts from cars – especially audio equipment. Always take out your ignition key when you leave the car and lock the doors, even if you are just popping out for a short time. An important precaution when you park is to look for somewhere secure with plenty of street lighting.

If you can't park the car overnight in a garage, choose somewhere well lit and busy, a spot that is overlooked by houses for instance. When you use a multi-storey car park look for one with good lighting and restricted access and exit points. Some car parks are 'pay and display', where you leave the ticket on your windscreen to show you have paid the parking fee. But if the car park is one which issues a ticket on entry, and the ticket is presented and the fee paid on

The streetwise tourist blends in with the crowd.

leaving the car park, do remember to take the ticket with you when you leave the car – a thief will find it difficult to get past the exit booth without it.

Thieves are also looking for what is inside your car, so don't leave cameras, bags and luggage in view. If the car has a boot, lock valuables in there. And it's a good idea to put coats in the boot, too, as they're often stolen in the hope that there's money in the pockets.

Bicycles are another popular target for thieves, as they're easily sold. Never leave a cycle unlocked, and always secure it to something immovable, such as a lamp post or railing (but ensure that it's out of people's way).

For holidaymakers, perhaps the most worrying problem is pick-pocketing. If you use a handbag or purse make sure that it can be closed, preferably with a clasp or zip, and that your money and cards are out of view. Keep hold of your bag in any public place and when travelling on public transport. If possible keep your keys in a separate place, so that if your bag is lost or stolen, you won't be locked out! For men, the safest place to carry a wallet is in the front trouser pocket or in the inside pocket of a jacket.

If you carry cash, don't carry a large amount with you, and certainly don't flash your money in public – pubs, restaurants or shops – where you could be advertising yourself as a target. If one of your credit cards is stolen, report it to your card company (see telephone numbers of major credit card companies in the *Health and Emergency* section) and the police straight away. And be careful of your passport too: it is easily sold. If you're travelling around the country, you might feel happier with your money and travel documents in a moneybelt (or 'bum-bag').

While violent crimes are comparatively rare in Britain, many people are still frightened that they might become the victim of a mugging or assault. Women may feel especially vulnerable, especially after dark. When you walk, avoid dimly lit streets and short cuts across waste ground. When walking along a road, face oncoming traffic so that you won't be surprised by a car coming up from behind and stick to the street side of the pavement in case someone's lurking in a doorway or alleyway. If you think you are being followed make a bee-line for somewhere light with people around – a pub, launderette or well-lit house – and telephone for the police.

Public transport can feel especially lonely late at night – this could be the time to book or hail a taxi. Only licensed taxis are allowed to ply for hire on the street and to call themselves 'taxis' – they also carry a licence plate. Other cars offering rides should be treated with suspicion. On trains, beware of carriages without connecting corridors. Choose one which is well lit, with several other passengers. If the train is nearly empty, let the driver know you're there and sit immediately behind his cab.

USEFUL INFORMATION

MONEY

Britain changed its shillings and pence for a decimal system 20 years ago. There are 100 pence to a pound. Coins, produced by the Royal Mint, are of the following values: 1p, 2p, 5p, 10p, 20p, 50p and £1 (100p). In England and Wales banknotes are issued by the Bank of England in denominations of £5, £10, £20 and £50. In Scotland notes are issued by the Bank of Scotland, Royal Bank of Scotland and Clydesdale Bank in the same denominations, with the addition of a £1 note. Scottish banknotes, like Bank of England notes, are legal tender throughout Britain.

Some pre-decimal coins and terms are still common; two shilling (10p) coins crop up frequently. The Royal Mint and Bank of England have recently been redesigning the coins and notes that they issue and the Mint has plans to issue new coins and notes in the future.

When you use money in automatic machines – such as railway ticket machines or public telephone boxes – check to see which notes and coins they accept. Some have not been updated to take the new issues.

BANKS AND BUREAUX DE CHANGE

There are four main banking groups in England and Wales: Barclays, Lloyds, Midland and National Westminster. They have branches in most towns, open Monday to Friday 9.30am to 3.30pm (except in the City of London where they close at 3pm). Some branches are experimenting with longer opening hours in the week and a service on Saturday morning. Scottish banks have broadly the same opening times as their counterparts in England and Wales.

All banks are closed on bank holidays (the dates of some bank holidays differ north and south of the border; see *Public Holidays*, below).

The larger branches of most banks offer a comprehensive exchange service, which are also provided by Bureaux de Change and some travel agents, department stores and hotels.

Exchange rates and commission charges can vary significantly, so when you change foreign currency it can pay to shop around.

CREDIT CARDS

Access/Mastercard, Barclaycard/Visa and American Express are widely accepted in Britain. There is usually a notice in shops, restaurants and hotels telling customers which credit cards are accepted. At present there is no difference between the cash price of goods and services, and the price when paying with cards. However, there is some discussion about putting a surcharge on credit card sales to cover the retailer's costs in processing the payment. A few stores, including Marks and Spencer, only accept their own credit card.

ELECTRICITY

The electricity supply is 220 volts, usually with three-pin plugs, for which you can buy adaptors to convert from Continental plugs. Electrical appliances from the USA and Canada will not work in Britain, and attempts to try them could be explosive!

TELEPHONES

By far the largest telephone company in Britain is British Telecom, though it has growing competition – Mercury payphones, for instance, can be seen in major towns.

Public telephones were once well known for their sturdy red kiosks, but these are now being replaced with more basic glass and steel booths. British Telecom operate two types of public telephone – coin operated and Phonecard operated. All telephones have clear instructions explaining their use.

Pay telephones take 10p, 20p, 50p and £1 coins. It's best to use a lot of low denomination coins when you make a short call, as pay telephones only return completely unused coins. Any residue of money in the machine is cancelled when you replace the receiver. If you want to make a second call, press the blue button.

Phonecard operated telephones use prepaid British Telecom Phonecards, valued in units of 10p. The smallest card is 20 units and costs £2. Cards are also available in 40, 100 and 200 units, and can be bought from post offices and shops displaying the green Phonecard logo.

All telephones have standard tones: dialling (continuous purring or high pitched hum); ringing (repeated burr, burr); number engaged (repeated single tone); number unobtainable (steady tone); and pay tone (rapid 'pips'). If you are not familiar with these tones, you can dial 191 and ask the operator to demonstrate them to you.

If you have any difficulties making a call contact the operator by dialling 100. Other useful numbers are 192 for directory (number) enquiries for outside London, and 142 for London area directory enquiries.

International Calls International directory enquiries are on 153; the international operator is on 155. To make a call abroad from a pay telephone, you'll need to put in at least £1 or 10 Phonecard units. Direct dialling is cheaper than making an operator controlled call. International direct dialling is a simple four-step operation. First dial 010 and then dial the country code (1 for the United States and Canada), following this with the area code (for Canada, omit the first 0) and then finally the telephone number. The cheapest time to call the United States and Canada is between 8pm and 8am (British time) Monday to Friday, and any time on Saturday or Sunday.

For advice on making reverse charge (collect) calls or using Calling Cards, contact the international operator.

POSTAL SERVICES

Britain's postal service – the Royal Mail – is run by the Post Office. Post offices and sub post offices (usually local shops which also provide basic postal services) display red signs with the 'Post Office' logo in yellow. Opening times are usually 9am to 5pm Monday to Friday and 9am to midday on Saturday, but check locally as these times may vary. Letter boxes come in different shapes and sizes, but they are all 'pillarbox red' and display a small notice giving details of the post collection time and the local post office.

Postage stamps can be bought from post offices and sub post offices, coin-operated stamp machines and increasingly from shops and newsagents.

Post within Britain can be sent either first class, which is generally a next day delivery, or second class, which is cheaper but means a slower delivery. Airmail letters to the east coast of the United States and to urban Canada take about a week from posting to delivery. Surface mail is cheaper, but it takes far longer.

If you want to get a written message to America in a hurry, British Telecom offer a telemessage service. If you telephone 100 with your message before 10pm Monday to Saturday, or 7pm on Sunday and bank holidays, your message should arrive by mailgram in the United States the next day. The cost for the first 50 words (addressee's name and full postal address are free of charge) is £11.95; £5.95 for each additional 50 words.

TIME

Time is uniform throughout Britain. Standard time is Greenwich Mean Time (GMT). In March the clocks are put forward an hour to British Summer Time (BST) which continues until October. The clocks change at midnight on the last Saturday of the month.

EMBASSIES

United States of America
Embassy: 24 Grosvenor Square, London W1A 1AE, telephone 071-499 9000
Consulate: 3 Regent Terrace, Edinburgh, Lothian, Scotland, telephone 031-556 8315
Canada
High Commission: Canada House, Trafalgar Square, London SW1 5BJ; and also McDonald House, 1 Grosvenor Square, London W1A, telephone 071-629 9492
Consulate: Glasgow, telephone 041-221 4415

PUBLIC HOLIDAYS

There are eight statutory holidays – called bank holidays – when banks, offices, factories and shops are closed and some services are restricted. Six of the holidays are the same in England and Wales and in Scotland:
New Year's Day   January 1
Good Friday   Friday before Easter in late March or April
May Day   first Monday in May
Spring Bank Holiday   last Monday in May
Christmas Day   25 December
Boxing Day   26 December
In England and Wales the other two holidays are Easter Monday (the Monday after Easter)

The AA Patrol is a very welcome sight.

26

and Summer Bank Holiday (the last Monday in August). In Scotland the other holidays are New Year Holiday (2 January) and Summer Bank Holiday (the first Monday in August).

HEALTH AND EMERGENCIES

EMERGENCIES

If you need help urgently you can telephone for the police, ambulance and fire service (also cave rescue, coast guards, and mountain rescue) by calling the free 999 emergency line from any telephone. The operator will ask for the number from which you are calling and which service you want. When you get through to the emergency service give the address where help is needed, and any other useful information.

Emergency hospital treatment is free to anyone under the National Health Service. Any non-emergency treatment, however, has to be paid for by anyone who is not from Britain or certain European countries. Check before leaving home to see whether you need any health insurance, and if you do make sure you are adequately covered.

DOCTORS

Family doctors, known as general practitioners or GPs, are listed in the Yellow Pages, commercial telephone directory. Visitors must give a temporary address to register as a temporary patient. If you are visiting Britain from America you will have to pay to see the doctor, except in an emergency when you are entitled to free treatment.

MEDICATION

Local pharmacists are listed in the Yellow Pages. If you want a prescription made up, there is a set rate per item under the NHS. Pharmacies which are near doctors' surgeries usually operate outside usual opening hours to fit in with surgery hours. Pharmacists can also give you helpful advice on health matters and suggest treatments for minor ailments. Outside normal working hours, pharmacies operate emergency services, advertised in local newspapers or on pharmacy doors. Overnight or at a weekend, contact the police for advice on getting an emergency prescription.

Strict drugs laws operate in Britain. Anyone holding illegal drugs will be prosecuted or deported. Overseas visitors on a drug regime should obtain a letter from their doctor giving details of the medication to show at Customs.

DENTISTS

Most towns have a dental practice, although in some country areas they are a bit sparse. If you are eligible for National Health Service treatment check that the dentist provides an NHS service, as private treatment tends to be more expensive.

General advice on the health service is available from local Community Health Councils (in England and Wales) and the Local Health Council (in Scotland).

CAR BREAKDOWNS

Several motoring organisations in Britain provide a 24-hour breakdown service. The largest is the Automobile Association (AA), Fanum House, Basingstoke, Hampshire, RG21 2EA, telephone 0256 20123. The AA offers overseas visitors associate membership. If you are already a member of a motoring organisation outside Britain, check to see if it has any reciprocal agreements. If you do break down and you are not a member of any organisation you can join the AA on the spot; telephone 0800 887766 for breakdown assistance (no charge for calls).

CREDIT CARD LOSS

Make sure you always keep your credit cards in a safe place, separate from cash and travellers cheques. Lost or stolen credit cards should be reported immediately to your credit card company. Access/Mastercard runs a card holders' enquiry line on 0702 352211. The number to contact about lost Barclaycard/Visa cards is 0604 230230. Diners Club members should call 0252 513500, and for American Express contact 0273 696933. Remember to report the loss to the police.

LOST AND STOLEN PROPERTY

Lost or stolen property should be reported to the police (local station addresses and telephone numbers are in the telephone book under 'Police'; only dial 999 if it is an emergency). Be prepared to give a description of what is missing and where you think it happened.

If you lose something on a bus, note the service you were using and get in touch with the operating company. Any local railway station will be able to give you details of British Rail's lost property if you lose something on a train.

LANGUAGE TIPS

No matter if you thought you'd been speaking English all your life – you could still find yourself at a loss when you are asked in Cardiff 'where you to?'(where are you?), or a Scottish café presents you with the choice of 'neeps and tatties' (turnip or swede and potatoes). As well as getting to grips with the wide range of regional dialects, with their unique vocabularies, you may have to take time out to decipher some of the local accents. And English isn't the only language in Britain. The much older Celtic languages – Gaelic in parts of Scotland and especially Welsh in Wales – are still significant; and in the larger cities languages from all over the world can be heard.

These are some of the differences North American visitors need to know:

Accommodation

boiler/geyser   *water heater*
corridor/passageway   *hall*
first floor, second floor etc   *second floor, third floor, etc.*
flannel   *washcloth*
flat   *apartment*
folding bed/z-bed   *murphy bed*
ground floor   *first floor*
hall   *large room (for functions)*
let   *rent (accommodation)*
lift   *elevator*
self-catering flat   *efficiency apartment*
tap   *faucet/spigot*

toilet/loo/lavatory/WC   *wash-room/rest-room*

Children

nappies   *diapers*
pram   *baby carriage/buggy*

Food

ale   *beer*
aubergine   *eggplant*
bap   *soft bun*
bill   *check*
biscuit   *cookie*
chips   *french fries*
courgette   *zucchini*
crisps   *chips (potato)*
faggots   *meatballs*
grilled   *broiled (meat, etc)*
jelly   *Jell-O*
maize   *corn*
minced meat   *ground meat*
porridge   *oatmeal (boiled)*
scone   *biscuit*
sweets   *candy*

Medication

(NB the same drugs are often given different names in Britain and North America. If you take medication regularly, ask your doctor to give the drug's generic name to avoid any confusion)
chemist/pharmacy   *drugstore*
chemist   *druggist*
cotton wool   *absorbent cotton*

Clothing

braces   *suspenders (men's)*
dressing gown   *bathrobe*
jumper   *sweater (pullover)*
pants/underpants   *men's underwear*
plimsolls   *sneakers*
tights   *panti-hose*
trainers   *athletic shoes*
trousers   *pants*
vest or singlet   *undershirt*
waistcoat   *vest*

Travel, transport

big end   *larger end of connecting rod in car engine*
bumper   *fender*
caravan   *trailer house/mobile home*
(car) bonnet   *(car) hood*
(car) boot   *trunk*
car park   *parking lot*
central reservation   *traffic island*
coach   *long-distance bus*
dual carriageway   *divided highway*
estate car   *station wagon*
level crossing   *railroad crossing*
lorry   *truck*
pavement   *sidewalk*

pedestrian/zebra crossing   *crossway*
petrol   *gasoline/gas*
railway   *railroad*
roundabout   *rotary interchange/traffic circle*
single ticket   *one way ticket*
windscreen   *windshield*

Miscellaneous

bank holiday   *legal holiday*
banknote   *bill (paper money)*
biro   *ballpoint pen*
garden   *yard*
handbag   *pocketbook/purse*
hire purchase   *instalment plan*
holiday   *vacation*
kiosk   *booth*
letter/post box   *mailbox*
long weekend   *Friday and/or Monday as well as Saturday and Sunday*
newsagent   *newspaper store*
purse   *coin purse*
queue   *line (of people)*
reverse charge call   *call collect*
rubber   *eraser*
shop   *store*
summer time   *daylight saving time*
theatre interval   *intermission*

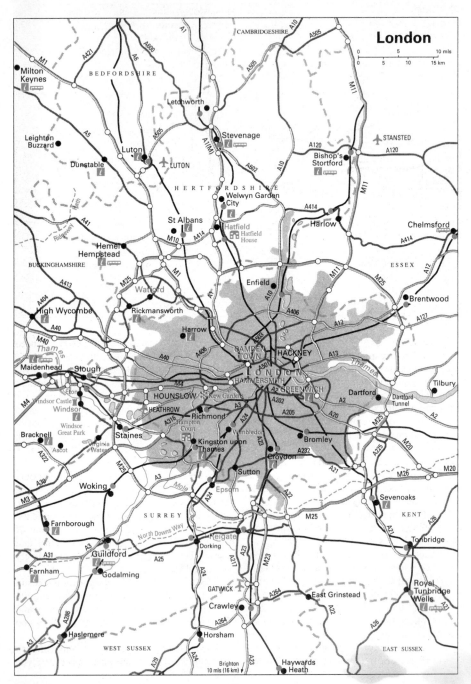

London

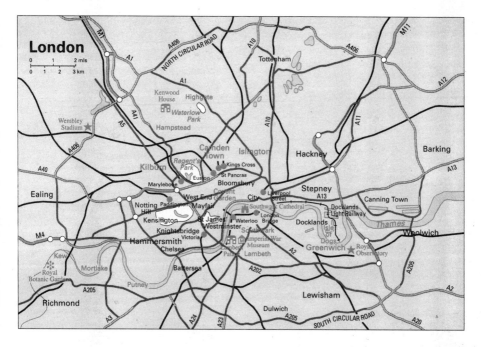

London is a huge, sprawling city, bigger than New York, more populous than Paris. It's where the Government, national newspapers, television and radio stations are based, and the focal point for trains, planes and buses. It has great national art collections, museums to rival any in the world, cathedrals, theatres and concert halls and other music venues catering for all tastes, cinemas, clubs, and some splendid architecture. In spite of all that it isn't the easiest city to know, partly because it's so big – but tackle it patiently and you'll discover a city of character that's like nowhere else in the world.

There are some famous sights which even those who've never been near London know well – the Houses of Parliament, Buckingham Palace and the Tower of London. Those places aren't the whole story though, and if you want to get the real flavour of London you'll spend some time on the bits in between. If the noise, crowds and traffic fumes become unbearable, you're never far away from spacious green parks and gardens.

The easiest way to tackle London is to concentrate on one area at a time, and this chapter is arranged with that in mind. That way you need only do the minimum travelling on London's expensive and crowded transport. The City, which is the oldest part of London, includes St Paul's Cathedral and the Tower of London. It's also London's financial centre, and is packed with places to visit, both ancient and modern.

Bloomsbury, Marylebone and Regents' Park includes the British Museum, Madame Tussaud's and London Zoo.

The West End takes in the main shopping streets, Piccadilly, Mayfair with its exclusive designer boutiques and art galleries, and Soho, which has lively, low price restaurants, and the shops, restaurants and unique atmosphere of London's Chinatown; plus theatreland and Covent Garden, one of London's most lively and popular areas.

Westminster and St James's section takes in the landmarks of Buckingham Palace. the Houses of Parliament, Westminster Abbey and the art collections of the National Gallery and the Tate.

Knightsbridge, Kensington and Chelsea includes the huge green open space of Hyde

Park, plus the Victoria and Albert and other big museums. Chelsea was the epicentre of 'swinging' London in the 1960s and is still fun to see, with much older places to explore.

In the *Discovering Outer London* section you will find London's liveliest markets, plus Docklands, Greenwich, and Hampstead Heath. The *Outings from London* section tells you how to reach the three great palaces of Hampton Court, Windsor Castle and Hatfield House.

Local flavour
In the last few years London has seen a phenomenal rise in the number of young people begging a living on its streets. Opinions are divided about just why they have no homes or jobs, but one thing's for sure — once a person's fallen down the slippery slope of destitution in London, there's no easy way out

Sightseeing   London Transport runs sightseeing buses from Baker Street Station, Marble Arch, Piccadilly Circus and Victoria, at frequent intervals every day. Open-topped buses are used in fine weather, and guides give a commentary. Tours last about 1½ hours and costs about £8 if you get the ticket on the bus, less if you buy it in advance. For around £10.50 you can get a combined ticket to a major attraction such as Madame Tussaud's, which works out as a saving. There are evening tours too. Other companies do tours, but they may have a taped commentary.

There is a huge range of guided walks with a theme: ghosts, Shakespeare, pubs, Sherlock Holmes, wildlife, the Lord Mayor and cemeteries are all things you might come across. Prices range up to around £4, but some are free. Look in *Time Out* and *City Limits* magazines, or ask tourist information centres.

Getting around   Travelcards, available from London Transport Travel Information Centres, give unlimited travel for set periods by Underground, local British Rail, most buses and the Docklands Light Railway. They can be used after 9.30am on weekdays, otherwise all day. You'll need a photocard if you want to buy a

one-week or one-month travelcard. Photocards are free – all you have to do is take a passport-type photograph.

Local flavour
Life on the tube is cheered up by London Transport's specially commissioned art posters, and theme décor, like the British Museum-inspired decorations at Holborn. Poetry sometimes replaces advertisements inside the trains.

Children under five travel free, five to 15-year-olds get reduced rate travel. Children aged 14 or 15 must have a child rate card to get child rate tickets. The cards are free, but you need a passport size photograph.

London Transport Travel Information Centres at mainline stations, Piccadilly Circus station and Heathrow airport sell travelcards, tickets for special tours, and guide books. They also supply free maps and other information.

No smoking is allowed on the tube system, either on trains or at stations.

Buses and tubes are nearly always busy, but they're especially crowded in the rush hours: roughly 7am to 9.30am and 4pm to 7pm.

Buses cover London in a dense network of routes, some of which go well into the suburbs. Buses come in traditional red and in other colours too, but if they have the London Transport symbol then they're part of the system. Note that the number 15 bus is the one to the Tower of London. The 15B takes a more northerly route, but they're easily confused.

Take an ordinary service for a cut-price sightseeing tour. The number 11 goes past the Bank of England, St Paul's Cathedral, Trafalgar Square, the Houses of Parliament and the King's Road. Bus number 6 goes a similar way to Trafalgar Square, then to Piccadilly Circus and Oxford Street.

Between midnight and 6am you can catch night buses from the centre right across London. The main stop is in Trafalgar Square: night buses and stops are marked N. Travelcards can't be used. There's generally a good atmosphere on these night time rides.

You're never far from a tube station in the centre. There are no all-night services: last trains leave the centre up to about midnight. Some stations close at weekends, services may be restricted on public holidays. Crime isn't a major problem, but avoid empty carriages and think twice about catching the tube late at night, especially if you're a lone woman. Chances are your journey will be trouble free, but steel yourself for grime, drunks, crowds and sometimes long delays.

All stations and station platforms have tube maps. Each line has its own colour, and interchanges are marked. Check the destination on the front of the train – trains often don't run to the end of the line, and some lines fork.

Tube and bus fares are calculated by zone. Zone 1 means central London, zone 5 stretches to Heathrow. Stations in the centre have automatic ticket machines. They're designed to give change, but it's wise to carry a supply of coins. You need your ticket to get in and out of the tube, so hang on to it. In the centre you usually have to feed your ticket through automatic entrance and exit gates. There should be an official near by to help those with pushchairs or luggage.

The traditional London 'black cab' comes in other colours nowadays, but if it carries the 'Hackney Carriage' licence plate and number on the back, it's part of the system. These are the only cars allowed to ply for passengers. Hail a taxi if the yellow For Hire sign is lit, or try a taxi rank (all main stations have them). They're also listed in telephone directories. Charges are recorded on the meter, and mount up for 'extras' like luggage and night-time rides. It's usual but not compulsory to give a tip of 10 to 15 per cent.

Driving in central London isn't encouraged or recommended, but shortfalls in the public transport system may mean there's no alternative. Car parks are expensive, but illegal parking is penalised by fines, clamping and towing away, with huge fees to pay (at inconvenient locations) before you can retrieve your car.

The Docklands Light Railway is London's most scenic train route: an overhead line from the City to the Isle of Dogs and Stratford in the east part of the East End. Travelcards are valid,

or buy a ticket from the machine at stations.

You can also travel along the Thames on a river bus: the boats run from early morning between Greenwich and Chelsea, calling at several stops on the way. Boats go all year from Westminster and Charing Cross Piers down river to the Tower of London (about 20 minutes) and other places.

Entertainment   You'd be hard put not to find something to entertain you in London – there is always a huge range, whether your taste is for grand opera, Shakespeare, Andrew Lloyd Webber or spotting new talent among fledgeling comedians.

One of the main venues for events is the Barbican Centre, in the heart of the modern, pedestrian-only Barbican complex of apartments and offices on the edge of the City. It offers masses of music, drama, films and art exhibitions all under one roof, plus places to eat, shops, a library, an indoor garden and a lake overlooked by a medieval church. The trouble is finding it – even regulars get lost. Once you're in the Barbican housing/office complex, follow the yellow line on the ground.

Moneysaver

The Barbican has free jazz concerts most Sundays in the Terrace foyer (level 5). There are free daytime entertainments and children's workshops over bank holidays and school holidays, and free foyer exhibitions and entertainment in the evenings. Previews, press nights and Thursday matinées are cheapest at the Barbican Theatre. The Barbican Gallery costs less after 5pm.

The Barbican Theatre and The Pit are the London base of the renowned Royal Shakespeare Company (RSC). They always keep some tickets back for sale on the day. The 2,000-seat Barbican Hall has concerts most nights, by visiting performers or the resident London Symphony Orchestra. Exhibitions at the Barbican Gallery tend to be widely reviewed, and it's open until 8pm on Thursdays.

Details of everything are in the free monthly Barbican Centre calendar, available there and from information centres.

The South Bank Centre is a slightly older concrete arts complex, with an equally big range of events, and a wide choice of impressive productions. Forty tickets are kept for sale on the day at 10am.

The Coliseum packs in crowds of all ages for English National Opera's performances. Productions here are always interesting, often enthralling, and are sung in English. Dancers, including top international companies, take over in the summer.

Summer at the Royal Albert Hall means the BBC Henry Wood Promenade Concerts, affectionately known as 'the Proms'. This is arguably the world's best music festival, running from mid July to mid September. 'Promenaders' line up for same-day, standing room tickets in the arena or high up in the gallery. Tickets for seats aren't very expensive, but they do get booked up. For the rest of the year the hall stages a wide range of events.

The Royal Opera House is London's grandest theatre, home of the Royal Ballet and Royal Opera, and host to international companies and stars. Tickets range from around £17.50 (opera), £10.50 (ballet) to over £100. Booking is essential, but 65 rear amphitheatre seats are always kept back for sale on the day, plus 50 standing places when all seats are sold out. Join the line at the Floral Street box office, early.

Sadler's Wells is the home of the National Youth Theatre, the Academy of Ancient Music and the English Shakespeare Company. It hosts various productions but especially dance. Standby tickets are usually kept back for the day, but be there early.

Behind Sadler's Wells is the 200-seat Lilian Baylis Theatre, where prices start low for music, dance and theatre, often of an experimental nature.

St John's, Smith Square is a church converted into a concert hall, with a programme of recitals and chamber music. BBC Radio 3 broadcasts concerts from St John's Smith Square at 1pm on most Mondays (not bank holidays or summer). If you want to attend, they're excellent value. Similar fare is on offer at the Wigmore Hall, a favourite with both artists and audience, where the civilised Sunday morning coffee concerts include coffee or sherry.

The main concentration of theatres is around Shaftesbury Avenue (Leicester Square tube station), where you'll find over 20 productions within a few minutes walk – comedies, farces, musicals and some serious 'quality' drama – often in wonderfully ornate Edwardian surroundings. Tickets for the likes of Andrew Lloyd Webber musicals are rare and expensive. Preview nights and matinées are usually cheaper, but you may miss out on atmosphere.

The Open Air Theatre in Regent's Park is the perfect setting for Shakespeare from May to September. They also do children's shows and concerts. Kenwood House at Hampstead has open air concerts by the lake every Saturday from June to August, sometimes with fireworks. Holland Park's open air theatre puts on Shakespeare plays, opera and Royal Ballet School productions in summer. Waterlow Park in Highgate has free jazz, big band and other music; bands play free in all the large London parks.

Moneysaver

The Society of West End Theatres (SWET) ticket booth in Leicester Square sells half-price tickets for the same day. It's open from noon for matinées, from 2.30pm for evening shows. They also supply a useful guide to shows. Four tickets per applicant is the limit, and you must pay in cash.

For rock, club and pub music, London's venues range from the 100,000 capacity Wembley Stadium, to innumerable pubs, bars and clubs providing rock, reggae, jazz, pop, blues, disco, etc, every night.

Venues are sometimes here today and gone tomorrow – but places that look firmly rooted are Dingwalls in Camden, the Marquee and the Astoria, both in Charing Cross Road, the 100 Club in Oxford Street and the Town & Country Club in Highgate. The Dominion in Tottenham Court Road sometimes has very famous names;

Ronnie Scotts in Frith Street has been providing the best in international jazz for many years (it's fairly expensive at £10, less for students). Your best bet is to consult *Time Out* or *City Limits* magazines.

The same goes for nightclubs, of which London has many. The city may look deserted after 11pm, but you can dance to 3am every night of the week. Most clubs are for members only, but membership fees are often included in the admission price. It often costs less to get in before 10pm or 11pm, more at weekends. Women may get in free. Some clubs are choosy about what you wear: not jeans and trainers, for instance. They range from smart disco places to wild and sweaty cellars. Drinks may cost double what they'd cost in a pub.

> **Local flavour**
> Some of the nicest musical entertainment is provided free in pubs, especially Irish ones. The players may just be sitting round a table, but the atmosphere is unbeatable. See *Time Out* magazine

For comedy and cabaret, either have a hilarious time or writhe with embarrassment watching comedians and other acts braving the hecklers. Again, the venues are many and ever-changing, but try the Comedy Store in Leicester Square or the Hackney Empire.

For people with disabilities, Artsline advises on access to arts and entertainment venues. Contact them at 5 Crowndale Road, London N1 1TU, telephone 071-388 2227.

The choice of films is huge too, but beware high prices in the big cinemas around Leicester Square. For less commercial films, try the arts centres, and independent cinemas like the Electric in Portobello Road, and the Scala, near King's Cross train station. They may be for members only, but membership is usually a nominal 50p or so on the ticket price.

Pageantry and ceremony One of the bargains for the budget traveller in London is the city's wealth of pageantry. The Changing of the Guard at Buckingham Palace is at 11.30am daily from April to July, otherwise alternate days. You'll need to arrive early to get a good viewpoint.

The Mounting of the Guard in Whitehall is quieter: daily at 11am (10am on Sundays). The Tower of London has a ceremony at 11am (daily in summer). There's nothing spectacular about the Ceremony of the Keys, which is just a matter of locking up the Tower of London and putting the keys away, but it has happened every night for the last 700 years. You have to apply to attend: write to the Resident Governor at the Tower of London, London EC1.

The Queen's 'official' birthday is celebrated on the second Saturday in June by Trooping the Colour, when the flags (colours) of a regiment are trooped before her. Tickets are only available by post: write before the end of January to the Brigade Major (Trooping the Colour), Household Division, Horse Guards, London SW1, telephone 071 439 7438. Or get in place early to watch the procession along the Mall from Buckingham Palace. There's another chance to see the Queen on her way to the State Opening of Parliament in early November.

The Lord Mayor's procession is in early November.

The Lord Mayor's Show cheers up the City of London on the second Saturday morning in November, when the newly elected Lord Mayor of London is taken round the City in the State Coach to be 'shown' to the citizens. He's accompanied by floats, bands and much cheering and flagwaving, with fireworks on the Thames later. Telephone 071-606 3030 for information.

The Oxford and Cambridge Boat Race takes place along the Thames from Putney to Mortlake in late March/early April. Get free (but crowded) views from Thames bridges and riverside pubs like the Dove in Hammersmith.

About 25,000 runners take part in the London Marathon (April/May) from Greenwich to Westminster Bridge. It starts at 9.30am; fastest runners complete the course in less than three hours, others take an hour or three longer, but most finish.

The Chelsea Flower Show is a horticultural spectacular in the third week in May with cascades of flowers, specially created gardens and every kind of gardening gadget. Public days are Wednesday, Thursday and Friday. Tickets are about £15.

> **Moneysaver**
> Tickets for the Chelsea Flower Show are reduced after 4pm for one hour on one of the days.

Royal Ascot Races take place in the third week in June. The Royal Family is always there. Entry to the Royal Enclosure is a matter of money and contacts, but anyone can join the fun at the Silver Ring. The Thursday is Ladies Day, when hats are *de rigeur* for lady spectators. Again, special trains run from Waterloo.

The third week in June also means the start of the Lawn Tennis Championships at Wimbledon. This top-rank international event is so popular that tickets are issued by ballot: send a stamped addressed envelope for an application form between April and December the previous year, to the All England Club, PO Box 98, Church Road, London SW19 5AE. Or join the queue for tickets very early in the morning (or the night before). Wimbledon's ticket touts are notorious for their prices. There's also good tennis at Queen's Club, which hosts the Stella Artois tournament in June, and other events: telephone 081-381 4213.

The Notting Hill Carnival is on August Bank Holiday Sunday and Monday. Go for the daytime street celebrations; avoid evenings, when the atmosphere can be menacing.

Only cars from before 1905 can enter the London to Brighton Veteran Car Run on the first Sunday in November, and the drivers are often splendidly attired. They start in Hyde Park and head out of London via Westminster Bridge.

Avoid New Year's Eve in Trafalgar Square unless you like dense, drunk and strangely joyless crowds. You'll have far more fun in any pleasant pub. Chinese New Year in early February is a different matter, with dragons dancing round the Gerrard Street area among cheerful crowds, music and stalls.

Accommodation London accommodation is expensive by British standards. If you want to be sure of somewhere reasonably priced, you should book before you arrive. It's cheaper outside the centre, but the saving may be offset by the cost and discomfort of travelling.

For advice and free advance bookings (at least six weeks ahead), contact the London Tourist Board, 26 Grosvenor Gardens, London SW1W 0DU, or telephone the LTB Central Accommodation Unit on 071-730 2699. *London Where to Stay* lists all types of accommodation and costs about £2.50 – available overseas through tourist offices. It includes a booking form which lets you book by type and price.

If you're booking a long way ahead, you may have to pay a deposit. If you haven't booked, you may be asked to pay on arrival. Refusal isn't easy, but you can expect to see the room first.

The best way to get an inside view of London is to stay with a family. You can book by writing to the London Tourist Board, or ask for their leaflet *Staying with Families* if you'd prefer to book yourself.

If you're travelling in a group, it might be worth renting an apartment: they're available in a wide range of prices. You can book through the London Tourist Board, or ask for their leaflet *Self Catering Apartments and Agencies* if you want to book yourself.

People with disabilities can get advice on accommodation from the London Tourist Board, or from Holiday Care Service, 2 Old Bank Chambers, Station Road, Horley, Surrey RH6 9HW, telephone 0293 774535.

> **Moneysaver**
> Accommodation prices may be much lower out of season or for longer stays.

DISCOVERING CENTRAL LONDON

THE CITY

The City is the oldest part of London. The Romans built a wall and had a temple, baths and amphitheatre in this area, and it has flourished more or less ever since, celebrated in fairy tale, nursery rhyme and history book. The Tower of London and St Paul's Cathedral are both here, but this is also where the big banks, Stock Exchange and other centres of financial activity are based, in buildings which make London's most exciting skyline. The new glass and steel buildings lie on a medieval street plan, and among them you'll find much older churches, pubs and markets, with a ceremonial life rooted in medieval times.

Visit the Museum of London (St Paul's/Barbican tube stations) to see why the capital is the way it is. Everyone seems to like this museum. Displays are in order of age, so you walk through time from prehistory to the present day. Open daily except Mondays, and free.

It's wise to start at the Tower of London (Tower Hill tube station), not just because of its history but also because it's very popular, and the queues can be long. William the Conqueror built the White Tower at the core, and the rest has been added on as fortification, palace, prison, and place of execution. It's expensive but more than justifies the price. And the Tower's generally grim saga of death and wrongdoing seems to be just what children like.

Moneysaver
Guided tours of the Tower of London are free (after you pay the admission price) and last one hour.

The White Tower now contains the Royal Armouries, including four of Henry VIII's own suits, and a tiny, ancient chapel. The Bloody Tower may have been the site of the murder of

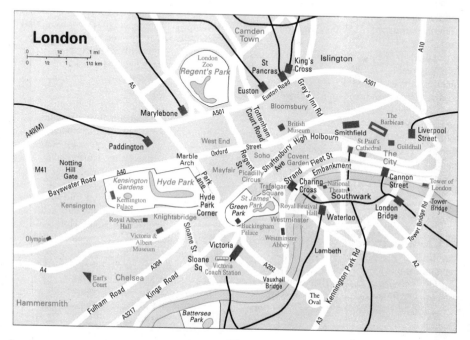

the 'little princes', and Sir Walter Raleigh was certainly imprisoned here. Underneath, a gateway opens on to Tower Green where royal prisoners were executed, having arrived via the Thames at Traitor's Gate (ordinary mortals ended their lives more publicly on Tower Hill). Torture instruments are on view; more engaging are the Crown Jewels, kept in an underground Jewel House (closed February).

The Tower is guarded by 'Yeoman Warders', better known as Beefeaters, whose uniforms haven't changed since the days of Henry VIII. The other inhabitants are the ravens which live and breed in the inner ward. It is said that if they leave, the tower will fall.

Crossing the Thames at this point is Tower Bridge, built in 1894 to match the Tower of London. It's worth a visit for the views from the enclosed walkway along the top.

Across the City, St Paul's Cathedral still feels like London's grandest building, even though it's dwarfed and obscured by 20th-century offices. Ultra-modern in its time, the cathedral was Sir Christopher Wren's greatest work: 'if you seek his monument, look around you' says the Latin inscription on his tomb. It was a target during the blitz bombing of World War II, but volunteers brushed the bombs off the roof and put out the fires.

Be there before 4.15pm to climb 259 steps to the Whispering Gallery which runs round the inside of dome. A word whispered into the wall on one side should be heard 112ft away on the other and return to the whisperer, but other noise obscures the effect. Another 120 steps take you to the Stone Gallery, for outside views of London. From there, stepladders lead to the

St Paul's Cathedral is a major London landmark.

Golden Gallery at the very top – wonderful views, but for the healthy and adventurous only (not open Sunday). Evensong at St Paul's is at 5.30pm. Or time your visit round an organ recital – every Friday at 12.30pm (tube station: St Pauls).

Cross Ludgate Hill and go down Carter Lane to an odd little corner of London, with narrow streets and hidden gardens on the sites of long-gone monastic buildings. Visit the Black Friar pub on for an amazing Art Nouveau reminder of the vanished local monks.

The Monument column commemorates the Great Fire of London in 1666. It stands 202ft high and 202ft from the fire's starting point in the king's baker's house in Pudding Lane. It looks lost among later developments, but climb the 311 winding, claustrophobic steps inside for a view for miles across London.

The Great Fire of London in 1666 destroyed much of the City and boosted London's fire insurance business. Plaques on buildings showed which company they were insured by: the Chartered Insurance Institute at 20 Aldermanbury (near the Guildhall) has a display.

Local flavour
Leadenhall market has stalls selling oysters and lobsters in an arcade of Victorian glass and iron.

At Leadenhall you're at the foot of the Lloyds building, designed by Richard Rogers – all gleaming glass and steel with pipes, ventilation shafts, glass lifts and other working bits on the outside. At night it's bathed in blue light; by day you can go in free, and it's well worth a look. An enclosed lift takes you up to the Visitors' Gallery, with its view 100ft down the middle of the building to the Underwriting Room – the hub of operations. Focal point here is the Lutine Bell, traditionally rung twice for good news, once for bad. An exhibition explains Lloyds' business (open Monday to Friday).

For a lot more action, watch the London International Financial Futures market, or LIFFE. They're based in the Royal Exchange building. Traders here speculate in currencies with much shouting and gesticulation. Free, and only from 11.30am to 1.45pm, Monday to Friday.

You can't go inside the Bank of England, but it does have a free museum, with chunks of gold (some of them real), a big display of old bank notes, interactive videos to test your knowledge, uniforms and all sorts of other Bank items on display (open Monday to Friday).

Local flavour

Street crime is rare in the City, but a messenger was robbed in 1990. He was carrying £300 million worth of bonds – such an everyday transaction around here that no one had thought to give him a bodyguard.

Centre of City government is the Guildhall. This cathedral-like 15th-century hall is the meeting place of the Court of Common Council which administers the area, and the site of the annual Lord Mayor's Banquet. The big wooden figures are Gog and Magog, British giants said to have fought off Trojan invaders in around 1000BC (open daily, free). The Guildhall Library has the best collection of manuscripts and books concerned with London; the Guildhall Clock Museum is a peaceful place where you can study intricate little watches to the soothing background tick-tocking of clocks (free). If you're at the Guildhall in late July/early August, you may see horsedrawn carts arriving to be marked with the City crest. 'Cart Marking' was required by law in the days when the City controlled all carts within its boundaries.

Moneysaver

Broadgate Arena has free lunchtime concerts from April to September: jazz, classical, Caribbean and others. From October to March this is an ice rink (admission charged).

The National Postal Museum has a huge collection of stamps and art work for stamps from all over the world. The way in is inside London's most handsome post office (King Edward Street), and admission is free.

City pubs and wine bars are good for wine and a very traditional atmosphere, but they usually close early in the evening.

Take the tube to Blackfriars to emerge near the east end of Fleet Street. A tiny street called St Bride's Avenue leads to St Bride's Church, built by Wren. The steeple is said to have inspired the traditional tiered wedding cake. Below you can see finds from excavations, going back to the Romans through 2,000 years of London life: open Monday to Friday and free.

Dr Johnson, Mark Twain, Theodore Roosevelt and many other notables have frequented Ye Olde Cheshire Cheese in Wine Office Court (off Fleet Street). Newly built after the Great Fire of London in 1666, it's a place of low ceilings and open fires. Next to the pub is the way into Gough Square, where Dr Johnson's house is open Monday to Saturday (closed bank holidays). There are more old houses (all offices today) in Red Lion Court and Bolt Court.

Prince Henry's Room at 17 Fleet Street is named after King Charles I's elder brother. It probably had nothing to do with him, but it is London's oldest domestic building, with a decorated plaster ceiling and carved panelling. Open Monday to Saturday afternoons, and free.

London's barristers and some solicitors work in the Inns of Court, in surroundings with a distinctly Dickensian flavour. Go through the gatehouse in Middle Temple Lane off Fleet Street for the Temple, an area of green courtyards, gardens and mellow brick buildings running down towards the River Thames. The Devereux pub, down an alley opposite the Law Courts, is a nice place for a pint.

The legal connection with the area goes back to the 15th century, but the name comes from the Knights Templar, who were soldier monks of the Middle Ages. They built round churches as a reminder of the Holy Sepulchre in Jerusalem, and one of them is in the Temple. It's much bigger inside than you expect, with ancient carvings around the south door and stone effigies of knights in the round nave.

Lincoln's Inn is another haven of the legal world. Wildy and Son's bookshop (piled high with old legal tomes) is by a gateway into New Square, a green lawn surrounded by 18th-century buildings. You can't walk on the grass unless you belong here though. Beyond is Lincoln's Inn gardens, with more green tranquillity, trees and permission to sit and picnic – quietly – from 12 noon to 2.30pm. Inigo Jones designed the chapel – open Monday to Friday, free.

Gray's Inn is the last of the Inns of Court, and lies northwards on the other side of High Holborn. Sir Francis Bacon designed the gardens in the 16th century, and Shakespeare's *Comedy of Errors* was first performed here in 1594. There's a 16th-century hall, but you have to apply to the Under Treasurer in writing to see it. The gardens (including a catalpa tree planted by Bacon) are open daily from 12 noon to 2.30pm, from May to mid September (free).

Lincoln's Inn Fields have a much less reverent atmosphere. Duels used to be fought here and the plane trees were sometimes used for hanging people; today it's become a camping ground for homeless people. There's a netball court and a kiosk with tables and chairs for snacks and ice creams.

The strangest-looking house was the home of the architect Sir John Soane, who designed the Bank of England. Not only is it filled from floor to ceiling with art and bits and pieces he collected, it's also just as he left it, with his colour schemes and layout. For a free lecture tour go on Saturday at 2.30pm – numbers are limited to 25, no parties allowed. Open Tuesday to Saturday, and free.

The Courtauld Institute's collection of priceless paintings is in Somerset House, at the Fleet Street end of the Strand.

BLOOMSBURY, MARYLEBONE AND REGENT'S PARK

Bloomsbury has Georgian squares, bookshops, literary links, budget ethnic eating – and a giant of a museum.

The British Museum (Holborn or Russell Square tube stations) started modestly in 1753 with an 80,000-item collection belonging to Sir Hans Sloane. Since then it has grown. The theme is 'the works of man' from prehistoric times.

Highlights include the Egyptian mummies (of cats as well as people), and the Rosetta Stone. The Elgin marbles are a sculpted frieze from the Parthenon in Athens (and the Greeks would like them back). Follow the sequence round to get the sense of excitement as horses and riders prepare for a procession, then gradually pick up speed. Finds from Britain include the Sutton Hoo Treasure, an 89ft Anglo-Saxon ship from the 7th century containing important artefacts. A big Oriental section has jolly Buddhas and other deities. The new Japanese galleries have changing displays of lacquer and other delicate items – nothing is permanently on show, because it's all too fragile. There's a lot more, but you could easily spend an entire visit among the illuminated manuscripts and the scribbles of Keats, Virginia Woolf and others, just right of the main entrance.

The Portland Vase is one of the British Museum's most prized items. It dates from the early years AD. Smashed by a vandal in 1845, it has been repaired three times – the last effort, in 1989, is very impressive.

If an Egyptian cat or even the Rosetta Stone has caught your fancy, you might be able to buy a copy in the museum shop; also here are books, postcards and posters.

Moneysaver
From October to April, the South Place Ethical Society holds concerts at 6.30pm every Sunday at Conway Hall, 25 Red Lion Square. Tickets cost £2.50 at the door. (Holborn tube station.)

Gordon Square was the home of Virginia Woolf and others of the Bloomsbury Group of intellectuals and artists in the first decades of the 20th century. The Bloomsbury Workshop (free) in Galen Place (off Bury Place) is a bookshop and gallery which specialises in Bloomsbury Group art and literature. They can advise on Bloomsbury Group places in and outside

London (closed at weekends).

Charles Dickens lived not very far away at 48 Doughty Street, from 1837 to 1839 – you can visit the house from Monday to Saturday (not bank holidays).

On the other (west) side of the British Museum, Charlotte Street has numerous low-price Greek and other restaurants, plus a cluster of galleries (free) around Windmill Street.

Local flavour

The Princess Louise at 208 High Holborne has wonderful etched mirrors and Victorian décor, installed in 1891. You'll also find a range of 'real ales' and bitters here.

Madame Tussaud's, in Marylebone, is always busy. Get there before opening time to avoid longer waiting later on. The usual opening time is 10am, but it's 9.30am at weekends and 9am in July and August. It isn't a budget outing, but if you want to see re-creations of famous people, past and present, then it rewards the payment and the waiting with a quality show. It's certainly instructive to see how tall or short famous people really are, although US visitors may be worried by the unhealthy look of Presidents Lincoln, Reagan and Bush. The Chamber of Horrors includes an excellent re-creation of a London back street among its nasty scenes, and the prison officer with moving eyes is a big hit. Photography is allowed.

Local flavour

Madame Tussaud founded her waxworks show in Paris in 1770. She made death masks of guillotine victims during the French Revolution. The show settled in Marylebone Road in 1835.

The London Planetarium is a lot more wholesome: you sit back in your chair and see the glories of the night sky projected on to the dome while a commentator tells you about them. The first show is at 10.20am, and they start every 40 minutes after that until 5pm (starting time is 12.20pm on weekdays in school holidays. In the evening it becomes the Laserium, with laser shows to rock music at 6pm and 7.45pm, except Mondays.

Moneysaver

Family tickets (two adults and two children) and combined tickets reduce the cost of visiting Madame Tussaud's and the Planetarium.

The Wallace Collection in Manchester Square is one of London's less-visited places, but it's well worth some time (and it's free). The most famous painting here is Franz Hals' *Laughing Cavalier*, but there are also pictures by Canaletto and Titian and other notables, lots of porcelain, fine furniture, clocks and a sizeable display of armoury – all in a very handsome 18th-century town house.

London Zoo began as a small collection of animals in Regents Park, and has grown into one of the world's biggest zoos. It has changed a lot in recent years, as doubts have grown about the ethics of keeping animals. The old cages have been replaced by enclosures which re-create natural environments, and there are breeding programmes to preserve threatened species. In the Charles Clore pavilion for small animals, the 'Moonlight World' reverses night and day so you can see nocturnal animals going about their business.

The zoo is in Regents Park, which is one of London's vaster green open spaces. It has a sizeable boating lake and a rose garden at the centre, and it's dotted with elegant houses. The Regent's Canal runs along the north side and you can take narrowboat rides between March and early October: telephone Jason's Trip on 071-286 3428 to book. *Jason* starts at Little Venice, opposite 60 Blomfield Road: the nearest tube station is Warwick Avenue.

THE WEST END

Oxford Street The main stretch for big stores is from Marble Arch to Oxford Circus.

Numerous high street chain stores for shoes and clothes have branches here. Oxford Street is usually crowded, and very crowded on Saturday, at lunchtime or during sales.

Marks and Spencer's biggest branch is near Marble Arch: their high reputation is for quality and value in men's, women's and children's wear, especially underwear and knitwear. They do household goods too.

C&A offers a big choice of clothes for men, women and children, including good value ski wear. Selfridges is immense, and includes a food hall and big selection of household goods. John Lewis has an extensive range of household goods too, and a wonderful fabrics department. Off-cuts are sold at a reduced price. Between Oxford Circus and Tottenham Court Road there are more small shops, often selling clothes at very low prices: worth investigating for jeans and other casual wear. There are some chain store branches here too.

The vast HMV store on this section of Oxford Street sells music of all sorts on record, tape and CD.

Regent Street   Regent Street runs from Oxford Circus to Piccadilly Circus. There are some exclusive stores here, but chains such as Laura Ashley have arrived in recent years.

Near the northern end, Liberty is arguably London's most attractive department store. Walk round the back to admire the timber-frame construction of the building; the inside has panelling to match. The great speciality here is fabrics, which need not cost the earth; and the high quality clothes, Oriental goods, antiques, accessories, glass and china which may not be within budget range but are usually interesting to see.

Hamleys is a big, long-established toy shop, with several floors of toys and games of all sorts, from teddies to electronics and including the the most 'in' toys of the moment. The pre-Christmas crowds are legendary. Classic clothes shops in Regent Street include Jaeger, Aquascutum and Burberry – go at sale time for one of their distinctive raincoats. Garrard are the Queen's jewellers, and have responsibility for the upkeep of the Crown Jewels.

Tower Records is at the end of the street, where it meets Piccadilly Circus: a huge range of music here, and it's open until midnight.

Charing Cross Road   The street of bookshops, including low-price second-hand and remainder titles. Tottenham Court Road tube station is at the north end. For new books, Books Etc at number 120 has a good range of fiction and fact, including a large travel section. It's easy to find your way around and the staff are helpful. Over the road, Foyles is famous, chaotic and infuriating, but it has nearly every English book in print and will almost certainly have the one you want – somewhere. Waterstones next door is a good general bookshop on several floors (with a useful travel section).

Mayfair   This is the area south of Oxford Street (west end). The very name suggests London life at its classiest, thanks to a history as one of London's wealthiest residential areas. Businesses have a strong presence here now, which has dulled the old social focus, but you still get more than a whiff of opulence in the streets. Start at Bond Street for some wonderful window shopping.

Running from Oxford Street to Piccadilly, 'New' Bond Street is at the top – north – end and 'Old' at the bottom. Some of the world's more expensive clothes, shoes and jewellery are on sale here, under the labels of Yves St Laurent and other international names. Among the shops with no price tags (if you need to ask, you can't afford it) look out for Fenwicks department store – it has a good name for its wide range of women's wear (and underwear), with prices starting at reasonable levels. South Moulton Street is the place to see designer clothes.

Sotheby's at 34 New Bond Street is one of the world's leading auction rooms. It looks rather private, but it's open to all from 9am to 4.30pm should you wish to sit in on the sales (no charge). In the surrounding rooms you can view the lots which are coming up for sale, including the kinds of things that are otherwise seen only in museums.

Walk north along Queen Street and beyond to catch the spirit of old times in Mayfair. It can be rewarding to delve down down narrower streets and through archways into quiet 'mews' back streets. Only a few of the larger houses are still family homes, but plaques commemorate the great and famous (and often forgotten).

The squares of this area are peaceful oases with big leafy screens of trees. Grosvenor Square is dominated by the vast the US embassy. You won't hear any nightingales in Berkeley Square today, though you will hear the ringing tones of the English aristocracy at pubs in the area. St George's Church, just off Hanover Square, has lunchtime recitals at 1.10pm (free, but donations invited). The gardens in the squares are open (free) on weekdays, and they're packed at lunchtimes with office workers coming up for air.

Eros - the famous statue in Piccadilly Circus.

Moneysaver

Vidal Sassoon's Hairdressing School in Davies Mews will remodel your hair for only £6.50 (less if you are a student) if you're willing to put yourself in the hands of a student; telephone 071-499 5808.

Burlington Arcade   This Regency-style shopping mall now shelters expensive gift-type shops. Take a stroll along the arcade, but don't whistle, run or sing – there are beadles on patrol to enforce decorous behaviour. On the south side it opens into Piccadilly.

The Museum of Mankind is a branch of the British Museum, but much less famous and much more peaceful. Straight ahead as you go in is the Café de Colombia: a cool, light and stylish place for a tasty but not very cheap light lunch (about £5) and good coffee (but no tea). It's in Burlington Gardens, a street on what used to be the gardens of Burlington House (now the Royal Academy).

Shepherd Market   This is an oasis of life, with the roar of Piccadilly on one side, and the beautiful but largely unlived-in streets and squares of Mayfair on the other. It's a cluster of shops, restaurants and sandwich bars, with tables spilling out over the pavements in summer and a 'village' feel. Among the more expensive eating places there are cheaper pasta style joints. Don't expect pure sweetness and light though: traditionally this is a red light district.

Piccadilly   The first impression of Piccadilly is of airline offices and tourist boards, but it

repays a closer look. And there's only one place to start . . . Piccadilly Circus.

Piccadilly Circus is always packed with sightseers and other lingerers, though the attraction isn't easy to explain. Perhaps it's the neon lights or the formation dancing of the traffic, perhaps it's the statue known as *Eros*, who is actually an all-aluminium Spirit of Charity. The Trocadero has shops and ethnic food, and stays open till midnight (11pm on Sunday). Also here is the Guinness World of Records exhibition, which is all based on the *Guinness Book of Records* – tallest man, shortest women etc. It's open from 10am to 10pm, which is a plus, but it is expensive, as is the Rock Circus at the London Pavilion, which is run by Madame Tussaud's and has 'bionic' wax model rock stars performing. Open till 9pm from Sunday to Thursday, other nights till 10pm.

Simpson of Piccadilly is a department store with a name for classic clothes, usually at classic prices. But go at sale time, and you might pick up a high quality bargain. Hatchards bookshop has an attractive setting in an old building, with good all-round stock and helpful staff.

Fortnum and Mason is a classy department store, like a smaller, quainter Harrods, but is best known for its food hall (expensive) on the ground floor. Fun to look though, and the building is a treasure.

The beautiful St James's Church was designed by Sir Christopher Wren, with inside woodwork by Grinling Gibbons. Lunchtime concerts are on Thursdays and Fridays at 1pm – free, but donations invited. There are evening concerts too, for which you have to buy tickets, but they're not expensive. On Fridays and Saturdays there's a craft market in the churchyard, and the Wren Café at the west end of the church is open every day.

The Royal Academy puts on major international art exhibitions, and they're widely publicised. The Summer Exhibition comes round every year, in June, July and August, with an enjoyable hotchpotch of all sorts of pictures. This is an art academy too: if the students' summer show is on, take the opportunity to get a glimpse behind the scenes. The admission charge varies.

The narrower streets south of Piccadilly have some venerable specialist shops. James Lock at 6 St James's Street has been making hats for over 200 years: they made the first bowler hat and called it the Coke after the client. Paxton and Whitfield at 93 Jermyn Street are cheese specialists, with a splendid array of well kept varieties.

Local flavour

Mayfair takes it's name from an annual fair which was held for two riotous weeks every year. The area only became respectable after the fair closed down in the 18th century.

Soho   Once a sleazy red light area, Soho has become much more respectable in recent years. Some people say it's now too bland, but it still has colour thanks to the ethnic communities that have settled here over the years. French Protestants arrived in 17th century; later there were Greeks and Italians, and today it has a big Chinese community. Ethnic food shops and above all restaurants are the great attraction here. Leicester Square tube station is central.

The Camisa food stores at 1A Berwick Street and 61 Old Compton Street are family-run concerns selling the best in Italian pasta, cheeses, olive oil, salami and the like – prices aren't high, and off-cuts may be sold at a reduced rate. You don't have to look hard to find somewhere to eat in Soho. There are some very low priced cafés and restaurants with good reputations.

Soho's Chinatown centres on Gerrard Street – easy to identify by the pagoda-style street furniture. You could spend a long time just browsing among the local supermarkets and other stores. There's also a big choice of restaurants and cafés.

Covent Garden   Huge crowds are drawn here during the day, for the shops, bars, markets and street entertainers, and it's one of the very few areas in London which really fizzes in the evening and on Sundays. This is ideal territory for ambling about and enjoying the atmosphere by night or day. Covent Garden tube station is central.

The Covent Garden Piazza used to be a wholesale fruit, vegetable and flower market, and at night you'd have seen the market porters rubbing shoulders with the dressed-up opera goers emerging from the nearby Royal Opera House. The opera house is still there (see *Orientation*), but the market moved out in 1974, and the buildings now house stylish and fairly pricey shops. The streets around here include numerous clothes shops, and some unusual specialist stores.

On a typical day, the crowd could be applauding a juggler at one end of the Piazza and a string quartet at the other.

Shops in Covent Garden are regularly open till 7.30pm, as well as on Sunday afternoons. The markets close earlier, but Jubilee market is open all day Sunday.

Local flavour

Eliza Doolittle was a Covent Garden flower seller in George Bernard Shaw's play *Pygmalion*, filmed as *My Fair Lady*.

Overlooking the scene is St Paul's Church, known as the 'actors' church' – go round the side for the way in and memorials to familiar names from stage and screen.

The Theatre Museum is a treasurehouse of props, posters and costumes, including many used by the famous from Sarah Siddons to John Lennon and Mick Jagger. Open Tuesday to Sunday, until 7pm. There's a little theatre inside – if you go for a performance, you can see the museum free. Whether you visit the museum or not, keep the café in mind for a light lunch or tea, telephone 071-836 7891.

What used to be the flower market at Covent Garden is now the London Transport Museum, with lots of old vehicles like steam locomotives and buses. You can sit in a bus driver's seat, 'drive' a Circle Line tube train, watch working models and get an insight into the system. Good value, although there aren't as many chances to look round inside the vehicles as children might like.

Moneysaver
Look out for art school degree shows around June, when graduates display their work – not just paintings, but pots, jewellery, furniture and other specialities. The shows are free and fun, and there's always a chance of buying something beautiful and unique.

WESTMINSTER AND ST JAMES'S

BUDGET FOR A DAY

Westminster Abbey	(donation) 2·00
Cabinet War Rooms	3·50
Tate Gallery	Free
Lunch	3·50
Dinner	9·50
	£ 18·50

plus accommodation

Trafalgar Square   This famous square celebrates Nelson, the hero of the Battle of Trafalgar in 1805. His 17ft 4in statue surveys the scene from the top of his granite column (total height about 185ft), with lions and fountains at the base. Thousands of pigeons live in and around the square, and they're viewed with delight or suspicion according to temperament. Nearest tube stations are Charing Cross and Leicester Square.

The lions are by Landseer, and you can see a painting of him with lions in the National Portrait Gallery (behind the National Gallery, which runs along the top of the square). The huge collection is arranged by date and by theme: the Romantic poets' room has Byron in a turban and Keats looking pale and poetic; elsewhere, Elizabeth I in full finery is close to a dark little portrait of Shakespeare wearing an earring. The 20th-century section is an entertaining hotchpotch of the famous, in photos, cartoons and other media as well as paintings. Free except for some special exhibitions, and there are free lunchtime lectures from Tuesday to Friday, and special events on Saturday afternoons such as readings or recitals. Children's events are arranged in the school holidays.

The National Gallery is the home of some very famous pictures, like Constable's *Haywain* and the 'Rokeby' *Venus*. If you want to see some highlights, use *A Quick Visit to the National Gallery*, which includes a map and commentary on 16 great works of art. There are 2,000 pictures here from all the great areas of European painting, from the 14th to the 20th centuries. (Most British paintings and international 20th-century paintings are at the Tate Gallery.) Free except for some special exhibitions; and the National Gallery, too, has free lunchtime lectures and twice-daily guided tours from Tuesday to Saturday, plus lunchtime films about art and artists on Monday and children's events in school holidays. On summer Wednesdays it stays open to 8pm, with talks and recitals at 6.30pm.

St Martin-in-the-Fields has a galleried interior with royal boxes, because Buckingham Palace is in the same parish. This is an active church with a lot going on, including concerts (free at lunchtime, but donations invited). It includes a refuge for homeless people.

Whitehall   Leading off Trafalgar Square, this is where you'll find a detachment of the plumed and helmeted Household Cavalry staring stolidly through ranks of sightseers taking photographs.

The Banqueting House is all that's left of the former Palace of Whitehall, most of which was destroyed by fire. It was designed by Inigo Jones and has extraordinary ceiling paintings by Rubens. Inside is a huge room: go to the far end to view the ceiling paintings from where they were meant to be seen by King Charles I. He was executed outside in 1649. (Closed Monday.)

Number 10 Downing Street has been the official residence of the Prime Minister since Robert Walpole lived there in 1735. Number 11 is the residence of the Chancellor of the Exchequer. The street has been closed to the public for some time, but former Prime Minister, Margaret Thatcher had large gates put across the entrance.

Signs direct you to the Cabinet War Rooms, the weird heart of British operations in World War II. The rooms are in a heavily reinforced underground bunker, where Winston Churchill and many others worked (and often slept) to evade wartime bombing. You see things much as they were, complete with 1930s-40s telephones and typewriters, and maps showing different armies in coloured wool.

Local flavour
The Cabinet War Rooms include the telephone room which had Churchill's transatlantic hotline to the US President. It was so secret that people working there assumed the door led to Churchill's private lavatory.

Westminster   The Houses of Parliament have been transformed in recent years, because they've been cleaned to reveal the fine detail of

The Houses of Parliament have public galleries.

the Gothic design by Sir Charles Barry and Augustus Pugin. Most people know the clock tower at the north end as Big Ben, though properly speaking Big Ben is the 13 ton bell inside.

This is where politicians debate and decide the country's future, and it's a fascinating spectacle. You can watch them at work (and sometimes at sleep) from the visitors' galleries: Monday to Thursday from 2.30pm, Friday from 9.30am until about 3pm for the House of Commons. Hours for the House of Lords are Monday to Wednesday from 2.30pm, Thursday from 3pm and Friday from 11am. From Monday to Thursday the talking in the Commons goes on until 10pm or later: if you haven't got a ticket, you're advised to go at around 5pm. If you want to be there for Prime Minister's Question Time at 3.15pm on Tuesday and Thursday, a ticket is essential – write to your MP or embassy weeks ahead. The procedure is the same if you want a guided tour (Monday to Thursday only). This is the only way to see Westminster Hall, which dates from Norman times and has a 600-ton roof supported by ingeniously engineered beams. For information telephone 071-219 3000 (Commons), 071-219 3107 (Lords). Tube station: Westminster.

English monarchs have been crowned at Westminster Abbey since the 11th century, when Edward the Confessor had it enlarged just for that purpose. The tombs of Elizabeth I and other royals are here, together with memorials to numerous notable people. Poets' Corner and the Tomb of the Unknown Warrior always seem special places; and at the heart of the abbey is the shrine of Edward the Confessor. Donations are expected, and there is a charge for certain parts of the Abbey. Prepare yourself for long queues in the summer.

Among the abbey buildings is the little College Garden (open till 4pm from October to March, but otherwise until 6pm). A combined ticket lets you into the abbey museum to see coronation regalia, the Pyx chamber for treasures, and the Chapter House, which has medieval tiles, painting and sculpture.

Westminster Cathedral is about half a mile up Victoria Street. Buses run this way, or you could catch a tube to Victoria. This is London's Roman

Catholic cathedral, built in Byzantine style. The interior decoration isn't finished yet, but the combination of dark brick vaulting, shadowy domes, glittering mosaics and coloured stone make a wonderful effect. Along one side of the square you'll find the Royal Horticultural Society Old Hall, with the New Hall close by. There are flower and produce shows here about once a month. The shows aren't as glamorous as the Chelsea Flower Show, but they're more frequent and less crowded.

 You could walk to the Tate Gallery from here; other ways to get there are by bus or by walking along the river from Parliament Square, or by bus from Victoria train station. The nearest tube is Pimlico station (not very near). The Tate has British art from Elizabethan times, and modern art from all over the world, so you can choose between Constable's landscapes and the most abstract of abstract expressionists. If you've visited before but not recently, you'll almost certainly find the new layout exciting. Attached is the new Clore Gallery, which houses the collection of paintings by Turner: this is the best collection of his work, and includes some wild and wonderful studies of light. Free except for some special exhibitions.

Moneysaver
Posters for portable and reasonably priced souvenirs are on sale at the National Gallery, National Portrait Gallery and the Tate.

St James's This is aristocratic London, with royal palaces and exclusive shops. St James's Palace was started by Henry VIII as his official London home. It's still used by the Crown and isn't open, but you can walk through (not drive, ride or cycle) to the Mall. The streets around here are secluded and usually peaceful. St James's Park is arguably London's prettiest, with lawns for lazing, lots of trees, and water with black swans and pelicans, homely coots and mallard ducks.

 You can tell when the Queen is at Buckingham Palace because the Royal

Standard (flag) is hoisted over the building. The house isn't open, but the outbuildings offer two good-value outings. On Wednesday and Thursday afternoons you can visit the Royal Mews (the stables) to meet splendid horses and get a close look at the royal carriages and tack. The Queen's Gallery has changing exhibitions of art and other items from the royal collections; closed Monday.

KNIGHTSBRIDGE, KENSINGTON AND CHELSEA

London's most famous shop, and it's free just to look.

Knightsbridge Just a few yards from South Kensington tube station, Daquise is a Polish café and restaurant with a real Eastern European feel to it, thanks to lots of elderly Polish ladies having their coffee and cakes while they chat and put on their lipstick.

Some of London's most luxurious and expensive stores and smaller shops are found here, but by far the most famous is Harrods. This is Europe's largest department store, and the legend is that they sell everything. If it isn't in stock they'll order it for you. It can delight you with touches like harpists playing in the perfume department, though you may be shocked at the sheer excess. The whole store is good for a wander, with some truly sumptuous displays. The Food Halls are the most spectacular. At night the façade is lit by 11,000 light bulbs. Harrods sales in January and July are a celebrated fight for bargains (Knightsbridge tube station.)

South Kensington South Kensington puts you in touch with the ideals of the Victorian age.

It's dominated by a row of huge museums, which were planned by Prince Albert as part of a centre of learning. There are colleges in this area too: in summer you can usually climb the tower of Imperial College on Exhibition Road for good views over London. The museums are linked to the tube station by a foot tunnel, which is the also the easiest way to reach the Royal Albert Hall (see *Entertainment*, page 55).

The Victoria and Albert Museum, affectionately known as the V&A, specialises in art and design of all periods and parts of the world. Exhibits range from Japanese ivories to 20th-century creations in plastic. You'll find sculpture, carvings, ceramics of all ages, fashions, enamels and tapestries and very modern items too. If you want to take in the most famous bits, like the Raphael cartoons, use *100 Things To See in the V&A*.

Admission to the V&A is free, despite the battery of cashiers at the entrance. They're there to accept voluntary donations. You can just walk past, and many do. That said, it's a fantastic place, and you may feel inclined to give more than the suggested donation (£2) when you leave. The shop is full of beautiful things.

There are free tours four times a day Monday to Saturday, plus daily tours of the British collections, family tours in school holidays, daily talks and lectures at 2.30pm (Sunday 3.30pm), children's events, sometimes free lunchtime concerts and various special events.

The Science Museum concentrates on science in life, and it has always been good on participation. All ages can have fun activating the exhibits. The very popular Launch Pad on the first floor is full of games and tests which demonstrate scientific principles. There are galleries on chemistry, nuclear physics, electricity and all sorts of other aspects of science, including a big new display on food. Upstairs is the maze of the Wellcome Museum of the History of Medicine, not easy to get out of in a hurry.

The Science Museum and Natural History Museum are free from 4.30pm onwards (5pm at weekends). You should miss the school parties after that time too. The Natural History Museum's family ticket is a sizeable saving if you use it for the maximum two adults and four children.

Take time to admire the building at the Natural History Museum, including inside details like the monkeys climbing the pillars. You know that you're on to a winner for children when you see the dinosaur in the great entrance hall. There are lots of interactive displays to explain evolution and biology; the oil and gas section is designed as an offshore rig; and the Creepie-Crawlies gallery has hundreds of insects and spiders. The geological section includes a piece of the moon among thousands of rock samples. Downstairs, the Discovery Centre offers more activities, and is open to families at weekends and school holidays (they recommend it for seven to 11-year-olds).

Take a breather among the trees and flowers of Kensington Gardens. Kensington Palace is the London base of Princess Margaret and the Prince and Princess of Wales, but you can visit the State Apartments – the big attraction is the collection of court dress from 1750 onwards. Across the park, the statue of Peter Pan has been charming children since the early 1900s. Go over the bridge for the 340 acres of lawns and trees of Hyde Park, which is less formal. The best free show is watching the waterfowl on the Serpentine (where you can also hire a boat). On Sundays, anyone can take to a soapbox at Speaker's Corner and harangue the crowd. The park cafés don't live up to the surroundings.

Local flavour

Hyde Park and other London open spaces are royal parks, which were first opened to the public by kings Charles I and II. They originate from land set aside for hunting by Henry VIII.

Kensington   Kensington itself is west of Kensington Gardens. Kensington market has a reputation for good buys in streetwise clothes for the young. The Commonwealth Institute on Kensington High Street offers three floors of exhibitions on the 49 countries that make up the Commonwealth – no charge, except for some special exhibitions, and the building is very dramatic. Activities like craft sessions are held here, either free or for a minimal fee, and both children and adults can get involved. The shop sells lots of crafts and other products, and prices start low.

Moneysaver

The Commonwealth Institute puts on free entertainment on Sunday afternoons. The setting is in the midst of the colourful exhibitions, and you're encouraged to meet the artists at half-time. The shop has a sale in January.

There is also no charge for visiting the house and garden of the Victorian artist Lord Leighton, on Holland Park Road, off Melbury Road (near the Commonwealth Institute). The house is closed Sunday and bank holidays.

Chelsea The King's Road, Chelsea, starts at Sloane Square. Mary Quant opened her first boutique in the King's Road in the 1950s; in the 1970s, punks stalked along the road, shocking and enthralling with their multicoloured hair. The King's Road doesn't exude character like that any more, but it still has some strange shops. Buses run along it from Sloane Square, take the tube to Sloane Square station.

The National Army Museum on Royal Hospital Road has the weapons and uniforms you'd expect, but the displays add up to a vivid picture of life for the ordinary soldier. Interesting even if you're not especially keen on war, and free.

DISCOVERING OUTER LONDON

Some of London's liveliest districts lie just outside central London, a matter of minutes by tube, bus or sometimes boat.

DOCKLANDS

The River Thames used to be a busy working waterway, but its docks are no longer open to shipping. Instead they've been restored for leisure, housing and offices, with urban farms, sailing, a dry-ski slope and an airport among other facilities, plus the 12,000-seat London Arena. The area is heavily promoted and has a visitor centre handing out free maps and information seven days a week (Limeharbour, Docklands Light Railway), telephone 071-512 3000.

DLR is the Docklands Light Railway, and it is the best way to see the area. The section through the Isle of Dogs runs past open water and dramatic modern buildings such as vast Canary Wharf. The trains have 'Captains' but no drivers (unless the computer is broken, which is often the case).

St Katharine Docks are now a picturesque place to wander round, looking at the yachts and sailing barges on the water. Former warehouses have been converted into shops; the Dickens Inn is a barn-like but popular pub – all close to the Tower of London (Tower Hill tube station, Tower Gateway DLR).

Tobacco Dock is a shopping mall in old warehouse buildings: lots of shops, places to eat and some street entertainment, but crowds aren't usually a problem (Shadwell DLR). Hay's Galleria is on similar lines, on the south side of the river between London Bridge and Tower Bridge.

The Prospect of Whitby is a picturesque riverside pub, but a steady stream of coach parties detracts from the atmosphere. An alternative with river views (through glass) is the Grapes on Narrow Street (Limehouse DLR). Away from the river are two much friendlier pubs. The House They Left Behind is in Narrow Street; the Five Bells and Bladebone is in Three Colts Street, behind the wonderful Hawksmoor Church of St Anne. The name refers to the five bells that rang at closing time for the docks. On the south side of the river, the Angel is off Jamaica Road and gives one of the best views of Tower Bridge. The Mayflower is a beautiful and friendly pub on the river front off Brunel Road (both close to Rotherhithe tube station): sit on the jetty to enjoy the view.

EAST END MARKETS

This is the London of the television series *East Enders*, though you won't find their exact location, because it's a studio fabrication. This is a great area for street markets and ethnic eating.

Petticoat Lane market is from 9am to 2pm along Middlesex Street and others, near Liverpool Street train station. Hundreds of stalls sell clothes and household goods. Flowers and plants are sold at Columbia Road from 8am to 1pm. Quality might not always be as high as elsewhere, but prices are low.

Brick Lane market is partly along Brick Lane but mainly along Cheshire Street. Some new household goods and clothes are sold here, but the real speciality is second-hand goods – from antiques (a few), to reasonable second-hand, to junk. A bargain hunter's paradise, but not for the fastidious. To get here go to Aldgate East tube station and walk up Brick Lane. As in all busy shopping areas, be careful of money and valuables at London street markets.

Local flavour

Tubby Isaac's stall sells ready-to-eat shellfish and jellied eels near Aldgate East tube. Other places to buy shellfish include Brick Lane market.

GREENWICH

Cutty Sark is just one of Greenwich's attractions.

BUDGET FOR A DAY		
One-day travel card		2·60
Cutty Sark		2·90
Gipsy Moth IV		·30
National Maritime Museum & Old Royal Observatory		3·00
Royal Naval College	Free	
Lunch		3·50
Dinner		7·00
		£ 19·30
plus accommodation		

The scenic way to reach Greenwich is by boat: trips start from from Tower, Westminster and Charing Cross Piers for a 30 to 45-minute journey. An alternative is to take the Docklands Light Railway or bus to Island Gardens on the Isle of Dogs, and then walk under the river through a Victorian foot tunnel.

Greenwich feels leafy and villagey after central London, and besides visiting the many sights, you can take breezy parkland walks. The best free thing is the view back to London from the top of the park by the Old Royal Observatory.

One of the first things you'll see is a sailing ship, the *Cutty Sark*, a record-breaking tea clipper built in 1869. She's now in dry dock and open to visitors. Near by is *Gypsy Moth IV*, the tiny yacht in which Sir Francis Chichester became the first to sail single-handed round the world, in 1966-67.

Inigo Jones designed the Queen's House, and it has been restored to look as it would have done in the 1660s, when freshly fitted out. The rush matting and plain white walls are authentic, as are the amazing colours in the Queen's own apartments. Even the furniture has been newly made, using appropriate techniques. Fascinating, but don't expect the mellow look of most old houses. The admission charge includes a wand to activate a recorded commentary.

The National Maritime Museum has a huge collection of all things nautical, including ship models and figureheads, charts and marine pictures, and the jacket worn by Nelson at the Battle of Trafalgar, complete with bullet hole. For the same price you can visit the Old Royal Observatory up the hill. The Greenwich Meridian is marked here, so you can stand in the eastern and western hemispheres at the same time. And set your watch by the timeball, which drops at 1pm precisely.

Moneysaver
The *Cutty Sark*, Queen's House, National Maritime Museum and Old Royal Observatory can be visited on a Passport Ticket. It is valid for a year. The 18th-century Ranger's House is free (near the Observatory).

Visit on Saturday or Sunday for Greenwich market – a great hunting ground for collectable things and second-hand clothing. It starts at 7am and goes on to 5.30pm. Greenwich Theatre has a reputation for interesting productions.

HAMPSTEAD AND HIGHGATE

The leafy heights of Hampstead make a refreshing change from city streets (Hampstead Town tube station). Hampstead Heath covers 700 acres including plenty of open grassland for bracing walks and flying kites. Writers and artists have made this their home since the 1700s, when the local spring water made Hampstead a fashionable spa. There are lots of pretty streets, historic pubs and homes of the famous.

Sigmund Freud lived at 20 Maresfield Gardens, telephone 071-435 2002/5167, and the contents include his now-famous couch. Open Wednesday to Sunday afternoons, signposted from Finchley Road tube station. John Keats lived at Wentworth Place, Keats Grove. *Ode to a Nightingale* was written in the garden. Open every afternoon, and on Saturday morning (free).

Hampstead and Highgate ponds offer deep fresh water swimming, free. There are pools for mixed, men's and women's bathing, but the latter have the nicest wooded settings. Only for confident swimmers, telephone 081-340 4044. (Nearest tube station is Kentish Town.)

Highgate is on the other side of the heath from Hampstead. Highgate Cemetery has the tomb of Karl Marx on the east side, but the western section is the most evocative, with splendid Victorian tombs in tangled greenery. You can usually only visit this part on guided tours: 12

noon, 2pm and 4pm on weekdays, every hour from 11am to 4pm on Saturday, and about every 20 minutes on Sunday afternoon. Winter tours stop earlier: telephone 081-340 1834 to check. Waterlow Park off the High Street is attractive too; nearest tube station is Highgate.

Local flavour
London cemeteries may sound gloomy places for free sightseeing, but they're remarkable for Victorian sculpture, famous names and wildlife. Highgate is the most famous; others are at Kensal Green (W10) and Abney Park (N16).

KEW GARDENS

Boats run to Kew from Westminster Pier taking about 1½ hours; faster alternatives are by tube to Kew Gardens station and British Rail to Kew Bridge station.

The Royal Botanic Gardens (generally known as 'Kew Gardens') offer idyllic walking among 300 acres of woodland and formal gardens, with spectacular glass houses where you can bask in the tropics on the chilliest winter days. The plants and trees form an internationally important collection, and world-leading research is done at Kew – but you don't have to be a botanist to enjoy it. Many precious trees were lost in 1980s storms however. The gardens always open at 9.30am; closing time ranges from 4pm in winter to 6.30pm in summer (8pm on Sunday and bank holidays).

Inside the gardens is Kew Palace, a country retreat for the first three King Georges: open April to September, and you can visit Queen Charlotte's Cottage, a rustic fantasy house where royalty used to take tea.

LAMBETH

An ex-church by Lambeth Palace houses the Museum of Garden History, founded to commemorate John Tradescant and his son, who were gardeners to Charles I. It includes a garden. Open Monday to Friday but only from

11am to 3pm, and on Sunday 10.30am to 5pm, free. Waterloo tube station is about three quarters of a mile away.

The Imperial War Museum looks at war in the 20th century, and aims to 'bring the past alive' without trivialising or glorifying it. Besides planes, bombs and rockets on show, there are re-creations of wartime scenes, including a World War I trench. The collection of war art is impressive. Lambeth North or Elephant and Castle tube stations are near.

Moneysaver
The Imperial War Museum is free on Fridays.

SOUTHWARK

Southwark is on the south side of the river, close to London Bridge tube station, or a short walk over the bridge from the City. It is also close to the river boat stop at Tower Pier.

Southwark Cathedral is a beautiful old church, tucked close beside the river and easy to miss. Lunchtime and other concerts are held here. HMS *Belfast* is an 11,000-ton Royal Navy cruiser, now moored on the Thames as a floating museum. It's signposted off Tooley Street, and for boat trippers there's a shuttle boat from Tower Pier.

The London Dungeon in Tooley Street offers grisly scenes in slimy surroundings: black witchcraft, ghastly aspects of medicine, execution methods and other subjects are illustrated. Naturally it's very popular, though not a budget outing; telephone 071-403 0606.

NOTTING HILL

Visit on Saturday for Portobello Road market (Notting Hill tube station), with hundreds of stalls selling antiques, collectables and second-hand items, including clothes. Beyond the antiques are fruit and vegetable stalls (including Caribbean specialities), and beyond those are the junkiest stalls, where you're most likely to rootle out a bargain. The atmosphere is usually good, with street entertainers and lots of ethnic eating in the area.

Whiteley's is an old-established department store which has been transformed into a multi-shop mall, with several eating places: fun for browsing. It's a short walk or bus ride away along Queensway (or Bayswater or Queensway tube stations).

OUTINGS FROM LONDON

All the main towns in the *South East England* section could be visited on a day out of London. Oxford, Cambridge and Bath are feasible outings too: see *Central England*, *East Anglia* and *West Country* sections. If you don't mind being at the mercy of someone else's schedule, coach operators offer good value sightseeing tours: ask tourist information centres (addresses in *Orientation in London*).

HAMPTON COURT PALACE

Hampton Court is a splendid Tudor palace, and was once the residence of Henry VIII. You can get there by boat from Westminster Pier, but it takes three or four hours (telephone 071-930 2062). British Rail trains run from London Waterloo to Hampton Court.

The palace was actually built by Cardinal Wolsey, who offered it to Henry VIII in an effort to placate him. The king wasn't appeased, but took the palace anyway and added the great hall, the huge kitchens and the tennis courts. Later rulers made their own additions: William and Mary commissioned Sir Christopher Wren to remodel parts of the palace. The hedge maze also dates from their time and still provides happy puzzlement for visitors. The last ruler to live here was George II, but it is still very much the grand palace, full of tapestries and pictures. No charge for the gardens and grounds, which are open until dusk. There's a restaurant and café, or you could take a picnic.

HATFIELD HOUSE

This splendid Jacobean mansion was built by Robert Cecil in the early 1600s and is still a Cecil family home. It replaced an older house where Elizabeth I grew up, and has mementoes like a pair of her silk stockings and some famous portraits. There are lots of other pictures to see, suits of armour and tapestries, model soldiers, formal gardens and parkland. Part of the young Elizabeth's home survives as the Old Palace, where Tudor banquets are held.

There's a coffee shop restaurant, and a place for picnics (indoors if necessary). The house is open from late March to mid October, but closed on Mondays except bank holidays. Visits are by afternoon guided tours, except on Sunday or bank holidays. The park is open all day until 8pm; the West Gardens are open slightly shorter hours. Trains run from British Rail King's Cross station to Hatfield station, which is opposite the park gate.

WINDSOR

Windsor, the largest inhabited castle in the world, is the official residence of the Queen. William I built the first fortress here in wood in 1070, and it has been added to and altered by nearly every monarch since. It covers 13 acres, and makes a dramatic battlemented skyline. Trains run from London Waterloo; or catch a Greenline Bus which gives you a discount on the Guide Friday open top bus tour. Be prepared for astonishing crowds at Windsor. Different parts of it are open at different times: telephone 0753 831118 to confirm access before you visit, but you can almost always go into the castle precincts and see the chapels and some other buildings from the outside. In this lower part of the castle, St George's Chapel is very grand,

Windsor is the world's largest inhabited castle.

with royal tombs and banners: usually open, except in January. The State Apartments are splendid: they close for most of June and December, as does Queen Mary's Dolls' House – the last word in miniature houses. It was designed by the architect Sir Edwin Lutyens with the minutest details in perfect, tiny replica.

While in Windsor you could visit Eton College, a public (ie private) school founded in the 15th century. Some of the buildings are open in the afternoons. The Royalty and Empire Exhibition (a Madame Tussaud's creation) at Windsor and Eton Central station re-creates Queen Victoria's arrival for her Diamond Jubilee celebration in 1897, with full size waxworks in the original surroundings.

Guide Friday run frequent open-top bus tours around Windsor, and stops include the castle and Eton. The ticket is valid for a day, so you can get on and off as you please.

Windsor Great Park was a hunting place in Norman times, and it's a wonderful place for walks in wooded and open parkland. There's also a lake (Virginia Water), and masses of azaleas and other shrubs in the Valley Gardens. You pay to park; otherwise admission is free. There is a charge to visit the Savile Garden, where hundreds of different types of plants make a dense display. It's best in spring but is open all year and always has something interesting.

ORIENTATION IN LONDON

INFORMATION
TOURIST OFFICES
The following are the main tourist information centres of the London Tourist Board. In addition to these, there are several local tourist information centres around the capital.

Victoria train station forecourt, SW1 open April to October, 8am to 6pm.
Selfridges Oxford Street W1 (basement services arcade) open store hours.

Harrods *Knightsbridge SW1 (basement banking hall) open store hours.*
Heathrow airport *Heathrow Underground station concourse, open daily 8am to 6.30pm.*
Liverpool Street *train station, open Monday to Saturday 9.30am to 6.30pm, Sunday 8.30am to 3.30pm.*
Tower of London *EC3 (West Gate) open daily April to October 10am to 6pm – telephone enquiries 071-730 3488, Monday to Friday 9am to 5.30pm.*
POST OFFICE
The London Chief Office is in King Edward Street, EC1 and is open Monday to Friday 8.30 to 6pm, except on public holidays. The Trafalgar Square post office is at 22-28 William IV Street WC2, ☎ 071-930 9580, open Monday to Saturday 8am to 8pm. Each district in London has its own chief post office and there are many smaller sub-offices.
TELEPHONES
There are two telephone number prefixes. Dial 071 for inner London; dial 081 for outer London. No prefix is needed if you are dialling within either of these areas, but is required for dialling from one area to the other.
POLICE
In an emergency, dial 999 and ask for the police (calls are free). For reporting thefts and other crimes which take place on London public transport, ☎ 071-222 5600 for London Transport Police.

TRANSPORT

LONDON TRANSPORT
How to get there:
☎ *071-222 1234. How services are running:*
☎ *071-222 1200*
UNDERGROUND
☎ *071-222 5600*
BICYCLE HIRE
For advice on any aspect of cycling in London, ring the London Cycling Campaign, ☎ *071-928 7220.*
On Your Bike *22 Duke Street Hill (south side of London Bridge).* ☎ *071-407 1309.*
Yellow Jersey *44 Chalk Farm Road, Camden Town.* ☎ *071-485 8090. Prices start at around £6 a day, £25 a week, plus deposit*
Bikefix *48 Lambs Conduit Street WC1 stays open for repairs until 7pm, and reckons to offer a faster, friendlier service*

ACCOMMODATION

HOTELS – CENTRAL LONDON
Mentone Hotel *54-55 Cartwright Gardens WC1H 9EL.* ☎ *071-387 3927 or 071-387 4671. Double bed and breakfast from £40.*
Edward Lear Hotel *30 Seymouth Street W1.* ☎ *071-402 5401. Double bed and breakfast from £49.50.*
Chesham House *64-66 Ebury Street SW1N 9QD.* ☎ *071-730 8513. Double bed and breakfast from £43.*
HOTELS – OUTER LONDON
Aber Hotel *89 Crouch Hill N8 9EG.* ☎ *081-340 2847 Single bed and breakfast from £16, double from £30.*
Clearview House *161 Fordwych Road NW2 2NL.*

☎ *081-452 9773. Bed and breakfast from £16 per person.*
Crystal Palace Tower Hotel *114 Church Road SE19 2UB.* ☎ *081-653 0176. Single bed and breakfast from £18, double from £30.*
UNIVERSITY ACCOMMODATION
This is a selection, ask the London Tourist Board about others.
King's Campus Vacation Bureau *Kings College, 552 King's Road SW10 0UA.* ☎ *071-351 6011. All college vacations, one hall of residence available all year.*
Imperial College *Contact Summer Accommodation Centre, Linstead Hall, Watts Way SW7.* ☎ *071-589 5111. Usually not available at Easter.*
Passfield Hall *1 Endsleigh Place WC1.* ☎ *071-387 3584/7743. Only available at Easter and summer.*
CAMPING
Abbey Wood *Federation Road SE2. Five minutes from Abbey Wood tube station (a 35-minute journey into central London).* ☎ *081-310 2233. £2 per person plus £3 per tent (£4.50 if you have a car).*
Pickett's Lock *Pickett's Lock Lane N9.* ☎ *081-803 4756. £3 per person. You get a free pass to the Pickett's Lock Centre, which has a restaurant and bar, and golf and other outdoor sports facilities (pay extra for those).*
Tent City *Old Oak Common Lane W3.* ☎ *081-743 5708. The really budget option at £4 a night per person, whether you bring your own*

tent or sleep in one of the communal tents (beds provided). Free blankets, hot showers and luggage store.
YOUTH HOSTELS ASSOCIATION London has several YHA hostels, with dormitory accommodation from £8.60 to £11.10 a night, depending on your age. You should book ahead and must be a member (you can join on arrival though, and special family rates are available). Two of the hostels are well placed for the city centre:
Holland House Holland Walk, Holland Park W8. ☎ 071-937 0748.
Carter Lane EC4, near St Paul's Cathedral. ☎ 071-236 4950. A Renaissance former choir school of St Paul's Cathedral.

ENTERTAINMENT
The Barbican EC2: box office ☎ 071-658 8891. Nearest Underground stations Moorgate, Barbican (weekdays only), Farringdon, St Paul's.
South Bank Arts Complex SE1. Royal Festival Hall, Purcell Room, Queen Elizabeth Hall: box office ☎ 071-928 8800. National Theatre: box office ☎ 071-928 2252. Nearest Underground station Waterloo, or from Embankment Underground station walk over the Thames on the footbridge (alongside the railway).
The London Coliseum St Martin's Lane WC2: box office ☎ 071-836 3161. Nearest Underground stations Charing Cross,

Leicester Square.
Royal Albert Hall Kensington Gore, SW7: box office ☎ 071-589 8212. Nearest Underground station South Kensington (a 20 minute walk).
Royal Opera House Covent Garden WC2: box office ☎ 071-240 1066 (listen to opera recordings while you wait to be connected). Nearest Underground station Covent Garden.
Sadler's Wells Rosebery Avenue, EC1: box office ☎ 071-278 8916. Nearest Underground station Angel.

EATING OUT
THE CITY
Cranks Crowcross Street near Smithfield market. Vegetarian and wholefood café.
Croissant Express Leadenhall market. Filled French sticks from £1.30.
Fox and Anchor Smithfield market. Traditional hefty English breakfasts.
Marina's Leadenhall market. Light lunches, pasta for about £4.
Sweetings Restaurant on the corner of Queen Victoria Street near Bank tube station. A very traditional City eating place. Fish specialities (oysters £8 for six – a special non-budget treat) and less expensive dishes.
Wainwright and Daughter Leadenhall market. Classy snacks.
Also try other pubs and cafés in the area for similar fare.
FLEET STREET
British Museum Café Good meals, snacks and drinks, but

not very cheap.
Pizza Express Coptic Street, in an old dairy building. Pizzas from £2 to £5, as well as other dishes.
Poons of Russel Square 50 Woburn Place. ☎ 071-580 1188. A stylish Chinese restaurant, set menus from £8.50.
Spaghetti Tratt 4 Victoria House, Southampton Row. ☎ 071-405 6658. Good pasta; you can eat here for under £10.
COVENT GARDEN
Calabash Restaurant Downstairs at the Africa Centre crafts shop on King Street. ☎ 071-836 1973.
Diana's Diner, and the **Fish Restaurant** are side by side in Endell Street. They have tables outside, and are popular for well cooked fried food (under about £5).
Food for Thought 31 Neal Street. ☎ 071-836 0239. A vegetarian restaurant and takeaway for lunch, afternoon or early evening.
Lamb and Flag Rose Street. An old and very popular pub; well worth seeking out in its hidden corner.
Porters 17 Henrietta Street. ☎ 071-836 6466. A simple menu – just pies and puddings.
SOHO
Amalfi 29 Old Compton Street. Old-fashioned charm and style; meals about £8 (also a pâtisserie).
Dragon Inn 12 Gerrard Street. Specialises in dim sum, from about £7.
Ed's Easy Diner 12 Moor Street. ☎ 071-439 1055. Burgers for homesick

Americans from £3.35, and a jukebox for every two seats.

Gaby's Continental Bar Charing Cross Road. Café and takeaways, useful location for theatre-goers. Dishes include humus and falafel (deep-fried chick pea ball) and tasty vegetable salads.

Lorelei Bateman Street. Fairly basic, but good budget pizzas.

Mildred's 58 Greek Street. Quality vegetarian and vegan wholefood snacks and meals from noon to 10pm. About £5 for lunch.

Pollo Old Compton Street. Simple, with a good reputation.

Poons 4 Leicester Street. In Soho's Chinatown. Specialises in wind-dried meats to eat with rice, about £6.

MAYFAIR

Brown's Hotel Dover Street/Albermarle Street. Afternoon teas here are reckoned the best. £10.50 for an afternoon's indulgence in scones, cakes and pastries (no bookings).

May Fair Inter-Continental Stratton Street. Fairly up-market, but try the coffee shop for afternoon tea – £7.50 for sandwiches, pastries, scones, etc.

PICCADILLY AND ST JAMES'S

Hard Rock Café Piccadilly. Another spot for homesick Americans. You might have to wait a long time for a table.

Ritz Hotel Piccadilly. ☎ 071-493 8181. Elegant afternoon teas in glittering surroundings for £11, but you need to book a week or two ahead (no jeans, and gentlemen should wear a jacket and tie).

Wren Café at the west end of St James's Church. Reasonably priced teas, coffees and light meals.

SOUTH KENSINGTON

Daquise just a few yards from South Kensington tube station. A Polish café and restaurant with plenty of Eastern European atmosphere.

Victoria and Albert Museum Cromwell Road, in the back of the museum. Pleasant, but not especially cheap.

TRAFALGAR SQUARE AND WESTMINSTER

St John's Church Smith Square. Wine bar and gallery open weekdays for lunch and on concert evenings for buffet salads and hot dishes. Eat here for around £5; there is also a more expensive restaurant section.

St Martin-in-the-Fields Trafalgar Square. This church has a stylish, friendly café serving coffee and meals.

DOCKLANDS

Pubs to try in the area are **The Grapes**, and also **The House They Left Behind**, both in Narrow Street; **Five Bells**, and also **The Bladebone**, both in Three Colts Street. On the south side of the Thames try **The Angel**, off Jamaica Road; and **The Mayflower**, off Brunel Road.

EAST END

Bagel Bake 159 Brick Lane. ☎ 071-729 0616. Open from 12 noon till 6am Monday to Thursday and non-stop from Friday to Sunday.

GREENWICH

Eel and Pie Shop Greenwich Church Street. They don't do eels any more, but you can get homemade pies with mashed potatoes and peas, then fruit pie and custard for 'afters' for less than £5. Open at weekends.

Trafalgar Tavern Park Row. ☎ 081-858 2437. Fried whitebait is the speciality here, but they do other food as well.

HAMPSTEAD

The Spaniard's Inn Spaniard's End. A delightful 15th-century inn that also does lunchtime and evening food – hot dishes for under £5. It's cosy in winter and has a pretty garden in summer. It's popular, so be prepared for crowds.

NOTTING HILL

Whiteleys Shopping Centre Queensway, nearest tube stations are Bayswater or Queensway. An entire floor of this shopping precinct is devoted to eating places and food and drink shops.

WINDSOR

There are several places to eat in the town of Windsor, or you could picnic by the Thames.

Country Kitchen is in the middle of the town. ☎ 0753 868681. A range of main dishes always includes something for vegetarians; you could eat here for under £5. The three-course Sunday carvery lunch is £7.50.

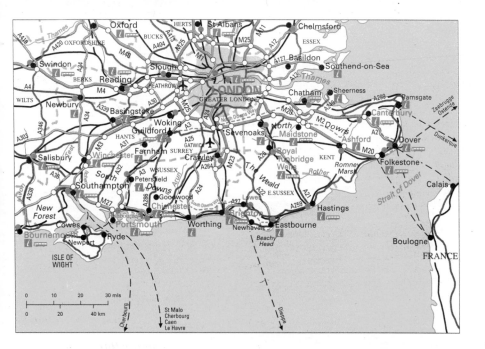

This corner of England between London and the Channel is a region with nearly every sort of scenery except high mountains, and it compensates for those with fine hilltop walking and some of Britain's best cliffs. It's a good region for tracking down links with favourite writers and characters: Jane Austen (Chawton and Winchester), Geoffrey Chaucer (Canterbury), Charles Dickens and even Rupert Bear. Henry James and Rudyard Kipling lived in this region too.

The scenery is the first attraction. The region is crossed by two steep-sided spines of chalk hills – The North Downs and South Downs – which offer breezy walks and far-reaching views. They end in spectacular cliffs, most famously at the 'white cliffs' of Dover, but most dramatically at Beachy Head, just southwest of Eastbourne. In between the two is the Weald, where you'll find rolling hills, woods and pretty villages where idyllic cottages have roses round the door.

For a taste of something wilder, head for the west side of the region, to the woods and heathland of the New Forest. William the Conqueror made this tract of land a royal hunting ground, and today it's a pleasure ground for everyone, with miles of walking and plenty of opportunities for horse riding.

Canterbury has one of the region's old and beautiful cathedrals, and the city centre has some picturesque streets – best in the evening, when the day trippers have gone. Brighton has had a raffish sort of reputation ever since it became a seaside resort in the 1700s. It's a lively town all year round, with many restaurants, music pubs and arts events, but without some of the disadvantages of a big city. Inland is the great hulk of the South Downs, with several attractive villages and towns to visit within easy reach; along the coast Chichester is a mellow cathedral city, with little streets, old pubs and some stylish shops. Portsmouth a big, busy city, where the Royal Navy has had a base for nearly 500 years. Portsmouth isn't beautiful, but its

57

naval history means there's a lot to see.

In the county of Hampshire, Winchester is yet another very old city, with Roman origins and a beautiful cathedral. King Alfred made Winchester his capital city, and today it's a prosperous, pretty place with good shopping.

Bournemouth, a sophisticated seaside resort on a lavish scale, has miles of sandy beach, and you can see the New Forest from here. Bournemouth is also within easy reach of the eastern places in the *West Country* chapter.

Getting into the region from London is easy – there are frequent trains and buses from London to all the main centres. Gatwick airport is in the middle of the region; travellers to and from mainland Europe can use cross-Channel ports right round the coast. Within the region, bus services range from meagre to good. Summer sees an outbreak of open-topped buses; elsewhere, horses, bicycles and boats may be recommended transport.

A typical Wealden farmhouse at Singleton

and shellfish on the coast. Around Winchester the fish to eat is trout, fresh or smoked. In the New Forest the local speciality is venison. Brighton and other coastal places have an astonishing number of fish and chip shops for traditional refuelling. The region is much more health conscious than some other parts of Britain, though. Vegetarian dishes and salads are often included on menus as a matter of course. Look out also for 'Pick Your Own' signs, which could mean a chance to select your own asparagus and strawberries from the fields in early summer, or apples later on. There are local wines to enjoy too, from vineyards scattered throughout the region. Local beers include the range made by Gales of Horndean, near Portsmouth.

Local flavour

Chichester, Winchester and Canterbury were all Roman towns, and Canterbury has Roman forts near by. Chichester is close to the site of a huge Roman palace, Fishbourne, with a big area of mosaic floors on view.

A car will allow you to get to out of the way places, but driving is restricted in the centres of smaller cities like Winchester and Chichester. Traffic can be heavy too – despite the away-from-it-all feeling that parts of this region encourage, you're never very far from towns. Avoid the commuting hours, and allow time for traffic on the main roads. On Sundays the whole population seems to be on the move in cars, and the end of the M3 near Winchester is a notorious traffic bottleneck.

The big cities and seaside resorts have plenty of budget bed and breakfast places. In the smaller towns and cities they may be harder to find, so book ahead. Summer will always be busy; booking is virtually essential when there's an arts festival or other event on.

For eating, look out for freshly caught fish

Local flavour

Antiques shops are part of the scene in the region's more picturesque places, and antiques fairs are often advertised. For collectors on a budget, there are huge fairs at Ardingly near Brighton in January, April, July, September and November.

You could time your visit to coincide with one of the region's arts festivals – Canterbury, Brighton, Winchester and Chichester all have one. In spring there's the free spectacle of apple blossom in Kent's orchards; in summer the seaside resorts can be great fun, with special holiday open-topped bus rides and band music in the parks. Another common summer sight is cricket on village greens all over the region, and bigger matches at county grounds. Winter offers a chance to explore towns in relative peace; the drawback is that historic houses and other places to visit will often be closed. If you're in Brighton in November you'll see the arrival of the RAC (Royal Automobile Club) London to Brighton veteran car run. On 5 November, nearby Lewes puts on a spectacular torchlit procession.

CANTERBURY

BUDGET FOR A DAY

Cathedral	(donation)	2·00
Canterbury Heritage		1·20
Guided Walk		2·00
Lunch		3·50
Dinner		10·00
		£ 18·70

plus accommodation

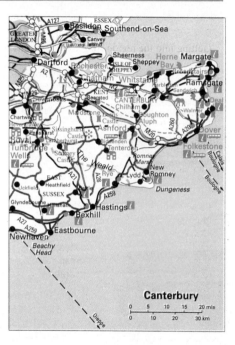

Canterbury

This is a natural starting point for a tour of the southeast. For one thing it's in easy reach of London and the Channel ports (and eventually, the Channel Tunnel); for another it's the historic starting point – the Romans landed on the coast north of Canterbury. Canterbury itself is an interesting city with one of the great cathedrals, and from there it's easy to explore Kent. The northern side of the county has impressive Roman remains, but it's short of spectacular scenery. The prettiest countryside is southwards, along river valleys and up into the North Downs. Beyond the downs lies Romney Marsh, once beloved of smugglers and still mysterious.

Moneysaver

Canterbury has a park-and-ride scheme for drivers – free parking with regular free transport to the city centre, from early morning to 6pm. Signs direct you from main roads.

This is London commuter country, where rustic villages are more likely to house office workers than farmhands. Both railways and buses run to most of the places suggested for outings. Lanes linking quiet villages make for pleasant cycling, and bicycles can be carried on the local trains for combined rail/cycle outings. Tourist information centres sell *Kent for Cycling* (small charge), with many miles of cycle routes and other information.

Canterbury is just under two hours from London by coach, 80 minutes by rail. Trains from London's Victoria train station arrive at Canterbury East train station just south of the city centre; trains from London Charing Cross station arrive at Canterbury West station, which is just north. Drivers can get there along the A2 through Harbledown, which follows the route of the medieval pilgrims.

Most of the interesting parts of Canterbury

are in the old city area, which is still half enclosed by a medieval wall built on Roman foundations. Don't expect a complete medieval city – this one was partly flattened by World War II bombs, but it's still rewarding to explore.

'From every shire's end of England, to Canterbury they wend' wrote Geoffrey Chaucer in his *Canterbury Tales* – the classic series of stories told as if by pilgrims travelling from London to Canterbury. Today he might have truthfully said that they wend here from the other side of the earth, but the best starting point is still the cathedral, where medieval pilgrims flocked to see St Thomas Becket's shrine.

Look at the cathedral from outside first, to admire the soaring tower called Bell Harry. The cathedral's story begins back in Saxon times, but its days of glory came after 1170, when Archbishop Thomas Becket was murdered in the north transept by four knights. They were acting on the orders (perhaps unintended) of King Henry II, who had a close but stormy relationship with Becket. Miracles were reported soon after Becket's death, and pilgrims began pouring in to visit his tomb. Hence Chaucer's *Canterbury Tales*, and also T S Eliot's play *Murder in the Cathedral*.

Admission to the cathedral is free, but a donation is suggested, and you have to pay for cathedral tours, for which you get tickets from the Friends Desk at the south door. The nave is impressive, and the stained glass is wonderful, especially around the east end. It's worth taking binoculars to have a good look.

Canterbury has innumerable old buildings with stories to tell. The most evocative is Eastbridge Hospital in the High Street, where medieval budget travellers stayed – entrance is free, and you get a real sense of the past here. Through daunting West Gate, St Dunstan's church has the head of Sir Thomas More, brought here in secret after being cut off by Henry VIII. The church is mentioned in Charles Dickens's *David Copperfield*. The Falstaff on St Dunstan's Street is a picturesque place for a pint: it dates back to the early 1400s.

Through Queningate you'll reach the abbey founded by St Augustine in AD598 (English Heritage), and St Martin's Church, which may be England's oldest working church. Walk along the wall at Dane John Gardens, where William the Conqueror built a castle in 1066.

Top spot for photographers is off the High Street – a row of weavers' cottages which overhang the River Stour. You go through them for rowing boat trips on the river, 30 minutes with a guide or 40 minutes self-row; available Easter to October, price £2.

Local flavour
Pilgrim Father James Chilton was born in Canterbury in 1583. He is said to have been the first to step off the *Mayflower* at Plymouth Rock.

The Royal Museum in the High Street is free. Canterbury Heritage in Stour Street surveys Canterbury's past, taking in *Mayflower* traveller Robert Cushman and nursery-book personality, Rupert Bear, with treasures and everyday items on display. It's open Monday to Saturday all year, and Sunday afternoons from July to October. Canterbury Tales in St Margaret's Street 're-creates' the medieval journey from London to Canterbury, with five of the Canterbury tales told on the way. Lots of audio-visual wizardry and famous actors' voices; open all year.

Guided walks start from the tourist information centre Easter to November on Sunday at 2pm; April and May, Monday to Saturday 2pm; June to September Monday to Saturday 11am and 2pm, and Friday at 8pm – including ghosts. Walks take about 1½ hours. Tours on an open-topped bus start at Canterbury East train station, but you can join them en route. Telephone 0227 764669 for details.

For evenings, the Marlowe Theatre offers plays, music and ballet (it's named after playwright Christopher Marlowe, born in Canterbury in 1564). Out of town on the Whitstable road the University of Kent's Gulbenkian Theatre is worth checking out for plays in school term time, including children's shows. While you're on the campus, enjoy the view of the city. The richest time for culture is during the September/October arts festival.

ORIENTATION IN CANTERBURY

INFORMATION
TOURIST OFFICE
34 St Margaret's Street.
☎ 0227 766567.
POST OFFICE
High Street
PUBLIC LAVATORIES
By the cathedral; by the footbridge to East train station.

TRANSPORT
LOCAL BUSES
East Kent Road Car Company, St George's bus station, St George's Lane. For bus enquiries ☎ 0227 472082. Some Sunday services are operated by Westbus of Ashford, ☎ 0233 636001.
LONG-DISTANCE BUSES/COACHES
National Express, tickets available from the East Kent Road Car Company, above.
RAILWAY
East train station (south of centre) or West train station

(north of centre). For enquiries ☎ 0227 454411 or 463460.
CAR HIRE
Avis 130 Sturry Road.
☎ 0227 768339.
Renault Rentals Northgate Garage, Northgate. ☎ 0227 765561.
BICYCLE HIRE
Canterbury Cycle Mart 23 Lower Bridge Street.
☎ 0227 738818.

ACCOMMODATION
HOTELS
Castle Court 8 Castle Street.
☎ 0227 563441. Bed and breakfast starts at £15 single, £28 double.
Magnolia House 36 St Dunstan's Terrace, close to West Gate. ☎ 0227 765121. Prices start at under £25 for single bed and breakfast.
UNIVERSITY ACCOMMODATION
University of Kent Conference Office, Canterbury CT2 7NZ.
☎ 0227 769186. College vacations only, bed and

breakfast around £17 - booking advisable. Also self-catering apartments in summer vacation.
YOUTH HOSTEL
Canterbury Youth Hostel 54 New Dover Road. ☎ 0277 462911.
CAMPING
St Martins Touring and Camping Site Bekesbourne Lane, off A257 Canterbury-Sandwich road.
☎ 0227 463216.

EATING OUT
Chaucer Hotel Ivy Lane.
☎ 0227 464427. Lunches for £10 and dinner around £12.50.
Crotchets Wine and Piano Bar 59 Northgate. ☎ 0227 458857. Vegetarian dishes available; tortilla and salad £3.75.
George's Brasserie 71-72 Castle Street. ☎ 0227 451011. Open for lunch or evening meals, or just coffee. Daily 'specials' £4-£5. Garden.

OUTINGS FROM CANTERBURY

THE KENT COAST

Dover   Buses and trains run to the port of Dover, where the North Downs end abruptly in sheer white cliffs. Most people come here just to embark for France; but Dover Castle is worth the journey in its own right. It's one of the biggest in England, with massive walls and a keep above a network of underground operations rooms, last used in World War II. A Roman lighthouse has survived 2,000 years of change within the walls; open daily, English Heritage.

In the town you can also see the remains of a

Impressive Dover Castle overlooks the Channel port.

Roman house, in New Street. It has rare wall paintings, and is open April to October (not

Monday), price £1. It costs £2.50 for a 45-minute guided tour of the old town jail at Dover Town Hall in Biggin Street, with sights and sounds to bring history alive (this is a bit gruesome). Open all year, but closed on Monday and Tuesday from September to June. A walk along the cliffs gives views of France on a clear day.

If you decide to visit the Continent, check that you have the right documentation. Non EEC nationals often need a visa to visit France.

Moneysaver

Fares for day trips to France are slashed in off-peak months. For duty-free shopping, try shops in Boulogne – the prices and range of goods will almost certainly be better than in duty free shops on the ferry.

Folkestone   There is more of a seaside holiday atmosphere here than Dover, with promenade and sandy beach. You'll soon become aware of Channel Tunnel workings in this area – buses run to the Eurotunnel Exhibition Centre which explains the engineering of the tunnel underneath the Channel; open Tuesday to Sunday.

Deal and Walmer   The coastal castles at Deal and Walmer were built by Henry VIII – Deal Castle is the most complete, but Walmer has more charm because it's the official home of the Lord Warden of the Cinque Ports. In the 19th century the Lord Warden was Lord Wellington, whose rooms have been kept in the sparse style he liked. Both castles are run by English Heritage; Deal is open all year but Walmer closes in January and February, and when the Lord Warden is there.

Sandwich   The landscape gets very bleak around Sandwich, which makes this town all the more amazing. You enter through an ancient gateway to a town which hasn't changed very much since Queen Elizabeth I visited in 1573. Its winding streets are lined with flawless old houses, all set within medieval walls. The one thing that has gone is the sea – Sandwich was once a prosperous port until silt deposits 'moved' it

inland. Tom Paine, author of the *Rights of Man*, lived in New Street in 1759. Nearby Richborough Castle (English Heritage), has some of the best-preserved Roman walls in England.

Broadstairs   Charles Dickens used to take his family for holidays at Broadstairs. The cliffs drop down here to small sandy bays, and the streets are a warren of old houses (there may be crowds though). Dickens stayed at what's now called Bleak House, which includes a maritime and smuggling display: open all year, with late opening to 9pm from July to September. Dickens House Museum (telephone 0843 62853) is open April to October afternoons, and other Dickens connections abound. So do fish and chip shops and other unpretentious eating places, but for budget eating with flair try the Mad Chef in Harbour Street.

Local flavour

Visit Broadstairs in June for the Dickens Festival, when people dress up in Victorian costume, and the town celebrates Dickens with music and other entertainments.

Moneysaver

Two can share a main course at the Mad Chef in Broadstairs if you want to eat well but not heavily. They'll also do 'half meals' for children.

Whitstable   One of the major attractions here is the food: the speciality is oysters. There are no bright lights or amusements – just the harbour and higgledy piggledy old streets where they say smugglers used to live. The Royal Native Oyster Store specialises in seafood, and the tourist information centre supplies a list of other places to try.

The Whitstable Oyster Festival in July includes the Blessing of the Waters ceremony held on Reeves Beach. The Romans ate Whitstable oysters, and today they're served in many local pubs and restaurants. The traditional drink to wash them down is stout.

NORTH DOWNS

The North Downs south of Canterbury offer breezy walks along chalk hills. You can join the North Downs Way long-distance footpath for walks at Barham.

Howletts Zoo at Bekesbourne is one of two in Kent run by John Aspinall (the other is at Port Lympne). The world's largest captive gorilla colony is here, as are many rarities. Aspinall likes his animals to have plenty of space, so give yourself time. You can get there by bus to Littlebourne or train to Bekesbourne – it's a 20-minute walk from either.

The Stour Valley is a pretty, inland route, which includes the perfect, picture-book village of Chilham (you pay to park). Chilham Castle's splendid gardens (telephone 0227 730319) are open late March to mid October. The energetic can join the Pilgrim's Way at Chilham.

RYE AND ROMNEY MARSH

Trains take 1¼ hours to reach Rye, which is the prettiest place on Romney Marsh – but beware crowds in summer. Once a port, now stranded from the sea, it stands on a conical hill with narrow cobbled streets, a windmill and a river full of boats. The novelist Henry James lived at Lamb House; both James and fellow-writer E F Benson are said to have met ghosts there. Three rooms are open from April to October, on Wednesday and Saturday afternoons (National Trust). The most romantic pub is the Mermaid, all low ceilings and sloping floors, which, as the plaque on the outside wall says, was 'rebuilt in 1420'! Trains go from Canterbury West station, change at Ashford.

The Saxon Shore Way takes walkers into Romney Marsh itself, which is still mysterious even though it's no longer strictly marshland. If you're a birdwatcher, or interested in old churches, then Romney Marsh will be a treat. You'll need independent transport to get there.

ROCHESTER AND CHATHAM

Rochester is 45 minutes to one hour by train. It's a great place for Charles Dickens devotees: he lived locally and many of the places along the pretty High Street appear in his novels. There's a Dickens Centre at Eastgate House (telephone 0634 844176), where you can see the Swiss chalet where he used to write.

Rochester Castle was first built by the Romans, but what you see today is one of the finest Norman castle keeps in England. English Heritage, open daily. The cathedral is close by: the carvings around the great west door are arguably the best feature.

> **Moneysaver**
> The family ticket to Chatham dockyard saves money for two adults and two children (or one adult, three children). Tickets are stamped for each area you see – no charge for coming back to tour the parts you missed the first time.

Chatham is reached by walking down Rochester High Street; or you can get there direct by train from Canterbury East station. The place to visit is the Chatham Historic Dockyard (telephone 0634 812551), where a heritage of over 300 years of shipbuilding included Nelson's *Victory*. The navy departed in 1984, but left behind an interesting place to visit. The buildings are exceptional, and you can also watch people carrying out traditional shipbuilding crafts like ropemaking and sailmaking. Draught horses used to work here too, so you can meet some of them as well. Most of the site is accessible to wheelchairs and pushchairs.

There's a restaurant, and open and covered picnic areas are provided. This outing is expensive but you could spend some time here so it is quite good value (see also *Moneysaver*). Coaches run once a day between Canterbury and Rochester/Chatham.

TUNBRIDGE WELLS

Royal Tunbridge Wells is the correct name, but the abbreviated form is more common. It's an attractive town, and it lies close to some stunning places. From Canterbury (either train station), the journey takes about 1½ hours. Unfortunately, public transport is limited in Tunbridge Wells.

Before the 1600s Tunbridge Wells was nothing but a spring in a wood. Then in 1606 its iron-rich water was discovered by the court of King Charles I, and the area became a royal summer holiday camp: queen and courtiers came down here to stay in tents and take the waters. Permanent buildings followed, and the town grew from there. Today it's a sizeable place, but you'll still find the atmosphere of an elegant spa town.

Local flavour

Taste the spa water of Tunbridge Wells from the spring at the Pantiles in the centre of town.

The place where it all began is the Pantiles. The name comes from the tiles that were used to pave the area after one of Queen Anne's sons slipped on the original grass. A few of original pantiles are left, near the point where the spring emerges.

MAIDSTONE

Maidstone is the county town of Kent, and main road, bus routes and trains radiate from here to all corners of the county.

The town itself has a handsome high street, and the Medway riverbanks offer peaceful walks near the centre. Beside the river you reach a cluster of mellow medieval buildings, including the parish church, one of England's biggest. Inside, look at the carvings under the choir stall seats, and look out for the Washington memorial. It commemorates an earlier member of the family of the US President, George Washington, and carries the family crest of stars and stripes. Nearby is the Tyrwhitt Drake Museum of Carriages, which is free to visitors and has all sorts of coaches and carriages, including some royal ones on loan.

THE WEALD

The Weald is very rich in beautiful old houses and gardens to visit, in a setting wooded hills and picturebook villages. These are some of the highlights.

Scotney Castle   One of the Weald's most romantic spots is Scotney Castle (telephone 0892 890651), where flowering shrubs cascade down the hill to a little ruined castle in a moat. Run by the National Trust, it's open April to mid November, Wednesday to Sunday and bank holiday Mondays. It's about seven miles south east of Tunbridge Wells; there is no practical bus service.

Moneysaver

It costs a little less to visit Scotney Castle on a weekday, rather than a weekend or bank holiday.

Chiddingstone and Penshurst   You won't find any great National Trust houses immediately west of Tunbridge Wells, but they do own most of Chiddingstone. It's a tiny village of 16th- and 17th-century houses, complete with post office, shop and pub. These are real-life places where you can shop and eat, although you may feel there's an unnatural perfection about the place. The Castle Inn does bar lunches.

Penshurst is on the same bus route: a little place of Tudor houses tucked into the wooded hills. You can look around Penshurst Vineyards free, or take a guided tour with tasting.

Penshurst Place was the home of the Elizabethan poet-soldier Sir Philip Sidney, and is still owned by one of his descendants. Its great medieval hall has hardly changed since the 14th century. Admission is cheaper if you just want to see the grounds, which include a Tudor-style garden and an adventure playground. Open from April to September in the afternoons, and closed Monday except bank holiday Mondays.

Hever Castle   Hever Castle was the childhood home of Anne Boleyn – first of Henry VIII's wives to be beheaded, and mother of Queen

Elizabeth I. It had fallen on hard times by the early 1900s, and might have crumbled away if American millionaire William Waldorf Astor hadn't snapped it up. He brought it back to life in style, and added little Tudor village for friends to stay in. Open March to November afternoons (gardens from 11am).

Knole House Knole House is one of the biggest stately homes in Britain, in an unlikely setting just off the High Street in Sevenoaks. It's also one of the oddest – a rambling series of courtyards and wings added on through the ages. This is the setting of Virginia Wolfe's strange novel *Orlando*. You can't see everything, because it's still the Sackville family home, as it has been since 1566. National Trust; open summer, Wednesday to Saturday and bank holidays.

Chartwell Sir Winston Churchill lived at Chartwell, which lies about five miles west of Sevenoaks. It's kept as it was when he lived here, with items like his paintbox ready to hand, and correspondence with people like General Eisenhower on display. All visitors get timed tickets, which means that you might well have to wait to get in at the height of the summer. Open from April to October weekday afternoons and from 11am at weekends and bank holidays; closed Fridays and Mondays (except bank holidays, in which case it closes the day after).

Igtham Mote Lanes on the other side of Sevenoaks take you to Ightham Mote, a moated manor house with a romantic story – Charles Henry Robinson of Maine, USA, fell in love with a picture of it in his youth and managed to buy it years later. He rescued and restored it, and his ashes are buried here.

Sissinghurst and Biddenden Vita Sackville-West and Harold Nicolson created a cluster of gardens around the old castle tower. They came and fell in love with the scene, even . though it was a cabbage patch at the time (1930). This is one of the most admired gardens in Kent – most famous of all is the ethereal White Garden, where everything including foliage is in shades of white. Open April to mid October in the afternoon, and from 10am on Saturday, Sunday and Good Friday. Closed every Monday.

Biddenden's village sign features its famous twins.

Moneysaver
You can look round many of the Kent and Sussex vineyards free; others charge a fee, but offer would-be buyers tastings as well. See *Vineyards in South East England* (from tourist offices).

Just east is Biddenden, which became rich on the wool trade in medieval times and then stopped changing – the high street is lined with old Wealden houses. You have to make an appointment to see the Baby Carriage Collection at Bettenham Manor (telephone 0622 872068), an enthusiast's array of babies' transport, from 18th-century 'stickwagons' and grand Edwardian perambulators to simple modern buggies (admission free).

Local flavour
Elisa and Mary Chulkhurst were Siamese twins who lived in Biddenden in the 12th century. They lived to the age of 34, and left land to pay for the annual 'dole' to the poor. It is still handed out each Easter Monday in the form of bread, cheese, tea and biscuits.

There's no charge for Biddenden Vineyards either, if you're happy to take a self-guided tour (tasting included). Grape harvesting and pressing usually begins in mid to late October.

Tenterden You won't be the first if you decide that Tenterden is the prettiest place in the

Weald – the long main street climbs a hill lined with boarded, tile-hung and chequered brick houses, among which you'll find pleasant pubs and teashops, and some stylish shops for browsing. At weekends from Easter to Christmas you can take a steam train for a seven-mile, 80-minute return trip on a stretch of restored railway line. Trains also run from Tuesday to Thursday in June and July, and every day in August.

Two miles south is Smallhythe Place, home of the Edwardian actress Ellen Terry, and full of evocative possessions. Run by the National Trust, open afternoons from April to October (not Thursday or Friday).

Aylesford   The Friars is a Carmelite priory and pilgrimage centre at Aylesford. On certain special Pilgrimage Days you could find yourself visiting the shrine with thousands of others; at other times this is a very peaceful place, where you can wander around the old buildings and gardens. Free, but donations welcome.

A walk north of the town takes you to Kit's Coty and Little Kit's Coty (both free), the remains of Neolithic tombs on a hillside high above the Medway Valley (no charge).

Leeds   Leeds Castle is the kind of place that people know well even if they've never been near it – it's a photographer's dream, with battlemented walls rising from two islands in a lake-like moat. Its romance was spotted early on by King Edward I, who made a gift of it to Queen Eleanor. Inside, there are rooms with tapestries and Impressionist paintings; outside, you can explore woods and gardens, a maze and a grotto. The admission price for all this is high, but for many people this 'loveliest castle in the world' will be the one they mustn't miss. Open daily in summer, and at weekends from November to March.

BRIGHTON

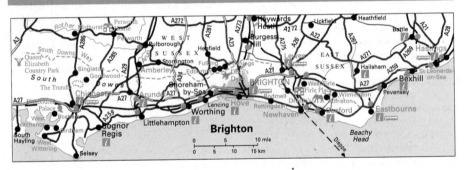

Not so long ago this south coast resort had a decidedly sleazy reputation: it was the place for illicit weekends out of London. Today it's justifiably promoted as one of the more sophisticated out-of-London spots – a place for jazz clubs, smart little restaurants, business conferences, shopping and stylish hotels. A flavour of the old Brighton lingers on, but the mix of the old sleaze and the sophisticated new style is a major part of Brighton's charm.

If you want to see the town at its most vibrant, visit during the Brighton International Arts Festival in May. In the height of the summer you'll discover Brighton's appeal as one of the

oldest English seaside resorts.

Brighton lies on the seaward side of the South Downs. Spacious, thinly populated landscapes, secret-seeming flint-built villages, ancient churches and white chalk cliffs are the attractions here.

Bus services include some special summer scenic routes. Ask the tourist information centre for *Bus Times* (free), which brings together timetables from Brighton's various bus companies in one easy-to-use magazine. Cycling on the South Downs is wonderful once you're at the top, though climbing up is laborious. For accommodation there are lots of small hotels, often in easy reach of the sea. Booking is advisable at holiday and festival times.

Brighton is an hour from London (Victoria station) by rail, two hours by bus. Gatwick airport is 30 minutes away by rail; nearby Newhaven has four-hour ferry crossings to France.

Cars are a headache in Brighton. Parking in the centre is expensive, and the police are ruthless about towing illegally parked cars away. Car theft figures are high, too.

Brighton's story begins with Dr Richard Russell, who wrote a book in the mid 1700s extolling the virtues of sea air and sea bathing on this coast. This attracted the Prince of Wales (known here as 'Prinny': he later became Prince Regent and then George IV).

The sea bathing doesn't seem very remarkable today: it's a pebble beach rather than sand, open to a stiff breeze off the Channel. The beach is fun though: if you want to sample traditional English seaside pleasures Brighton is the place to do it.

Walk along Palace Pier (free) for popcorn, sticks of Brighton rock, shellfish stalls and end-to-end pop music, plus ornate Victorian ironwork and free use of deck chairs. Romany gypsies will tell your fortune for an exotic fee. There's a carousel and other rides at the far end; at night the pier closes and the lights go on from end to end.

Local flavour
Required reading is Graham Greene's nasty thriller *Brighton Rock*, though it describes a much more disreputable Brighton than the one you'll find today.

In the town, the first place to see is the Royal Pavilion. It grew from a farmhouse which 'Prinny' rented in order to be near his mistress Mrs Fitzherbert (who became his secret wife). Outside you see Indian moghul-style domes and minarets; inside it's Chinese, with staircases made of cast iron to look like the frailest bamboo. The Royal Pavilion has suffered over the years from bad drainage and other problems,

The utterly frivolous Royal Pavilion in Brighton.

and restoration work may be going on when you visit. But it doesn't detract from the general splendour. Even the kitchen has splendour – it was one of the most advanced of the time. Look out for the 36-course menu for 15 January 1817. There's a café for snacks and light lunches. The Pavilion is open all year.

Next door to the Pavilion, the Prince's riding school is now the Brighton Dome, a 2,000-seat venue for events from rock to opera. There used to be stables where you'll now find the Brighton Museum – a must if you like Art Nouveau or Art Deco, with a delightful fashion section and some good paintings too (closed Mondays except bank holidays, and free).

The Lanes are a warren of narrow, car-free, brick-paved streets off Old Steine: one way in is behind the tourist office. The original fishing village stood here, and today a browse among the antiques shops and little eating places is an essential part of a visit to the town. Guided tours run from the tourist office at 2.30pm every Sunday, three times a week in summer.

Since 1883 Volk's electric railway has been shuttling passengers along the seafront from Palace Pier to Brighton Marina – a hugely ambitious 20th-century project, with permanent moorings for over 1,000 boats plus shops, cafés and street entertainment in summer. Open-topped buses run this way in summer, and there's free parking. Brighton's naturist beach is at this end of town too.

Best time to visit for day and night culture and entertainment is in May for the Brighton International Arts Festival. You'll find visiting symphony orchestras, lunchtime concerts, theatre, dance, exhibitions and other events –

but you will need to book for the big-name shows. Late-night happenings like writers' workshops also occur (with a late-night bar); and look out for the Town Plays – free theatre in the streets.

Arts festival programmes are published in March and include a booking form. Write to Marlborough House, 54 Old Steine, Brighton BN1 1ER, or telephone 0273 676926.

Year-round entertainment ranges from London productions at the Theatre Royal to alternative drama at Sussex University's Gardner Theatre. The Brighton Centre tends to have the glitziest names in pop and sport; check the daily *Evening Argus* and monthly tourist sheet *Brighton Scene* for Brighton's numerous

jazz clubs, music pubs and other smaller music venues (or ask the tourist information centre). Sussex County Cricket ground is at Brighton's neighbouring town Hove (telephone 0273 73216 for fixtures).

Moneysaver

The Beach Deck (west of Palace Pier) has free shows all summer, including theatre and children's events; no charge either for brass band music in the Pavilion Gardens. The arts festival includes numerous reasonably priced shows, and some free ones.

ORIENTATION IN BRIGHTON

INFORMATION

TOURIST OFFICE
Marlborough House, 54 Old Steine. ☎ 0273 23755.
POST OFFICE
Ship Street
PUBLIC LAVATORIES
Pavilion Theatre; Old Steine; Grand Junction Road.

TRANSPORT

LOCAL BUSES
Enquire at the tourist office.
LONG-DISTANCE BUSES/COACHES
National Express, Pool Valley.
TRAINS
Brighton station, Queen's Road, near the city centre. For information ☎ 0273 206755.
CAR HIRE
Avis Unit 6a, Brighton Marina. ☎ 0273 673738.
Budget Rent-a-Car 87 Preston Street. ☎ 0273

27351.
BUH 35-36 Lewes Road. ☎ 0273 689215.
Endeavour 90 Preston Road. ☎ 0273 550211.
BICYCLE HIRE
Harmans Hire 21-24 Montpelier Road. ☎ 0273 550211.

ACCOMMODATION

HOTELS
New Steine Hotel 12a New Steine. ☎ 0273 681546. Price around £15 per person.
Regency 28 Regency Square. ☎ 0273 202690. Double rooms from £48. Close to an NCP car park - £7 for 24 hours parking.
Trouville 11 New Steine. ☎ 0273 697384. Immaculate accommodation from £15 per person.
UNIVERSITY ACCOMMODATION
University of Sussex East Slope Social Centre, Falmer, Brighton BN1 9RP. ☎ 0273 606755. Summer

vacation self-catering apartment for six to eight people, from £200 per week - book well in advance.
YOUTH HOSTEL
Patcham Youth Hostel
Patcham Place, London Road. ☎ 0273 556196.

EATING OUT

Al Duomo 7 Pavilion Buildings. ☎ 0273 26741. Pasta from £3.50, pizza from £3.20.
Al Forno 36 East Street. ☎ 0273 26741. Similar to Al Duomo, above.
D'Arcy's 49 Market Street, in the Lanes. ☎ 0273 25560. Specialises in seafood, minimum charge £10, main courses start at £6.
Pinocchio 22 New Road. ☎ 0273 677676. You can also choose from an amazing number of fish and chip shops in the town.

OUTINGS FROM BRIGHTON

THE DOWNS

There are free or low-price guided walks all summer on the South Downs, and signed walks start at several points near Brighton. Ask the tourist information office for details. The most spectacular point for walking near Brighton is above the Devil's Dyke (four miles from Poynings). The devil is said to have made this cleft in the chalk in an effort to flood the churches of the Weald.

> **Local flavour**
> The tiny village of Edburton near Fulking has a family-run fish smokery where you can buy delectable smoked salmon and other products. You'll need a car or bicycle to get here, there are no buses.

Open-topped bus 24 runs from Palace Pier to Devil's Dyke three times a day on Sunday from May to September, and daily from mid July to mid August. The 2.15pm bus does a two-hour tour via Lewes, Rottingdean and good scenery: £2.50 for the whole journey.

Firle Firle is a tiny village and a large house (Firle Place) in a most beautiful setting under the South Downs. There are paths across the parkland, and Firle Place has Sèvres porcelain and fine paintings. Guided tours start at 2pm on Wednesday, Thursday and Sunday from June to September, plus bank holiday Sundays and Mondays.

A long lane near Firle takes you to Charleston Farmhouse, haunt of the Bloomsbury Group of writers, artists and intellectuals. Clive and Vanessa Bell lived here from 1916; Virginia Woolf and T S Eliot were regular visitors. The walls and furniture are covered with paintings, and the house is realistically messy. Open on weekend, Wednesday, Thursday and bank holiday afternoons April to October. Buses takes you to the end of the long drive (not Sunday). Charleston Farmhouse is one of a

number of Bloomsbury Group places in Sussex. Berwick church is covered in murals by Duncan Grant and Vanessa Bell. Virginia Woolf lived near by in the Monk's House at Rodmell (National Trust).

Alfriston Nearly every cottage in Alfriston seems to be a craft shop or tea shop, and it's very pretty indeed. The church is called the Cathedral of the Downs; next to it is the 14th-century Clergy House (telephone 0323 870001), the first property bought by the National Trust (it cost £10); open April to October. The Star Inn was used by pilgrims travelling to Chichester, and has carved and painted beams. The George has been an inn since 1397, and offers cream teas in a garden overlooked by the South Downs. Drusilla's Zoo Park near Alfriston specialises in small animals and rare breeds; other attractions include a pottery. Children are especially welcome; open daily.

Goodwood Northwest of Brighton is Goodwood House, where you can see treasures like Sèvres porcelain on summer afternoons (telephone 0243 774107 for details). Goodwood racecourse sweeps along the hills above the house. The peak of the summer racing season is the July/August Festival meeting.

> **Moneysaver**
> Budget grandstand for Goodwood Races is the Trundle, an Iron Age hill fort and natural viewpoint. You can place a bet here, but the real draw is the atmosphere. Buses run from Chichester on race days. Binoculars and sun/rain protection are advisable.

Trundle Hill near Goodwood makes a starting point for walks (it's about a mile's walk from the nearest bus stop, at Singleton).

Singleton At the Weald and Downland Museum, you can wander in and around some 35 historic buildings, all rescued, moved and rebuilt in this peaceful valley – a tiny school, farmhouses and all sorts of others. There are several breeds of farm animals, and the watermill earns its keep by grinding flour.

Petworth The pretty town of Petworth climbs up a hill to the enormous stately home of Petworth House (National Trust). The house is full of treasures including pictures by Van Dyck and Turner, carvings by Grinling Gibbons and sculptures; the gardens are beautiful, and there's no admission charge for Petworth deer park (open April to October).

Amberley Chalk Pits Museum The Amberley Chalk Pits Museum shows traditional industries in the spacious setting of an old chalk quarry. 'Exhibits' include a working blacksmith and a potter, and you can ride on a narrow gauge workers' train complete with authentic discomfort; there are also boat trips. This is a place to spend a few hours, with a lot to offer for children. Open from late March to October, Wednesday to Sunday, bank holiday Mondays and daily in school holidays.

LEWES

Lewes is clustered round a castle – one of a chain built by the Normans soon after the Battle of Hastings, to guard the route to France. It's a town of cottages and elegant brick houses, with antique shops and bookshops for browsing. There's a good view of it all from the towers of the castle. The green below the castle has been used for bowling since 1640; before that it was a medieval jousting ground.

Thousands of people in costume take part in the torchlight procession on 5 November in Lewes. The procession commemorates the 17 martyrs burnt at the stake in the 1550s. They were imprisoned first in the Star Inn, now the Town Hall.

Tom Paine, supporter of American independence, lived in Lewes at what is now the Bull House Restaurant. He debated politics in the Headstrong Club at the White Hart. Another resident was John Harvard, after whom the American university is named.

Anne of Cleves House was part of the divorce settlement of Henry VIII's fourth wife. She never lived here, but it's interesting to visit for its displays on the vanished Wealden iron industry. Open mid February to October; you get a slight reduction on a combined ticket to the house and castle.

> **Moneysaver**
> The Southdown Explorer ticket costs £3.75 for a day's bus travel on Southdown and some other buses from Brighton.

THE COAST

Rottingdean Numerous buses (including an open-topped service in summer) run to the pretty village of Rottingdean, where Rudyard Kipling wrote *Kim* and other books (the house is private but you can wander in his garden). Another resident was a bank clerk called Reuter, who collected news by pigeon post and thus started a worldwide news service. Rottingdean Grange is open daily except Wednesday, with a small museum and travelling art shows (free).

Seaford Seaford offers magnificent views along the white chalk cliffs called the Seven Sisters. There's good walking here on downland and seashore, with rock pools to explore.

Eastbourne Eastbourne is the stateliest resort near Brighton, with a Victorian pier, sandy beaches, theatres and miles of well kept promenades. From here it's a 15-minute bus ride or two-hour walk up to Beachy Head, where the South Downs end abruptly with a 534ft drop to the sea. Boat trips give views of the cliffs from the sea. Chez Duprée at 48 Grove Road does lunches. They say they'll cook anything if you order it in advance and if they can find it; telephone 0323 24637.

Hastings Hastings is scruffy but interesting. The name covers two towns – the old fishing port of Hastings, and the Victorian/Edwardian resort of St Leonard's on Sea. The Old Town is the most interesting, with steep streets running down to a beach packed with fishing boats and nets. Antique/second-hand shops abound, but the oddest and most enticing window displays belong to the Old Town Museum (free – closed on summer Sundays, but only open Sunday afternoons in winter).

The East Hill cliff railway climbs 267ft to a country park and gives good views. West Hill cliff railway goes up to the ruins of Hastings Castle. A train journey to Hastings involves a change at Eastbourne.

Local flavour
The tall dark structures on the beach at Hastings are net houses, built for drying nets. There's a fish market near by in summer, and one stall stays open all year. Shellfish is sold by the beach.

The Bluebell Railway is a preserved line with steam train rides through the wooded hilly country of the Sussex Weald from Sheffield Park station. There is a bus service from Lewes, or go by train from Brighton to Haywards Heath and then bus. On Sundays and public holidays, there's an inclusive ticket for bus and Bluebell Line, and the Bluebell sometimes puts on free bus services.

CHICHESTER AND ITS HARBOUR

BUDGET FOR A DAY

Train fare	4·90
Guided Walk	1·50
Cathedral	Free
Pallant House	1·50
Bus to Fishbourne	1·20
Roman Palace	2·00
Lunch	5·00
Afternoon tea	3·50
	£19·60
plus accommodation	

Chichester is quiet and compact; there are just four main streets, and traffic is banned from much of the centre, which is easy to reach from bus and rail stations by bus or walking. Most of the interesting parts of the city are still within the walls first built by the Romans.

Guided walking tours of about 1¼ hours

tours set off the tourist centre three times a week, and the Rotary Club does a walking tour on Sunday afternoons (free, but donations invited).

The cathedral is free (again, donations are invited). You may have seen the spire as you approached the city – it's visible from miles around. Most of the building is Norman, and it has some striking 20th-century work inside, including a huge tapestry by John Piper behind the high altar.

Just off South Street is Pallant House, easy to identify by the stone dodos on the gateposts. Twenty years ago this grand Queen Anne-style house was crumbling away; now pictures by Henry Moore, Frank Auerbach and other 20th-century artists are displayed in the panelled rooms, along with porcelain and glass. It's open Tuesday to Saturday.

Eastwards out of the old city in Church Road, Portfield, is something different – the barrel organs, musical boxes and other ingenious devices of the Mechanical Music and Doll Collection. The admission price includes the guided tour and demonstrations. Buses run to within easy walking distance: (ask for Sainsbury's superstore, or Uving Road).

The most exciting time to visit is for the Festivities in July, when the city is transformed with street theatre, children's shows and especially music – inside, outside, classical, jazz and a capella, from an equally huge range of performers. You'd be hard put not to find something to suit your taste and budget: obtain a programme from Amanda Sharp, Canongate House, South Street, Chichester, West Sussex PO19 1PU, telephone 0243 785718. Booking opens at the beginning of May.

Moneysaver
The Chichester Festivities include low-price and free events.

The Chichester Festival Theatre is the culture flagship all year round: information on what's on there is widely available. There's also an arts centre, tucked away in a converted 13th-century church off East Street, with visiting exhibitions and evenings of music.

Chichester Harbour isn't a harbour in the usual sense, but miles of sea, marsh and mudflats, with inlets running inland. Footpaths wind round it.

Bosham The prettiest place to visit is Bosham (say 'Bozzum') – you could encounter crowds here. This may be where King Canute ordered the waves to go back in about AD1020. (The story is that he was showing he couldn't do everything people said he could.) Southampton Water claims the story too, but in Bosham a child's grave has been found where Canute's daughter was said to be buried. The little church appears in the Bayeux Tapestry, with Bosham spelled as it is today.

The *Chichester Harbour Guide* is a map of the harbour with basic information on places, lavatories and buses, with angling, wildlife and history as well. It's aimed at sailors but useful for others – from the Chichester tourist information centre or Itchenor harbour office.

Wildlife-watching is one of the best pastimes in Chichester Harbour. Winter attracts thousands of ducks and waders, and some locals (but not the farmers) enjoy the arrival of huge numbers of brent geese. In summer you'll see salt-loving plants and flowers.

> **Local flavour**
> Shellfish are the speciality of Selsey. They're cooked straight off the boat on the East Beach, ready for eating among the lobster pots.

Itchenor The road to Itchenor ends at the boatyard and jetty in a mass of sailing boats. Harbour tours get you amongst it all: the Wingate does a 1½-hour round trip but times depend on the tides: telephone 0243 786418 for information. A ferryboat sometimes crosses between Itchenor to Bosham: ring the Itchenor harbour office to check, telephone 0243 512301.

West Wittering Windsurfers go to West Wittering to sail off the sand, naturalists visit for the nature trail along the sand and shingle of East Head (National Trust). From the bus, there's a walk to the beach. If you drive, you pay to park: cheaper after 3pm.

Fishbourne Fishbourne looks unpromising, but it has one of Britain's great Roman sites: the remains of a huge palace with numerous mosaic floors. What you can see is extensive (at ground level), although it's only a fraction of the original building. The remains are roofed over, but there's also a garden. Buses go to the village, but then it's a long walk.

ARUNDEL

Arundel stands on a hill, with a mighty castle and tall-spired cathedral making a fairytale picture. Steep streets climb up to the top of town, and shops for browsing include three covered antique markets during the week, plus a Saturday antiques market in Crown Yard. The town museum is at 61 High Street; at 23 you'll find the little Toy and Military Museum with its enormous collections of toy soldiers, egg cups and other small things. Open most days Easter to October. The Swan Pub opposite does lunches.

The Dukes of Norfolk have owned Arundel Castle for 700 years: inside it has pictures, tapestries and other treasures accumulated over the generations. Open April to October in the afternoons (not Saturday).

For many people there's only one place to go in Arundel – the Wildfowl and Wetlands Trust centre on the river. Hundreds of waterfowl live among the pools and reed beds here – some have been brought here from distant parts of the world, others are wild birds. The ducks are fed at 4pm in summer, 3.30pm in winter; the restaurant feeds people all day.

WINCHESTER

Winchester's hero is King Alfred, who made it his capital city, defeated the Vikings and brought peace and prosperity to southern England. His great granite statue looms over one end of the city's main street by the River Itchen. Peace and prosperity still rule here – there's

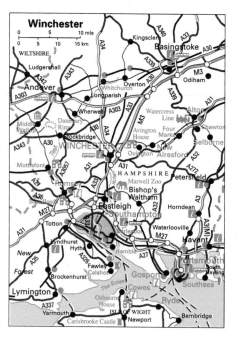

Winchester

London, or two hours by bus.

A good place to start looking around is the High Street, a Roman road running through the city. The tourist information centre is in the Guildhall at the lower (east) end of the street, where it opens out into Broadway. The City Mill is open in the afternoon from April to September, but not Monday and Friday. It is open on Good Friday and bank holiday Mondays, in which case it closes on the following Tuesday (National Trust).

Guided walks start from the Guildhall twice a day from May to September (once a day on Sundays and less frequently at other times of year). From late July through the summer there are also walking 'drama tours', during which you might meet King Alfred or another Winchester celebrity; and special interest tours take place in winter.

Moneysaver

The City Museum is free and full of evocative objects from the past – including a 9th-century child's shoe and early versions of the fork. Upstairs are Roman mosaics, an Edwardian bathroom and a splendid old-fashioned pharmacy reconstruction.

At the top end of the High Street is Westgate, only survivor of four original ways into the city. It may be under repair, but you should be able to visit the tiny museum upstairs for treasures like one of Charles II's boots, and graffiti scratched into the stone by 17th-century prisoners (closed on Monday in winter).

Local flavour

Domesday Book was compiled in Winchester in 1086 on the orders of William the Conqueror. The name means 'day of judgement' because it was a final authority for property litigation.

---

plenty of modern commercial activity, but in the city centres you can still wander beside the crystal clear waters of the river and explore quiet streets of centuries-old buildings around a fine cathedral.

The surrounding scenery is chalk country, cut through by some enchanting river valleys with a lot of scope for rural outings. The valley of the River Itchen offers a string of tiny villages and a preserved railway line. Along the Test Valley you'll find mellow old towns with a range of places to see. You're never really very far from other people in this part of the world, but you don't have to travel far from Winchester to feel that you're in the heart of rural England.

The main places are linked by bus services, but independent transport would be useful for exploring the villages. Cyclists can enjoy many miles of quiet lanes between the main roads. The nearest place to rent bicycles is at Southampton (see *Orientation*). You should book if you want to stay in Winchester, because accommodation is limited. There's a bigger and less expensive range in Southampton. Winchester is just over an hour by train from

William the Conqueror founded a castle at this elevated end of town. All that's left is the

Great Hall, an airy, elegant building some 750 years old. Inside hangs the Round Table, marked with the names of King Arthur and his knights. Weighing over a ton, it dates from the 1200s, well after King Arthur's time (if he existed) but romantic all the same (free).

Cars are banned from much of the High Street, and it's lined with an evocative hotchpotch of medieval and Georgian buildings (mostly shops now). Just by the City Cross, an arch leads to the Square, where you'll find the City Museum. Places for light lunches, coffee and the like are Waltons (popular with younger people) and Betjeman and Barton's upstairs tearoom.

The origins of the cathedral lie back in the 7th century, and the present building was begun in 1079. This is Europe's longest medieval cathedral, a beautiful, lofty place inside and out. It's good for memorials too. There's a little window to Izaak Walton, who fished the local trout streams and died in 1683 aged 90 – his motto was 'study to be quiet'. Jane Austen is buried in the cathedral having lived her last days in Winchester.

From Easter to September there are usually tours of the cathedral at 11am and 3pm – these are free, although a donation of £1.50 is suggested. There are also tours of the crypt, if it isn't flooded. (No tours Sunday.)

You can also visit the library of 1150 from the south transept: climb the steps and knock at the door to see treasures like the gorgeously illustrated 700-year-old Winchester Bible. Admission to the library costs £1, open from

Monday to Saturday, but closed for lunch and on Monday afternoon. There's no charge for visiting the cathedral, but a donation is suggested. The cathedral grounds are dotted with old buildings, and in one of them you'll find refreshments – a pot of tea, cake and hospitality for about £1.30 – with lavatories downstairs. Wisteria-draped Priory Gate leads out to Kingsgate, with tiny St Swithun's Church on top and tiny Wells bookshop below. Beyond that is leafy College Street, where Jane Austen lived her last days.

The high walls hereabouts enclose the lads at Winchester College, founded for 70 poor boys by William of Wykeham in 1382. It's now much larger, and is one the most exclusive public (ie private) schools in the country. The chapel, cloisters and chantry can usually be visited. Closing time is 5pm, or 4pm in winter, free. Guided tours set off at 11am, 2pm and 3.15pm (Sunday 2pm and 3.15pm).

Nearby Wolvesey Castle dates from the 12th century and used to be the bishop's palace but is now a massive ruin. Run by English Heritage it's open from Easter to September. There are good walks from here. You can amble for about a mile south via river and meadows to the Hospital of St Cross, which was founded in 1136 to care for old people (and still does).

For evenings, the Theatre Royal in Jewry Street is a handsome Edwardian venue for drama and films. There are several restaurants around here. Other culture spots are the King Alfred Arts Centre and the Tower, with very reasonably priced music and drama.

ORIENTATION IN WINCHESTER

INFORMATION
TOURIST OFFICE
Guildhall, The Broadway.
☎ 0962 840500.
POST OFFICE
Middlebrook Street.
PUBLIC LAVATORIES
By Abbey Gardens; St Norris Coverts.

TRANSPORT

BUSES
Bus station opposite the tourist office. For information ☎ 0962 52352.
TRAINS
Winchester station, 10 minutes walk from the city centre. For information ☎ 0703 229393.
CAR HIRE
Balldown Garage
Stockbridge Road. ☎ 0962 872744.
Churchfields Vehicle Rental

Railway Station, Stockbridge Road. ☎ 0962 844022.
Graysons Moorside Garage, North Wall. ☎ 0962 856471.
BICYCLE HIRE
Peter Hargroves 453 Millbrook Road, Southampton. ☎ 0703 789160. Mountain bikes at £10 a day, £30 a week, or £40 a fortnight, plus deposit.

ACCOMMODATION
GUESTHOUSE

Aerie Guesthouse *142 Teg Down Meads (off Dean Lane), Winchester SO22 5NS.* ☎ *0962 862519. Bed and breakfast from £15. No children under 10 years of age.*
COLLEGE ACCOMMODATION
Sparsholt College
Conference Officer, Sparsholt College, Sparsholt, Winchester SO21 2NF.

☎ *0962 72441. Summer vacation only, bed and breakfast from about £14. Booking advisable.*

EATING OUT
Mr So *3 Jewry Street.* ☎ *0962 61234. This Chinese restaurant does lunches and set evening meals from £10.*
Elizabethan Restaurant

Jewry Street. ☎ *0962 53566. Fixed-price three-course lunches and early dinners (both £7.95)in a 1509 building.*
Wykeham Arms *between the cathedral and Winchester College. This pub does midday and evening food (not Sunday) as well as real ales: starters are around £2.75, main course salad is £4.*

OUTINGS FROM WINCHESTER

PORTSMOUTH

Portsmouth and the navy have been linked ever since 1495 when Henry VII decided to build a dry dock there. The main sights today are the historic ships – especially Nelson's *Victory* and the *Mary Rose* – but you get good views of modern ships too. Portsmouth has a resort side at Southsea, with traditional seaside attractions including a funfair, and great green lawns backing the promenade.

Portsmouth is hemmed in on three sides by the sea, but within it the different areas are quite distinct. The one to see if time is restricted is the harbour, with HM Naval Base. South is the Old Town, where the coastal fortifications make a fine promenade to Southsea. Then there's the city centre which lies inland. The navy connection meant that Portsmouth was a prime target for bombs in World War II, so this part is modern.

This isn't the prettiest city in the world and walking between the different areas is tedious, but you can reach them all by bus. Buses are worth considering even if you arrive by car – finding parking spaces in different parts of the city can be difficult.

From Winchester it's 50 minutes by train; go to Portsmouth Harbour train station for the Old Town, Southsea and HM Naval Base. Portsmouth and Southsea is a separate train station close to the city centre.

You can go into the dockyard free of charge, and stroll among the figureheads in the public area. Lavatories and refreshments are available, but don't expect great sophistication.

Visits to the *Victory* are by guided tour. Tickets are for a set time, and there may be a long wait. Avoid weekends and school holidays (including half term breaks), or arrive early. The *Victory* was the ship in which Nelson fought and won the Battle of Trafalgar on 21 October 1805, and died in the process. Admission includes the Royal Naval Museum.

Moneysaver
Combined tickets save money on *Mary Rose*, *Victory* and Royal Naval Museum; also on the Submarine and Royal Marines Museums.

The *Mary Rose* was Henry VIII's flagship, but on 19 July 1545 she sank in view of the king while fighting the French off Southsea. It took years of preparation to excavate her from the sea bed in 1982. A walkway takes you past the starboard side, which is virtually intact. The exhibition (same ticket) shows thousands of artefacts found on the ship – guns, games, musical instruments, pocket sun dial, bowls and spoons.

HMS *Warrior* was the Royal Navy's first iron warship (1860), and visitors can wander at will: good for children, but steep steps could be tricky for the very young. She looks ready to set off, with everything from cannons to kitbags stored

HMS Warrior, one of Portsmouth's historic ships.

away but ingeniously easy to reach. Guides are on hand to answer questions.

The Royal Naval Museum occupies a series of dockyard buildings (start at the *Victory* end). It's a lively display, with figureheads, ship models and a huge range of other naval items.

> **Local flavour**
> The term 'a square meal' dates from the days when sailors ate their rations off square wooden boards – you can see one at the Royal Naval Museum.

The other vessel to visit is HM Submarine *Alliance*, in service until 1973 but now chief exhibit at the Submarine Museum in Gosport. You can look round the entire craft (which is big) and visit *Holland I*, launched in 1901, besides seeing the museum. Open from 10am, last tour 4.30pm. The quick way from Portsmouth is by the Gosport ferry, which takes five minutes. The crossing to Gosport is free, but you pay to come back. For cars there's a small parking charge.

Take a harbour boat trip to see warships and merchant ships, and get views of the coastal fortifications. Trips are advertised on the Hard, with lists of the ships that are in Portsmouth on the day.

Ferries and hovercraft cross to the Isle of Wight from Portsmouth and Southsea. Prices vary: Solent Enterprise do a day trip to Cowes on Thursday or Ryde on Wednesday, and should give you time to visit a major sight like Carisbrooke Castle or Osborne House on the

island. Ask at the tourist information centre about coach tours of the Isle of Wight. Various boats also do tours of the Solent from Portsmouth.

In August, the Cowes Week yacht races are the best free show: Cowes Pier and the Esplanade are good vantage points. Power-boat races start from Cowes on the Sunday before bank holiday Monday in August.

From the harbour it's a bus ride or 20-minute trudge to the Old Town – nicknamed Spice Island in the days when its main purpose was to entertain sailors. Now it's a pretty little corner with winding streets and views of the harbour inlet called the Camber. This is a good part of town for restaurants. Portsmouth Cathedral is in the High Street. If you're a sailor, touch the Golden Barque here for luck. Open-topped buses run between the Hard, Old Town and Southsea on Sundays in summer.

Walk along the sea defence wall in the Old Town for a breezy route to Southsea, the smart residential and holiday-making side of town. On the way you pass Henry VIII's Southsea Castle, open all year. Out to sea is Spitbank Fort, which dates back to the 1850s – open from Easter to October. The admission fee includes the ferry. It takes a good hour to look round, and the views are wonderful. Ferries leave every 75 minutes from 11am to 3pm, and take 10 minutes to get there.

You'll find traditional seaside attractions at Southsea, plus the Sea Life Centre, which is a spectacular modern aquarium. The Pyramids Leisure Centre has 170ft waterchutes, wave machines and poolside bars, all in a summery 84° Fahrenheit micro-climate. The D-Day Museum celebrates the Allied landings in Normandy of 1944. You're lent a headset with commentary for viewing the Overlord Embroidery, a 50yd illustration of Operation Overlord.

Portsmouth's other 'sight' is Charles Dickens' birthplace, on the north side of town. It's signposted on the road and reachable by bus from the centre (open from October to March).

QUEEN ELIZABETH COUTRY PARK

Queen Elizabeth Country Park offers miles of

walking in woodland and open pasture on the South Downs. You can book barbecue hearths and pony trekking at the park centre; mountain biking, hang gliding and grass-skiing are also possible. There is a charge for parking: make sure you have the right change to open the automatic exit gate. Maps and information are available at the park centre, open daily from March to October but otherwise only at weekends. Best free shows are the sheep management days in summer, including dipping, shearing and chats with the shepherd.

The Iron Age Farm at Butser Hill near the country park has re-created homes and fields as they would have been over 2,000 years ago. Telephone 0705 598838 to check on bus access; for drivers, it's signed off the A3. Open every day except Saturday in school holidays; otherwise Sundays and bank holidays all day, and Saturday afternoons.

SOUTHAMPTON

People often underestimate Southampton because they stick to the main shopping area and never discover the rest. The shopping's good, but the really interesting bits are to the south, around the Old Town and the waterside. Start by picking up a street map at the tourist information centre on Above Bar (the main shopping street, round the corner from the bus station, a little further from the rail station).

You can get to Southampton from Winchester in 40 minutes by bus or 20 minutes by rail. If driving, follow signs for the Old Town or Waterside. Be careful – if you deviate from the signed route you're liable to be swept off into remote parts of the city.

The Old Town lies behind the present day waterfront. It's flanked by amazing medieval walls – some of Europe's finest, still standing to their original height in places. The best place to start is Bargate, at the end of Above Bar. From there you can walk a stretch along the top of the wall above Western Esplanade, which used to be a quayside. Free guided walks start at Bargate all year on Sunday and Monday at 10.30am, July and August at 10.30am and 2.30pm.

At ground level you can see West Gate,

through which some of Henry V's soldiers set off for Agincourt in 1415; later the Pilgrim Fathers left from here too. As you wind up Blue Anchor Lane the high wall on your right shields the Tudor garden of the Tudor House – now a museum, and free. God's House Tower in Winkle Street was one of the first artillery fortifications. Porters Lane has the remains of Norman houses, and in French Street there's a merchant's house, intact and dating from the late 1200s (English Heritage).

Local flavour
Southampton has festivals for films, jazz, women, senior citizens and others. The Balloon and Flower Festival in July involves over 100 balloons and two marquees full of flowers. For details of all events, ring the Special Events Hotline: 0703 832525.

Mayflower Park is the scene of the annual Southampton International Boat Show. Fifteen minutes walk away, Ocean Village is a classy marina, with shops and places to eat. Southampton's maritime museum is due to move here.

Moneysaver
Admission to the boat show is most expensive on the first day, cheapest after 4.30pm in the last week (it stays open till 7pm after the first day).

The Hall of Aviation close by celebrates the lesser known achievements of Southampton's many aircraft companies – this was the birthplace of the *Spitfire*, and has an enormous Sandringham Passenger Flying Boat that you can climb aboard; closed Monday except bank holidays and school holidays.

Eling Tide Mill is on the western edge of the city, but worth the trek. There has been a mill here for at least 900 years. Tidal energy drives the millstones, and flour ground at the mill is on sale; open Wednesday to Sunday. The waterside here is a good place for watching sailing boats and larger shipping.

EAST OF WINCHESTER

A peaceful lane runs along the Itchen valley from Winchester to New Alresford. It's ideal for cycling, and you can walk this way too, along a network of lanes and paths between villages (use Ordnance Survey Landranger sheet 185). The whole route to New Alresford is several miles, but you could do part of it by bus. There's also a faster road, the A31.

New Alresford and the Watercress Line
New Alresford (say 'awlsford') was new in the early 1200s, when it was created by the Bishop of Winchester. A lot of the houses are Georgian, dating from just after a fire in 1689. This isn't a big town but it's pretty, and you could spend a long time browsing among the shops selling antiques, books, arts and crafts. Tiffins in West Street do teas and light lunches.

Signs direct you to the train station for the Watercress Line, which has preserved steam train services on a route through beautiful countryside. The line used to carry enormous hampers of locally grown watercress to London. Watercress is still grown locally – you can see the beds from the train, and it's often on sale on trains or at the station buffet. Trains run mainly between March and October, with several services a day at the height of summer. 'Specials' at other times include pre-Christmas 'Santaland' runs.

The trains run to Alton, but you can stop at Ropley for the picnic area and view of locomotives being restored. There are also halts at Medstead and Four Marks, where on certain days trains connect with a free vintage bus service to Chawton and Selborne. Check dates on the Watercress Line leaflets (widely available).

A return ticket on the Watercress Line costs only a little more than a single, and gives you unlimited steam train travel for the day; price £4.65, family ticket £12.95.

Chawton Chawton was Jane Austen's home from 1806 to 1817. She lived in the red brick house opposite the Grey Friar pub, and wrote *Emma, Persuasion* and other novels there. It has been restored to look as it would have done in her day. It's open daily from April to October, at weekends in January and February, and otherwise from Wednesday to Sunday.

Selborne Selborne is known to many who've never been near it because of the *Natural History of Selborne*, written in 1789 by curate Gilbert White. A lot of the land is owned by the National Trust – if you arrive by car, their free car park behind the Selborne Arms pub. From here you can walk up to Selborne Common on the Zig Zag path, built by Gilbert and his brother. Gilbert White's house, The Wakes, has a five-acre garden and displays on the Oates brothers, who were explorers. Open March to October, Wednesday to Sunday and bank holidays (and Tuesday in school holidays). There's also a Romany gypsy museum in the village; and don't miss the delightful church.

Regular buses run to Chawton and Selborne from Alton, but not very frequently. Special Tuesday and Friday buses run right to Jane Austen's house; otherwise it's about half an hour's walk.

Marwell Zoo Marwell Zoo is southeast of Winchester (no Sunday bus in winter). There are hundreds of animals here, and they are given plenty of space in natural-like enclosures, so you need time to see it all. There's a train if you don't want to walk, and for an extra charge you can drive round (but not encouraged). The emphasis is on conservation and breeding: an information board brings you up to date with recent births and other events. Features for children include a periscope which shows the world as a giraffe sees it. Price £4.30.

NORTH, AND THE RIVER TEST

Whitchurch The main reason for visiting Whitchurch is the silk mill, powered by a mighty waterwheel on the River Test. The old but beautifully maintained machinery is interesting in its own right, and you can buy silk by the metre. There's also a tearoom for light meals. Open Tuesday to Saturday, bank holidays and summer Sundays. Whitchurch is north out of Winchester (no bus Sunday).

Local flavour
Whitchurch Silk Mill makes the heavy black silk for the gowns worn by judges: that's why judges are nicknamed silks.

Middle Wallop   This is the home of the Museum of Army Flying. The army aircraft in the impressive display range from kites and balloons to the latest in helicopters. Buses run from Andover, but not very frequently; they also run to within about a mile of Danebury – an Iron Age hill fort, with high, well preserved earthworks that make a good walk.

ROMSEY AND MOTTISFONT

Romsey is small in size but big in interest. Bus travellers arrive close to the tourist information office, and there's also a car park here. Romsey Abbey is a beautiful (and huge) Norman church, which the townspeople bought for £100 when the former monastery was closed in the 1500s (free, but donations invited). King John's House, over 700 years old, has graffiti (of a devout sort) that can be dated 15 February 1306. The Cobweb Tearooms at 49 The Hundred do lunches and teas and you can get a light lunch at the Three Tuns in Middlebridge Street

On the edge of town is Broadlands, once the home of Victorian Prime Minister Lord Palmerston (you will have seen his statue in the

Broadlands , the Hampshire home of Lord Romsey.

town centre). More recently this was the home of the late Earl Mountbatten of Burma, who is buried in the abbey. The house has Van Dyck paintings, splendid rooms, and a good garden; it's expensive to visit, but offers several hours of interest. Open Easter to September, but closed on Fridays except Good Friday. The last tour starts at 4pm, although it's open until 5.30pm.

Trains run from Romsey to Mottisfont Dunbridge (but avoid Sunday), which is three-quarters of a mile from Mottisfont Abbey (National Trust). The walled gardens have wonderful old-fashioned roses: visit in the rose season for fragrant evening openings. These are usually in June and July, from 7pm to 9pm from Tuesday to Thursday and Sunday, but check first, telephone 0794 41220. Otherwise the gardens are open April to September daily (except Friday and Saturday) 2pm to 6pm. For an extra charge on Wednesdays, you can see a room with *trompe l'oeil* (optical illusion) paintings by Rex Whistler. There may be a long wait however.

BOURNEMOUTH

Bournemouth is the fun metropolis of the south, an essential destination if you want sandy beaches, seaside attractions and night-time entertainment. For business people Bournemouth is a popular venue for conferences, for shoppers it has department stores and arcades, and for culture the flagship is the Bournemouth Symphony Orchestra.

Bournemouth has a huge amount of accommodation of all sorts and prices, but in summer it can be very hard to find places. The tourist information centre in Westover Road has a computerised booking service and masses of local information.

Bournemouth is three hours from London by bus, 90 minutes by rail. From Winchester it's an hour by bus. Bournemouth airport destinations include Glasgow and Brussels.

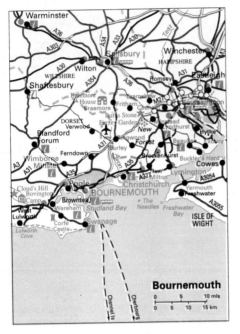

Bournemouth

0   5   10 mls
0 5   10   15 km

similar fare on a larger scale. The Winter Gardens theatre has occasional concerts by the Bournemouth Symphony Orchestra; Poole Arts Centre has plays by local and touring companies, plus films, ballet, opera and pantomime. The Regents Centre in Christchurch has a varied programme too.

Visit in late June/early July for the Music Festival (classical, choral, jazz bands); or late July/early August for the Folk Festival. August brings the regatta and carnival, plus entertainments in the Lower Gardens for the Children's Festival.

Sports events include good value international tennis at the Bournemouth Open in August, and there are other tournaments too; watch the cricket at Hampshire County Cricket Ground, or visit in September to watch power boats.

> **Moneysaver**
> Hotels and children's entertainments reduce prices for the young during the Children's Festival in August.

> **Moneysaver**
> *Where to go in and around Bournemouth* costs 75p from tourist information centres, and includes discount vouchers for outings, entertainments and places to eat.

The Russell Cotes Art Gallery and Museum on East Cliff is a treasure trove of exotica, pictures and ship models (price £1, closed Sunday).

Go west of Bournemouth for Poole, with Georgian streets, lots of bustle in the harbour and Brownsea Island (National Trust) offshore. This is the place for wandering among woodland haunts of red squirrels, deer, feral peacocks and wild birds. Ferries operate from April to September between 10am and 8pm, or sunset if earlier.

Behind the miles of sandy beach are cliffs cut through by little valleys called chines, now mostly public gardens and pine-scented pathways. The Pavilion and Pier theatres have summer spectaculars and other shows; the Bournemouth International Centre (BIC) offers

ORIENTATION IN BOURNEMOUTH

INFORMATION
TOURIST OFFICE
Westover Road. ☎ *0202 291715.*
POST OFFICE
Post Office Road.
PUBLIC LAVATORIES

West Cliff Promenade; Undercliff Drive; next to tourist office.

TRANSPORT
BUSES
For outings from Bournemouth, Wilts and Dorset Travel Office, 29 Gervis Place.
☎ *0202 673535 or ask at*

the tourist office.
TRAINS
Bournemouth Central station, Holdenhurst Road, about ⅔ of a mile from the centre. For train information, ☎ *0202 292474.*
CAR HIRE
Avis 17A Christchurch Road.

☎ *0202 293218.*
Budget Rent-a-Car *The Wessex Hotel. West Cliff Road.* ☎ *0202 296163.*
Hendy Hire *8-14 Palmerston Road, Boscombe.* ☎ *0202 309331.*
BICYCLE HIRE
Pedals *290 Holdenhurst Road.* ☎ *0202 301683.*
Bikes *431-33 Poole Road, Branksome.* ☎ *0202 769202.*

ACCOMMODATION
HOTELS
Amitie *1247 Christchurch*

Road. ☎ *0202 427255. Prices start at about £12 for single bed and breakfast.*
Cliff House Hotel *113 Alumhurst Road.* ☎ *0202 763003. Dinner, bed and breakfast from £29.*
CAMP SITE
Chesildene Touring Caravan Park *2 Chesildene Avenue, close to the town centre.* ☎ *0202 513238.*

EATING OUT
There is a wide variety and choice of places to eat in

Bournemouth.
Durley Grange Hotel *6 Durley Road, Westcliff.* ☎ *0202 24473. Fixed-price evening menu at £11.50, which may include seafood. (They sometimes do good-value off-season breaks for dinner, bed and breakfast.)*
Flossie's *73 Seamoor Road, Westbourne.* ☎ *0202 764459. Substantial vegetarian lunches for under £5; a non-vegetarian section downstairs.*

OUTINGS FROM BOURNEMOUTH

THE NEW FOREST

Expect neither newness nor a vast tract of trees here – 'forest' in this sense means hunting ground, and it was a new one for William the Conqueror in 1079. Ever since then, the New Forest has had its own laws and its own ways of doing things. Originally the idea was to preserve the deer for hunting, with draconian penalties for poachers and other lawbreakers. Now it's open to all, with especially good walking and horseback riding across open country, plus golf courses, fresh and saltwater fishing and a variety of places to visit. It's worth trying to avoid school and public holidays, though, especially in summer.

The feature that always thrills first-time visitors and draws others back again is the free-roaming livestock. Donkeys and cattle stroll round the villages with a lofty disdain for the highway code; pigs still rootle for acorns in autumn; and there are ponies everywhere. If you are driving watch out: they have no road sense.

New Forest ponies may be direct descendants of the wild horses of primeval Britain. All of them have owners and there are regular round-ups, or 'drifts'. Officials called 'agisters' collect a fee for each pony, and in return patrol the Forest to help animals in trouble.

Local flavour
The death penalty no longer applies, but the byelaws should be observed. Some of them are: don't light fires, do close gates, park only in car parks (there are plenty), keep dogs on a lead. Never feed the local livestock.

From April to October you may be able to take a horse and wagon ride: telephone Brockenhurst 0590 23633 or Burley 0425 75276 to book. For many people the only way to see the New Forest is on horseback. You're more likely to see wild animals like foxes and deer this way too. Numerous stables offer half-hour to two-hour rides, independently or in a group. Brockenhurst and Burley have several stables near by; the New Forest Visitor Centre at Lyndhurst has a list of stables that offer rides.

Drivers are catered for with car parks throughout the Forest, but there aren't many buses. Cycling along the tracks and paths is allowed, but remember to close all gates.

Many animals roam free in the New Forest.

Lyndhurst A useful starting point is the New Forest Visitor Centre (free parking) at Lyndhurst. Pride of the town is the parish church, which has pre-Raphaelite stained glass, and the tomb of Alice Liddell (the original for Lewis Carroll's *Alice in Wonderland*). The 14th-century Verderers' Court is the traditional administration centre for the Forest and stands next door to the modern equivalent, the office of the Forestry Commission.

Local flavour

New Forest venison is on sale at John Strange's shop, near the church in Lyndhurst High Street. The venison sausages are famous well outside the area, and local trout is also sold.

North of Lyndhurst are some of the prettiest places in the New Forest – Fritham, Eyeworth and Minstead, with its lanes and cottages (it's on a bus route too, but no services on Sunday). Sir Arthur Conan Doyle and his wife are buried in the churchyard. Furzey Gardens offer eight acres of colourful strolling.

Close to Lyndhurst you can join the Bolderwood and Rhinefield Ornamental Drives. Both are narrow roads through woodland, with car parking and ways to walk. Off the Bolderwood Drive you can have a look at the Knightwood Oak, one of the oldest trees in the forest. There's also a deer sanctuary with observation platforms from which you'll almost certainly see fallow deer.

The Rhinefield route is at its best in early summer, when the rhododendrons are in flower. Along the way is Rhinefield House which is a splendid mock-baronial hotel – stop for tea or lunch, if only for a look at the panelled Armada Room.

Beaulieu and Exbury Leave Lyndhurst on the road to Beaulieu, and you'll instantly be in the most evocative type of New Forest landscape – one of heathland and close-nibbled turf. Pony sales take place at Beaulieu Road Station in April, August, September, October and November. Beaulieu Heath (on the way to Lymington) is another wide open expanse, part bog but mostly heather, and dotted with ancient burial mounds. Hatchet Pond has coarse fishing: licences from the post offices in Bramshaw and East Boldre, Forestry Commission camp site offices and other places.

Beaulieu in the southeast of the New Forest is a pretty little village which has the New Forest's major tourist spot – half a million visitors a year come for the complex of attractions old and new, all linked by high level monorail. The heart of it all is the ancestral home (since the 17th century) of Lord Montagu: Beaulieu Palace is a beautiful Tudor pile, though it's just the gateway of an abbey which stood here before. The basic visitor's package includes the house, National Motor Museum and a 'time capsule' ride through vehicles down the ages, plus two vouchers for other features like the monorail and veteran bus rides. Services include wheelchairs on loan, and a room for tending to babies. Not a budget event, but good of its kind. Buses run to Beaulieu on Sunday in summer.

Buckler's Hard village is two miles south on a wide stretch of the Beaulieu River. In its 18th-century heyday the village was entirely geared to building timber ships – the timbers were seasoned in the one broad street, and the ships were built at the end of it, including Nelson's favourite, the *Agamemnon*. Some of the cottages are a maritime museum, from which you enter reconstructions of scenes 200 years ago. Don't go into the houses marked 'Resident' – real-life people live there.

South of Beaulieu you can get lost in the the 200-odd acres of Exbury Gardens – best in late spring when hundreds of varieties of rhododendron and azalea burst into heavy scented flower. Autumn brings a more soothing show of colour and a lower entrance fee. Open early March to early July, and early September to mid October.

Moneysaver
No charge for visiting the Reptiliary at Holidays Hill (west of Lyndhurst). The Forestry Commission breeds snakes and lizards here, and some are released back into the forest. Open April to September till 8pm; best on warm days.

Lymington The best day to visit Lymington is Saturday, when the steep main street is lined with market stalls. Beware traffic congestion if you're in a car though. The Georgian houses along the street were built on the profits from sea salt, of which Lymington used to produce several thousand tons a year.

The nearby harbour is among a mass of little sailing boats, fishing craft and children fishing off the jetty. There are river trips on the *Water Rat* from the Quay.

A journey that's fun to make from Lymington is over the Solent to the Isle of Wight. The ferry takes about 30 minutes to reach Yarmouth which is at the western, more peaceful side of the island.

BREAMORE

One of a variety of things to see at Breamore House.

Breamore has an Elizabethan house and countryside museum in unspoiled country just over the northern boundary of the New Forest, between Fordingbridge and Salisbury. The ticket covers the house, carriage collection and workshops of a wheelwright, blacksmith and other rural craftsmen. Open May to September afternoons, closed Monday and Friday except bank holiday Mondays, but open daily in August. There's no charge for following the walk through the woods to a yew grove, where a maze pattern is outlined on the ground. Some say it's Celtic, others that medieval monks crawled round it to atone for sins.

WIMBORNE MINSTER

This charming little Dorset town lies in the shadow of its famous Minster – a great, twin-towered building which embraces almost every known architectural style, from Norman to Gothic. The west tower has a quarter-jack clock, the quarter-hour bells being struck by the figure of a grenadier bearing a hammer in each hand.

Opposite the Minster you'll find the Priest's House Museum which displays a wealth of exhibits of local interest. The gardens are open to the public too, (open from Easter to September, daily 10.30am to 4.30pm).

Knoll Gardens in Staplehill Road have a rare, unusual and exotic collection plants from all over the world, begun some 20 years ago. In recent years the gardens have been completely refurbished, and water gardens, ponds, waterfalls, streams, rockeries and herbaceous borders have been added (open from March daily 10am to 6pm or dusk if earlier.

Moneysaver
You can visit just the gardens and parkland of Kingston Lacy at reduced admission cost. National Trust members, of course, visit free of charge.

Kingston Lacy is the place for art lovers. One of the finest houses of its period in Dorset, it has only been open to the public since 1986 and is full of pictures by Titian, Rubens, Van Dyck and others. It was bequeathed, along with 1,500 acres of its land, to the National Trust and is open from April to early November, Saturday to Wednesday from 12 noon to 5.30pm, although the park is open from 11.30am to 6pm.

WEST TO PURBECK

Swanage is a cheerful resort today with a beach and bandstand. There are plenty of seaside cafés. Steam trains run on a preserved railway line all year – daily in summer, weekends in winter.

Buses (or a longish coast walk) take you north from Swanage to the beach of Studland Bay, which is owned by the National Trust (no free parking). The good beach is renowned for its naturist section; the heathland behind is special for naturalists. Look south for Old Harry and his Wife, which are the great limestone rocks detached from Handfast Point. South Purbeck has a high cliff coast with fine walking and occasional places for bathing off rocks

Corfe Castle has stone-walled, stone-roofed cottages, with the skeletal castle brooding above – the castle is run by the National Trust (it closes for winter, except at weekends).

A little farther west the Tank Museum at Bovington Camp has a huge number of tanks and other military vehicles, plus plenty of weaponry and other things to appeal to children. Bovington's most famous soldier was T E Lawrence, better known as Lawrence of Arabia. He lived very simply near by at Clouds Hill, which is a tiny National Trust cottage, open in the afternoon from Wednesday to Friday, Sunday and bank holidays, but Sundays only in winter.

SOUTHWEST BRITAIN – THE WEST COUNTRY

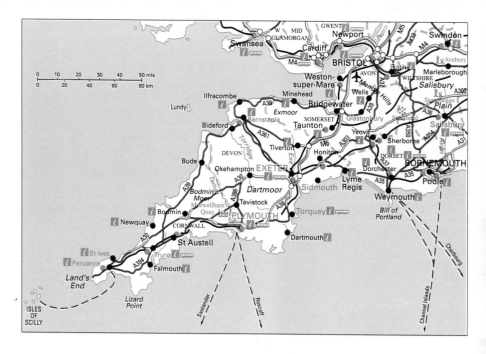

This chapter covers the southwestern counties of England. It includes interesting old towns and a couple of big cities, but a major attraction is the scenery outside them. There are hundreds of miles of unspoilt coastline, and the inland scenery ranges from picture-book rustic to wild.

Local flavour
If you are thinking about bringing a pet along, bear in mind that dogs are banned from most West Country resort beaches in the summer.

Tucked away within it are some stunning gardens and beautiful old houses. This is also a great area for tracking down prehistoric sites, and literary associations. As a major holiday area, it's well supplied with purpose-designed leisure parks and other all-weather attractions, especially towards the west.

A car would undoubtedly be useful, but you can explore by train. There's an unusually good railway network, and nearly every route is worth taking just for the views. There are plenty of buses throughout the region, and they are geared to taking visitors to the prime sights. As usual though, bus services become infrequent or non-existent in winter and on Sundays throughout the year.

A good place to start is Bath, where you can stroll around the most elegant of 18th-century cityscapes, and visit some impresssive Roman remains. Bath is a lively city, with some great shops. The drawback is that it's begun to attract more summer visitors than it can bear. If you have the flexibility to do so, it would be worth timing your visit to avoid the May to September months. Bath is also in easy reach of some natural showpieces: the Cheddar Gorge in the Mendip Hills, and the cave complexes below them. A bit further off is Glastonbury, intricately linked with the legend of the Holy Grail, and there are some celebrated historic houses to visit.

Southeast from Bath is Salisbury, where medieval streets surround a graceful cathedral. Salisbury is a good base for visits to the ancient stone circles at Stonehenge and Avebury. The other big attraction is Stourhead, which is one of England's most beautiful gardens.

Southwest on the coast, at the head of a large estuary, is Exeter, where the centrepiece is another mellow old cathedral. There's also a huge collection of ships at the Maritime Museum. Resorts range from glamorous Torquay, self-styled rival of Cannes, to traditional Sidmouth, with miles of sandy beaches all along the coast.

West again, Dartmoor is a wilderness of rocks and moorland where Sherlock Holmes cracked the mystery of *The Hound of the Baskervilles*. In good weather it's wonderful walking country – accessible on day trips from Exeter or Plymouth, but you'll need independent transport if you want to explore it.

Cornwall is the western-most county of all, noted for its coastal scenery and associations with King Arthur. The north coast is famous for its cliffs and beaches, the south coast for its wooded estuaries. The port towns and fishing villages on both coasts somehow keep their character despite being major holiday areas. The suggested base is Truro, a reasonably central point; if you preferred, it would be easy to stay by the sea.

Return eastwards along the north coast to Barnstaple, for the coastline and for Exmoor, another moorland, cut by secret wooded valleys,

The West Country is well known for its regional food specialities - notably cream teas, Cornish pasties, Cheddar cheese and 'Scrumpy'.

with spectacular cliffs at its northern edge. There are some exceptionally picturesque little harbour villages along this coast.

May/June (apart from public holidays) and September/October are the best times to visit if you want to avoid crowds; the countryside looks best then too, with masses of wild flowers in the lanes in early summer. Many historic houses and other attractions close in winter.

This region has some of the warmest weather in Britain, which attracts crowds and makes the roads very busy. Traffic jams on the main roads to the southwest are an integral part of the British summer. If you want to enjoy the festive holiday atmosphere, time your driving to avoid the peak times and book train tickets and accommodation well in advance.

The holiday traditions of the area mean plenty of budget accommodation: bed-and-breakfast establishments abound, as do places to rent.

Moneysaver
Eat out for tea rather than lunch – good teashops are easier to find than budget restaurants.

Regional food includes some notable sweet treats. Devon and Cornwall are dairying areas, and clotted cream is traditional in both. In Cornwall you'll also see saffron cakes – fruit buns coloured yellow with saffron. Bath has Bath buns, which are a variation on the fruit bun theme. It also has Sally Lunn teacakes, which are like the French brioche.

On the savoury side, Cheddar cheese

originated in the Mendip Hills south of Bath, and is still made by traditional methods in the area. Cornish pasties are advertised everywhere in Cornwall.

Devon, Somerset and Dorset are the places to look for locally made cider, sold on the farm and in pubs. Traditional 'scrumpy', as it's known, is designed to produce quick oblivion, but more palatable (a personal view) ciders are also made.

Traditional festivals are faithfully observed, like the big October/November carnivals around the Bristol area, and the Cornish May celebrations.

The smartest shopping in the region is in Bath, where enticing specialist shops range from high class chocolates to craftsman-made violins. You'll find souvenir shops selling hard

to tourists everywhere.

This is also a good region for craft workshops: Devon has more than its share of potters and weavers, and nowhere in Cornwall is far from a craft centre. Artists are thick on the ground in St Ives in Cornwall: again, prices vary, but you may find just the right picture to take home. Somerset baskets are an ancient craft tradition – you may see them advertised at the roadside

Local flavour

The West Country was England's gateway to the New World. John Cabot and other early explorers set off from Bristol, and the *Mayflower* sailed from Plymouth.

BATH

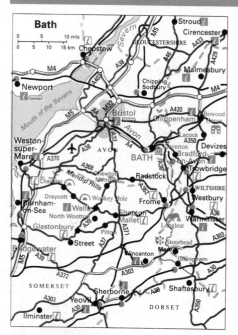

Bath is one of England's most popular places to visit – an especially handsome town with some

of the country's best Roman remains, and streets full of interesting, unusual and tempting shops. A word of warning, though. Bath is suffering from tourist overload, and locals maddened by open-topped bus tours have been known to pelt passengers with apples, and even turn hose-pipes on them. Overcrowding is severe from May to September, and you will enjoy the city more if you visit earlier or later in the year.

It's feasible to live in Bath or Bristol and work in London, so you'll find these two cities more sophisticated (and expensive) than some other parts of the West Country. Inexpensive accommodation does exist, but is best booked ahead.

Bath is just over an hour from London (Paddington) by rail or three hours by bus. Trains from London link with the Rail-Air bus from Heathrow airport at Reading train station, which also has a train link with Gatwick. The nearest airport is at Bristol, which has flights to other cities in Britain and mainland Europe.

Bath is special because of its combination of elegant Georgian architecture with honey-coloured Bath stone. It's set in a bowl of hills, so you can be in the middle of the city and still get glimpses of green open spaces. Even though it attracts a lot of visitors, it hasn't fossilised like some old cities; it feels like a lively place. Bath is a city of a hills, so be prepared for steep walking.

The reason for the city's existence is a hot spring which gushes out at 120° Fahrenheit. According to legend, Bath's hot springs were discovered by Prince Bladud, who was banished because he was a leper. He became a swineherd, and was cured when he followed his pigs' example by bathing in the water.

The Romans built a bathing establishment on the spot within 10 years of occupying Britain, but Bath is mostly Georgian – the period when it was very fashionable. Jane Austen and other writers visited Bath in its Georgian heyday and wrote about it, not always flatteringly. The tourist office stocks various guides to literary connections. Free guided walks start outside the Pump Room at least twice a day (but not Monday or Saturday) all year. They're led by members of the Mayor's corps of honorary guides.

Guide Friday runs regular, one-hour open-topped bus tours round the city, and you can join them at several points, including the bus station and Bath Abbey. There's a guide on every bus to give a commentary.

The Roman baths and museum are below street level now, and you go down to the evocative remains of heated rooms once used for lounging about, warm water baths for soaking and a cold plunge pool. There was a temple here, and all sorts of small offerings are on view – the museum has 16,000 coins, plus gems, jewellery and other objects such as plates. You'll also see curses on display. Open all year with late opening till 7pm in July and August.

> **Moneysaver**
> If you want to visit the Roman baths and the Museum of Costume, you may be able to buy combined tickets. There's no charge for visiting the Pump Room.

The Pump Room above the Roman Baths was the fashionable meeting place of Georgian times. You can still taste the water there (free), but they also serve coffee and light lunches (not very cheap), sometimes to the strains of a string ensemble.

> **Local flavour**
> The Bath Carnival is celebrated in early September, with events such as chariot racing, processions and fireworks.

For Georgian elegance, the most admired streets are Royal Crescent, high above Royal Victoria Park, The Circus, and the Pulteney Bridge over the river. Number 1 Royal Crescent has been restored and furnished as it would have been in Georgian times – open March to mid December (not Mondays except bank holidays). The Museum of Costume is in the Assembly Rooms – this is a wonderful collection of high fashion, from exquisite 18th-century dresses to the present day.

Pulteney Bridge is one of Bath's many attractions.

> **Moneysaver**
> Make lunch the main meal of the day: More expensive restaurants often charge less for a fixed-price midday meal than the evening menu.

The American Museum is a little out of town at Claverton. Eighteen period furnished rooms and galleries in this handsome mansion show American artefacts, including quilts and work by the Shakers, Pennsylvania Germans and American Indians, as well as others. The gardens include an American arboretum, and you can tuck into real American cookies in the restaurant. Open in the afternoon from April to October (except Mondays). Buses run there direct in summer, otherwise there's a 10-minute walk from the nearest bus stop.

The annual arts festival in late May/early June coincides with the International Contemporary Art Fair in Bath and with the Bath Balloon Festival. The opening weekend is the most festive, with bands and fireworks in Victoria Park, and candles in the windows round the Circus. If you want to book for concerts and other festival events, write to the Festival Office at Linley House, Pierrepont Place, Bath BA1 1JY. Places for year-round culture include the Theatre Royal, which is one of England's oldest.

ORIENTATION IN BATH

INFORMATION
Tourist Office
Colonnades, Bath Street.
☎ *0225 462831.*
Post Office
New Bond Street.
Public Lavatories
Pump Room/Roman Baths complex; Saw Close (by Theatre Royal); Ham Gardens (24 hours).

TRANSPORT
Local Buses
Manvers Street bus station. The suggested outings are mostly on Badgerline bus routes. ☎ *0225 464446.*
Long-Distance Buses/Coaches
National Express, tickets from Badgerline office (see above).
Car Hire
Avis Unit 4b, Riverside Bus Park, Lower Bristol Road. ☎ *0225 446680.*
City Rent-a-Car Century House, 4-5 Pierpoint Street.

☎ *0225 46963.*
H G Self Drive 3 Ham Gardens. ☎ *0225 466229.*
Bicycle Hire
Avon Valley Cyclery behind and below the railway station. 24 hours costs £9.95 for a three-speed cycle, £21.95 for a mountain bike, £22.95 for a tandem. Booking advisable in summer.

ACCOMMODATION
Hotels
Laura Place Hotel 3 Laura Place, Great Pulteney Street, near the city centre. ☎ *0225 468351. Single rooms start at £18, doubles at £40.*
Somerset House Hotel 35 Bathwick Hill. ☎ *466451. There is a serious interest in food here. Single bed and breakfast starts at £19.35, a week with dinner from £229.*
University Accommodation
University of Bath Vacation Lettings Claverton Down, Bath BA2 7AY. ☎ *0225 826826. College vacations*

only; bed and breakfast from about £10. Booking advisable.
Camp Sites
Newton Mill Touring Centre Newton St Loe, 3 miles northwest of the A4. ☎ *0225 333909.*
Newbridge Caravan Park Brassmill Lane, Newbridge (on the edge of Bath). ☎ *0225 428778.*
Youth Hostel
Bath Youth Hostel Bathwick Hill. ☎ *0225 465674.*

EATING OUT
David's Pulteney Bridge. Meals served all day; lots of cakes, choice of tea blends.
The Canary ☎ *0225 424846. Tempting cakes and teabreads, and a choice of teas.*
Popjoys ☎ *0225 460494.*
The Hole in the Wall ☎ *0225 25242.*
Clos du Roy ☎ *0225 64356.*
Rajput Tandoori ☎ *0225 66933 or 64758.*

BRISTOL

Bristol is 45 minutes by bus from Bath, less by train. Bristol is bigger and less immediately attractive; but you may grow to prefer its seafaring and industrial flavour. It has been a port for over 1,000 years, though the docks have moved out of the centre to Avonmouth on the Severn estuary. The hub of the city is the streets north of the old docks (the 'Floating Harbour'), where a lot of the warehouses have been transformed for new uses.

On the way there from the bus station, you could pause to see the world's oldest Methodist church, built by John Wesley himself in 1739–48, preserved inside the modern Broadmead shopping centre. It's open all year from 10am to 4pm, but not for sightseers on Sundays (or Wednesdays in winter); from 1–2pm the upstairs rooms close (no charge).

> **Local flavour**
> John Cabot sailed from Bristol to North America on 24 June 1497 – a year before Columbus set foot on the mainland. Cabot Tower in Bristol (1897–99) commemorates the event.

Colston Hall in the city centre is one of the city's main venues for arts and other events. This is the side of town for Red Lodge and the Georgian House: the first has 16th-century rooms, the latter is a handsome town house, built for one of Bristol's wealthy merchants. It's furnished in the style of the period (both are closed on Sunday and at lunch time). The cathedral is in this area too, and has some beautiful craftsmanship in wood and stone.

The oldest city streets are on the other side of the main roads which slice through the centre. In Corn Street look out for the pillars called the Nails: Bristol merchants settled deals on them, hence the saying 'to pay on the nail'. The 1766 Theatre Royal in King Street is England's oldest continuously used theatre.

On the waterside are two arts complexes: the Watershed is the more mainstream, the Arnolfini more unconventional.

The old docks have been brought back to life in recent years, with watersports and other things going on. There are various museums here, but the main sight to see is SS *Great Britain*. She was designed by Isambard Kingdom Brunel and launched in 1843; now she's back in the dry dock where she was built, and open to visitors. There's a free maritime heritage centre close by, as well as the Bristol Industrial Museum.

If you're travelling in a group with children,

a family ticket to the Exploratory Hands-On Science Centre might be a good investment (by Temple Meads train station).

Clifton Suspension Bridge is a bus ride from the town centre. It's another inspired Brunel design, with a 702ft span, 245ft above the Avon Gorge; it opened in 1864.

BRADFORD-ON-AVON

Bradford-on-Avon is an old, stone town, which used to have a cloth industry. It's pleasant to wander around the narrow lanes and steps between old cloth-makers' cottages and their employers' finer houses. There is no charge for the great Tithe Barn which is well signposted in Bradford-on-Avon, open April to October 10am to 6pm, November to March 10am to 4pm (English Heritage).

LACOCK

If you think that the village of Lacock feels somehow unreal, that may be because it's owned by the National Trust and is a little too perfect. Lacock Abbey was converted to a house in the 16th century, but still has the old monastery cloisters: open in the afternoon from April to early November (grounds only on Tuesday). If you just want to see the grounds and cloisters it costs £1.20. Next to the house is something special: the Fox Talbot Museum shows the work of photography pioneer William Henry Fox Talbot, including the world's first photograph showing one of Lacock Abbey's windows. Open March to early November. If travelling by bus you have to change at Chippenham – ask for the Day Rambler ticket.

BOWOOD HOUSE

Bowood House is handsome, but the best thing is the gardens, which were designed by the 18th-century landscape garden supremo, 'Capability' Brown. Visit in spring for daffodils and bluebells, summer for roses, any time for the lake, cascade and picturesque features like the 'hermit's cave' lined with fossils. There's a big adventure playground, a restaurant and café, and a place for picnics; open late March to early November. It's possible but not very easy by bus.

LONGLEAT AND STOURHEAD

Longleat and Stourhead are both within reach of Bath if you're driving, but there's no pubic transport to either place. You can visit them on a weekly Wiltshire Tours bus in summer however. Longleat is the palatial Elizabethan home of the Marquess of Bath. Apart from the house, the big attraction is the wildlife safari park, with wandering lions and other animals. There are also lots of rail rides and other amusements.

Stourhead is the last word in English landscaped gardens. It was created in the mid 1700s by a banker called Henry Hoare, who was inspired by artists like Claude Lorraine. Lakes reflect the different colours of deciduous and evergreen woodland, and mock temples and other 'eyecatchers' add romance to the scene. Visit in spring for bluebells and other spring flowers, or around October for the reds and browns of the trees. The house can also be visited, but the gardens are the main attraction. It's owned by the National Trust, which also runs the Spread Eagle Inn at the entrance – you can get lunches and teas here. There are places to picnic too. There's no public transport right to the garden.

WELLS AND GLASTONBURY

BUDGET FOR A DAY	
Bus Rover ticket	3·75
Glastonbury Abbey	1·00
Tribunal	·85
Somerset Rural Life Museum	1·00
Lunch	6·00
Afternoon tea	2·30
plus accommodation	£14·90

Wells Wells is an exquisite tiny cathedral city. Binoculars would be useful for the 356 medieval statues across the spectacular west front of the cathedral; inside, admire the view down the nave. A 14th-century astronomical clock features jousting knights, which delight visitors every hour.

There are guided walks round Wells all summer on Friday afternoons, or with the town crier on summer Thursday afternoons.

The Market Place has a big general market on Wednesday and Saturday, and a gateway leads into the moated, still-used Bishop's Palace – open in the afternoon on Thursday and Sunday from Easter to October, most Wednesdays and Fridays from May to September, and daily in August. Within the grounds but outside the moat, you can see the wells that give the city its name. The Somerset Guild of Craftsmen usually has an exhibition here. The most remarkable street in Wells is Vicar's Close, hardly changed since medieval times.

Glastonbury You don't have to be a New Age mystic to feel there's something special about Glastonbury. A very old tradition identifies Glastonbury Tor as the Isle of Avalon (King Arthur's resting place). There's a legend that Jesus visited Glastonbury with Joseph of Arimathea; and another that Joseph brought the Holy Grail to Glastonbury. He is said to have founded a church where his staff took root in the ground. The staff became the Holy Thorn, which flowers in May and December. The church became the abbey, which was once very wealthy but is now a collection of massive ruins. Pilgrims used to stay at the George and Pilgrim, which has a wonderfully ornate façade.

The Holy Grail is said to be hidden in the Chalice Well on Chilkwell Street. You can walk up Glastonbury Tor to the ruined church tower on top, which is a very atmospheric place.

Moneysaver
There's no charge for looking round some of Somerset's vineyards, though a charge may be made for guided tours. Pilton Manor at Pilton is the biggest, and there are others at North Wootton and Shepton Mallet.

91

Local flavour
Some farms and pubs make cider from local apples, and the very old craft of basket making still goes on locally.

Finds from an Iron Age marsh village are on view at the medieval Tribunal in the town (closed on Mondays in winter). Traditional crafts are the subject of the Somerset Rural Life Museum, which is set out in the abbey barn and farmhouse with real farm animals outside. The Glastonbury Festival is a weekend of outdoor music at Pilton – avoid it if you don't like crowds or offbeat people, visit to recapture the flavour of the 1960s.

THE MENDIPS

Beneath the Mendip Hills there's another landscape of caverns and pools etched out of the limestone rock. Most of it is for serious potholers only, but Wookey Hole and Cheddar Caves and Gorge are accessible to all. A guide takes you along a paved, lit path through Wookey Hole – an underworld of pools and caverns weirdly draped with stalactites and stalagmites. One shape is said to be the petrified Witch of Wookey. A papermaking demonstration and the Penny Pier Arcade – lots of old slot machines, with big old British pennies to work them – are included in the admission fee (you pay for the pennies). Ebbor Gorge is a few hundred yards from Wookey Hole: paths lead through the wild-looking

scenery, where there's a good chance of seeing buzzards and other birds.

The way into the Cheddar Showcaves is at the southern end of Cheddar Gorge, which is a big attraction in itself. This is another complex of dramatically lit galleries and huge caverns, and the admission fee covers an above-ground route up to a high viewpoint. Adventure caving expeditions set off three times a day all year: hard hat, lamp and boilersuit provided. No under-12s allowed, and you have to book: telephone 0934 742343. Buses run to Cheddar from Wells. If you want to see Cheddar Gorge, alight at Tweentown, from where it's a 10 to 15 minute walk.

Local flavour
Cheddar cheese is a hard, yellow cheese, traditionally made with milk from the Somerset Levels. It was highly esteemed as far back as the 17th century.

The Cheddar Cheese Company in Cheddar does demonstrations of cheese-making and other crafts, and the Chewton Cheese Dairy at Chewton Mendip also has demonstrations in the school holidays (not Thursday or Sunday). You can see the process free at Times Past, Westfield Lane, Draycott (telephone 0934 743465). They're open from 7.30am, but between 12 noon and 2pm is the best time to see cheese-making. Buses run from Wells, contact Badgerline in Wells (telephone 0749 73084): service 126 to Draycott and 376 to Chewton Mendip.

SALISBURY

Salisbury is one of southern England's prosperous cathedral cities, and the cathedral is certainly worth a visit, soaring as it does above pretty water meadows and a network of medieval streets around an old market. The spire is England's tallest at 404ft. A few miles north is something much more famous however: the ancient stone circle of Stonehenge, one of the finest prehistoric monuments in Europe.

Buses run from Salisbury to most of the main sights. For car drivers, main roads out of Salisbury cut across Salisbury Plain, which is used by the army – hence the 'Tanks Crossing' warning signs. It's more fun to take the minor roads which wriggle out of town along narrow river valleys lined with peaceful villages. Keep the peace by seeing them by bicycle.

Wiltshire Cycleway is a free map and guide

to cycle routes all over Wiltshire, including rides out of Salisbury; you'll find copies at the tourist office in the city.

> **Moneysaver**
> There are several hill forts and other prehistoric sites in the area, and most of them can be visited free of charge. Use the Ordnance Survey Landranger map sheet 184 to seek them out, but stick to public footpaths.

Salisbury is two hours from London by rail and approximately 3½ hours by coach. It's 50 minutes from Bath.

The centre of Salisbury is compact and easy to see on foot. The best days to visit are Tuesdays and Saturdays, when the open air market is in full swing in the Market Square. All around here are medieval streets and alleys, some with timber-framed houses. Most amazing is the 1470 house of John Halle in New Canal. It forms the entrance to the Odeon

Salisbury Cathedral has a beautiful setting.

Cinema, and there's no charge for having a look.

A five-minute walk down High Street takes you to the Cathedral Close, a big green open space which can only be reached through massive stone gates – a sign of strained relations in medieval times. In the middle is the cathedral, free in theory, but in practice a 'voluntary' donation is expected. The effect is sombre but elegant. For a small extra charge you can see one of the original copies of the Magna Carta, and for a bit more you can tour the roof repairs and get a good view of the city. Roof tours are conducted daily except Sunday at 10.30am and 2.30pm.

The best view of the cathedral is from the water meadows a few minutes walk away across the River Avon. The artist Constable painted many views from here, and it's pleasant for picnics.

> **Local flavour**
> Choristers provide enthralling singing at the cathedral, usually daily (but not Wednesday or during the summer vacation, mid July to mid September) at 5.30pm, and on Sunday at 10am, 11.30am and 3pm.

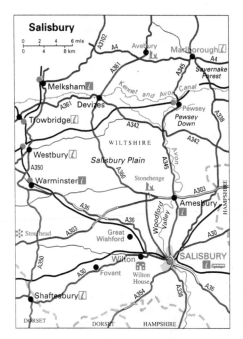

The Close is lined with attractive old houses, the homes of famous people past and present. Two places you can visit are the Salisbury and South Wiltshire Museum, which has a good section on Stonehenge; another is Queen Anne-style Mompesson House (National Trust).

The Salisbury Arts Festival runs for two

weeks in September, and there's year-round culture at the Playhouse and the Arts Centre. At 9.30am on 29 May villagers from nearby Great Wishford arrive *en masse* at the cathedral to reaffirm ancient rights, having got up at dawn to collect oak boughs from their local wood. Join the festivities at Great Wishford in the afternoon (bus from Salisbury, not Sunday).

ORIENTATION IN SALISBURY

INFORMATION
TOURIST OFFICE
Fish Row. ☎ 0722 334959.
POST OFFICE
Castle Street.
PUBLIC LAVATORIES
Market Square.

TRANSPORT
LOCAL BUSES
Bus station, Endless Street.
Buses for most of the suggested outings are Wilts and Dorset, ☎ 0722 336855.
LONG-DISTANCE BUSES/COACHES
Bus station, Endless Street.
Operator is National Express, ☎ 0722 336855.

TRAINS
Salisbury train station, a few minutes walk from the city centre, at the western end of Fisherton Street. ☎ *0722 27591.*
BICYCLE HIRE
Hayball Cycles *All-terrain and sports cycles, £5 per day, £25 per week, plus deposit.*
Salisbury Youth Hostel *(see below) hires bicycles to YHA members.*

ACCOMMODATION
HOTELS
Glen Lyon *6 Bellamy Lane, Milford Hill, in a quiet road near the city centre.* ☎ *0722 29885. Single bed and breakfast starts at £13.*

CAMPING
Coombe Nurseries Touring Park *Race Plain, Netherhampton, 2 miles southwest off the A3094.* ☎ *28451.*
YOUTH HOSTEL
Salisbury Youth Hostel *Mill Hill House, Milford Hill.* ☎ *0722 27527.*

EATING OUT
Coach and Horses
Winchester Street. ☎ *0722 336254. Bar food all day, 10am-10pm. You can eat well here for around £5.*
Mo's Restaurant *Milford Street.* ☎ *0722 331377. Fun, and not too expensive if you're careful.*

OUTINGS FROM SALISBURY

WILTON

Just a few minutes away from Salisbury, Wilton is a much older town, which used to be the regional capital until Salisbury virtually eclipsed it. The main sight here is Wilton House, a splendid stately home part of which was designed by Inigo Jones. Admission includes the spacious gardens and an adventure playground which is highly rated by children. It's open from Easter to October (not Monday except bank holidays).

STONEHENGE

Work started at Stonehenge some 5,000 years ago, before the Egyptian pyramids, and much, much earlier than the Druids. It's a circle and inner horseshoe shape of massive stones, some of which were brought from Wales – no one knows how or why, though it must have been a place for ceremonies. You can view it from behind a rope if you pay at the car park.

Actually it's best seen from a distance: the car park itself is free and from here you can walk to a vantage point which also overlooks all sorts of other prehistoric features. Get the National Trust leaflet to walks in the Stonehenge Estate from the Salisbury tourist office. Cyclists should take the very pretty Woodford Valley route along the River Avon; you can catch a bus this way too, but not on Sunday.

Avoid Stonehenge around the time of the summer solstice (21 June). In recent years it has been the scene of violent clashes between police and motley crowds who believe the site has spiritual significance – the main axis of the circle is aligned with the sun on that day.

MARLBOROUGH

The best part of Marlborough is the wide main street, which is lined with old inns and shops with bow-fronted windows. Market days are Wednesday and Saturday. At the west end is Marlborough College, a public school (private and expensive) with an ancient burial mound in the grounds. There's an old tradition that Merlin is buried underneath.

East of Marlborough is the Savernake Forest, with picnic spots and walks through leafy glades. A few miles west of Marlborough is an amazing complex of ancient sites, all free. The main one is Avebury, a pretty little village in the middle of a large prehistoric circle of huge stones. A well-marked path leads round them, and there are various museums in the village.

EXETER

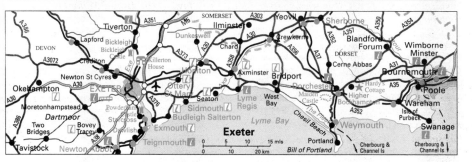

People who take the road to Exeter often rush past the city without stopping, on their way to the seaside places of Devon and Cornwall. The city is worth a look however, partly because of its history, partly because it's a lively place with plenty to offer the visitor.

Don't expect an untouched old city – much of Exeter had to be rebuilt after being bombed flat in World War II. The cathedral survived however, and the city centre is still surrounded by stretches of Roman walls, topped with medieval reinforcements. The other focal point is the quay area, which made Exeter rich in the old days and is still a great attraction.

Out of town the biggest attraction is the south Devon coast – you have a wide choice of resorts here, from homely spots like Teignmouth to glamorous Torquay – focal point of the self-styled 'English Riviera'.

The resorts are easy to reach from Exeter by train or bus, and in summer you'll find endless possibilities for boat rides and fishing trips. Away from the coast you're instantly in deep Devon countryside, with traditional towns and thatched villages set amid hilly farmland.

There's a huge supply of accommodation along the coast around Exeter, which tends not to get fully booked except at the peak holiday times. Renting a self-catering place is the most popular option on the coast.

Local flavour

Devon is a popular place with craft workers, especially potters. Pottery is worth bearing in mind as a souvenir; as a bonus, some not very old Devon wares are now collectable items.

Exeter lies at the end of the M5 motorway, which is the main holiday route into the West Country. Twenty-mile traffic jams aren't unknown during fine weekends and holiday times – listen to local and national radio stations for travel bulletins and use a good map to find alternative minor roads.

Exeter is 2½ hours by rail from London's

95

Paddington station and there's a slower line which runs from London's Waterloo station via Salisbury. Buses from London take four hours. The M5 motorway makes a fast (usually) link to Bristol and all points north by car; you can also use it to join the M4 to London. Exeter airport has a weekly flight to Toronto, plus flights to Europe.

The cathedral was the most amazing survivor of the World War II bombing. Stand at the main west door and you get a view 300ft along the nave, lined with clusters of pillars that spread into a web of stone across the roof. But it's the detail that's the real pleasure here, from the extravagantly carved 52ft-high bishop's throne to the curious creatures hidden under the choir stall seats.

The mighty stone front in the High Street belongs to the Guildhall. It dates back to 1330 and is still in use, but you can visit if there's no special function going on (free, closed Sunday). Across Fore Street, a narrow path takes you to the ancient house of St Nicholas Priory (open Tuesday to Saturday, closed lunchtime).

Off the High Street are the Underground Passages – low and medieval medieval tunnels which brought water into the city. The way in is by Boots the Chemist; guided tours are Tuesday to Saturday afternoons (they lend you a hard hat).

The Marimite Museum is on Exeter's old quay.

Rougemont House has a costume collection displayed in period settings; it's also a museum of lace, a speciality of nearby Honiton. The gardens spread into the moat of Exeter's former castle, and there a restaurant and tea room (closed Sundays, except July and August).

> **Moneysaver**
> Admission to Rougemont House Museum is free on Friday, and half price from November to April.

The Royal Albert Memorial Museum is part filled with Devon arts and crafts, part an Aladdin's cave of exotica. Open Tuesday to Saturday, free, and there are free lunchtime lectures. Next door on Gandy Street is the Exeter Arts Centre, the main venue for the annual arts festival, with films, drama, music and other events all year. You can get drinks and food here. Other theatres are the Barnfield and the Northcott Theatre at Exeter University, where shows include touring opera and dance companies – it's out of town, but there's a minibus service.

Visit in June, for drama, music, exhibitions and open air events; during July and August there is free street entertainment on Thursday evenings. 'Entertainment in Exeter' is a series of light music concerts in October. Details from the Festival Office, Civic Centre, Exeter EX1 1JN, telephone 0392 265875.

The Exeter Maritime Museum has a huge collection of boats (157 at the last count) ashore and afloat, from steam tugs to tiny fishing coracles. Some are for climbing aboard, and there's a huge workshop where you'll probably see shipwrights or volunteers restoring old boats. For a quiet break from city streets, the Exeter Ship Canal and the River Exe offer waterside walking near the museum.

ORIENTATION IN EXETER

INFORMATION
TOURIST OFFICE
Civic Centre, Paris Street.
☎ 0392 256297.

POST OFFICE
Bedford Street.
PUBLIC LAVATORIES
Guildhall Shopping Centre;
Granby Street; The Quay.

TRANSPORT

LOCAL BUSES
Bus and coach station, Paris Street, Most services are Devon General, ☎ 0392 56231. Or Devon bus public transport information,
☎ 0392 382070.

LONG-DISTANCE BUSES/COACHES
Bus and coach station, Paris
Street, where Devon General
will organise bookings on the
National Express network.
TRAINS
Exeter St David's station for
fast trains to London. Local
trains go southwest from here
via St Thomas station (south of
centre); or southeast via
Exeter Central station (north
of the city centre).
CAR HIRE
Olympic Mazda ☎ 0392
412333.
BICYCLE HIRE
Flash Gordon 14 Old Park
Road. ☎ 0392 213141.
Three-speed bicycles cost £6
a day, £25 a week, plus
deposit.

ACCOMMODATION
The local seaside resorts also
have a huge range of

accommodation, especially
around Torbay.
HOTELS
Telstar 77 St David's Hill.
☎ 0392 72466.
Park View Hotel 8 Howell
Road. ☎ 0392 71772/53047.
Prices start at £15 single,
£22 double.
UNIVERSITY ACCOMMODATION
Hospitality Services St
Luke's, University of Exeter,
Heavitree Road, Exeter EX1
2LU. ☎ 0392 264970. Bed
and breakfast from about £10
- book well in advance; also
self-catering in summer
vacation.
CAMP SITE
*Kennford International
Caravan Park* 4 miles south
of Exeter. ☎ 0392 833046.
YOUTH HOSTEL
Exeter Youth Hostel 47
Countess Wear Road.
☎ 0392 873329.

EATING OUT
Devon Foods 15 Gandy
Street. Do your shopping for
a picnic here; specialities
include locally made cheeses
and sausages.
Great Western Hotel Station
Approach. ☎ 0392 74039.
Includes Brunel's Restaurant,
which has fixed price
three-course menus at
around £9.
Tinleys Cathedral Close,
opposite the cathedral.
☎ 0392 72865. Light
lunches under £5; afternoon
tea £2.95.
White Hart 65 South Street.
☎ 0392 70897. An old
coaching inn with bars that
go back over 500 years - they
serve food at three price
levels, from snacks to à la
carte, with bar lunches in
between (about £4).

OUTINGS FROM EXETER

KILLERTON HOUSE

This National Trust property has a costume collection in appropriately furnished rooms (April to October, not Tuesday). The admission charge is much less if you just want to see the splendid hillside gardens. Visit in spring to see the azaleas in bloom. Devon General run a bus to within about three-quarters of a mile, but there is no bus on Sunday.

BICKLEIGH

Bickleigh is a village of thatched and whitewashed cottages in the valley of the River Exe. Bickleigh Castle began as a Norman castle, then became a fortified house and then a farmhouse; today it's a romantic place to visit,

but is still lived in. Curiosities inside include spy and escape gadgets used in World War II. The castle is open twice a week from Easter to late May; then daily except Saturday until early October. The Devonshires Centre has fishing, crafts, farm animals and all sorts of other attractions around an old watermill; open weekends only in winter, otherwise daily.

EAST ALONG THE COAST

Exmouth   Exmouth is south of Exeter, where the River Exe meets the sea. On hot days it offers soft, gold sand for roasting on – if you want to swim, watch out for the red flags which warn of dangerous conditions. There's a busy dock area too, which adds a bit of spice to the scene. Boat trips are advertised on the seafront in summer –

besides pleasure trips there are boats along the coast to Torquay, and hourly ferries over the estuary to Starcross (see *South Along the Coast*).

(see *South Along the Coast*)

> **Moneysaver**
> The Coastlink bus ticket, available after 9am, gives you a day's unlimited travel on most bus routes along the coast, including a return journey across the Exe from Exmouth to Starcross. Buy it on the first bus you board.

Budleigh Salterton   Budleigh Salterton is better for confident swimmers: instead of soft sand you'll find a beach of flat rounded stones (tempting as souvenirs), which plunges steeply into the water. You can follow the coastal footpath from here along high red cliffs. Sir Walter Raleigh grew up locally, and Sir John Everett Millais painted his picture *The Boyhood of Raleigh* while staying at the Octagon house.

On the main street look out for the Singing Teapot café, which has a small-scale model railway running through it with a child-height viewing point. They offer a range of leaf teas, and serve cream teas and light lunches.

Sidmouth   Sidmouth was one of Queen Victoria's childhood homes – her parents came here in 'gilded poverty' hoping for a quiet refuge from creditors. It has Georgian terraces and villas, a beach with rock pools, and huge red cliffs rising to 500ft on either side. Visit in August for the International Folklore Festival, with music and dancing from all over the world.

> **Local flavour**
> Inland from Sidmouth, Ottery St Mary celebrates 5 November (Bonfire Night) with a huge bonfire followed by a wild race (the competitors carry burning barrels of tar). At any time of year it's an interesting unspoilt town.

Lyme Regis   Lyme Regis is a little port and seaside resort with houses in pastel ice cream shades. The harbour is protected by the mighty 13th-century breakwater called the Cobb. This is where the anguished Meryl Streep walks in the film *The French Lieutenant's Woman*. The beach isn't beautiful but it is a good place to look for fossils – prising them from the cliffs isn't advised, as the soft rock is far from stable, and landslips are common.

WEYMOUTH

King George III made Weymouth fashionable back in the late 1700s. Today it's a sprawling seaside resort, but the centre has a nicely old-fashioned flavour. George III's statue is a local landmark (it's where the bus stops are), and elegant Georgian houses line the seafront. The harbour area is the place to get a flavour of old Weymouth, before King George, with its fish market, narrow streets and alleyways, beside a waterway full of boats. There are a lot of places to eat around here.

The station is near the beach – a wide curve of gently sloping sand complete with bandstand, very fancy clock and ornate little shelters along the seafront. Look out for sand-carver Fred Darrington, who shapes this fragile medium into amazingly solid-looking shapes.

See wild birds close to the town centre on Radipole Lake, a bird reserve with hides on the River Wey; east of town is Lodmoore, which also has walks and hides – both free.

A road leads south over a bridge from Weymouth to the bleak Isle of Portland, totally unlike the rest of Dorset, but so odd it's worth a mention. Visit in spring or autumn if you're a bird-watcher, because it's a kind of Heathrow airport of the bird world, with thousands of long-distance fliers checking in and out.

Portland isn't quite an island – it's linked to the mainland by Chesil Beach, a shingle bank stretching 15 miles along the coast from West Bay. The brackish water behind it is the Fleet; both beach and water are protected for wild birds and water plants.

DORCHESTER

This is the 'Casterbridge' of Thomas Hardy's

novels, and Hardy's statue stands in the town. You can still walk on the Roman ramparts he describes in *The Mayor of Casterbridge*. Hardy was born nearby at Higher Bockhampton and lived in the town. *Discover the Hardy Country* is a free tourist office guide to places linked to Hardy's life and novels. The County Museum in High West Street is good if you want background on Hardy and other Dorset specialities: prehistoric sites, geology, rural life and the dialect poet William Barnes (closed Sunday). The Dinosaur Museum includes life-size models, computers and videos to please children.

Moneysaver

Two historic places are free: The Old Crown Court, where in 1834, the Tolpuddle Martyrs were sentenced to transportation (really for forming a trade union); at the Antelope Hotel, the infamous Judge Jeffreys tried 340 rebels after the unsuccessful Monmouth Rebellion in 1685.

Maumbury Rings in Dorchester is a Stone Age site used as a Roman amphitheatre. Just west of the town is Maiden Castle, where you can walk along the high, huge and complicated earth ramparts of an Iron Age fort. There are no buses, but you can reach Maiden Castle by car, or walk from Dorchester, which takes about 20 minutes. The views are wonderful, and it's free.

SHERBORNE

Sherborne is a town of honey-coloured stone buildings around a splendid old abbey church. It was a cathedral in Saxon times, but it's most admired for the intricate 15th-century fan vaulting inside. The old abbey buildings are part of Sherborne School. East of town you can visit the ruin of the 12th-century Old Castle (English Heritage, open daily except for winter Sundays). It was bought by Sir Walter Raleigh in 1592 but he gave up trying to convert it into a house and built Sherborne Castle instead – this

is a much grander affair which is still lived in. It's open from Easter to September on Thursday, weekend and bank holiday afternoons. The grounds were landscaped by 'Capability' Brown and include a lake and Gothic-style dairy (which now serves teas). It costs much less to visit the grounds only, if you don't mind missing the house.

SOUTH ALONG THE COAST

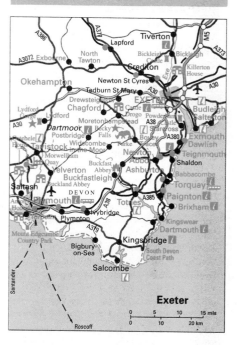

Exeter

The railway along this part of the coast from Exeter is the kind of route people take just for the scenery – it runs down the Exe estuary then weaves in and out of the red cliffs along the coast. Red rock, lush greenery and blue sea make a startling combination.

Starcross The Atmospheric Railway Museum at Starcross is a preserved part of a scheme designed by Brunel, to help trains up a steep incline by a vacuum pumping system, open March to October. Powderham Castle is about a mile away. It was built by Sir Philip Courtenay in 1390 and is still lived in by his descendants. Inside are the elegant rooms and treasures you might expect; outside is a scented rose garden. Open in the afternoons from late May to mid September (not Friday or Saturday). Buses run within about a mile.

Dawlish Dawlish Warren is a stretch of dunes which looks like the end of the earth in winter, but becomes a holiday playground in hot weather – you can buy buckets, spades and other beach essentials from the shops near the train station. Part of the Warren is a nature reserve – visit in winter for birdwatching. The town of Dawlish is a delight, with well kept Victorian houses, and Dawlish Water bustling down through pretty gardens towards the sea.

Teignmouth Teignmouth (say 'tinmuth') is special for its harbour area on the River Teign, and for the river ferry to Shaldon which began over 700 years ago. It has interesting old winding streets, but don't expect glamour.

Moneysaver

Teign Valley Glass Studios is on the Newton Abbot road out of Teignmouth – no charge for watching the glass blowing and other processes, and there's a shop selling samples and seconds and well as perfect goods. Marbles are a speciality.

Torquay The Torquay coast is sold as the 'English Riviera': the hinterland is rustic Devon rather than Mediterranean cork groves, but Torquay does have palm trees, gardens and grand buildings. In summer the sea is peppered with leisure boats, there are pretty lights along the front, and shops stay open late at night for the strolling throng. Several beaches in the area have European 'Blue Flag' awards.

Torquay doesn't have a wild nightlife, but it does have the Hollywood Bowl, which is open till midnight. The Model Village at Babbacombe is a much older attraction – a landscape in miniature, including streams and waterfalls as well as village scenes, with sound effects. It's open till 10pm.

Kent's Cavern is an underground network of passages and caves studded with stalactites and stalagmites. Open daily (with extended opening

until 9pm on July and August, except on Saturday).

Paignton A short rail or bus ride takes you to Paignton, which is very much a family resort. It's also the starting point of the Paignton and Dartmouth railway – a preserved line where steam engines cross high viaducts with huge views (sit on the seaward side). The terminus is at Kingswear, where you can take a ferry to Dartmouth. Or stop for the beach at Goodrington Sands, open from Easter to September, and some other days.

Brixham Brixham is a centuries old fishing port, with steps and alleys leading down to the quayside and a mass of pleasure craft and fishing boats.

DARTMOOR

People who've never been near Dartmoor usually have a vivid idea of it – a moorland wilderness, possibly wreathed in dim recollections of Sherlock Holmes, pursuing the Hound of the Baskervilles across the treacherous mire. A large part of Dartmoor really is like that, but it has other scenery too.

Around the edge of Dartmoor you'll find deep green valleys with villages and farms. The next level up is common land, where ponies and cattle nibble at treeless pastureland. The highest parts of Dartmoor are the peat moorland – a gigantic soaked sponge of bogs and streams. This is the wildest and most mysterious part, but all three types of landscape make up Dartmoor National Park – 365 square miles, including 100,000 acres of open space.

The little Dartmoor pony is a sturdy breed.

The common land is peppered with Bronze Age stone rows and circles, burial mounds and other reminders of people who lived here when the climate was warmer. You'll find sites marked on Ordnance Survey maps.

Local flavour

Dartmoor has a granite foundation; where it breaks the surface there are tors (bare outcrops of rock), which have been worn into weird shapes over thousands of years. Nelson's Column in London is made of Dartmoor granite.

The Exeter–Plymouth Transmoor Link bus takes you right into the middle of Dartmoor. It runs three times a day at weekends and bank holidays from late May to September, and daily from late July to the end of August. Bus times coincide with Dartmoor guided walks – get a free leaflet and timetable from tourist information centres. The other relevant bus service is the Exeter–Plymouth X38, which runs along the southern edge of the moor via Ashburton and Buckfastleigh. Trains don't run within the national park, but if you're cycling the branch railway from Plymouth to Gunnislake could be useful.

Walking and horse riding are the only ways to see large parts of the moor. For getting about the lanes that link the villages and towns of the eastern side you'll need a car or bicycle. Roads are graded according to difficulty – look out for the signs. Ponies and other livestock wander freely over big areas of Dartmoor, so drive carefully. Cattle grids tell you when you're entering an unfenced road.

If you're walking any distance on the high moor you'll need serious walking gear – boots, waterproofs, emergency rations, warm clothes, a map – and ability to read a compass. The weather can change very quickly.

You can rent mountain bikes, touring bicycles or tandems from Dartmoor Bike and Tandem Hire, North Tawton. Bicycles can be delivered to you, and collected at the end of your journey (there's a charge for this). You could also try Monro Bikes at Exbourne. Cycling is

allowed on bridleways, but you need permission to go across open land.

There are several stables with horses and ponies for all levels of experience. They will always supply hard hats, but you may have to pay extra.

Buzzards can often be seen soaring above Dartmoor; you may see ravens and ring ouzels around the tors. By rivers look out for kingfishers, herons and dippers, which walk under water. You'd be lucky to see otters, but you might see feral mink.

The army uses parts of Dartmoor for firing practice, mainly in the northern part. Check local papers for firing times, or ask information centres. Red flags give warnings.

There are handsome old market towns at strategic points round the edge of the moor. Tavistock, Chagford and Moretonhampstead are all attractive stone towns; Okehampton has a romantic ruined castle and Dartmoor museum.

Lydford Gorge is a natural spectacular south of Lydford village where the river foams in potholes as it rushes through a ravine. You can follow the river on through a deep valley to a 90ft waterfall. There's also a castle in the village (English Heritage and free).

Moneysaver

There's no admission charge to the park around the Dartmoor National Park headquarters at Parke; it offers some beautiful woodland and waterside walking.

Visit Drewsteignton (buses from Exeter) for Castle Drogo, looming on a 900ft crag above River Teign. Sir Edwin Lutyens designed this great granite castle, which looks medieval but was only started in 1910. Open April to October (National Trust).

Widecombe in the Moor is possibly the best known place in Dartmoor because of the song *Widecombe Fair* – thousands of people visit every year to find out what the attraction was for 'Old Uncle Tom Cobley and all'. The village isn't too spoilt by all this attention, and it does mean that you'll find plenty of teashops.

Postbridge is on the Transmoor Link bus

route and also has an information centre – the main sight is the clapper bridge, made with nine huge slabs of granite.

Buckfastleigh is an attractive little town, but the main place to see is Buckfast Abbey. It was abandoned in the 16th century but then rebuilt by a handful of monks in the 20th. Buckfast monks are expert beekeepers, and Dartmoor heather honey is prized. The bees were bred by Brother Adam after a plague virtually wiped out the native honey bee in the early 1900s. You can get snacks or meals in the tearooms. Admission is free, but if you bring a car there's a parking charge.

The Buckfast Steam Railway runs from Buckfastleigh along the River Dart – travel in spring to see why it's called the Primrose Line. Trains run daily in summer holiday months, and other days as well.

Francis Drake's statue looks out over Plymouth Hoe.

PLYMOUTH

Plymouth is a must in the itinerary if you're interested in history, because it has witnessed some of the momentous events of the past – the sort that are part of folklore. It's the place from which Elizabethan sailors set forth to claim new corners of the world (and to raid Spanish treasure ships); and most famously, the Pilgrim Fathers sailed from Plymouth in search of new lives in the New World.

Plymouth was also a prime target for World War II bombs, but they didn't obliterate the character of the place. Its business has always been with the sea – the Royal Navy has been here for 300 years and runs Europe's largest naval base here.

Plymouth is a big busy city – in fact it's a combination of three towns, Devonport, Plymouth and Stonehouse – but most of the interesting bits are concentrated in a small area best explored on foot. A good place to start is on the Hoe, the high point overlooking the sea to the south of the city. This is where Sir Francis Drake earned a niche in history in 1588; while others were worried about the Spanish Armada invasion fleet sailing up the Channel, Drake played an unruffled game of bowls. There's still a bowling green, and a statue of Drake

overlooks the wide bay, with its sailing boats and navy vessels.

The best all-round views are from Smeaton's Tower on the Hoe, where 93 steps lead up to a viewpoint over the city, docks and sea, with Dartmoor and the coast beyond. The tower was built by Smeaton as a lighthouse for the notoriously dangerous Eddystone Rocks, but was rebuilt here when Eddystone acquired a larger lighthouse.

The Plymouth Dome on the Hoe gives you centuries of Plymouth history all at one gulp: inside, you can walk down a mock-up Elizabethan Street, experience the gun-deck of a sailing ship, and get radar and satellite views of the harbour today.

Local flavour
Plymouth Gin has been made in the distillery in Southside Street since 1793. Distillery tours can be arranged.

Sutton Harbour has been the historic heart of Plymouth for hundreds of years. On 6 September 1620 the Pilgrim Fathers set sail for North America from the point marked by an arch and stone set into the pavement. They spent their last evening at nearby Island House, and a board outside tells you their names. The whole quayside is dotted with plaques celebrating the Pilgrims and other famous and unsung voyages, including convicts bound for Australia in 1787, and countless Devon and Cornish miners and farmers heading for new lives in the New World.

This is the area known as the Barbican. New

Street is a narrow cobbled way flanked by old stone warehouses and timber-framed buildings such as the Elizabethan House, which you can visit (closed Monday except bank holidays).

> **Moneysaver**
> The Barbican Pannier market in Southside Street is open every day for good value local produce and may have bargains in bric-a-brac.

Other survivors of 16th-century Plymouth are off Notte Street. The Merchant's House belonged to an Elizabethan sea captain, and has the same opening times and admission fees as the Elizabethan House. The main city art gallery is free.

Plymouth Boat Cruises run one-hour river cruises from Phoenix Wharf, between the Hoe and Barbican. Mount Edgcumbe House and Country Park are just the other side of the Tamar estuary. Cars use the Torpoint ferry, which is signed from the city centre. Foot passengers can take the Cremyll ferry from Admiral's Hard at Stonehouse, a bus ride or 20-minute walk from the city centre (telephone 0752 822105 for crossing times). The ferry takes you virtually to the gates of the 800-acre park, for Cornwall's earliest landscaped garden. These gardens open every day, and the country park runs along 10 miles of coastline. The house (Tudor style outside, classical inside) and the Earl's Garden are open from Easter to October, Wednesday to Sunday and bank holiday Mondays. A restaurant and shop are open in summer.

Antony is an 18th-century house of stone and brick, with panelled rooms inside. There are gardens here too. It's less than two miles from the Torpoint ferry, and you can get there on the Ferrybus 80A. Another National Trust property; it's open April to October, midweek and bank holiday afternoons, plus Sundays in mid summer.

ALONG THE TAMAR

Cotehele House The Edgcumbe family stopped living here in 1553 and it is just as they left it, complete with the original furnishings. No one ever got round to installing electricity, so visit on a bright day if you want a good look at the tapestries and armour inside. The gardens run down to the river, where you can also see a working watermill, a cider press and a Tamar sailing barge called Shamrock. (National Trust; open April to October, not Friday except Good Friday). The gardens are open every day.

Morwellham Quay Morwellham Quay was a boom town of the mid 1800s. Huge quantities of copper used to be exported from here; when the copper ran out, the quay settlement sank into oblivion. In the last 20 years it has been meticulously restored, with cottages, workshops, a Victorian farm, and staff in costume. Public transport isn't easy. The nearest station is Gunnislake, about four miles away, but there may be a special bus service from Plymouth in the summer.

BUCKLAND ABBEY

> **Local flavour**
> One of the prized exhibits at Buckland Abbey is Drake's Drum, which is said to sound a warning when danger threatens England's shores.

The medieval monastery of Buckland Abbey was cunningly converted into a family home by Sir Richard Grenville in 1541, and later became the home of Sir Francis Drake. (National Trust; open April to October – not Thursday). Admission may be higher on the Living History days in June, when Elizabethan music, crafts and other skills are demonstrated by people in appropriate costume.

TOTNES AND DARTMOUTH

Totnes is a riverside town with a working harbour and a neat Norman castle on a hill. The best free activity is just exploring the old streets and market, where stallholders wear picturesque costume on summer Tuesdays.

There was a fire here in 1990, so rebuilding may be going on at Eastgate. You can climb up to the castle ramparts for views over the Dart Valley – it's open all year, except Monday in winter (English Heritage). Other places to see are the museum and the 16th-century Guildhall – still in use but you can visit from Easter to September (closed for lunch). The quay is attractive too, and you can catch boats from here to Dartmouth.

If you want to look around Dartmouth, check ferry times – they change according to the tides. Dartmouth is a very old port indeed – soldiers sailed from here to fight in the Crusades in the 12th century, and there's still a busy, boat-filled harbour. The cobbled quayside of Bayards Cove gives the best flavour of the old port and there's a little ruined fort (admission free). It was built to supplement Dartmouth Castle, which goes back to 1481 (English Heritage). In the town you'll find some delightfully picturesque streets.

A plaque at Bayards Cove in Dartmouth marks where the Pilgrim Fathers landed in the *Speedwell* and *Mayflower* in 1620. This was on their first attempt to reach North America – they later abandoned the *Speedwell* and set off again from Plymouth in the Mayflower alone.

TRURO

Truro is Cornwall's only city and proud of the fact. It isn't big, but it's trim and pretty, with interesting old streets and a handsome cathedral.

Cornwall is a mysterious place, despite the fact that it attracts millions of visitors every year. It's mostly surrounded by sea and is virtually cut off from its only neighbouring county of Devon by the River Tamar. Until 200 years ago there were Cornish people who spoke Cornish rather than English. Another reason could be that Cornwall is Celtic, more closely related to Wales and Brittany than to other parts of England. Like other Celtic places, it's wreathed in myth and legend. King Arthur may have had his base here.

All over Cornwall you'll see mine engine houses – tall thin buildings with taller chimneys. They once housed huge steam engines, which pumped water out of deep mines or hauled men and ore up and down.

Cornwall isn't exactly a wild, natural landscape – this county has been dug up, picked over and tunnelled to an extreme degree in the search for china clay, tin and other minerals, and the remnants of that activity make for some haunting landscapes. You'll find evidence of recent mineral extraction alongside remarkable prehistoric remains.

The best free thing is the stunning coastline: cliffs and good beaches to the north, beautiful wooded estuaries to the south, with picturesque fishing ports right round. Long stretches of the Cornwall coastline are owned by the National Trust, which protects them from development. The best way to see the scenery is from the coastal footpath, which runs for 268 miles.

For wide open spaces go to Bodmin Moor, which is like a smaller version of Dartmoor. Cornwall needn't cost you much. It isn't an

Truro

expensive holiday area, but it isn't a very sophisticated one either. You'll find a huge number of attractions and amusements advertised, but, surprisingly, it can be hard to find really good fresh seafood.

> **Local flavour**
> Cornwall has mixed feelings about visitors. They're referred to as 'emmets' (ants).

Cornwall has no motorways, and roads can get crowded, but outside the July/August summer peak it isn't too bad. Historic houses and other places may be closed in winter, but Cornwall's climate makes it a good winter destination if you want the picturesque spots to yourself.

For transport, use ferries where they're offered, because the alternative will probably be several miles by road around a river estuary. On land, double-decker buses and rural rail routes give the best views and take you to interesting places. Against the independence of a car you have to weigh your taste for winding, narrow roads with occasional precipitous gradients. Some popular destinations are barred to cars, and parking fees can be high.

Cyclists don't have those problems, and lanes usually roll along without too many steep hills. You may meet heavy traffic in tight spots, and when hills are steep, they're very steep.

Accommodation can be very cheap – you'll see farmhouses advertising bed and breakfast for £8 a night or less, and seaside places have plenty of low-priced hotels and bargain breaks. Places to rent range from caravans to cottages, and there are plenty of camp sites.

Truro is about 4¾ hours from London by rail, 6½ hours by coach. The nearest airports are Newquay (flights from London Heathrow), and Plymouth (flights from London Heathrow and Gatwick).

Truro is Cornwall's main administrative centre – it also feels proud, with neat streets and lots of flowers. Around the cathedral are narrow lanes and a traffic-free area with interesting shops – the Guild of Ten is worth a look for its pottery and other craft items. The three-spired cathedral is the main landmark and focal point, though it's relatively new, being completed in 1910. The County Museum in River Street has prehistoric finds and paintings by Cornish artists, and an exceptional collection of minerals (closed Sunday).

ORIENTATION IN TRURO

INFORMATION

TOURIST OFFICE
Boscawen Street, Truro.
☎ 0872 74555.

POST OFFICE
High Cross, Truro.

PUBLIC LAVATORIES
Lemon Street; Green Street;
the Leats.

TRANSPORT

LOCAL BUSES
Bus station, Lemon Quay,
Truro. Most of the
suggested outings are
Western National, 21A
Pydar Street, Truro.
☎ 0872 40404. Or ask at

the tourist office.

LONG-DISTANCE BUSES/ COACHES
National Express in
conjunction with Western
National. ☎ 0872 40404.

TRAINS
Truro station, 15 minutes'
walk from the centre. For
train information ☎ 0872
76244.

CAR HIRE
Carental Infirmary Hill,
Truro. ☎ 0872 76797.

Vospers Richmond Hill,
Station Yard, Truro. ☎ 0872
73933.

BICYCLE HIRE
Truro City Cycles 110
Kenwyn Street, Truro.
☎ 0872 71703.

ACCOMMODATION

HOTELS
Harbour Hotel 1 Harbour
Terrace, Falmouth. ☎ 0326
311344. Bed and breakfast
for one from £10 per night.

Marcorrie Hotel 20
Falmouth Road, Truro.
Central for bed and
breakfast: prices start at
£15.50 single, £30 double;
evening meals can be
provided.

CAMP SITES
**Carnon Downs Caravan
and Camping Park** Carnon
Downs, 3 miles off A39.
☎ 0872 862283.

Chacewater Park 5 miles
from both coasts and Truro
city. ☎ 0209 820762.

Chiverton Caravan and Touring Park *Blackwater, Truro, ¼mile from junction of A30 and A390, of B3277 St Agnes Road.* ☎ *0872 560667.*

Leverton Place *Greenbottom, Chacewater, 3 ½miles west of Truro off*

A390 at Threemilestone roundabout. ☎ *0872 560462.*

Liskey Touring Park *Greenbottom, 3 miles west off 390.* ☎ *0872 560274.*

Ringwell Holiday Park *Bissoe Road, Carnon Downs, 3 miles southwest off*

A39. ☎ *0872 862194.*

Summer Valley *Shortlanesend, 3 miles northwest off B3284.* ☎ *0872 77878.*

Tretheake Manor Tourist Park *Veryan, Truro, adjacent to A39 Falmouth–Truro road.* ☎ *0872 501658.*

OUTINGS FROM TRURO

TRELISSICK GARDEN

Trelissick Garden is high above the estuary with wonderful views down to the sea inlet of Carrick Roads. The setting alone is worth the journey, but the big gardens are special too, with a mass of shrubs and trees, and woodland where you can walk all year. The gardens are National Trust and open March to October. You can get there by bus from Truro in about 40 minutes. Western National run one bus a day at 1.40pm on weekdays and 12.50pm on Saturday.

FALMOUTH BAY

BUDGET FOR A DAY	
Bus fare	2·00
Pendennis Castle	1·40
St Mawes Castle	·85
Two-hour river cruise	3·50
Lunch	3·00
Dinner	7·00
	£17·75
plus accommodation	

Boats run to Falmouth from the town quay in summer. If the tide is wrong, a bus will take you to the start point at Malpas.

Falmouth is where seven rivers meet the sea, having first run into the deep sheltered waters of the Carrick Roads. This was once Britain's second busiest port; tankers still anchor in Carrick Roads – a surprising sight from villages that you might have thought were well inland.

People visit today for the beaches near by, and for the sailing. The shops have an individual air – you'll find some traditional firms here, with a sprinkling of arts and crafts, and a bookstore specialising in marine matters.

There are lots of restaurants and other places to eat. You could get tea or a light lunch at the Cavendish Coffee House, or at de Wynns, which also sells speciality teas and coffees. For evenings the Continental at 29 High Street has main courses at a reasonable price.

Running up from this main street is The Moor, where you'll find Jacob's Ladder, a steep flight of 111 steps. The pub at the top issues certificates for climbers (the Sea View pub round the corner has a better outlook though). On the edge of town, Pendennis Castle was built by Henry VIII to guard the Carrick Roads and still looks stout today (English Heritage and open all year, but not Monday in winter).

> **Moneysaver**
> For a budget outing try the ferry over the river to the pretty village of Flushing. Flushing's name and its Dutch-style houses originated with Dutch builders who came to Falmouth to build sea walls.

The St Mawes ferry takes you over the Carrick Roads. This is the quickest way to reach St Mawes Castle, which is a smaller companion to Pendennis (open the same times). St Mawes is another idyllic place, with yachts in the harbour and lanes of cottages.

Cruise boats do two-hour tours of the river and its creeks. For a little more you can sail on *Pentreath Laity*, which is a traditional sailing lugger, telephone 0860 755343.

There are paths through the woods by the river too, and it's a good spot for bird-watching in winter. Trebah is an all-year ravine garden, with giant ferns and palm trees running down to a beach on the Helford River.

EAST ALONG THE COAST

Mevagissey   Mevagissey is one of Cornwall's showpiece fishing ports, with quaint cottages along narrow streets running down to a harbour full of boats. It used to have a name for smuggling and for pilchards. The fishing still goes on, although the days of local fishwives packing pilchards into barrels have gone. It's still a place of character, although a lot of the old harbour buildings have changed their uses. The Sharksfin hotel occupies an ex-sardine warehouse and cannery and serves fish dishes at a reasonable price; other places do simpler food at lower prices. Buses run from Truro, but change for Mevagissey at St Austell.

Charlestown   Charlestown was purpose built in the 18th century for exporting china clay, which it still does, though the harbour entrance is tortuous for modern vessels. It's a tiny but perfect little settlement of Georgian houses around a quay, with obvious attractions as a filming location. *Poldark*, *The Onedin Line*, and *The Eagle has Landed* were all partly filmed here. Between April and October you can visit the Shipwreck and Heritage Museum. Buses run from Truro, but change for Charlestown at St Austell.

Local flavour

The Cornish Smoked Fish Company in Charlestown is a factory with shop. You might find bargains here in smoked salmon, mackerel and other fish.

Fowey   Fowey (say 'foy') is one of the most appealing of Cornwall's picturesque ports. It has quaint narrow streets to explore, but it's big enough to give a bit of breathing room as well.

The wooded estuary and coast make for beautiful walks. South along the coast path is Menabilly – Daphne du Maurier lived here, and it's identified as the Manderley of her haunting novel *Rebecca*. The house isn't open, but you can walk across the beach below it.

Kenneth Grahame's children's classic *The Wind in the Willows* was partly inspired by Fowey. It would still be a great place for characters like Ratty, happiest just 'messing about in boats'.

LOOE

Looe is one of Cornwall's quaint fishing ports. Tourists rather than pilchards are the main haul nowadays, but the harbour is still full of fishing boats and opportunities for fishing trips and pleasure cruises. Inland, the old part of East Looe is the place to wander in timeless-feeling narrow streets. If you have a car, use a park-and-ride scheme at Liskeard.

LANHYDROCK

Lanhydrock is a longer journey, but you could make this a whole day out. It's a very grand house, originally built in the 17th century but rebuilt after a fire in 1881, so what you see is a luxurious Victorian home. Most people find the 'below stairs' domestic quarters at least as interesting as the grander rooms. There are formal gardens with clipped yew hedges, and beyond those you can walk in the attractive riverside park.

The nearest public transport is Bodmin Parkway train station, where signs direct you along the drive once used by carriages. It's nearly two miles; open April to October.

THE NORTH CORNISH COAST

For long beaches, head for the north coast. Perranporth, half an hour by bus from Truro, is a family resort with three miles of sandy beaches. Newquay is Cornwall's biggest and most popular resort, with plenty of amusements and sheltered beaches for a day out (about an hour by bus from Truro). It's also a mecca for surfers, who visit for the Atlantic rollers on Fistral beach.

Moneysaver

Eat out at lunch time rather than in the evening – fixed price lunches are usually cheaper than equivalent evening meals.

'Obby 'Oss celebrations on May Day in Padstow.

Padstow is a north coast fishing port, with steep old streets winding down to the harbour. The May Day celebrations here attract big crowds with the 'Obby 'Oss, a masked and black clad figure with swirling skirts who parades through the crowds to the beat of a drum. How the 'Obby 'Oss began isn't clear, but it may be pre-Christian.

Ferries take you over the estuary of the River Camel to Rock, which despite the name offers a sandy beach. Also on this side is Polzeath, where the poet John Betjeman spent childhood holidays – it's an attractive spot, with cliffs and rock pools, and more good surfers' beaches.

North of Padstow are Boscastle and Tintagel – both worth visiting, and both set on dramatic cliff coastline.

Boscastle is one of the rare havens for boats on a long stretch of black cliff coastline. The tiny harbour is at the end of a jagged cleft in the rocks. Even on calm days you feel the waves

booming, and when the tide is right the sea water comes whooshing out of a blowhole in the cliffs. The main part of the village runs up a steep hill inland – an attractive place with old pubs, cottages and stylish Edwardian houses.

You can see the coast from the water on the little boat *Lucky*, telephone 08405 245. Or stick to dry land and follow the footpath along the National Trust coast.

Tintagel has been identified with King Arthur's Camelot since at least the Middle Ages. Whether the legendary king existed or not, the remains of a 5th-century stronghold have been discovered at Tintagel, which would be just right for his time. Today he's the town's main industry. The castle you see today dates from the 12th century, and it has a spectacular cliff-top setting (English Heritage). The other place to see is the Old Post Office, originally a medieval manor house and now bowed with age under its stone roof (National Trust, open April to October).

PENZANCE

Penzance is the end of the railway line – the last stop west. It's a natural target for visitors, but. Penzance has a life of its own.

Local flavour

Cornish heavy cakes or 'heavies' are a flat, sweet and fruit-filled cross between cake and bread. They're not as indigestible as the name suggests, but they're very filling.

Buses take useful routes around this corner of Cornwall; bicycles can be hired at both Penzance and St Ives. Most of the scenery is clifftop plateau, so cycling's usually not too strenuous.

The picturesque way to arrive is by train, which runs right beside the beach before ending close to the harbour. Penzance occupies a sheltered spot on Mount's Bay, which means it basks in a sub-tropical microclimate. Across the bay is the rocky islet and romantic-looking castle of St Michael's Mount. You can reach it by walking over a causeway from Marazion at low tide; otherwise by ferry, but only if weather permits. It's now owned by the National Trust, but is still the home of the family that has lived here since 1660. The house is open on weekdays from March to October, with guided tours at other times – telephone 0736 710507. Avoid peak times because you may have to wait to get in.

Causewayhead is a traffic-free street with some individual shops, but the showpiece of the town is Chapel Street. This is where you'll find the Egyptian House, so named because of its ornate façade. The National Trust has a shop here. It faces the plain-looking Union Hotel, which is Elizabethan behind its façade. Nelson's victory and death at the battle of Trafalgar were first announced at the hotel.

The Isles of Scilly are 28 miles out in the Atlantic. You can reach them by air or sea, but most routes start at Penzance. On a good day these islands seem a kind of paradise, with subtropical plants, dolphins and seals just offshore, and plenty of birds for bird-watchers.

Boats take two hours to get there and you could see whale or shark on the way, but remember that you have to cross a stretch of the heaving Atlantic, which isn't for everyone.

St Michael's Mount is reached from Marazion.

HELSTON AND THE LIZARD

Crowds pour into Helston for Floral Day on 8 May. The celebration starts with a medieval play (the Hal-an-tow), and then townsfolk dance through the streets to the tune of the Helston Furry Dance. Visit on a Monday for the market down Coinagehall Street; at other times, expect a quiet, local town with winding streets.

Two of Cornwall's bigger all-weather, all-ages attractions are near by. Special excursion tickets from Penzance include entrance fee to Flambards Theme Park, which offers full-size rides (for adults too), a reconstructed Victorian village and a 'Britain in the Blitz' street among other amusements – the admission fee is steep, but it covers all the attractions (and see *Moneysaver*).

Local flavour

The Blue Anchor pub in Helston brews its own tasty Spingo beer and serves a good pasty too. The premises were built for monks in the 1400s, and the furnishings can't have changed much in the last 100 years or so.

Moneysaver

Admission to Flambards Theme Park is reduced by £2 after 5pm in the peak season; otherwise after 3pm. If you're hooked on the place, 30p will buy you a return card for further reductions.

Poldark Mine offers a reconstructed village based on Winston Graham's *Poldark* novels, and a real tin mine to explore (it's not deep and there's no chance of getting lost). It's kept dry by a mighty Cornish engine, pumping out 30,000 gallons of water a day.

The best free show near Helston is the Royal Navy Air Station (RNAS), Culdrose, which has a public viewing area on the Gweek road. RNAS Culdrose always has an air show on the last Wednesday in July.

South of Helston lies the Lizard – a strange moorland peninsula which ends in jagged cliffs at Lizard Point. This is mainland Britain's southern-most point. A lot of the coast is looked after by the National Trust, which means it remains unspoilt, and there's fine walking on the cliff-top coastal path (you need to be cautious though because the path isn't fenced). North of the Lizard Point on the way to Mullion is Kynance Cove, which can only be reached by walking along the coast path or by a steep route down from the National Trust car park. This is a wonderful place, where a cleft in the cliffs meets the sea at a white sand beach and huge rocks.

AROUND THE LAND'S END PENINSULA

Mousehole The poet Dylan Thomas called Mousehole (pronounced 'mouzel') 'the loveliest village in England'. It has narrow streets of cottages around a little harbour where hundreds of pilchard-fishing boats once moored. The Ship Inn celebrates Tom Bawcock's Eve on 23 December with 'stargazey pie' – a pie with fishes heads sticking through the crust. The story is that Tom Bawcock saved the village from famine by catching seven sorts of fish.

Porthcurno Porthcurno is the home of the Minack open-air theatre – a Greek style amphitheatre cut into the cliff with just the white beach and the Atlantic beyond. It was created in 1923 and now has touring productions between May and September. You can make reservations if you're a party of 12 or more; otherwise you have to join the line for tickets. Buses from Penzance suit matinée performances, but you'll need independent transport for evening shows. You can visit just to look around.

Moneysaver
You can get that 'next stop America' feeling, without the crowds or the expense of Land's End. Other westward viewpoints are Cape Cornwall (down a lane from St Just); Gwennap Head (a walk from Porthcurno); and Pendeen lighthouse.

Land's End This is the western-most point of mainland England – next stop across the Atlantic is New York if you bypass the Isles of Scilly. The land is privately owned and you have to pay to get in, plus a parking fee, but the admission charge covers all sorts of attractions and exhibitions. The coastline lives up to expectations with rocks and jagged cliffs. Beyond those lie the Longships lighthouse and notorious Seven Stones reef. On a clear day you can see the Wolf Rock lighthouse and beyond to the Isles of Scilly, 28 miles away.

Whitesand and St Just The biggest local beach is north of Land's End on Whitesand Bay. Bed and breakfast places around here have paths down to the beach; day-trippers can get there by road to Sennen Cove. It's a wide, soft sand beach, with rock pools when the tide is out. The southern end is the more sheltered; the northern end is open to the Atlantic and can be dangerous. The lifeboat is on view when not in use (free, but donations invited). Boats used to be hauled out of the water by the windlass in the Round House, but it's now gallery shop and a good place to look for reasonably priced pictures of the area. The Singing Teapot serves lunches and teas and has outdoor tables overlooking the sea.

St Just is the last town west, and it's unexpectedly industrial in feel, with streets of terraced houses. The reason is the local tin mines. Signs direct you to the viewpoint of Cape Cornwall; you can also hire bicycles at Penwith Mountain Bikes. You'll need some sort of independent transport to reach Carn Euny, the remains of an Iron Age village on the road to Sancreed – the house walls are still a few feet high. The other remarkable ancient place is Chysauster, the remains of a village of the 2nd century AD. Both are English Heritage sites.

Local flavour
D H Lawrence wrote part of *Women in Love* while living at tiny Zennor near St Ives in World War I. He drank at the Tinners' Arms, where you'll probably get a much warmer welcome than he did – the villagers suspected Lawrence and his wife of being German spies.

St Ives St Ives is like bit of the Mediterranean on the Cornish coast – it has white sand beaches, blue seas, even topless sunbathers and Mediterranean-style aeroplanes with advertising banners streaming behind. It's an appealing place which, not surprisingly, attracts crowds. Around the harbour and beaches lies a maze of narrow streets. Day visitors' cars are not welcome in the heart of St Ives. The nearest car parks to the centre have bus links to town. Or use the rail park-and-ride at Lelant Saltings. Trains take a cliffside run with wide sea views, arriving at a tiny station that's all but on the beach.

The clear light of St Ives attracts artists, but it's especially associated with a mid 20th-century group of artists that included Alfred Wallis, Ben Nicolson and Barbara Hepworth. The Tate Gallery is hoping to open a collection of their work in the town in 1992. In the meantime the coolest place to visit on a hot day is Barbara Hepworth's house and sculpture studio. Behind it is a dense, green garden, where sculptures are set among the trees. It's open Monday to Saturday (and Sundays in summer).

BARNSTAPLE

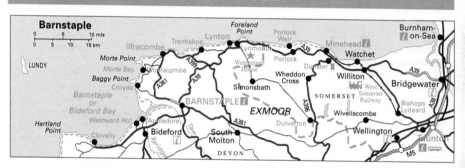

Devon ends with a flourish on the north side: it rises up to the high moorland of Exmoor, and then drops in 500ft cliffs to the sea. Westwards is another dramatic and rocky coast; inland the high country is cut through with deep wooded river valleys: good for walking, fishing and riding, with pleasant old towns. The coast doesn't have many settlements, partly because it's hard to find a foothold on this shore: those that do exist include traditional resorts and fishing havens.

West of Exmoor, Barnstaple is a nice old town, full of character, with good transport links to the coast and inland places. This area is easy to reach from the M5 motorway, which is the southwest tentacle of Britain's motorway network – useful, but it means a lot of visitors. The advantage is that you'll find plenty of low-price tours in the peak season, and there's also plentiful accommodation.

Tour buses go to the main sights in summer, and there's a network of regular local services;

but you'll get most out of this coastline if you're prepared to do some walking. Bicycles can be rented for exploring the lanes or for rougher moorland. On Exmoor, several stables offer horse riding at reasonable prices. If you're driving on Exmoor, beware of free-range ponies or livestock, and be prepared for very steep hills on the coast road. You can rent bicycles from Tarka Trail Cycle Hire at the train station. The daily rate gets cheaper the longer you have the bike. It's advisable to book for summer periods.

Camping is popular in this generally rural area; otherwise cottages and other places to rent will work out cheapest. The Devon farm liaison group operates a hotline for last-minute enquiries about renting a place to stay. Telephone Sandra Gay on 07693 259. You needn't pay much more than £100 a week to be cossetted with good home cooking on a farmhouse. Contact Let Devon Farms Accommodate You for details of all types of farmhouse accommodation: telephone 0626 833266.

The Domesday survey of England in 1086 makes Barnstaple sound a solidly prosperous place, and it still feels the same way today. The bridge goes back to the 13th century, although it's been much altered over the years – take the riverside walk to get a look at the old structure underneath. The market has been here even longer and it still makes a good free show today.

The potteries around the town are part of the medieval tradition too, and they're fun to visit quite apart from the chance of buying something.

The best day to be in Barnstaple is on Friday, when the pannier market in Boutport Street has over 400 stalls. Barnstaple has the West Country's biggest pannier market, traditionally for local produce – home baking, butter, cut flowers, vegetables or other fresh goods – all of which could be carried in panniers by ponies or donkeys in former times. There's also a Friday cattle market, and a market selling antiques. In summer, smaller pannier markets are held on Tuesday and Saturday (250 stalls), with craft markets on Monday and Thursday.

Moneysaver
Brannam's pottery has a shop selling seconds at reduced prices.

ORIENTATION IN BARNSTAPLE

INFORMATION
TOURIST OFFICE
North Devon Library, Tuly Street. ☎ *0271 47177.*
PUBLIC LAVATORIES
Bus station; Pannier Market; The Square car park; multi-storey car park; North Walk.

TRANSPORT
BUSES
Most of the suggested outings are on Red Bus North Devon services; ☎ *0271 45444, or ask at the tourist office.*
TRAINS
Railway station, town centre. ☎ *0271 22200*
CAR HIRE
Godfrey Davis Europcar Taw Garage, Victoria Road.

☎ *0271 72809.*
Practical Car Rentals Astra Garage, Exeter Road, Braunton. ☎ *0271 817000 (take Ilfracombe bus 3 or 62 from Barnstaple Strand bus station).*
Western Car and Truck Rental Roundswell Trading Estate, Barnstaple. ☎ *0271 79321. This firm will deliver to you.*

ACCOMMODATION
HOTELS
Yeo Dale Pilton Bridge. ☎ *0272 42954. A house with 16th-century origins; bed and breakfast starts at £13.50 single, or £94.50 for the week (£112 with evening meals).*
Rowden Barton Roundswell, 2 miles out of town. ☎ *0271 44365. A modern farmhouse overlooking north Devon*

scenery; single bed and breakfast starts at £11, or £70 for the week (£112 with evening meals).
CAMP SITE
Chivenor Holiday Centre Adjacent to to A361 and RAF Chivenor. ☎ *0271 812017.*

EATING OUT
Lynwood House Bishops Tawton Road. ☎ *0271 43695. Good food in a range of places and prices, from bar lunches for under £5.*
Royal and Fortescue Boutport Street. ☎ *0271 42289. A handsome, traditional place - King Edward stayed here as Prince of Wales. Fixed price lunches are £5.25; fixed price evening meals are £9.25.*

OUTINGS FROM BARNSTAPLE

WEST ALONG THE COAST

Bideford   A cycle path along a former railway line links Barnstaple to Bideford, a busy little port, and the quay is a lively scene of pleasure boats and fishing vessels. There's a cattle and pannier market on Tuesday. Bideford is also the main departure point for Lundy Island.
Lundy   MS *Oldenburg* sails to Lundy from

Puffins can still be seen on Lundy Island.

Bideford all year round. (You can also sail from Ilfracombe in the summer). A return trip takes around two hours, which gives you some four hours ashore – enough to look around an island half a mile wide and less than four miles long. The coast is nearly all cliff, and you transfer to a launch to land because there isn't a harbour. It's an island of wild flowers, wild Soay sheep and sea birds. You could take a picnic, but the Marisco Tavern's hot meals might be welcome.

Appledore Appledore is a quaint fishing village of tiny cottages and lanes (no cars allowed). Boat building has gone on here since 1500, and the North Devon Maritime Museum at the top of the town is open Easter to October. Charles Kingsley's 1855 novel *Westward Ho!* inspired the creation of the Westward Ho! resort along the coast.

Clovelly Clovelly is an exceptional place, with white cottages tumbling down a steep, stepped, cobbled street to a harbour which is one of the few safe havens on this coast. Cars have to be parked at the top (for a fee): the locals get their deliveries by sledge, all year round. (A discreet Land Rover will carry passengers. Clovelly attracts a lot of visitors, but development is kept in check. Donkeys enhance the scene, and there's a crafts gallery to browse at on your way down to the harbour. The visitor centre at the top has a restaurant, or you could eat at the New Inn (no bus on Sundays, and regular services may be non-existent in winter).

EAST ALONG THE COAST

Morte Bay Morte Bay is popular for just soaking up the sun, but it does have Atlantic rollers for surfers, and rock pools at each end. There are good walks too, south to Baggy Point or north to Morte Point (both protected by the National Trust and both give good views). Woolacombe (north end) has more facilities, Croyde (south end) has more peace.

Ilfracombe Ilfracombe is the most popular resort, and it's a place of great character, with lots of Victorian and Edwardian buildings in terraces above the bay. A favourite activity is idling around the harbour, which is generally buzzing with fishing and pleasure boats. The Tunnels beach is something special – part has been constructed, and part is natural pools reached by tunnels and cleaned by the tides each day. By the pier you can see the working lifeboat (free, but donation please), and there's a very welcoming town museum. Among the 20,000 widely assorted items, it has lots of Victoriana, bygone kitchen equipment, plus exotica from Africa and Peru, bats and butterflies, and a ship-to-shore radio station, which children can 'operate'. It's open all year, and also has summer evening openings until 10pm.

> **Local flavour**
> Exmoor is the setting of R D Blackmore's novel *Lorna Doone*, about the wild Doone family who wrought terror from their stronghold in Doone Valley (near Lynton).

Beyond Ilfracombe you're within the Exmoor National Park, which includes the spectacular north Devon/Somerset coast. All these places are accessible by bus from Barnstaple or from Ilfracombe. Paths run off the coast road to the natural spectaculars – there are car parks along the road too.

The Hunter's Inn at Trentishoe is the starting point for wooded walks along the Heddon River to Heddon's Mouth, where it rushes out to sea. You can also reach Woody Bay on foot from Hunter's Inn – there's a sandy beach at low tide.

Lynton and Lynmouth Lynton is a bright, breezy (literally) town on top of a 600ft cliff; Lynmouth is at the bottom, reached by a zigzag path or cliff railway. The cliff has a gradient of

1 in 1.75, or 60 per cent; the railway works by the gravity pull of 700-gallon water tanks. A mile's walk from Lynton takes you to the Valley of the Rocks, scooped out of the heathland and dotted with oddly shaped rocks.

Lynmouth is at the meeting of the East and West Lyn rivers, with cliffs rising 800ft to either side. You can walk along the river past woods and waterfalls, or take fishing trips and boat tours. Some signed walks start at Watersmeet House, a National Trust centre about 1½ miles up river from Lynmouth. They're open from April to October with a café for lunches.

Minehead   Minehead is another resort with a lot of character and good beaches, although the sea may vanish to the far horizon at low tide. The best bit is around the harbour, where you may be able to find fishing trips. The *Waverley* paddle steamer does trips along the coast: telephone 0446 720656 for details.

The best walking is on North Hill between Porlock and Minehead. The National Trust has made a route 'for more experienced walkers' between the coast path and sea.

Minehead greets May Day with the 'hobby horse' – a masked figure with coloured 'horse' who capers among the crowd. The local legend is that the horse began as a way to scare off raiders from the sea; but many prefer more mystical theories.

The West Somerset Railway   The West Somerset Railway gives fine coast views before turning inland to run through woods to Bishops Lydeard, five miles from Taunton. There are plenty of trains between Easter and October, fewer out of the holiday season.

Dunster   The first stop on the West Somerset Railway is the attractive village of Dunster: alight here for a 15-minute walk to Dunster Castle, which has been the home of the Luttrell family since 1376. It's now run by the National Trust. The terraced gardens have sub-tropical exotica like the giant lemon tree and yuccas; inside you'll see centuries of family treasures.

> **Moneysaver**
> It costs £1.90 to see just the grounds and gardens of Dunster Castle.

Open Sunday to Thursday from April to September (and October afternoons). The gardens also open on Friday and Saturday .

EXMOOR – INLAND

This is the national park area stretching south from the coast between Ilfracombe and Minehead. It rises to 1,400ft, and is cut through by deep wooded valleys. It's great for walking, cycling and exploring on horseback; it's peppered with prehistoric sites; and the fishing's not bad either. In amongst it are remote villages and old towns.

> **Local flavour**
> Exmoor salmon and trout are on sale in local shops. You should be able to buy venison too. Exmoor is one of the rare places in England which can offer game fishing at a reasonable cost.

The information centre at Barnstaple can supply general sightseeing ideas and advise on where to walk/ride/fish etc. There are various information points around the park; for advance information write to the main office at Exmoor National Park Information Centre, Exmoor House, Dulverton, Somerset, or telephone 0398 23841. Guided walks are available right through the summer, and give you an instant feel of the area for a nominal fee. There are some 370 miles of footpaths to follow.

Exmoor has more wild red deer than anywhere else in England. They're elusive, but most in evidence in October and November, when the males' 'belling' calls resound as they fight with rivals and gather herds of hinds (the females). Exmoor ponies are a wild native breed.

One of the best ways to see Exmoor is on horseback. Some stables are geared towards experienced riders, and offer hunting in season. Others are for all levels of ability/inability. Stables near Lynton will probably offer rides along 'Doone Valley', setting for the novel *Lorna Doone*. See *Exmoor Visitor*, or ask one of the Exmoor visitor centres for advice.

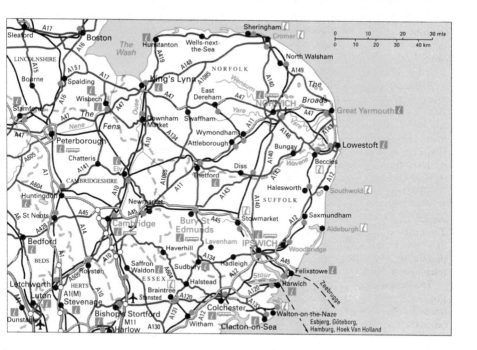

Just 50 miles outside London and its suburbs, you enter the totally different landscape of East Anglia, the region north east of the capital that bulges out into the North Sea. For some people, this is the prettiest English scenery, though it isn't obviously dramatic, because it has no high hills – in some places it has no hills at all. But it is beautiful in a more subtle way, with huge skies and an ever changing light.

In medieval times the region was very rich indeed because of the wool industry based here. When the industry died away, a lot of the region's towns and villages just stopped changing, so that today they're a wonderful collection of medieval streets and large old churches. This part of England also has a rich heritage of music and painting.

Cambridge is one of the oldest university cities – only just younger than Oxford. There are some beautiful old college buildings to visit, and it's worth spending a leisurely day wandering around them. North of the city is the strange, flat farming country of the Fens, which you cross to visit the little city of Ely with its immense cathedral.

Bury St Edmunds is geographically close to Cambridge but is quite different in atmosphere. It is a compact, friendly Suffolk market town with lots of medieval buildings, from where you can visit several towns and villages which haven't changed very much since medieval times. The painters Gainsborough and Constable both painted the surrounding landscape, and you can step into the real-life settings of Constable's most famous pictures.

The Suffolk coast is a romantic ensemble of estuaries and old harbour towns: Woodbridge, an old port town with a quay on the River Deben; Aldeburgh, home of the celebrated music festival; or Southwold, with its old fashioned seaside resort atmosphere. This is an ideal coast for people who like walking or bird-watching, or seaside holidays without bright lights.

Norwich is another long-established city, with its own strong character and rich cultural life. The central attraction is the cathedral, and there's also a huge market to visit. Between the

115

city and the coast, there's the unique, watery landscape of the Norfolk Broads. You'll need to rent a boat for a day or more to explore them. Then there's the coast, which offers family resorts such as Cromer, or bright lights and amusements at Great Yarmouth.

Bus services are reasonable – better in summer than in winter, and patchy in some areas, and there are some useful train routes which are worth taking just for the views. This is easy cycling country (if you're travelling with the wind), and the locals may look more kindly on cyclists than on cars.

There is plenty of reasonably priced bed and breakfast accommodation in small hotels, farmhouses and inns. The booklet *Stay on a Farm* gives details of a group of Norfolk and Suffolk farms that do bed and breakfast or rent out holiday accommodation. Write to Hillview Farm, Fressingfield, Near Eye, Suffolk IP21 5PY. Renting a cottage or apartment is very popular in this region, but you need to book a long way ahead for the busy season, which starts in April. Some places are booked up a year ahead, although it's always worth telephoning to see if there's been a cancellation. You should also book far ahead if you want to be in or near Aldeburgh during its music festivals.

On the food side, the area is well known for its fresh shellfish including crabs and oysters, and you can buy locally smoked fish. Look out for fresh delicacies such as asparagus. You might also find samphire for sale, which is a marsh plant known as 'poor man's asparagus'.

Local flavour

East Anglia has some renowned breweries, such as Adnams at Southwold and Greene King at Bury St Edmunds. You'll find their beers in pubs all over the region. East Anglia also has vineyards making their own wine.

Music festivals are another speciality of the area. The English composer Benjamin Britten founded the Aldeburgh Festival in 1948, which has now developed into a three-week feast of music that takes place just outside the town, and is followed by the more informal Maltings Proms in August. Norwich, Cambridge and Bury St Edmunds all have their own arts festivals, and they all have theatres. In summer you'd be unlucky not to stumble across local events such as village fêtes and carnivals, or 'garden open' days when private gardens are opened up to visitors for a small admission fee.

Moneysaver

The Maltings Proms at Aldeburgh are an inexpensive way to enjoy two weeks of music.

East Anglia is also a special place for spectacular medieval churches, built on wealth made in the wool industry. They're wonderful places to visit, if only to enjoy the craftsmanship in wood and stone. East Anglia also has an amazing number of windmills and watermills, some of which are open to visitors, and there are some very romantic moated manor houses too.

If you're looking for a souvenir of your visit, remember that this is a popular area with painters, whose pictures needn't cost the earth. East Anglia also has a lot of craftspeople, and you'll almost certainly come across crafts for sale. The quality can be very high indeed: Aldeburgh has an annual show for which buyers travel specially from the USA.

For forward planning, your best source of information on accommodation, places to see, transport and most other aspects of the region is the East Anglia Tourist Board, at Toppesfield Hall, Hadleigh, Suffolk IP7 5DN.

There are windmills all over East Anglia.

CAMBRIDGE

There are dozens of Cambridges around the world, but this is the original – a university city since medieval times, with a maze of ancient college courtyards and gardens to explore. Former Cambridge students range from Oliver Cromwell and Samuel Pepys to Byron, James Mason, and Princes Charles and Edward of today's royal family. From the sciences, Isaac Newton studied here and so did Ernest Rutherford and numerous other Nobel Prize winners. A hundred Cambridge students had emigrated to the New World by the mid 17th century. One was John Harvard, who gave his name to the American university and is commemorated by a plaque in the Emmanual College chapel.

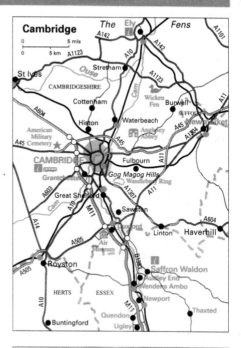

Behind the Cambridge colleges runs the River Cam, with lawns fringed by tall old trees – an area known as the Backs. Take a leisurely zigzag stroll to and fro across the river, admiring the mellow old buildings and the greenery.

Cambridge is 2½ hours by bus from London, or an hour by rail from London's Liverpool Street station. Take a bus from the Cambridge train station to the centre – it's a dreary walk. Cambridge airport has flights to Manchester and Amsterdam; Stansted airport is 45 minutes by bus, and has a growing international network. Driving to central Cambridge from London is very quick along the M11 motorway (an hour on a good day), but driving in central Cambridge is restricted. Cambridge's park-and-ride scheme provides low-cost out-of-centre car parking and a frequent return bus service to the centre. The car parks are signed from main roads into the city.

The origins of the university aren't known for sure, but the accepted version is that the first students arrived in 1209, because they couldn't afford the rents at Oxford. Hostels were founded for them, and those became the colleges of today. The Bishop of Ely founded the first one, Peterhouse, in 1280; millionaire David Robinson founded the newest, Robinson (built 1977-80). Colleges were strictly men-only until Girton College brought women on to the scene in 1869; now the numbers are nearly half and half. Students still live in the colleges, though not exclusively.

Moneysaver

You can see most college courtyards and chapels free of charge when they're open. Most of the museums, churches and other sights have no admission charge, though you may be asked to make a donation.

The colleges are private places for working and living, so follow the rules. Noise, games, picnics and walking on the grass will get you into trouble, as will venturing up forbidden stairs, and sometimes pushchairs. College porters (doormen) can be fierce.

Cambridge is worth a visit in March and April just for the sight of spring flowers on the Backs. Avoid late April and May if you want to see the colleges – most are closed so the students can study for exams, and many stay shut well into June. Otherwise they're usually open for part of the day. June is celebration time for students, with outdoor parties by day (not always an edifying sight) and dancing all night at the pricey 'May balls'.

More accessible to visitors are the Midsummer Fair on Midsummer Common, the May Bumps (actually in June), which are rowing races on the river outside the city, and the Footlights Revue – entertainment from the drama club which fostered the talents of many a media star. In July after the students have gone, the city comes into its own with the Cambridge Festival – a carnival, jazz and classical concerts, theatre indoors and out, mime and poetry and other events – many of them free. The Cambridge Folk Festival is a weekend of outdoor music by international artists at Cherry Hinton, on the edge of Cambridge. Year-round venues include the Arts Theatre, ADC Theatre and Arts Cinema.

Signs of autumn are fogs rolling in from the Fens and the funfair on Midsummer Common, with a big firework display on 5 November. On Christmas Eve the Festival of Nine Lessons and Carols is held at King's College Chapel, with unforgettable singing by the choir. This is free, but tickets are much sought after. It's on the radio however: check newspapers for details.

The best view of the city is from the tower of Great St Mary's Church (by the market) – the way up is a claustrophobia-inducing spiral staircase, so avoid peak times like weekend afternoons if you can. Two-hour guided walking tours start at the tourist information centre all year at 2pm, with two or three extra tours a day in summer. History tours and drama tours (to re-create the past more vividly) may also be available.

Guide Friday runs open-top bus tours, complete with a guide to point out the sights. You can join or leave at several stopping points, and the buses run every 15 minutes (every hour from November to February).

Several colleges are near the market: Corpus Christi has a mock-Gothic court at the front – walk through for the charming small-scale Old Court, Cambridge's oldest. Queens' College is reckoned the prettiest because of its timber-framed President's Lodge, but is only open from 10.15am to 12.45pm and from 1.45

to 4.30pm, April to September. Linking old and new buildings over the river is the Mathematical Bridge. The original is said to have been constructed without bolts by Isaac Newton, but students who took it apart couldn't put it together again.

King's College was founded by Henry VI for boys from the school he had started at Eton. The college has always had places for 16 choir boys – you might see them in their top hats marching between their school and King's College Chapel, which is best seen in the candlelight of an evening service when the choir is singing. Most services in term time are open to the public.

The chapel at King's is Cambridge's greatest glory, founded by Henry VI and completed with help from Henry VII and Henry VIII. It is stunning, a tall, airy building where the columns of the walls branch out into lacy fan vaulting across the roof. Intricate carving in the organ screen includes the initials H and A (for Henry VIII and his second wife Anne Boleyn). The altar picture is by Rubens; the windows show Old and New Testament stories. It closes for viewing during church services but otherwise is open daily, and free.

Trinity College was founded by Henry VIII, whose statue stands grandly over Great Gate – but his sceptre has been replaced by a chair leg. The film *Chariots of Fire* starts with a traditional Trinity challenge – to run right round Great Court while the clock strikes 12. Beyond it lies another architectural masterpiece – Sir Christopher Wren's library by the river (open weekdays 12 noon to 2pm and Saturdays in term time, free). St John's College has another ornate gateway, carved with curious creatures. Beyond it lie nine courtyards, from the 16th-century First Court to the 1960s Cripps Building. Cross the Cam by the Kitchen Bridge to see the romantic Bridge of Sighs, inspired by the one in Venice.

The Round Church in Bridge Street was built by the Knights Templar, medieval warrior monks. Their churches always copy the round shape of the Holy Sepulchre in Jerusalem, and only four of these strange buildings are left in England.

The handsome Fitzwilliam Museum on Trumpington Street is full of beautiful things – paintings by Titian and Cézanne among many others, lots of Chinese pots, Assyrian sculptures and Egyptian jewellery, Delft china cows and a room full of fans. There's a large gift shop and a café. Half is open till 2pm, the other half (mainly fine art) from 2pm till 5pm. Open daily except most Mondays, and free.

Local flavour

Thomas Hobson (1544-1630) hired out horses in Cambridge. Customers could take any horse so long as it was the one nearest the door – hence the phrase 'Hobson's choice', meaning no choice at all.

Punting on the Cam is a popular summer pastime.

The Scott Polar Research Institute (Lensfield Road) focuses on British polar explorations, with extra displays on polar people and wildlife. Open Monday to Saturday from 2.30pm to 4.30pm, free. Off Downing Street, a door in a car park leads to the Museum of Archaeology and Anthropology – good for children as well as adults, with all sorts of artefacts well displayed. Open Monday to Friday 2pm to 4pm, and Saturday from 10am to 12, free.

Two other museums which stand out are next door neighbours on Castle Hill, north of the city centre. The appeal of the Folk Museum has a lot to do with its steep old stairs and crooked floors - just right for a collection of bygones. Kettle's Yard was devised by Jim and Helen Ede between 1957 and 1973 to make art part of everyday life. The entire place is a welcoming work of art, not just the fine collection of 20th-century pictures and sculptures inside. Open every afternoon except Monday; free, but donation invited.

The Botanic Gardens lie south of town off Trumpington Street, and offer a scented garden, tall old trees and a little lake with bold ducks, as well as rare plants and glasshouses. Free except on Sunday.

Some of the best shopping (and window shopping) is close to the central colleges. Cheap-but-filling places to eat, aimed at students, can be found all over town. Riverside pubs that do food include the Mill, Spade and Becket and Fort St George.

Boats can be hired on the River Cam, including the traditional long flat punts, propelled and steered from the back by a long pole. The hilarious (for onlookers) error is to jam the pole into the riverbed and then hang on to it as the boat moves forward. Scudamore's and Trinity College rent out punts by the hour, but be prepared to pay a sizeable deposit. Chauffeured punts are also available for a 45-minute trip. You can rent the boats at Magdalene Bridge to go along the Backs, or near Silver Street Bridge for trips towards the village of Grantchester (a harder journey). They have rowing boats and canoes as well.

Cycling is the standard transport for students and many townspeople too. The central streets are mainly for bicycles and buses; elsewhere cycle-only lanes are clearly marked, and there's a spectacular special bridge over the railway for cyclists and pedestrians. Drakes on Hills Road rents out touring bicycles, and there are several others. Ask the tourist information centre for their leaflet on cycle hire.

Moneysaver

In winter bicycle rental rates are reduced at Student Bike Hire and Armada Cycles.

ORIENTATION IN CAMBRIDGE

INFORMATION
TOURIST OFFICE
Wheeler Street. ☎ *0223 322640.*

POST OFFICE
St Andrew's Street.
PUBLIC LAVATORIES
By the bus station, Lion Yard

shopping precinct, near Round Church, near Magdalene Bridge.

TRANSPORT
LOCAL BUSES
Drummond Street, near city centre. The suggested outings are on Cambus services, ☎ 0223 423554, or ask at the tourist office.
LONG-DISTANCE BUSES/COACHES
Express Stands, Drummer Street; for enquiries ☎ 0223 460711.

TRAINS
Cambridge station, Hills Road. ☎ 0223 311999.
BICYCLE HIRE
H Drake 56-60 Hills Road. ☎ 0223 63468.
Armada Cycles 47 Suez Road. ☎ 0223 210421.
Student Bike Hire 34 Kingston Street. ☎ 0223 311380.

ACCOMMODATION
HOTELS
Hamilton Hotel 156

Chesterton Road. ☎ 0223 65664. Single bed and breakfast from £18.
Antwerp Guest House Mill Road. ☎ 0223 24790. Evening meals available, single bed and breakfast from £20.

EATING OUT
Belinda's Trinity Street
Gonville Hotel Gonville Place. ☎ 0223 66611. Lunch from £7.45, dinner from £9.50.

OUTINGS FROM CAMBRIDGE

AROUND CAMBRIDGE

Grantchester The pleasantest way to get to the village of Grantchester, is to walk along the water meadows, just two miles along the River Cam. It feels miles away from the city bustle, and you can get bar lunches at the Red Lion or Rupert Brooke pub. Rupert Brooke lived at the Old Vicarage in the early 1900s, and wrote a poem about it, with the lines 'Stands the Church clock at ten to three? And is there honey still for tea?'

Local flavour
The Gog Magog Hills get their names from two legendary British giants.

Gog Magog and Wandlebury The Gog Magog Hills are sometimes called the Cambridge Alps because they rise to 250ft – very high in this low lying landscape – and they're an attractive place to walk. Wandlebury Ring is an Iron Age hill fort on the hills and is the burial place of the Godolphin Arab, one of the three horses from which many racehorses are descended. He died in 1753.
Duxford You don't have to be an aircraft freak to be impressed by the 120-plus aircraft on

show at Duxford Airfield, ranging from the frail-looking early bi-planes to the prototype Concord. On flying days (summer weekends) you can see some of them in the air, and for a price you can take a flight, if weather permits. Or take the ride simulator, which costs considerably less. An adventure playground and a huge array of military vehicles keep all the members of the party happy.
American Military Cemetery A hillside west of Cambridge makes a peaceful setting for the American Military Cemetery – a place of special significance for US visitors, but favoured by many locals because of its tranquillity. Guide Friday buses run this way on their Cambridge tour. The alternative is a taxi from Cambridge.
Anglesey Abbey Anglesey Abbey, a short distance to the northeast, is a National Trust house, but it's special for its Georgian-style garden, laid out by Lord Fairhaven in this century. He also gave the house its present character, by making it the home of his pictures and other collections. Open late March to mid October, Wednesday to Sunday and bank holiday Monday afternoons. The garden is open every afternoon from mid July to mid September, and it costs much less to visit the garden only.

NEWMARKET

Horse racing is the lifeblood of Newmarket. The Stuart kings liked riding here in the 1600s; the first race for a gold cup was in 1643. Today the big races are the Guineas in May, and there's regular racing from mid April to early November. On non-race days you might see horses going out for gallops, especially in the early morning. The National Horseracing Museum tells the story (April to December, closed most Mondays). Or book up for an 'equine tour' which includes a visit to the National Stud: it's expensive in the morning, when you see horses exercising, but half the price in the afternoons, when they rest. Telephone Newmarket 0638 667333.

SAFFRON WALDEN

Saffron Walden takes its name from the saffron crocus – once important here for dyeing cloth. The marketplace hasn't changed very much since medieval times, and the streets are lined with timber-framed buildings. The youth hostel dates from the 16th century (not open to day visitors, but best from the outside anyway); the church was worked on by the master mason for King's College Chapel in Cambridge. Out on the common is a mysterious maze marked on the ground, one of just a few scattered around England. Explanations range from dance patterns to pre-Christian symbols of rebirth.

Local flavour

Look out for the pargeting – the patterns in the plaster coating on Saffron Walden's old houses.

The mansion of Audley End is a mile's walk from Saffron Walden or from Audley End station. This house is enormous, but it's less than half of the Jacobean original, thanks to extensive reshaping in the 18th and 19th centuries. Now it has memorable though not always beautiful features of several periods.

'Capability' Brown designed the grounds, and they're dotted with appealing little 'eyecatcher' buildings by Robert Adam. There is a wonderful view of the wide, turreted stone front from the B1383 road. Open April to September in the afternoon, but closed Monday except bank holidays (English Heritage).

ELY AND THE FENS

Take the road or railway north out of Cambridge, and you're straight into the two-dimensional landscape of the Fens: no hills here, just a huge arc of sky, a few windmills, and fields of rich black soil stretching away to the horizon. In medieval times it was marshland – hostile to most, but an unlimited source of wealth for those who knew how to exploit it. Ely Abbey was one of several Fen monasteries which grew rich by draining some areas while leaving the rest to provide fish, wild birds, peat and reeds.

When first drained in the 17th century the Fens had a 60ft layer of peat soil. Drainage and farming have shrunk that to five feet, and in places the rivers and drainage ditches run above the present field level. There's speculation about the effect of rising sea levels.

The Isle of Ely has a special place in English folklore. It was the raiding base of Hereward the Wake, who defied the Normans after their invasion of Britain in 1066. The monks of Ely finally got fed up with the soldiers and betrayed them. What happened to Hereward is a mystery.

There's not a lot to Ely, and the cathedral dominates every view. Everything about this church seems larger than life, from the tall west doors onwards, and it's full of attractive details – don't miss the carvings under the choir stall seats, though you may have to ask permission to see them. Above the middle of the cathedral is the Octagon: 400 tons of wood, metal and stained glass through which (with luck) the sun will be pouring to make glowing colours on the floor. (If you're unlucky it will still be under repair, having taken a hammering in a 1990 gale.)

From March to October you can visit the cathedral's stained glass museum and see some fine examples, rescued from their endangered original sites and put on display here. There are also models explaining the craft.

Local flavour
Pike, pheasant and pigeon are all caught in the Fens.

Admission to the cathedral is free but a donation is suggested. Eat at the refectory to enjoy medieval surroundings and support a good cause: they do lunches and cream teas.

If you want to see how the Fens used to look, all marsh and reeds and butterflies, head for Wicken Fen (there is no practical bus service, but it is located about nine miles southeast of Ely off the A1123). These 600 acres have been left undrained – in fact the windmill is kept busy pumping water in. You can walk round – there is a boardwalk, but waterproof footwear is recommended in winter and spring, and the mosquitoes can be fearsome. Of the 700-odd types of butterfly, the star is the spectacular swallowtail; hides are provided for bird-watchers, who should remember to take binoculars. (National Trust.)

BURY ST EDMUNDS

Trim is the word for Bury St Edmunds. This is a prosperous little Suffolk country town, with a network of medieval streets, a cathedral, the ruins of a mighty abbey, and a renowned brewery.

Once here, you're within striking distance of what many consider England's prettiest

Bury St Edmunds

scenery: a string of villages and small towns where new building stopped in the 16th century. You'll find timber-framed houses and huge churches full of fine craftsmanship, some of them justly famous, others more secret and peaceful. A major attraction is visiting the scenes that Constable painted in famous pictures; and Gainsborough is another artist who had roots in the area.

This is rich farming country, and it's also good for gardens. Visit from May to July for a profusion of flowers in town and country, and ask tourist offices about dates when private gardens are open to the public. Admission fees (usually low) help named charities.

Moneysaver
N J Thake Cycles cuts the rental rate if you hire two bicycles. Reductions are also possible for older machines and children's bicycles, when available.

Buses run from Bury St Edmunds to the most popular sights, but independent transport will help you avoid crowded times at the most picturesque spots. N J Thake Cycles (Cycle King) hires bicycles and will advise on town and country routes. The Suffolk countryside is ideal for cycling: it has quiet lanes and enough ups and downs to be interesting, but no great hills.

Bury St Edmunds is 40 minutes from Cambridge by rail, 45 minutes by bus. From London it's two hours by rail or bus (change trains at Ipswich or Cambridge). Buses run here from Stansted airport.

The town name comes from Edmund, king of the East Angles, who was beheaded by Danish invaders in AD869. For no clear reason, the dead Edmund was soon being revered as a martyr. King Canute helped to found an abbey round his shrine, and pilgrims flocked here in medieval times. For the whole story, see the banners (made by local schools) in the cathedral.

Bury was laid out in a grid plan by an 11th-century bishop. Between the abbey and the old town is the open space called Angel Hill, and it makes a good place to start a visit. Overlooking the scene is the creeper-draped Angel Hotel, which has been an inn since 1482 (they do a rather pricey tea).

Charles Dickens put the Angel in his *Pickwick Papers*, and he also gave readings at the nearby Athenaeum assembly rooms – now home to the helpful tourist information centre. One-hour guided tours of the town start here on Tuesday afternoons from May to September, and Sundays in mid summer.

Follow Abbeygate Street from Angel Hill to explore the medieval network of streets and alleys. Timber framing sits side by side with neat Georgian façades, which often cloak a much older structure; public buildings include the old Corn Exchange and the market cross (now an art gallery). Market days are Wednesday and Saturday. Moyses Hall was a private house in the 12th century, and now makes a rare setting for the local museum (free).

Local flavour

Greene King started brewing in Bury St Edmunds in 1799. Among their beers are Abbot Ale and IPA bitter. You might be able to join a free guided tour of the brewery–telephone 0284 763222 to ask.

What looks like a pub doorway on Tavern Street is actually the whole of the Nutshell pub, the smallest in Britain – good for a novelty pint.

For a cosy local try the Dog and Partridge, in the shadow of the enormous Greene King Brewery.

In front of the brewery is the tiny Theatre Royal, a perfect little playhouse of 1819 (National Trust). Visitors can usually (not always) look around it during the day (no charge), but come back at night, if you can, to see it in action as a theatre. Productions range from local events to touring opera. The other special National Trust property is Angel Corner (off Angel Hill): a Queen Anne-style building which houses a clock and watch museum. Free; donations welcome.

The impressive gateway to the Abbey ruins.

The great portcullis gate on Angel Hill takes you to the ruins of the abbey buildings, with flower beds and lawns running to the River Lark and a medieval bridge. There's also a hidden rose garden, the inspiration of John T Appleby from the USA, who was stationed at nearby Rougham Airfield in World War II.

The abbey ruins include the site where 25 barons and the Archbishop of Canterbury vowed in 1214 to draw up a bill of rights (it became the Magna Carta). Close by is the very much intact 16th-century Cathedral of St Edmondsbury. Step inside and look towards the altar: above are painted angels in the roof, ahead stretch over 1,000 kneeling cushions sewn by local people with symbols of the saint or their neighbourhood.

Unusually, the cathedral has been extended in this century, and one gets the impression that it's a community concern – with some outside interest, like the US Dames of the Magna Carta who funded the barons' shields in the Quire. Admission to the cathedral is free; donation requested. 'First Sunday' concerts are on the first Sunday of the month at 4.30pm all year, plus organ recitals on August Thursday evenings at 7.30pm: no charge for either, but donations are invited. Along the road is the slightly older St Mary's, which has the tomb of Henry VIII's sister, Mary Tudor.

Visit in May for the Bury Festival – mostly jazz and classical music, with some chidren's events. Tickets vary in price, but start very low. The carnival is in June, with a parade on the last Saturday. In July the Arts Forum Festival features exhibitions, music, theatre and other entertainment.

ORIENTATION IN BURY ST EDMUNDS

INFORMATION
Tourist Office
The Athenaeum, Angel Hill.
☎ (0284) 764667.
Post Office
Cornhill.
Public Lavatories
Abbey Gardens; St Andrew's Street South, behind post office.

TRANSPORT
Local Buses
No bus station, buses stop in St Andrew's Street North. Chambers buses: ☎ Bures 0787 227233. Eastern Counties bus: ☎ 0284 766171. Or ☎ Suffolk County Council Transport Support: 0473 256676; or ask tourist office.
Trains
Bury St Edmunds Station, 15 minutes walk from centre along Northgate Street, ☎ (0473) 690744.
Bicycle Hire
N J Thake Cycles (Cycle King) 26 Angel Hill, ☎ (0284) 69902.

ACCOMMODATION
Hotel
Dunston House Hotel 8 Springfield Road, IP33 3AN. ☎ 0284 767981.
White Hart 35 Southgate Street, IP33 2AZ. ☎ 0284 755547.

EATING OUT
Porter's Whiting Street. ☎ 0284 706198.
Mortimer's Seafood 31 Churchgate, ☎ 0284 760623.

OUTINGS FROM BURY ST EDMUNDS

ICKWORTH HOUSE

If you think Ickworth House (National Trust) looks an odd place to live you'd be right: it was intended as a picture gallery as well as a home. It consists of a 100ft central rotunda with galleries leading to wings, and was dreamt up by Frederick Augustus Hervey (pronounced 'Harvey') in 1792. Frederick was Earl of Bristol and Bishop of Derry, and a great art collector too: you can see his paintings and fine furniture as well as the family's wonderful collection of silver. Open May to September (not Thursday or Monday except bank holidays), and weekends in April and October. It is much cheaper to visit just the grounds which offer landscaped parkland, a formal garden and miles of walking, with views of the eccentric building. Eastern Counties run a bus to nearby Horringer, then it's a 10 minute walk. There's usually no bus on Sundays, but you might find a special Sunday Rover service in summer.

SUFFOLK TOWNS AND VILLAGES

BUDGET FOR A DAY	
Explorer bus ticket	3·50
Lavenham Guildhall	1·50
Little Hall, Lavenham	1·00
Gainsborough's House, Sudbury	1·50
Melford Hall, Long Melford	2·20
Lunch	6·00
Afternoon tea	2·30
plus accommodation	£18·00

Lavenham When Henry VIII was king, this was the fourth richest town in England, with most of the population involved in weaving woollen 'blue cloth'. Then the industry went elsewhere, and Lavenham was left as if suspended in time. Now it's an extraordinary period piece, where nearly every street is lined with timber-framed houses, generally at odd angles. Chambers run a bus here from Bury St Edmunds (not Sunday). There may be a Sunday Rover bus service in summer.

Buses stop outside the Swan Inn. Rooms are quite expensive, but if you want to absorb the atmosphere try the teas; you get the works – sandwiches, rolls, scones and cakes (to the accompaniment of harpsichord music on Friday and weekends).

Suffolk grandest churches are the ones built on wealth from the medieval wool-weaving industry. The signs are tall towers, walls with 'more glass than stone', fine carving and sheer size, as at Lavenham, Long Melford and Blythburgh.

Local flavour
Look out for locally produced Suffolk ham at pubs and delicatessens in the area.

The wavy-timbered Guildhall (National Trust) has a display on the cloth industry; the neighbouring Little Hall was restored and furnished by identical twin army officers, who had travelled a lot in the Middle East – hence an exotic tendency among the objects inside. It's open on weekend afternoons, and good value. The Priory is the home of the Casey family, who have uncovered medieval wall paintings among other original features and gives an insight into the mammoth task of restoration. Open Easter to October. The Refectory Restaurant attached does good-value food all day (except Friday).

Kersey This is possibly the most picturesque spot of all, with pastel-shaded houses winding up from a ford at one end to a church at the other. Kersey cloth was a famous Suffolk product in medieval times. There's a pub, and not much else in the way of facilities. Access is not easy by bus, except when Sunday Rover services run in summer.

Sudbury Charles Dickens called Sudbury

'Eatanswill' in his *Pickwick Papers*; today he might choose something like 'Needsabypass' because the town centre traffic can be a headache. There is interesting eating though at Rafi's Spicebox – they do a monthly cookery demonstration with meal: telephone 0787 881992 for details. The place to visit is the birthplace of the artist Gainsborough (near the market place), which has several of his drawings and paintings. Closed Monday except bank holidays. The oldest part of Sudbury is by the river, where you'll find the Quay Arts Centre in a converted granary. Chambers run a bus to Sudbury: no Sunday service, but there may be a special Sunday Rover service in summer.

Moneysaver
Explorer tickets save money on a day's unlimited travel on Eastern Counties buses (Norfolk and Suffolk). Buy the ticket on the first bus you catch that day, or at an Eastern counties bus office.

Long Melford Long Melford lives up to its name – it has hardly any width, but it runs along the Bury–Sudbury road for about a mile. The lower stretch of the main street is lined with browsable antiques shops, 16th-century houses and old inns; above, it opens out into a big green, which is where the most interesting parts are. Near the top is the splendid church – all glittering glass and delicate flint and stone work.

Moneysaver
Overseas visitors can use a Heritage Card to visit Melford Hall. (See *Introduction* for details.)

Melford Hall (National Trust) is a turreted brick Tudor pile. Queen Elizabeth I (with 2,000 retainers) was entertained here in 1578; the children's author Beatrix Potter often came to stay in more recent times. This has been the home of the Parker family since 1786 – treasures inside include Chinese porcelain from a captured Spanish vessel and other reminders of the family's navy careers. Open midweek and weekend afternoons in summer, weekends only in April and October.

Further up the hill, an avenue of lime trees leads to the hidden, moated manor of Kentwell Hall. A family rescued it from oblivion in 1971, and it's open at intervals throughout the summer – ask tourist information offices, or telephone 0787 310207.

You can eat at both houses, but there's no shortage of picture-postcard inns and teashops. The Gladstone Tearooms at 4 Westgate Street offer very good value teas and light lunches.

Local flavour

Cavendish Manor has one of several vineyards in East Anglia. You can often look round free, or pay for a tour with wine tasting. Others are at Lexham Hall (near King's Lynn); Bruisyard, near Saxmundham; Boyton, Stoke-by-Clare; and Highwayman's in Risby.

Cavendish and Clare Cavendish is tiny and peaceful, with pastel-plastered houses set round a green. There's a 14th-century church, and – again – a plentiful supply of picturesque pubs. This is the unlikely setting of the Sue Ryder Foundation, a small but impressive philanthropic body. There's a salutary museum on Sue Ryder's work with Holocaust victims and others.

Clare is a busy little town with a 15th-century wool church in typically spacious style – and note the little face peering down at you in the porch. The aptly named Ancient House next door is Clare's museum, with elaborate pargeting (plaster patterns) on the outside walls, and hotchpotch of interesting things inside – open Wednesday to Saturday afternoons, and Sunday mornings. There are plenty of inns – the Bell does lunch from £5 upwards, or eat in the cosy little café behind the Ship Stores.

You get a good view of the town from the castle mound – there is no castle now, but it makes a focal point for a country park with a

nature trail and information centre.

Sunday Rover bus services run to Cavendish and Clare in summer. Otherwise the only bus is one that collects shoppers on Wednesday – it leaves Angel Hill in Bury St Edmunds at 12.15pm, goes to Cavendish and Clare and then comes straight back. It's worth considering as a round trip.

DEDHAM AND FLATFORD

Dedham Vale is the eastern end of the Stour Valley, accessible from Sudbury along minor roads with wide views. It takes skilful navigating to avoid the A12 dual carriageway however. If travelling by bus, you'll need to start at Colchester, which is worth spending time in for its Roman remains and huge castle keep – buses go back to Colchester from either side of the road, so check you're in the right place.

Dedham's wide main street has several medieval buildings, but a lot of them have 18th-century disguises. St Mary's church spire pops up in various Constable landscapes.

Dedham's other art connection is Alfred Munnings (1878-1959), whose house is now the Munnings Museum, with paintings, furniture and two studios (a mile from the church). The Dedham Centre is a former church, packed with arts and crafts shops. You can get teas and lunches here, and at the Essex Rose tearooms across the road.

It's a three-mile walk from Dedham to Flatford along the river, but much further by road. Flatford Mill belonged to Constable's father; next to it is Willy Lott's house, which appears in Constable's picture *The Haywain*. Visit early or late in the day if you want to avoid crowds, and don't expect house or mill to look exactly like Constable's pictures. Rowing boats can be hired by the hour. Car drivers will need some loose change for the large car park, a short walk away. The mill is a study centre for courses varying from watercolour painting to woodland management – no visitors are allowed. A minor road leads to East Bergholt, where Constable had a studio in what's now a private home opposite the post office.

WOODBRIDGE

Woodbridge is close to the Suffolk coast, in a landscape of winding estuaries that changes into shingle beach. It's little wonder that people get attached to this corner of East Anglia, and come back to it for their holidays year after year. The towns are small, but they're full of character, and the coast ranges from traditional seaside resorts (good for children) to creeks and inlets frequented by sea birds, yacht sailors and anglers. The immediate hinterland is quiet heathland and farmland, or sometimes conifer plantation, with small villages in between.

The Suffolk coast is popular for holidays, but the visitors tend to be self sufficient in their entertainments; this isn't a place for bright lights and nightlife. It's not entirely in a backwater, however: discerning people travel from London and further afield for Aldeburgh's annual music festival, and that's only one of many facets of the local cultural life.

Woodbridge is suggested as a base, because public transport is reasonable. If you have a car, you might prefer to make a base on the coast, perhaps at Aldeburgh or Southwold, which are both delightful seaside towns with plenty of places to stay.

Bus services are at their best in summer, when extra weekday routes are supplied. In summer you can also use the Suffolk Sunday Rover scheme, which provides lots of extra buses all over the county on Sundays. Outside summer, getting about by public transport isn't so easy. A combination of train and bicycle is feasible.

Renting a cottage or apartment for a week or two is popular on this coast – in fact the resort of Thorpeness is famed for its holiday homes. You have to book well ahead however: it's not unknown for owners to start the season fully booked. Seaside hotels and other places offering bed and breakfast are fairly plentiful, but again booking is always advisable. Booking is essential for during July and August, the Aldeburgh Festival (June) and Maltings Proms (August).

Woodbridge is four hours from London by coach and 1½ hours by rail. From Bury St Edmunds there are bus and rail connections via

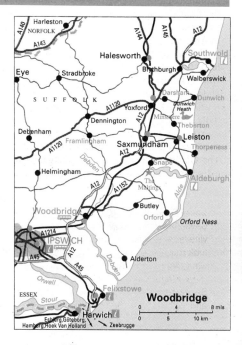

Woodbridge

Ipswich. National Express coaches run here via Stansted airport, which has international flights. Ferries for the Netherlands, Belgium, Germany and Scandinavia sail from Felixstowe and Harwich, a few miles south.

The main tourist information centre for this coast is at Felixstowe (see *Outings from Woodbridge*).

In Elizabethan times, shipbuilding, ropemaking and salt were big business in Woodbridge. Now the river's too silted up for large ships, but the water is still busy with boats. The tall, white, weather-boarded building overlooking the quay is the Woodbridge tide mill, standing where there has been a mill since 1170. This one dates from 1793. It works by catching water at high tide and releasing it slowly to power the mill machinery. It's open from mid July through August and many other times too, but working times depend on the tides. Telephone 0473 626618 for details.

The streets to explore in Woodbridge are the

medieval ways running up from the waterside. You'll find some elegant Georgian houses here, and shops catering for prosperous country and yachting people. There's a small museum at the top of the hill, and a theatre at the bottom.

Boats go over the Deben to Sutton Hoo, a group of mounds where in 1939 archaeologists found a ship 89ft long, loaded with treasure for the burial of an Anglo-Saxon king. An archaeological 'dig' is now investigating other mounds here, and finds include what seem to be the victims of executions or sacrifices. Site tours are on weekend afternoons from May to September. The Sutton Hoo treasure is in the British Museum in London, but you can see replicas in Ipswich Museum, and Woodbridge Museum also has a section on it.

Woodbridge Tide Mill of 1793 overlooks the quay.

ORIENTATION IN WOODBRIDGE

INFORMATION
TOURIST OFFICE
Felixstowe Leisure Centre, Felixstowe, IP11 8AB.
☎ *0394 276770.*

TRANSPORT
LOCAL BUSES
Buses leave from the Turban Centre, Hamblin Road. Buses for the suggested outings are Eastern Counties,
☎ *Ipswich 0473 253734.*

TRAINS
Woodbridge station, by the Quay. Information:
☎ *Ipswich 0473 690744.*
BICYCLE HIRE
Byways Bicycle Centre
Priory Farm, Darsham, near Saxmundham, Suffolk IP17 3QD, ☎ *072877 764/459*
Country Garden Nurseries
Sudbourne Hall, Orford.
☎ *0394 450733.*

ACCOMMODATION
Grove House *39 Grove Road, IP12 4LG.* ☎ *03943 2202. Bed and breakfast from £16 single, £30 double; £139 for a week with dinner.*
Oxfam B&B Scheme
☎ *03943 2740. Around £12 per person per night at various establishments in the area; a third of the bill is donated to the charity, Oxfam.*

EATING OUT
Captain's Table *3 Quay Street,* ☎ *03943 3145. Fixed price dinner around £10.50; seafood a speciality.*

OUTINGS FROM WOODBRIDGE

IPSWICH

Moneysaver
There's no charge for visiting Christchurch Mansion in Ipswich.

Ipswich is the nearest large town – if travelling by train or bus, you will have travelled through it on the way to Woodbridge. It isn't the prettiest of towns, but it does have something special in Christchurch Mansion. The mansion is an Elizabethan house, with rooms furnished in period style, and a gallery with pictures by Constable and Gainsborough – all in a beautiful park. The best introduction to the town's other sights might be to join one of the walking tours which start at the tourist information centre, on summer Tuesdays and Sunday afternoons; there's also a signed trail through the town.

FELIXTOWE

You could go on from Ipswich by train to the town of Felixstowe, an important port, but also a popular seaside resort, with 'hanging gardens' down the cliffs, clean beaches and lots of amusements. The main tourist information centre for the Suffolk coast is on the seafront. Ferries sail to Belgium from the port here.

ORFORD

Orford sits behind the shelter of Orford Ness, the shingle spit that starts at Aldeburgh and runs along the Suffolk coast. (Buses from Woodbridge run Saturday and Sunday only). Today the Ness is known and protected for wild flowers and birds, but ships have been wrecked on the seaward side, and smugglers once made use of its secluded inner waters. The ancient King's Head pub is said to have been a smugglers' haunt, but it's also worth a visit for fresh local seafood and Adnams ales (brewed up the coast at Southwold).

Overlooking the scene is the 90ft tall castle keep (English Heritage). Henry II built it because he felt threatened by Roger Bigod's mighty castle at nearby Framlingham (also English Heritage and well worth a visit).

Local flavour

The church at Orford has a font decorated with 'wodewoses', or wild men of the woods. Wodewoses are thought to be pagan in origin, but they're found on the fonts of many East Anglian churches.

Streets of pretty red brick houses go down to the quay and the end of the road. From here the *Lady Florence* sets off for a four-hour river cruise, six days a week in summer, three a week in winter. Not cheap, but a nice trip.

Local flavour

In the 12th century, legends say, local fishermen caught a merman near Orford. He was tortured in the castle to see if he would talk, but escaped and went back to the sea.

Turn right along the coast for views of Havergate Island nature reserve. The birds to look out for are graceful avocets, which bred here for the first time in 150 years when the area was flooded as a wartime defence measure. Visits are possible but have to be booked in advance.

ALDEBURGH

Aldeburgh is 45 minutes by bus. It's a seaside resort with a long history and a lot of charm. There are old cottages by the sea, and a wide main street with pubs and plenty of opportunities to browse among antiques, arts and crafts. In summer there's a booth for puppet shows on the beach, and all year round fishermen haul their boats up on the shore and sell their catch. Also on the beach is the Moot Hall (medieval meeting place). It used to be in the middle of town, which shows how much the sea has encroached on this coast.

The beach shelves steeply, but is safe for swimming. Behind it is the River Alde which almost, but not quite, reaches the sea at this point – it's cut off by the shingle bank of Orford Ness. There are lots of places to eat, from pubs to teashops and restaurants. The Aldeburgh Fish and Chip Shop in the High Street is not to be sneered at either – they cure their own salmon as well as serving traditional takeaways.

The composer Benjamin Britten was living in America when an article about the Aldeburgh poet George Crabbe made him feel that he must return to Suffolk. He founded the Aldeburgh Festival and is buried in Aldeburgh's church. The Festival now offers two weeks of excellent classical music in June. There are various venues – mostly very local, but including Bury St Edmunds. The main concert hall is Snape Maltings, outside Aldeburgh. Special transport runs from Aldeburgh to all the out-of-town venues.

You'll find three or four events a day from morning till night, including recitals, films, early music, opera and talks. Booking opens in April: write to the Aldeburgh Foundation, High Street, Aldeburgh, Suffolk IP15 5AX, telephone 0728 453543. It is followed by the festival of flowers, which takes over the local church for three days. It includes several organ and piano recitals too (all free, donations invited).

The Maltings Proms are in August, mostly at Snape Maltings concert hall, and almost every night (on one evening the Aldeburgh Carnival takes over). The range of music is very wide – Mozart, African, jazz, Schubert and cabaret could all feature. Booking opens early in July –or you could queue for standing/floor sitting space on the day. details from the Aldeburgh Foundation address above.

Moneysaver

Families of four (or groups of four people of 26 or under) can get cut price Square Deal seat tickets for some Maltings Proms concerts.

SNAPE

Snape is about six miles from Aldeburgh along the River Alde. The Maltings at Snape is the main place for the Aldeburgh Festival, but you'll find plenty of activity at other times of year. It's a group of big buildings which used to be granaries and malt kilns but now houses shops and the Pears Britten School of Music, as well as the concert hall.

Among a choice of places to eat, the little Plough and Sail pub does bar food. Beside all this is the river, winding through reed beds with paths for walkers and bird-watchers. River boats take trips along the Alde between April and October.

Snape Maltings hosts some fine musical events.

THORPENESS

Thorpeness is a couple of miles along the coast from Aldeburgh (buses run from Woodbridge on Tuesday and Thursday – it takes about 10 minutes by bus). This is a planned seaside resort, built in 1910 in mock-Tudor style with a boating lake called the Meare and a windmill – open summer weekend afternoons and every day except Monday in July and August, small charge. Look out for the 'house in the clouds' (actually a water tower). Not very much to stop for perhaps, but a real period piece. Careful beachcombers might find amber among the pebbles on the beach.

MINSMERE AND DUNWICH

Minsmere is one of the most renowned reserves of the Royal Society for the Protection of Birds, with 1,500 acres of heath and woodland, reeds and mud, and lots of birds. One of the hides is in the tree canopy to give you a close look at woodland birds, but the most famous residents at Minsmere are avocets, which are the RSPB's emblem. There's good access for pushchairs and wheelchairs too. Closed Tuesday, price £2. The nearest public transport is Darsham railway station, about four miles west.

Free public hides on Dunwich Heath overlook part of the Minsmere bird reserve. Dunwich Heath has cliffs and a beach as well as the heathland. It's run by the National Trust – you pay to park, but otherwise admission is free, and there's a shop/tearoom.

Dunwich is just north of Dunwich Heath (no buses). Stand on the cliffs here and you're looking over what was once a prosperous medieval town. Erosion has drawn it all under the sea – listen hard (it's said) and you might hear church bells ringing under the waves. The ruins of a monastery still stand on a cliff; the last church tower went under the waves in 1918. It isn't quite as romantic as it sounds – there's very big car park, and the beach café is a magnet for fish and chip eaters. The fish and chips are very good though (about £3 with tea) and the café also serves fresh-fried doughnuts.

SOUTHWOLD

This pretty little town and seaside resort is popular with families who want a good beach but don't want lots of amusement arcades and other attractions. The town's elegant look is partly due to a fire in 1659, after which Southwold was rebuilt in more spacious style around green lawns. Promenade and beach become hectic as families arrive for the summer, but Southwold isn't the sort of place that gets rowdy. In the town there's a local museum, and you may find art exhibitions. There's also a renowned brewery in the town, so a visit to one of the pubs is a must. The Sole Bay Inn is the one that always appears in pictures of the town, but the Lord Nelson is also recommended for food as well – and there's a good fish and chip shop. Walberswick Nature Reserve is about three miles' walk along the coast path.

NORWICH

When you've been travelling for many miles across East Anglia, Norwich takes you by surprise. In the midst of a very rural landscape, it's a sizeable, busy city, with a flourishing commercial life, lots of good shops, a university, theatres and things going on. At the heart of it all are medieval streets and a wonderful old cathedral, but Norwich doesn't live on its past – it's a lively and vibrant city as well as an old one.

Just east is the watery landscape of the Broads, where you can hire a boat for a day of exploring. Then there's the coastline – the east coast is known for its sandy beaches and holiday resorts, the north coast for its harbour villages and wild birds. Inland Norfolk is usually dismissed as dull – neither spectacularly flat like the Fens around Cambridge, nor pretty and rolling like Suffolk. But you might well find more local character in Norfolk towns and villages.

Norwich has several small hotels providing bed and breakfast. An alternative is to stay just outside the city on a farm. Renting a place for a week or so is popular in this area, and gives the best value if you're a travelling with a group.

On the transport side, railways take you to the Broads and the coast on journeys that are worth taking just for the views. Bus services run to most of the places mentioned, and the cycling is easy (unless you are pedalling against a strong wind).

Norwich is about three hours from London by road, just under two hours by rail. Norwich

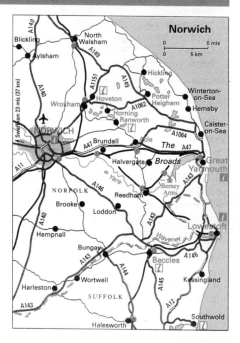

airport has flights to Paris and several other cities in mainland Europe and Britain; buses also run to Norwich from the international airport at Stansted.

Norwich is big, but it has grown around an ancient city centre. In medieval times the city was surrounded by four miles of wall, with 12 fortified gates. It also had a thriving cloth industry, but when textiles went elsewhere, Norwich found other trades. Mustard became a big business, and banking flourished too – a local bank called Gurneys combined with others to become Barclays. The medieval streets and alleys are still there, as are some 200 pubs – less than the thousand or so of Georgian days, but enough for most visitors. The University of East Anglia is on the edge of the city.

Local flavour

The Norwich firm of J J Colman is said to have made its fortune from what was left on the plate. Colman's have milled mustard for over 160 years. The Mustard Shop in Bridewell Alley stocks a wide range, and has a free museum.

The place to start looking around the city is at the market square, which is overlooked by the imposing City Hall. Along one side you'll see the grand medieval church of St Peter Mancroft, which is floodlit at night; on the other is the medieval Guildhall, now the tourist information centre. If you want an introduction, one-hour walking tours start from the Guildhall daily from late May to September, and twice a day in August. The market is a must – it's a little town in itself, with roofs of striped awnings and a mesh of alleys running between the stalls, called 'tilts', selling local fruit and vegetables, fresh fish from the coast, and all sorts of other interesting things.

Moneysaver

Some Norwich museums halve their admission fees in winter – the saving is nominal though, the summer fees are so low anyway.

Pedestrian-only streets take you towards the castle – it's a journey to linger over, because you pass some good specialist shops. The castle goes back to Norman times but was so refurbished in the last century that it looks brand new. It's now a museum and art gallery, with dungeons below which were used as a grim prison until the 1800s. The art collection is good, including

work by the 19th-century 'Norwich School' of painters, whose delicate oils and watercolours captured East Anglia's landscapes, water and sky, and the Twinings Teapot Gallery is a social history in itself.

Follow Bedford Street for Bridewell Alley, home of the Colman's Mustard Shop and Museum. The Bridewell Museum (next door) is a 14th-century merchant's house which used to be a prison but now shows Norwich trades. Elm Hill is a camera-ready cobbled street lined with timber-framed houses and shaded by trees; at the end you reach the Maid's Head Hotel, which goes back 700 years. It stands on the street called Tombland, where two great gates lead to the cathedral.

On the outside, Norwich Cathedral seems all flying buttresses and tall spire – second only in height to Salisbury Cathedral. Inside, with luck, the light will be drawing out the delicate colours in the warm stone. Ask to see the carvings under the choir stall seats if they're not already tipped up to reveal the graphic storytelling beneath. The cloisters are a must too. Free, but donations invited.

The cathedral serves cakes, light lunches and the like, in an ancient room over the cloisters. For something stronger the next port of call has to be the Adam and Eve pub, close by on Bishopsgate – it dates back to 1249 and is the oldest in Norwich.

October is the time for the Norfolk and Norwich Festival, with music, theatre, exhibitions, children's events and many others, ask for a programme from the Festival Office, St Andrew's Hall, Norwich NR3 1AU. There's also an October beer festival. You should find something going on at most times of the year however. The Theatre Royal offers a mixed bill of touring companies and touring London productions; the Maddermarket Theatre is the home of the semi-professional Guild of Norfolk Players, who do several plays a year; there's also the Puppet Theatre and the Arts Centre.

The Sainsbury Centre for Visual Arts is on the university campus (plenty of buses). Besides the permanent collection of art and sculpture, the centre has special exhibitions, including major shows from London.

ORIENTATION IN NORWICH

INFORMATION
TOURIST OFFICE
*The Guildhall, Gaol Hill,
NR2 1NF.* ☎ *0603 666071.*
POST OFFICE
Bank Plain.
PUBLIC LAVATORIES
Market Square.

TRANSPORT
BUSES
*Bus station, between Surrey
Street and Queens Road,*
about 10 minutes' walk from
city centre.
TRAINS
*Norwich (Thorpe) station, off
Thorpe Road, 10 minutes'
walk from city centre.*
CAR HIRE
Norwich Motor Company
79 Mile Cross Road.
☎ *0603 410661.*
BICYCLE HIRE
Dodgers ☎ *0603 622499.*

ACCOMMODATION
HOTEL
Marlborough House Hotel
*22 Stracey Road, Thorpe
Road, NR1 1EZ,* ☎ *0603
628005. Bed and breakfast
from £15*
FARMHOUSE
Salamanca Farm *Stoke
Holy Cross, NR14 8QJ.* ☎
*05086 2322. Bed and
breakfast from £15; 4 miles
from city.*

EATING OUT
Pinocchio *11 St Benedict
Street.* ☎ *0603 613318.
Pasta below £5, many other
dishes.*

OUTINGS FROM NORWICH

SWAFFHAM

Inland, visit Swaffham on Saturday for the long-established open market, where selling is conducted by auctioneers. The bidding makes a good free show, but you might just find a bargain in the huge array of local produce and second-hand goods. Country auctions are a popular way to buy and sell things in East Anglia. Lots range from bags of carrots to antique wardrobes, with a huge range of goods in between. If you bid, be prepared to pay in cash.

Swaffham has handsome streets from the days when prosperous Norfolk farmers had second homes here. In the church, look out for the carved figure of the Pedlar of Swaffham. The story goes that he went to London to seek his fortune – only to be told about someone's dream of a great treasure, hidden in the garden of a pedlar in Swaffham. The real person behind the story was John Chapman, who used his wealth to repair the church.

THE BROADS

The Broads are the watery landscape between Norwich and the sea. This is a place of marsh and lakes linked by five rivers, making about

BUDGET FOR A DAY	
Explorer bus ticket	3·50
One hour rowing boat hire	3·00
Berney Arms Windpump	·85
Hickling Broad Nature Reserve	2·00
Lunch	3·00
Dinner	7·00
plus accommodation	£19·35

125 miles of navigable waterway, with no locks. It all looks natural, but is actually a by-product of digging for peat in the Middle Ages. The Norfolk Broads have rare butterflies and birds· which have died out in other parts of Britain. The popular way to see it is by boat – there's a big choice of cruises and rental boats. There are also quiet lanes between waterways, and the landscape is easy on cyclists. Trains run to some areas that roads can't reach.

The tourist information centre at Norwich has information on the Broads, and from Easter to September there are Broads information centres at Hoveton, Ranworth and Beccles.

If you want to rent a motor cruiser for a few days, the main firms are Blakes Holidays Ltd, Wroxham, Norwich NR12 8DH and Hoseasons Holidays Ltd, B13 Sunway House, Lowestoft,

Suffolk NR32 3LT. The cost ranges from around £35 a day.

Water tours start from Horning on the Mississippi River Boat, telephone 0692 630262. Visit in summer for river races.

Moneysaver

Rent a rowing boat rather than a fuel-powered boat – it costs less and is better for the delicate environment of the Broads.

Local flavour

Norfolk reed is reputed to be the best material for thatching. It is still grown and harvested on the Broads.

Berney Arms can't be reached by road: you get there by boat, or by train from Norwich (£3.50 cheap day return). Berney Arms wind pump is the tallest marsh pump on the Broads. Climb the seven floors for a huge views: open Easter or April to September. There are more than 70 windmills and wind pumps on the Broads, and many of them can be visited. The wind pumps were used for draining the land and controlling the water level. Fuel-powered and electric pumps do the job now.

Hickling has boats for rent at the Whispering Reeds Boatyard. Hickling Broad is a nature reserve, about 1½ miles walk from Hickling. The reserve is open all year except for Tuesday, and it costs less to visit in winter. Paths lead through it and there are hides for bird-watching. In summer you can also book at the reserve for a nature tour on a reed-harvesting boat, including visits to hides. Telephone the reserve warden 069261 276 for details.

GREAT YARMOUTH

Great Yarmouth is East Anglia's biggest and busiest holiday resort. By train it's half an hour from Norwich; by bus it's an hour and 20 minutes.

The best free thing is the beach, which is wide, sandy and very long. The two piers have entertainments all summer, and you'll probably find a Punch and Judy show on the sand as well. If the weather's really bad, you can escape from it at the huge Marina Centre, which has artificial beaches and waves, plus summer entertainment. Great Yarmouth Pleasure Beach has around 70 rides and amusements, and lots of fast food places to keep you going. It's open on Sundays and bank holidays in April and May, and then daily from late May to late September. Admission is free, but for the rides you need from one to four tokens.

Attached to all this is a town with a long history. The Maritime Museum on Marine Parade tells the story, right up to todays North Sea oil and gas industries (closed on Saturdays). Merchants used to live in the old houses along South Quay; one of them is open to the public as the Elizabethan House Museum (closed Saturday). English Heritage owns an assortment of properties in the narrow 'Rows' behind: you can see them all on one ticket from April to October.

Best views inland and out to sea are from Nelson's Monument on the South Beach Parade, which commemorates the Battle of Trafalgar in 1805. The 217 steps take you 144 feet to the top. Open July and August afternoons (not Saturday), and on Trafalgar Day (21 October).

LOWESTOFT

Lowestoft has the Pleasurewood Hills American Theme Park – not exactly cheap, but once you're in all the amusements are free. It's open from mid May to late September, and some other weekends. Lowestoft also offers the five-mile South Beach, which has won a European Blue Flag award for cleanliness – you'll find piers, boating lakes and many other seaside amusements on this side of town, but more shops on the north side. In between is the harbour. From Norwich it's 45 minutes by train, 1½ hours by bus.

The tourist information centre at Lowestoft arranges 'fishing industry' tours three times a week in summer. Tours last about two hours and include a look at a trawler and a visit to the fish market (not usually open to the public). Tickets are £1.15; booking is essential.

Walk north along the sea wall to reach Lowestoft Ness, which is Britain's most easterly point. It's an easy stroll from central Lowestoft, and there's no charge.

THE NORTH NORFOLK COAST

Cromer was a fishing village which mushroomed into a seaside resort in Victorian times. The old fishing village streets are still there, and fishing boats are still hauled up on the beach. There are lots of seaside amusements, including a pier with pier theatre. Cromer has had a lifeboat since 1804 – no charge for seeing the present vessel in the lifeboat house, but donations are invited. It takes 45 minutes to reach Cromer by rail; a little further on is Sheringham, another resort which sprouted from a fishing village.

Local flavour
Cromer crabs are reputed to be especially tasty. Fishermen sell them on the beach, and they're served all over town. Whelks are the speciality of Wells-next-the-Sea, where you may also find fresh shrimps. Stewkey Blues are cockles, named after nearby Stiffkey (always pronounced 'stewkey').

BLICKLING HALL AND FELBRIGG HALL

Norfolk has some very grand historic houses, but they're not easy to reach by public transport. Blickling Hall is a wonderful combination of warm red brick and huge yew hedges. The nearest buses run to Aylsham, 1½ miles away along a main road (45 minutes). In the house you can admire tapestries and ornate plasterwork; outside are formal gardens and an orangery. The house is open late March to late October afternoons (not Thursday or Monday except bank holidays); the gardens are open daily in July and August, National Trust. Felbrigg Hall is a couple of miles from Cromer, and is special for its 18th-century grandeur. There's also a walled garden restored in traditional style. Open from late March to October in the afternoon (closed Tuesday and Friday), National Trust.

Moneysaver
The parks at Blickling and Felbrigg are always open for woodland and lakeside walks (no charge, except for parking). To visit just the gardens costs much less than the full admission charge.

WEST NORFOLK

King's Lynn The main town in west Norfolk, King's Lynn (1½ hours by bus), has been a port for as long as anyone knows and has medieval streets and lots of elegant 17th-century

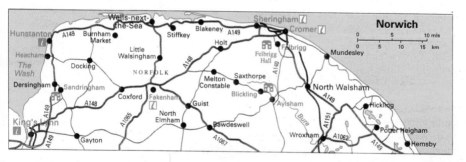

buildings. The best day to visit is Tuesday, for the market which has been held since 1146 on a spot surrounded by handsome old buildings. There's a tradition that William Shakespeare and his band of travelling players put on a show at St George's Guildhall (National Trust). It's used once again as a theatre today, and makes a focal point for the King's Lynn Festival, telephone 0553 773578 for details.

Chenery Travel does coach excursions from Norwich to this side of Norfolk: details from 20A Castle Meadow, Norwich NR1 3DH, telephone 0603 630676, or ask tourist information centres.

Moneysaver

There's no charge for visiting the country park at Sandringham, open late April to September every day for walks and a picnic area. Admission to Norfolk Lavender at Heacham is free as well.

Sandringham A few miles up the road is Sandringham, which has been a royal second home since Queen Victoria bought it for the Prince of Wales in 1862. The house and landscaped gardens are open from late April to September, except when the royal family is there – the house closes for three weeks between mid July and mid August, and the grounds close for several days in the same period. Just outside the grounds is the church of St Mary Magdalene, which is packed with precious gifts from royalty, including a silver altar. Chenery Travel do a tour to Sandringham from Norwich, taking in Hunstanton, or there's a bus from King's Lynn.

Norfolk Lavender At Caley Mill, Heacham, is Britain's biggest lavender farm and distillery. The grounds are open all year, but the most fragrant time to visit is usually from early July to mid August (earlier in a hot, dry summer). There's also a tearoom here, and a shop selling lavender-based soaps, scents and other gifts. Chenery Travel do a tour from Norwich, which takes in Sandringham and Hunstanton; or catch the bus from King's Lynn. Just north is Hunstanton, the only resort in Norfolk where you can watch the sun set over the sea. It's also special because of its boldly striped red and white cliffs.

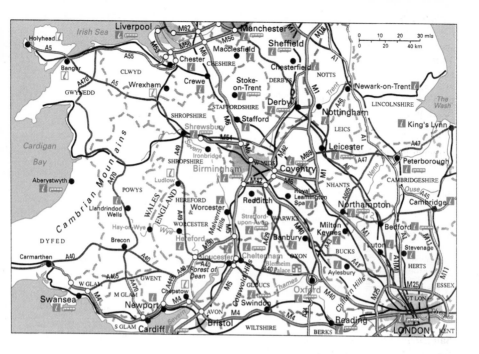

The tourist board calls most of this region the 'Heart of England', which sounds trite but catches the rural, traditional spirit of the region. The main centres include Oxford and Stratford-upon-Avon, which rank among England's best known towns, and some of its most photographed villages, in the Cotswold Hills. The next stages of the tour are through the Marches, the land of hills and rivers, market towns and traditional farms along the border with Wales.

Oxford is the home of an ancient university. It's a beautiful and also a very lively city, with music, plays and other cultural activities open to visitors. In Stratford-upon-Avon, known all over the world as Shakespeare's birthplace, you can visit several places linked with Shakespeare's life and family, and then take in a play at the Royal Shakespeare Theatre.

The handsome spa town of Cheltenham is a handy base for exploring the Cotswold Hills, where the honey-and-gold colours of the local stone make for enchanting towns and villages. • Hereford, a cathedral city and market town for a

big rural region, is the start of the Marches. From here onwards you'll see some quite remarkable timber-framed buildings, known in these parts as 'black-and-white' or 'magpie' style. Hereford is also a base for exploring the steep, gorgeous valley of the River Wye, the Malvern Hills or the quiet valleys towards the Welsh border.

> **Local flavour**
>
> Shakespeare isn't the only literary figure of this region. Others include the Dymock poets, including Robert Frost and Rupert Brooke (see *Hereford*); and Arnold Bennett, whose 'Five Towns' were the Potteries. Shropshire was the inspiration of A E Housman and Mary Webb.

Shrewsbury is noted for steep streets, black-and-white buildings and narrow alleys in between. The hills around Shropshire offer wonderful walks, and like Hereford it's in reach of some very peaceful places. Outings range

137

An example of local black and white architecture.

from the handsome little town of Ludlow, to the industrial museums at Ironbridge, to the big, busy urban sprawl of the Potteries, with dozens of china shops and factories to visit.

Oxford and Stratford are popular all year round, but they're especially busy in summer. The Cotswolds and Wye Valley are major tourist attractions too, but popularity means that visitors are well catered for. Gardens in the Cotswold villages should be full of flowers in May, the apple orchards around Hereford are prettiest in spring and have fruit for sale in October; and the leaf colour in the Wye Valley in October can be spectacular. All the towns in this chapter are regional centres or market towns with reasonable bus links to the outside world. You can get to most of the places suggested for outings by bus or train, although you may want independent transport to explore the surrounding rural landscapes.

Bed and breakfast accommodation is plentiful in most of the towns – Hereford and Shrewsbury have less than the others, but they have fewer tourists. You can usually choose between staying in town or on a farm just outside – good for local colour, but you'll need independent transport.

Moneysaver

Bed and breakfast prices may be lower out of the peak season and for stays of more than a couple of days. Self catering will usually be the cheapest option for families and other groups, but has to be booked well ahead.

The Marches are border country, with a string of castles dating from the medieval days of open warfare, and smaller historic houses – some are mentioned here, but there are many others which can be visited. There are prehistoric sites to seek out too, easiest with independent transport and Ordnance Survey maps. From Oxford visit Blenheim Palace, one of the stateliest of stately homes.

Try to time your visits to towns for market days, for the best atmosphere as well as for bargains. This is traditional farming country, and if you're catering for yourself there's some fine local produce to look out for – organically grown vegetables, traditionally reared meat, and local specialities such as Herefordshire cider and double Gloucester cheese. At the other extreme, Birmingham (see *Stratford-upon-Avon*) has a huge shopping centre, and big markets.

Oxford and Cheltenham are your best bet for snazzy stores and window shopping; Oxford also has the fine bookshops you'd expect of England's oldest university city. Bookshops and second-hand bookshops abound elsewhere – see *Hereford* for Hay-on-Wye, the town of second-hand bookshops on the Welsh border. See *Shrewsbury* for the Potteries, the home of numerous pottery factories, including famous names such as Wedgwood, Royal Doulton and Minton, and see *Hereford* for Worcester, home of Royal Worcester porcelain.

Moneysaver

Seconds and remaindered lines are sold at reduced prices in several shops in the Potteries. This is a good region for second-hand bookshops too.

Some of the best events to attend for local colour are county shows, with prize cattle and sheep alongside the latest in agricultural machinery, ploughing matches, craft stalls, show jumping and home produce competitions. Local village festivals are always worth a pause, and in summer look out for private gardens opened up to visitors for a day.

For advance information on all aspects of the

region, write to the regional tourist boards: most of the places in this chapter come within the area of the Heart of England Tourist Board, 2/4 Trinity Street, Worcester WR1 2PW, telephone 0905 29512; for Oxford it's the Thames and Chilterns Tourist Board, The Mount House, Witney, Oxfordshire OX8 8DZ, telephone 0993 778800.

OXFORD

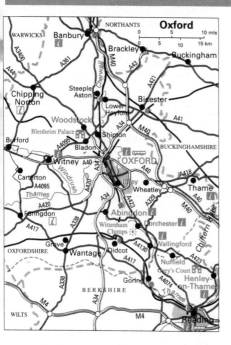

This is the 'city of dreaming spires', celebrated in poems and novels, films and plays. Oxford University is England's oldest and has a series of wonderfully ancient colleges, linked by winding, equally ancient lanes. Whichever way you arrive at Oxford, by road or rail, you really do see a skyline pierced by spires and pinnacles, although they're interspersed with less romantic buildings – Oxford is a sizeable city, with a commercial and industrial life of its own apart from the university. The combination makes for a lively atmosphere and for crowds – the High Street gets packed with traffic and people – but you need only walk a few yards to be in empty and beautiful old streets.

Oxford University wasn't formally founded – it was just a place where teachers and students met. The first college was Merton, built in the late 1200s, with chapel, dining room and accommodation in a quadrangle with a gate that was closed at night – which became the pattern for all later colleges.

The old college and university buildings are the main but not the only attraction: Oxford also has some extra special museums, and other things that really shouldn't be missed are the Botanic Garden, college gardens and parks, and the rivers Cherwell and Thames (called Isis here), for boat rides or walks. Then there are the stylish shops, the market, the Oxford Canal, memorable old pubs, and lots of theatre and music.

Drivers visiting for the day can avoid city centre traffic by using the park-and-ride service – free parking outside the centre, with fast, frequent transport into town (60p return). Park-and-ride car parks are signposted from the ring road round Oxford.

Local flavour
Frank Cooper began selling his wife's homemade marmalade at 84 High Street in 1874. The firm has bought the premises in recent years, and Cooper's excellent marmalade is on sale there once again. Senior citizens and students with cards get a discount.

For getting around Oxford, use buses, walk, or cycle as the locals and the university people do – Oxford is a city of cyclists, with a network of marked cycle routes. Cycling is a good way to see the surrounding scenery too, with plenty of quiet lanes linking the villages. For less energetic exploring, a car would be useful but isn't essential: buses take you to Blenheim and into the Chilterns, and there's a pretty train route through the Cotswolds.

There's a lot of bed and breakfast accommodation on the main roads out of town, but it isn't particularly cheap. For details of cottages, houses and apartments to rent, ask the tourist information centre. These should be booked well ahead, though it's always worth asking about cancellations.

Oxford is about an hour from London (Paddington station) by rail, a little over 1½ hours by coach. There are also fast, non-stop services from London Heathrow and Gatwick airports.

The magnificent Radcliffe Camera.

A useful starting point in Oxford is Carfax, which is the city's central crossroads. It's in reasonable walking distance of the bus and train stations, and most buses run this way. Carfax Tower is all that's left of a church which was knocked down to make way for traffic: climb up for an all-round city view (closed Sunday). The clock on the tower provides a free show each quarter hour, when the figures strike the time.

The main tourist information centre is close by on St Aldate's. Two-hour walking tours with official guides start here every day, up to five times a day in summer. You may also find non-official, alternative walking tours advertised. The other way to get an overview of Oxford is to take a Guide Friday open-topped bus tour: tour buses start every 15 minutes, every day, and a day ticket lets you get on and off at stops all round the city. The Oxford Classic Tour offers a similar service, April to October.

You can experience the Oxford Story on Broad Street, where you get carried through scenes of the past – but the real Oxford streets are so atmospheric that you may feel this is superfluous. The heart of the university is a series of beautiful buildings between Broad Street and The High, in easy walking distance of Carfax. They're in use and can't all be visited, but the outsides and the settings are unforgettable. The Radcliffe Camera (not open) is a great domed drum of a building, used as a reading room for the Bodleian Library, the university library, named after Sir Thomas Bodley who reorganised it in 1598. He arranged for it to receive a copy of every book published in Britain, which it still does. Part of the Bodleian is in Old Schools Quadrangle, where the Divinity School has an exhibition of treasures from the library's vast horde (admission free; closed Saturday afternoon and Sunday). Buy tickets here for guided tours of Duke Humfrey's Library, the original university library, founded in 1439 (mid March to October, price £2).

The Sheldonian Theatre was designed by Sir Christopher Wren in the 1660s as a place for university meetings and ceremonies, which it still is. This is another wonderful building, and another place to climb up for a good city view (closed Sunday). On the corner of Holywell Street is the King's Arms pub, which is big but full of character, and a favourite with students. Or take the alleyway between Holywell Street and New College Lane to reach the Turf Tavern; dating back to the 13th century, it's full of atmosphere, with extra tables outside in a leafy courtyard.

Required Oxford reading if you can find it is Max Beerbohm's *Zuleika Dobson*, published in 1911. It's an absurd but enthralling story which also gives a colourful picture of Oxford life.

The Oxford colleges are usually open from about 2pm to 5pm. To find them you have to root around a bit, but there's a rich cluster near the Radcliffe Camera. New College was new in 1379 – visit the beautiful old buildings and gardens by day, but come back in the evening to hear the choir in the chapel (service times are given at the gate). People live and work in the Oxford colleges, and visitors are asked to respect their privacy and peace. And spare a thought for nervous-looking students wearing gowns in early summer. They're probably on their way to take exams, for which full academic dress is required.

Moneysaver

Some colleges make a charge for visitors in the summer vacation, otherwise admission to most of them is free. There's no charge for the Botanic Garden or the various parks and meadows around the city.

Exeter College chapel has pre-Raphaelite tapestries, designed by Burne Jones and made by William Morris who was a student here. Further down The High is Magdalen (say 'mordlin'), easy to identify by its tower. The college choir greets summer by singing from the top at 6am on May Day. This is arguably the prettiest college, and can be visited in the afternoons.

A cobbled lane behind The High leads to Merton College, with the oldest buildings of all, next to imposing Christ Church College. Visitors enter from Christ Church Meadow – an admission fee lets you see the portrait collection in the hall, and the medieval chapel, which is also Oxford's cathedral. You pay less if hall or chapel are closed. The main gate is on the other side, with the landmark of Tom Tower above – it houses a bell called Great Tom, tolled 101 times at 9.05pm (originally a signal to 101 students that the gate was closing). The Christ Church Picture Gallery is reached from Oriel Square. Don't forget the college gardens, which are often enchanting, or the 1621 Botanic Garden – best of all early in the morning (it opens at 8.30am).

Local flavour

A Christ Church mathematician called Charles Dodgson is better known as Lewis Carroll, his pen name as author of *Alice in Wonderland*. The book began as a story told to a child called Alice Liddell.

Oxford's museums are special too. The Ashmolean began in 1677 as a home for curiosities collected by John Tradescant and inherited by Elias Ashmole – it's now a real treasure house with a big Oriental section.

(closed Mondays, free). The University Museum has dinosaur skeletons and other natural history exhibits, and is worth a visit just for the building. Next door the Pitt Rivers Museum is filled with masks and other exotic artefacts from round the world (both open Monday to Saturday afternoons, admission free). Among other places, the Museum of Modern Art's exhibitions are worth checking out; and the Museum of Oxford reminds you about non-university aspects of Oxford, such as its car industry (admission free; both are closed on Monday).

You can take a boat on the river from Cherwell Boathouse (Bardwell Road, north of the centre), Magdalen Bridge (down a slope by Magdalen) or Folly Bridge (south of the centre). The romantic option is one of the long, flat-bottomed punts, propelled and steered by pushing a pole into the riverbed. Don't push too hard, or your pole may get stuck – if it does, let go and paddle back to fetch it. Pole from the front (not the back, as in Cambridge), and leave yourself enough energy for the return journey.

On Wednesday there's an open air market at Gloucester Green; along Little Clarendon Street you'll find stores selling imported crafts and all sorts of other enticing things. Oxford's antique shops include a cluster at the Oxford Antiques Centre, best known as the Jam Factory, because that's what the building used to be (it's in Park End Street, by the station). Oxford is a shopping centre for the region, so it also has all the main British high street stores, as well as a classy souvenir shops such as the Oxford Collection, with gifts based on Oxford motifs.

Main events include the river races, known as 'Torpids' in February and 'Eights' in May. In September the wide street called St Giles is taken over by St Giles Fair. For details of events and entertainments all year see the *Daily Information* sheet, *What's On in Oxford* (monthly), the local press, and handbills proffered on the street. Or ring the recorded events information service on 0865 244888. Venues range from the Apollo Theatre (big shows, from touring opera to television comedians) to college gardens for open air theatre and concerts in summer (wonderful for atmosphere, and ticket prices start low). There are concerts at the Sheldonian Theatre and the Holywell Music Room; the Burton-Taylor Theatre has student productions and touring shows; the Pegasus is worth checking for offbeat shows; and the Old Fire Station arts centre has exhibitions and events.

ORIENTATION IN OXFORD

INFORMATION
Tourist Office
St Aldate's.
☎ *0865 726871.*
Post Office
St Aldate's.
Public Lavatories
Market Street bus station;
Blue Boar Street.

TRANSPORT
Local Buses
Gloucester Green. Most of the suggested outings are on Oxford Bus Company routes, for information ☎ *0865 711312, or ask at the tourist office.*
Long-distance Buses/Coaches
Long-distance coaches (to London etc) also leave from
Gloucester Green.
Trains
Oxford station, about 15 minutes walk west of the city centre. For information
☎ *0865 722333.*
Car Hire
J D Barclay Barclay House, Botley Road. ☎ *0865 722444.*
Bicycle Hire
Both of these firms have bicycles for around £5 a day, £30 a week.
Dentons 249 Banbury Road, Summertown. ☎ *0865 53859.*
Thakes 55 Walton Street. ☎ *0865 516122.*

ACCOMMODATION
Hotels
Cotswold House 363 Banbury Road. ☎ *0865 310558. Exceptional quality - bed and breakfast from £44 double.*
Green Gables 326 Abingdon Road. ☎ *0865 725870. Bed and breakfast from £30 double.*
Youth Hostel
Oxford Youth Hostel 32 Jack Straw's Lane. ☎ *0865 62997.*
Camp Site
Oxford Camping International 462 Abingdon Road. ☎ *0865 246551.*

EATING OUT
Both these pubs do meals for less than about £5
King's Arms Holywell Street.
Turf Tavern Between Holywell Street and New College Lane.

OUTINGS FROM OXFORD

WATERSIDE WALKS

Waterside walks start close to the city centre. Paths by the River Cherwell can be joined from Magdalen deer park and the University Parks. Walton Well Road on the west side of Oxford leads to Port Meadow, a wide pasture by the Thames: follow the river for the Perch pub, or the Trout, a bit further on. (Beware mud on all routes, but especially this one – Port Meadow is a flood plain, and may be a lake after heavy rain.) Join the towpath on the south side of the Thames/Isis at Folley Bridge for a walk to Iffley Lock – this is the stretch where the river races take place. Salter's river cruises start at Folly Bridge, from mid May to September. A two-hour boat trip takes you to the picturesque old town of Abingdon.

Further down river is Wallingford, an old market town with lots of Georgian buildings and the remains of a Norman castle. Walks can be taken from here along the River Thames. Henley-on-Thames is best known for its July regatta, with international rowing races and much drinking of champagne. Henley is worth visiting at any time, however, for its handsome streets, old inns and riverside setting.

Moneysaver
The Compass bus ticket gives a day's unlimited travel on Oxford Bus Company routes, including Citylink services.

If you're travelling this way by car, and if it's a Monday, Wednesday or Friday afternoon between April and September, go three miles west to Grey's Court, a mellow Jacobean house with medieval remains. The gardens are beautiful too, and they're open every afternoon except Sunday in the same months (National Trust).

WOODSTOCK AND BLENHEIM PALACE

BUDGET FOR A DAY	
Bus fare from Oxford	1·25
Blenheim Palace	4·90
Oxford County Museum	Free
Lunch	3·50
Dinner	8·00
	£17·65

plus accommodation

Local flavour
The Blenheim Orange apple variety was first grown in Woodstock.

Blenheim Palace is in the higher Cotswold hills. To get there, go first to Woodstock – there are several buses to choose from, including the X90 which gets you there in 14 minutes. You can alight at the park gates, but Woodstock is worth

a look too. It's a handsome little stone-built town, with old inns and tearooms, including a popular one called the Blenheim. There are some expensive little shops, and the Oxford County Museum is also in the town, with five-hole stocks outside (closed Monday; admission free). It has a garden where plays are sometimes performed in summer.

Blenheim Palace is beyond the Blenheim tearooms – the street takes you to a mighty gate, where you suddenly get a view of unreal perfection, taking in lake, parkland and golden-stoned house. It was started in 1705, as a reward for the first Duke of Marlborough's victory at Blenheim on the River Danube in 1704, and looks across the lake to the 134ft Column of Victory. The present-day Duke and Duchess of Marlborough still live in the house for much of the year. It's on a grand scale inside, with an entrance hall like a cathedral and lots of elaborate 18th-century furniture, porcelain and other treasures on show. One of the greatest attractions is a relatively modest room however: it was the birthplace on 30 November 1874 of Sir Winston Churchill, grandson of the seventh Duke of Marlborough.

Outside are the lake and Grand Cascade, ultra formal Italian gardens and water terraces, but you'll also find an adventure play area, butterfly house, garden centre and miniature railway rides, plus a range of restaurants. The palace is open from mid March to October; the park is open all year.

Sir Winston Churchill is buried in the church at Bladon, on the edge of the park, about 1½ mile's walk from Blenheim Palace.

STRATFORD-UPON-AVON

William Shakespeare was born in this small Warwickshire town in 1564, and made it one of the world's most famous places. People travel from all over the world to trace his life, and to see his plays at the Royal Shakespeare Theatre.

Despite all the attention, Stratford has kept its character as an old market town that existed long before Shakespeare was born. It's easiest to appreciate outside the May to September peak season, or in the early morning and

evening, after the crowds have gone. Those who stay a few days can explore a seemingly timeless corner of England, with cattle grazing in peaceful meadows beside the River Avon.

There are a lot of bed and breakfast places on the main roads into town, and farmhouses offer bed and breakfast near by. In summer and at weekends all year, it can be hard to find accommodation in a 10-mile radius of Stratford, so book ahead.

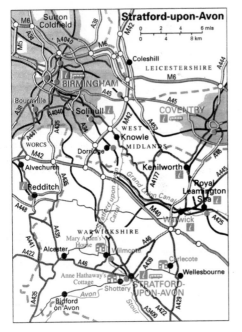

Stratford-upon-Avon is 40 minutes from Oxford by bus. (It's 2½ to three hours from London by train, change at Leamington.) Guide Friday operates a fast rail/road link: just over an hour to Coventry by train, then 35 minutes to Stratford by bus, with a late service back for theatre-goers.

If Shakespeare came back to Stratford-upon-Avon today, he would recognise quite a few of the buildings, and might even be able to find his way around. It's still a small-scale country town, as it was in his day. Guided walks are twice a week in summer, Sundays only in winter, price £1.50: details from the tourist information centre, once the house of Shakespeare's daughter Judith.

Clopton Bridge is said to give the best view of the town. There are small specialist shops for browsing, including an arcade of antiques stores, and plenty of places to pause for coffee. Stratford has a lot of reasonably priced restaurants too – Sheep Street is a good place to look. On Friday there are market stalls in Rother Street, and there's also a Tuesday cattle market.

One building that Shakespeare wouldn't

recognise is the Royal Shakespeare Theatre (RST): it was built in 1932, and stands a little apart, beside the river. This is where the Royal Shakespeare Company (RSC) puts on an intensive schedule of his plays, plus other works, old and new. Despite chronic financial troubles, the company remains one of the best in the world. The smaller Swan is behind the main theatre. For advance booking, write to the RST, Stratford-upon-Avon, CV37 6BB. Outside the summer peak period and weekends, you may not need to book. A limited number of standing and rear circle tickets are always sold on the day of performance.

Moneysaver
Students, senior citizens and some others can buy any unsold tickets at a reduced price just before curtain up. Families qualify for cut-price tickets for some matinées. In the January Armchair Proms, 200 stalls seats are sold at a very reasonable price to personal callers on the mornings of performances.

The RSC Collection has hundreds of props, costumes and other items and backstage tours include the Collection: telephone 0789 296655.

The Shakespeare Birthplace Trust looks after five buildings associated with his life and family. The house where Shakespeare was born is open daily; the others are closed on Sundays from late October to late March. Three of them can be seen on an easy stroll across the town centre: you save about £1 with a joint ticket from

Stratford and Shakespeare are synonymous.

the Birthplace if you buy the 30p town trail.

Shakespeare's Birthplace in Henley Street has attracted literary pilgrims since not long after his death. Admission includes the exhibition of costumes from BBC Shakespeare productions. His last home was New Place, which he bought in 1597. The house has gone, but a knot garden marks the site. It's reached through Nash's Place, home of Shakespeare's granddaughter and now a local history museum. The façade has been rebuilt, but the interior is Tudor. Along the street is Hall's Croft, the handsome home of Shakespeare's daughter Susanna, with a walled garden behind.

A footpath takes you just over a mile to Shottery for Anne Hathaway's Cottage, in a delightful setting. The last of the Shakespeare Trust properties is Mary Arden's House, which was Shakespeare's mother's family home. It lies three miles out of town at Wilmcote, and is a sizeable 16th-century farmhouse. It has a stone dovecote and its original barns and stables – now a rural life museum. It's five minutes by train to Wilmcote, or buy a day ticket for one of the Guide Friday tour buses, which take in all the Shakespeare places.

Charlecote Park is a gabled Elizabethan mansion, built for the Lucy family who had lived at Charlecote since 1247. It stands in a beautiful park, grazed by deer and sheep. Open April to October, closed Thursday and Monday except bank holidays (National Trust, 30 minutes by bus).

Shakespeare is said to have been caught poaching deer in Charlecote Park – hence his move to London, where he became an actor and then a playwright. There's no hard evidence for the poaching story however.

Shakespeare's tomb is at Holy Trinity Church, in the town near Hall's Croft: it's one of a line of plain Shakespeare stones in front of the altar, a donation is suggested. The Teddy Bear Museum has bears: large, small, mechanical and musical, bears of the famous and famous bears. There's also a shop.

Harvard House in the High Street is named after the grandfather of John Harvard, founder of the American university.

ORIENTATION IN STRATFORD-UPON-AVON

INFORMATION
Tourist Office
1 High Street. ☎ *0789 293127.*
Post Office
Bridge Street.
Public Lavatories
Waterside; Bridgeway car park; Fountain Way car park; by Tramway Bridge.

TRANSPORT
Buses
There is no bus station in Stratford; services by Stratford Blue and Midland Red, for information ☎ *0788 535555.*
Trains
Train station off Alcester Road, 10 minutes' walk west of the town centre. For information ☎ *Rugby train station, 0788 560116.*
Car Hire
Avis at the railway station. ☎ *0789 415000.*
Bicycle Hire
Clarke's Esso filling station,
Birmingham Road. ☎ *0789 2005507. £4.50 a day, £20 a week, plus deposit. Book in advance in summer.*

ACCOMMODATION
Youth Hostel
Stratford Youth Hostel
Hemingford House, Alveston. ☎ *0789 279093.*
Camp Site
Island Meadow Caravan Park *The Mill House, Aston Cantlow, 6 miles north off A34.* ☎ *0789 488273.*

OUTINGS FROM STRATFORD-UPON-AVON

WARWICK

Warwick Castle was rebuilt in the 14th century and lived in over the next 600 years. It's a rambling pile with towers and ramparts, dungeons and sumptuous interiors. Twelve rooms now have a Madame Tussaud's display, re-creating 'A Royal Weekend Party – 1898'. The grounds run by the river, with roses, woodland and a formal area, and you'll probably come across peacocks. It's near the centre of Warwick town, which has picturesque streets with lots of antiques shops and other specialist stores. There's also a fine church with banners of the Warwickshire regiment, and a doll museum at Oken's House (15 minutes by bus).

BIRMINGHAM

Birmingham is a shock if you've got used to compact little towns such as Stratford (an hour by bus). It's huge, crowded and confusing, with motorways carved through it and a disorientating covered area for pedestrians in the city centre. But if you like cities, then you'll probably enjoy its scale and its cultural life.

Local flavour
Cadbury's chocolate comes from Birmingham. Bournville is a model village, built for company workers. Cadbury World visitor centre has been built on the site of the old factory. Open every day (afternoons only on Sundays).

Moneysaver
Tickets for the Birmingham Rep cost more for Friday and Saturday evenings than for other evenings and all matinées.

You could start by picking up a map from the tourist information centre, at City Arcade, Union Street, near New Street train station. Once there you're in easy reach of the 18th-century cathedral, and of the Museum and Art Gallery, one of the best outside London. Famous actors and actresses have learned their craft with the Birmingham Repertory Theatre (the 'Birmingham Rep'); and its neighbours are the City of Birmingham Symphony Orchestra (CBSO) at the Symphony Hall. The music produced under the conductorship of Simon Rattle makes CBSO concerts a special experience, but you'll also be able to hear visiting musicians of all sorts here. The Birmingham Royal Ballet is the former Sadlers Wells Ballet, which moved to the city in 1990.

COVENTRY

Coventry has been rebuilt from the wartime ruins of a much older town (an hour by bus). The main thing to see is the dramatic new cathedral designed by Sir Basil Spence, with the bombed shell of its predecessor as a forecourt (free but donation suggested). A modern pedestrian shopping precinct fills a good deal of the city centre, with signposts to the handful of medieval buildings still standing. There is no charge for the Herbert Art Gallery and Museum, or the medieval guildhall. The British Museum of Road Transport has over 400 cars, motorbikes and other vehicles: open all year, but only Friday to Sunday from Christmas to Easter.

CHELTENHAM

At Cheltenham you're right on the edge of the Cotswold Hills, a limestone landscape strung through with old stone villages and towns. Cheltenham itself is a spa town, with flower-filled parks and gardens among its elegant Regency streets. If you're a horse racing enthusiast, the time to be here is March, when huge crowds arrive for the National Hunt Festival. Other big events are the International Festival of Music in July, and the Cheltenham Festival of Literature in October.

Just a few miles away is the larger city of Gloucester, which has a fine cathedral and some fascinating old corners. But the big attraction is the Cotswolds Hills, which rise in spectacular style close to town – Cheltenham is just below Cleeve Hill, their highest point. The hilltops are bleak and windswept: the charm is mainly in the valleys, where the towns and villages might have been created just to feature on calendars and postcards.

Cottage gardens, winding lanes and a

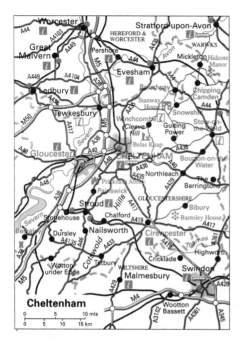

Cheltenham

crusting of lichen on old walls and roofs all add up to a lot of charm – and a lot of popularity. Brace yourself for crowds at any time, but especially in summer. Or make a point of avoiding all the places people say you should see, and use a map to devise your own routes by car or bicycle.

Public transport to surrounding towns is adequate, with a railway running through and buses radiating in all directions.

There are numerous bed and breakfast places in the town – some in the centre, but more on the main roads out. Shurdington Road has quite a few. Booking is advisable at any time of year, but especially in summer, the festival fortnight in October, and most of all for the National Hunt Festival in March. The Cotswolds have some idyllic cottages to rent for a week or more.

Cheltenham is an hour from Stratford-upon-Avon by bus. Buses also run from London Heathrow airport.

Cheltenham's career as a spa began in 1716 when some pigeons were seen pecking at what proved to be salt crystals formed by a spring. Visitors began arriving for the mineral-rich

water, and George III ensured Cheltenham's popularity by spending several weeks there in 1788. Stuccoed terraces in classical style, canopied balconies and delicate wrought iron work are all characteristic of Cheltenham's Regency streets.

Local flavour

Cheltenham has five public (ie private and expensive) schools. Cheltenham Ladies' College occupies the site of the original spa spring, and is one of England's more famous schools for girls. Cheltenham College was the main location for the film *If.*

A good starting point is the Promenade, a broad, tree-shaded street lined with tall Regency terraces and classy shops. The tourist information centre is towards the south end; turn right out of the tourist office for masses of floral colour in Imperial Gardens, and for Montpellier Walk, whose little shops are divided by caryatids. The domed building at the top is Montpellier Spa, started in 1817 – now a bank, but still splendid inside. This is the Montpellier and Suffolk end of town, with lots of enticing antique shops and other specialist stores, café-bar-style eating places and handsome architecture. Off the Promenade, the new Regent shopping arcade is worth a visit just for its extraordinary clock.

North of the centre there's more architectural splendour in the Pittville part of town. Pittville Park is a wide space of lawns, trees and boating

The exceptionally grand Pittville Pump Room.

lakes, with the colonnaded Pittville Pump Room as a centrepiece. There's no charge for going in and sampling Cheltenham's spa water in the Assembly Room – but beware, it doesn't taste very nice. You can also get brunch and tea here on Sundays only, between May and September. Upstairs is a fashion museum (closed on Mondays all year, and on Sundays from November to March). There is a small admission charge, but guided tours, starting at 2.30pm on Thursdays, are free.

The composer Gustav Holst was born in Cheltenham at 4 Clarence Road. His house is now a museum, furnished as a typical 19th-century home (closed Sunday and Monday; admission free). The Cheltenham Art Gallery and Museum is special for its Arts and Crafts furniture, metalwork and other artefacts (closed Sunday from October to April, admission free).

The Everyman Theatre offers a wide range of drama, including touring productions from London. The Playhouse has amateur shows; and touring companies visit the Shaftesbury Hall Theatre, which also offers films and music. Other venues for music of all sorts are the Pittville Pump Room and Town Hall, including regular dance nights, from ballroom-style to bop and ceilidh.

The National Hunt Festival at Cheltenham racecourse in March is the climax of the steeplechasing season (jump races). It attracts race-goers from all over the world but especially from Ireland, and there is a particularly lively atmosphere. Main race of the week is the Cheltenham Gold Cup. The racecourse is a mile or so from the town centre, at Prestbury. In July the Cheltenham International Festival of Music in July has master classes as well as concerts by international musicians, and it's accompanied by a Fringe Festival of theatre, film and other events. Visit in October for a packed schedule of readings, talks, debates, plays and other events of the literature festival, which has a reputation for participation from numerous eminent novelists, poets and other writers.

Moneysaver
The July festival period includes free and low-price events, and ticket prices for the literature festival start low – besides offering priceless opportunities to meet and talk to your favourite living author.

ORIENTATION IN CHELTENHAM

INFORMATION
TOURIST OFFICE
77 Promenade. ☎ 0242 522878.
POST OFFICE
225-27 High Street.
PUBLIC LAVATORIES
Promenade; Imperial Gardens; Montpellier Gardens; Regent Arcade; Pittville Park.

TRANSPORT
BUSES
Bus station at Royal Well, behind Promenade. For information ask at tourist office.
TRAINS
Train station at Queen's Road, west of city centre. For information ☎ Gloucester, 0242 237455.
CAR HIRE
Alpha Service Station Queen's Road. ☎ 0242 237455.
BICYCLE HIRE
Crabtrees 50 Winchcombe Street. ☎ 0242 515291. £5 per day, £20 per week; more for mountain bikes or tandems. Book in advance in summer.

ACCOMMODATION
HOTELS
Beaumont House Hotel 56 Shurdington Road. ☎ 0242 245986.
Knowle House 89 Leckhampton Road. ☎ 0242 516091. Single bed and breakfast from £12.
COLLEGE ACCOMMODATION
Cheltenham and Gloucester College of Further Education PO Box 220, The Park Campus, Cheltenham, Gloucestershire GL502QF. ☎ 0242 532774. Groups only (minimum number six), Easter and summer vacations. Advance booking essential.
YOUTH HOSTEL
Cleeve Hill Youth Hostel Cleeve Hill. ☎ 0242 672065. Open from March to October.
CAMP SITE
Longwillows Camping Site Station Road, Woodmancote. ☎ 0242 674113. 3½ miles north of Cheltenham.

OUTINGS FROM CHELTENHAM

GLOUCESTER

Gloucester is a few miles southwest (about 30 minutes by bus); it's a mixed bag of a place, with some drab stretches between exciting places. Guided walks start from the tourist information centre at 2.30pm on Sunday and Wednesday from June to September, and daily in August.

> **Local flavour**
> Near the cathedral, 9 College Court appears in Beatrix Potter's story *The Tailor of Gloucester*, which is based on a real event. Today the building is a shop and museum selling Beatrix Potter books and associated merchandise.

The 'must' is the cathedral, which dates back to Norman times and beyond, with fine craftsmanship in stone and wood, and a pinnacled tower rising high above the city (admission free, but donation suggested). There's a little rose garden in the delicately vaulted cloisters, which still have the stone basin where long-gone monks used to wash.

Gloucester Docks are on the other side of the city centre. Cargos used to be swapped here between sea-going vessels and inland boats, but most of the tall old warehouses have been transformed for new uses. The Albert Warehouse is now the Robert Opie Museum of Packaging and Advertising: a vast collection of cartons, tins, hoardings, bottles and other ephemera from Victorian times onwards, plus old television commercials, all shedding interesting light on changing tastes and styles. (Closed Monday except bank holidays.)

The Llanthony Warehouse is the National Waterways Museum, where besides the many exhibits you'll almost certainly see workers carrying out skills associated with the canal and river trade. Yet another warehouse is a pub restaurant, and another is the home of the Gloucester Antiques Centre, with five floors

and over 60 shops. A boat in the docks has been converted into a café, and the *Heather Spray* offers cruises.

Gloucester Arts Centre is on Eastgate, with a craft fair on the second Saturday of most months. Roman and medieval walls can be seen at the end of Eastgate; Gloucester also has a folk museum and a city museum with Roman finds (all free).

BERKELEY

Bus travellers should change buses at Gloucester for Berkeley Castle (1½ hours from Cheltenham). It has been the Berkeley family home for some 800 years, and has a huge medieval keep at its heart. The best known thing about Berkeley is that Edward II was murdered in gruesome fashion in the dungeons, but it's also special for well preserved medieval decorations. Berkeley was the home of Edward Jenner, who discovered vaccination in 1796. A wealthy Japanese philanthropist enabled Jenner's house to be converted into a museum. Open from April to September, and on October Sunday afternoons (closed Mondays except bank holidays).

PRINKNASH ABBEY AND PAINSWICK

Prinknash Abbey (say 'prinnash') is a new monastery, built in 1972 of bright gold Cotswold stone, on a high, steep hill above the Severn Plain (about 25 minutes by bus from Cheltenham). Beside the abbey is the Prinknash Pottery, started after clay was discovered when the foundations were dug – the speciality is pottery that looks like pewter or bronze. You can also visit the crypt church, and about half a mile's walk takes you to St Peter's Grange, an old manor house across the valley. Just below the pottery is Prinknash Bird Park, with waterfowl, peacocks, doves and deer among parkland and lakes, open Easter to October. The pottery has a teashop and picnic area.

Painswick's narrow streets of pale stone have some very quaint old buildings, but the strangest sight is the churchyard, which is full of clipped yew trees. According to legend, no more than 99 trees can grow here. Up the hill is the Rococo Garden, created in the 18th century with winding paths and carefully designed views. It was lost for many years, but is being restored to its appearance in a painting of 1748. Open from February to mid December, Wednesday to Sunday and bank holidays.

Local flavour
Each late May Bank Holiday, competitors hurl themselves down Cooper's Hill near Prinknash, in pursuit of Double Gloucester cheeses. The cheese-rolling races may be one of England's oldest customs,and they're a wild and extraordinary spectacle.

CIRENCESTER

The Corinium Museum has some important mosaics.

Cirencester was the Roman town of Corinium, second only to London in size. Today it's arguably the most beautiful town in the Cotswolds, with a wide marketplace dominated by the large, but very graceful parish church. An air of prosperity pervades, with picturesque old streets, several classy little fashion stores and some long-established local shops, besides the market on Mondays and Fridays. You'll also find a wide range of crafts at the Cirencester

Workshops (and a good self-service restaurant).

The Corinium Museum has an impressive collection of Roman finds, with reconstructions of Roman rooms and a section on the Cotswolds wool trade. Close by, one of the world's highest yew hedges hides Cirencester House, home of the Earl of Bathurst (not open). You can visit his vast wooded park, which spreads over 3,000 acres behind the house.

AROUND THE COTSWOLDS

Moneysaver
Cotswold Voluntary Wardens lead guided walks all year (free, but donation invited): ask the tourist information centres.

Bibury There's not a lot to Bibury, but what's there is very pretty, and a magnet for visitors – cottages clustered round a church, mellow old hotels, and ducks on the little River Coln. Weavers used to live at the ancient terrace called Arlington Row. The old cloth fulling mill is a rural museum, with Arts and Crafts furniture. (Open daily from mid March to mid November, otherwise at weekends.) Bibury Trout Farm has been open since 1902: visitors can feed the fish, and try their hand at fishing.

Snowshill Three miles south of Broadway is Snowshill, where the mellow old manor house is packed full of strange things collected by its former owner Charles Wade (so much so that he lived in a separate building). Open May to September from Wednesday to Sunday and bank holidays, weekends in April and October, and at Easter – you're advised to avoid Sundays and bank holidays however (National Trust.).

Bourton-on-the-Water A large coach and car park, lots of teashops and low price attractions can be found here, such as the long-established Model Village, the Motor Museum, with its huge collection of old advertising signs, and old breeds of domestic waterfowl at Folly Farm. The River Windrush runs along the main street, the village is cheerful and pretty, and the Bo-Peep tearooms do a hefty cream tea. Bourton is half an hour from

Cheltenham by bus.

Stow-on-the-Wold Stow-on-the-Wold sits high on a hill, with winding, camera-ready streets to explore around its central square (50 minutes by bus). Classy antiques shops, tearooms and old inns are the order of the day here. If you have independent transport, go a few miles west to Guiting Power, where the Cotswold Farm Park has rare and traditional breeds of farm animals in a farm setting. Sheep-shearing and other events take place according to the season. Open late March to late September (no bus).

Broadway Broadway really is a 'broad way' – it has a long, wide main street, lined with old inns (about 50 minutes by bus). It's a popular place to visit, with plenty of places to eat and several footpaths out of the village for local walks. The Cotswold Way leads from the higher end up to Broadway Tower, an 18th century folly with huge views from the top.

Chipping Campden This is a gorgeous place, built with local stone in rich gold colours (an hour by bus). It has a handsome church built with wealth from the wool trade, a market hall

and lots of inns and teashops along the main street. There may be crowds however – one US visitor compared it to being back home on the Fourth of July. The Cotswold Way long-distance footpath starts/finishes here, and leads out of town to Dover's Hill, scene of the Dover Games (or Cotswold Olympics) at the end of May. These rustic games were started by Robert Dover in 1612, and were revived in this century after being banned at various times for unruliness.

Winchcombe Another attractive old town, just the other side of Cleeve Hill from Cheltenham (20 minutes by bus). A side turning off the main road leads about a mile to Sudeley Castle, rebuilt in the 19th century from what had been the home of Katherine Parr, last wife of Henry VIII. It has tapestries, paintings and porcelain inside, and the large gardens include a collection of old fashioned roses. Refreshments and picnic places available; open April to October. The Cotswold Way and other paths climb Humblebee How to Belas Knap, a Neolithic burial mound.

HEREFORD

People driving past Hereford could be forgiven for underestimating its attractions, but it's well worth turning off the main road to spend a while in this old city. Hereford is the principal town for the southern Marches – the border country between England and Wales – and it has a lot of local colour and character, besides the obvious attractions of a cathedral and museums. It also makes a good touring base.

This part of England doesn't have huge stately homes, but it does have many old manor houses and others which can be visited. You may feel their small scale makes them all the more enchanting. There are some little gems among the churches; and not to be forgotten either are the pubs – it's a good area for traditional 'locals'.

Local flavour
Hereford cattle are easy to identify by their deep red colour and white faces. The breed dates back to the 18th century, and today there more than five million pedigree Herefords all over the world. The record price is £27,000 for Haven Reign On, bought by a Canadian dealer in 1980.

Local flavour
Orchards around Hereford grow apples for cider, and they're a sea of blossom in spring. H P Bulmer of Hereford is the UK's biggest cider firm, but cider is also made and sold on the farm by much smaller concerns.

On the transport side, a car would allow you to stay on one of the farms near Hereford, and

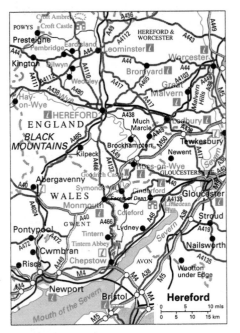

Hereford

explore the surrounding valleys and villages at your leisure. Independent transport would make it a lot easier to explore the Wye Valley and Forest of Dean. Otherwise, it's possible to take tours out of Hereford by public transport, so long as you're not too concerned about getting quickly round all the sights.

Hereford has bed and breakfast places, but not a huge number, so booking is always advisable. Beautiful old farms outside the city offer good value bed and breakfast too.

Hereford is between 1½ hours and 2½ hours from Cheltenham by rail (change at Worcester); the journey time depends on the connection in Worcester. To get from Cheltenham to Hereford by bus, go first to Gloucester, from where there's a direct service (half an hour to Gloucester, and a further 1½ hours from there to Hereford).

Walking is the best way to explore Hereford. It isn't a big city, and traffic is banned from some streets. Guided walks start opposite the tourist information centre every day from May to September at 10.30am. There's also a trail, marked by signs around the city. You can pick up a cheap guide to the trail at the tourist

information centre.

The best place to start looking around is on High Town, the broad traffic-free street just up the road from the tourist information centre. A market was set up here 1,000 years ago, and Hereford has been a shopping centre for the region ever since. There's a covered market hall – visit on Wednesday or Saturday for the full-scale market, with farm produce on sale and lots of local colour. You'll find plenty of modern stores as well, and a livestock market all week. Special sales of pedigree Hereford cattle are in January, March and November.

The huge timber-framed Old House stranded in the middle of High Town is all that remains of Butchers Row, the old meat market. It's now a museum (closed Sunday). Nearby Church Street offers some enticing window shopping – the Society of Craftsmen has a gallery here – and there's a group of craft workshops in Cappucin Yard. Organic produce may be on sale, and Nutters café serves wholefood.

Moneysaver
Old House Museum is free on Mondays, except bank holidays.

The present Hereford Cathedral was started some 900 years ago, but its origins are much older. It has effigies of knights, memorial brasses, African-made tapestries designed by John Piper, and two special things which you pay to see. A spiral staircase leads up to the 17th-century chained library (small charge), where the ancient books and manuscripts are secured to their shelves by chains. The opening hours are limited: usually 10.30am to 12.30pm and 2pm to 4pm, but only 11am to 11.30am, 3pm to 3.30pm from November to March.

The other treasure is the *Mappa Mundi*, a map of the world with Jerusalem at the centre – it was drawn in the 1200s and is full of Christian symbolism (tickets £2.50). A few years ago the cathedral caused an uproar by threatening to sell it. On weekdays in term time, come back to the cathedral at 5.30pm for evensong with the cathedral choir (not Wednesday).

The Three Choirs Festival takes place each

summer in Gloucester, Worcester or Hereford – the cathedrals take it in turn each year. The main programme of concerts and recitals is backed by other events all over the city, making this a lively time to visit.

Other places to see are the City Museum and Art Gallery (no charge), and the Cider Museum in the old Bulmer's cider factory (just outside the city centre ring road). Cider brandy is distilled here and sold at the shop, together with local cider and perry (made from pears). Open April to October. To see cider produced on an immense scale, make an appointment to tour H P Bulmer's modern factory: telephone 0432 352000.

ORIENTATION IN HEREFORD

INFORMATION
TOURIST OFFICE
Town Hall Annexe, St Owen Street. ☎ 0432 268430.
POST OFFICE
Broad Street
PUBLIC LAVATORIES
Bus station; Union Street; Bath Street; Castle Green; Maylord Orchards; Cattle Market; St Martins.

TRANSPORT
BUSES
Bus station in Commercial Road; services operated by various companies. For information ask at the touristoffice.
TRAINS
Hereford station, about 20 minutes' walk northwest of the centre. For information ☎ 0452 29501.
CAR HIRE
Europcar Commercial Road. ☎ 0432 2874886.
BICYCLE HIRE
Coombes Cycles 98 Widemarsh Street. ☎ 0432 54373.

ACCOMMODATION
HOTELS
Dinedor 3 miles southeast. ☎ 043273 481. Single bed and breakfast from 12.50.
Hopbine Hotel Roman Road. ☎ 0432 268722.
Single bed and breakfast from £17.50.
YOUTH HOSTEL
World's End Youth Hostel
World's End Lodge, Staunton-on-Wye. ☎ 09817 308. Closed Christmas week.
CAMP SITE
Caravan Club Site Hereford Racecourse, Roman Road. ☎ 0432 272364.

EATING OUT
French Corner 8 Church Street. ☎ 0432 274700. The speciality here is crêpes.
Taste of Raj 67 St Owen Street. ☎ 0432 351075. Curries for under £4, fixed-price meals for around £10.

OUTINGS FROM HEREFORD

ALONG THE WYE

Ross-on-Wye is at the start of the spectacular stretch of the River Wye (about 40 minutes by bus). It stands high above the river, with pleasant old streets radiating from the old stone market hall. Exploring the valley by bus would be laborious: it's easier by car. Or hire a bicycle from Little and Hall at 48 Broad Street, Ross-on-Wye, telephone 0989 62639.

About five miles south is Goodrich Castle – a massive red sandstone ruin above the Wye. It was battered into submission in 1640 by a locally made cannon called Roaring Meg, but is still impressively complete. It's closed on Monday from October to April. (You can join the Wye Valley Walk here.)

Symonds Yat is a couple of miles further. Here the river loops below a 500ft crag, creating a beautiful and much photographed view. A viewpoint plaque identifies distant landmarks. Follow the signs to Symonds Yat East, but don't expect romantic solitude – this is a popular spot. An attraction of recent years has been the peregrine falcons, which returned to nest in 1983 after an absence of 29 years. A forest trail for walkers starts at the car park.

The main road follows the winding course of the river past the nice old market town of Monmouth to Tintern, where the former train station is now an information centre. The main reason for visiting Tintern is Tintern Abbey, a graceful ruin beside the river, with delicate stone tracery outlined against the wooded hillside. You're just within Wales here, so it's looked after by the Welsh organisation, Cadw: open from late March to late October.

Moneysaver
The best free thing in the Wye Valley and Forest of Dean is miles of footpaths in beautiful scenery, including signed trails. For suggested walks and details of guided walks, ask tourist information centres at Ross-on-Wye or Coleford, or the Forestry Commission at Symonds Yat.

Local flavour
The River Wye has a reputation for enormous salmon – in 1923 a fish measuring 52 inches was caught. The other speciality is young eels (elvers), which travel up the river each spring.

Hay-on-Wye sits right on the Welsh border. It has grey stone streets overlooked by a gaunt grey castle, and is arguably Britain's oddest town. Nearly every shop has become a second-hand bookshop, and the biggest one of all is the former cinema. The person who started this transformation was Richard Booth, 'King of Hay' and owner of the castle. There's a craft centre near the main car park. Every now and then Hay bursts into life with a major event such as the summer jazz festival, with famous names on the bill. Buses to Hay take the beautiful Golden Valley route (one hour).

THE FOREST OF DEAN

The 35 square miles of the Forest of Dean are reserved for timber-growing and leisure, with picnic sites, barbecue hearths, viewpoints, and miles of paths for walkers. Rock climbing, canoeing and horseriding are possible too, and cyclists can travel along forest tracks and quiet lanes (but cyclists aren't allowed on marked trails for walkers). For information on all activities, call at the Royal Forest of Dean tourist information centre at Coleford, or at the Forestry Commission office, Symonds Yat.

The other side of the Forest of Dean's history is mining: iron was mined here well before Roman times, and coal mining goes back at least to the 13th century. The earliest mines were surface workings called scowles, found in various places but best at Puzzlewood, near Coleford, where a maze-like walk leads through woodland and mossy boulders. The paths were laid out as a picturesque curiosity in the 1800s. Open from Easter to October (not Monday).

Clearwell Caves near Coleford is a series of iron mines where the ore was extracted over some 2,500 years, right up to 1945. Eight caverns linked by ancient, uneven passageways can be visited (open April to October; guided tours can be booked at any time).

Littledean Hall near Cinderford is said to be England's oldest inhabited house. It dates back to the 11th century but stands on Roman foundations, and naturally has several ghosts. The gardens give fine views over the River Severn; open April to October.

THE MALVERN HILLS

Local flavour
Other spa waters are famous for their mineral content, but Malvern water is virtually pure. You can sample it straight from the spring at St Anne's Well.

At just nine miles long, the Malverns aren't a huge range of hills, but they're a landmark for miles. They're also very old – perhaps the oldest rock formation in Europe. A good starting point is Great Malvern, a Victorian spa town with steep streets leading on to the hills (27 minutes by train). The Worcestershire Beacon is the high point at 1,394ft, with wonderful views to Wales and across the Severn plain. The Malverns also have an Iron Age hill fort called British Camp. In the town, the church, Malvern Priory, contains fine 15th-century craftsmanship, and there's a healthy tradition of music and drama at the Festival Theatre and other venues. The Splash pool offers a late 20th-century way to take the waters, with a flume and waves.

Just down from the hills, markets take place at nearby Ledbury on Tuesday and Saturday, partly in the shelter of the old Market Hall (15 minutes by train). The composer Edward Elgar lived in the Malverns, and loved to walk on the hills. His birthplace at Broadheath near Worcester is now a museum.

Ledbury's funfair, in front of the old market hall.

WORCESTER

Worcester is a busy city, with a concentration of interesting things on the south side of the centre (40 minutes by train). First is the cathedral, rising high above the River Severn – it's worth seeing, but be prepared for scaffolding, because a major restoration is under way. King John is buried in front of the altar; Henry VIII's older brother Prince Arthur has a delicately carved chantry chapel near by. There's also an extensive crypt, with the boots of a medieval pilgrim on show. Near the cathedral, you can walk along the leafy banks of the Severn, or take a two-hour river cruise.

Telephone beforehand if you want to tour the Royal Worcester porcelain works, founded in in 1751. Tours last about 45 minutes and are available Monday to Friday, telephone 0905 23221. Collectors might prefer the two-hour Connoisseur's Tour, which costs extra. You don't have to join a tour to see the Dyson Perrins museum, which has the world's best collection of Royal Worcester, going right back to its early days (open Monday to Saturday; free, but 50p

donation suggested). There's a restaurant for snacks and lunches. Royal Worcester is open all year, except for Spring Bank Holiday week at the end of May and the Midlands Fortnight (late July, early August).

> **Moneysaver**
> Royal Worcester has a retail shop and a separate seconds shop, where items are sold at reduced prices. The seconds have flaws, but they're often hard to find.

The crooked timber-framed building called the Commandery was Charles II's headquarters during the Battle of Worcester in 1651. It has displays on the Civil War and on Charles II's escape route after his defeat.

AROUND LEOMINSTER

Leominster (say 'lemster') grew rich on the wool trade. It has elegant Georgian buildings, and an impressive medieval priory church, with three naves. There's a long tradition of livestock sales; antiques are a more recent attraction. Market day is Friday; 14 minutes by train.

Nearby Pembridge, Eardisland and Weobley (pronounced 'weeblee') are amazing (and famous) collections of black-and-white buildings, and there are others worth seeing in the area. Five miles northwest of Leominster, Croft Castle has been the home of the Croft family for some 900 years. It's run by the National Trust, open Wednesday to Sunday and bank holiday afternoons from May to September, and at weekends in April and October. A path leads to the Iron Age hill fort of Croft Ambrey. The nearest bus from Leominster stops just over two miles away at Cockgate .

> **Local flavour**
> Hops are a traditional crop around Hereford. A 'hop-picking morning' is the crisp, promising sort that starts with the sun clearing a light mist.

SHREWSBURY

Shrewsbury (say 'shrozebry') overlooks the northern part of the Marches (the border country between England and Wales). It's a sizeable, lively town, but it still has close ties with the surrounding country – it grew up as a market town around a castle, and is still a focal point for the region. Steep, ancient hills rise on three sides: the Wrekin to the east, Wenlock Edge, Stiperstones and Long Mynd to the south and west, leading to a green rolling landscape that climbs to the uplands of Wales.

You could spend a long time exploring the Shropshire hills, but don't miss Shropshire's industrial side. Modern industry owes a lot to Ironbridge, just a few miles away, where you can walk over the first iron bridge and visit a cluster of museums devoted to early industry. A longer journey will take you to Stoke-on-Trent, also known as 'The Potteries' – home of Wedgwood, Minton, Coalport and other eminent names in the world of china. Some of the pottery factories are open to visitors, many more have factory shops, and there are several museums with fine collections.

Independent transport is essential if you want to explore the villages and rural scenery. Outings to towns and some popular out-of-town sights can be made by public transport.

It's advisable to book accommodation during any of Shrewsbury's major annual events, and throughout the summer, when the town gets very busy. Bed and breakfast prices start at around £10; farmhouse accommodation outside the town is an attractive option if you have

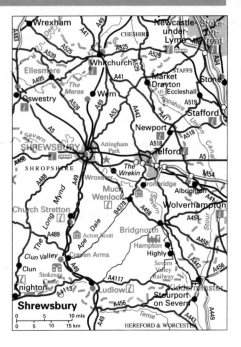

Ironbridge is an outing not to be missed. See p.159

independent transport. For a cottage you might pay anything from £70 to over £200 per week, depending on size and time of year.

The heart of the town is heaped up on a hill inside a tight-necked loop of the River Severn, with steep streets and narrow alleys (or 'shuts') running between spectacular black-and-white buildings and elegant Georgian brick.

Shrewsbury street names such as Mardol, Grope Lane and Peacock Passage date back to medieval times. Butcher Row and Fish Street are easy to explain, but the origins of Wyle Cop and Dogpole remain uncertain.

There's not much free parking in Shrewsbury, and traffic can be heavy. Drivers visiting for the day can use the park-and-ride scheme at weekends – free parking outside the centre, and frequent transport into town for a small fee.

The tourist information centre is in the middle of town, opposite the Old Market Hall. Guided walks start here at 2.30pm every day from May to October, with an extra walk at 11am on Sundays. Just down the hill is the covered market hall: market days are Wednesday, Friday and Saturday. One of the prettiest corners is Bear Steps, with an ancient timber-framed building over steps from St Alkmund's Square to cobbled Fish Street.

The Elizabethan poet and soldier Sir Philip Sydney was a pupil at Shrewsbury School, as was Charles Darwin. Clive House was the home of Robert Clive ('Clive of India'), who won significant victories in India in the 1750s. Rowley's House Museum is a black-and-white house on a grand scale; closed on Sundays from October to March. Exhibits include Roman finds from Wroxeter (see *Outings from Shrewsbury*). Shrewsbury Castle looms above the land route into town –

otherwise, the town can only be reached by bridges. The castle was founded soon after 1066, and is now the Shropshire Regimental Museum. Shrewsbury Abbey is equally old; it stands across the river, just over the English Bridge.

For entertainment, the Music Hall has everything from recitals to wrestling; there's also a film club and an arts centre. You might find horse shows, boat races and other happenings during the year, but the biggest events are the international music festival in July, and the flower show in August which is accompanied by show-jumping competitions and fireworks. For local colour, visit in May for the Mid West Agricultural Show, or September/October for ploughing championships, with separate contests for tractors and shire horses.

ORIENTATION IN SHREWSBURY

INFORMATION
Tourist Office
The Square. ☎ *0743 50761.*
Post Office
Corner of Pride Hill and St Mary's Street.
Public Lavatories
Fish Street; Quarry Park; bus station; by the abbey.

TRANSPORT
Buses
Bus station, Meadow place. For information go to Shearings in Barker Street.
Trains
Shrewsbury station, Castle Foregate (beside the castle). For information ☎ *0743 64041.*
Car Hire
Rent-a-Car Furrows Ltd,

Benbow House, Coton Hill. ☎ *0743 233631.*
Bicycle Hire
Jack Davies 22A Chester Street. ☎ *0743 53093.*
Drummond Outdoor Kayak and Canoe Centre, Southview, 8 Severn Bank. ☎ *0743 65022.For mountain bike tours (around £25 per day), or canoeing trips down the River Severn (around £10 per day).*

ACCOMMODATION
Hotel And Guesthouse
Cannock House Hotel 182A Abbley Foregate. ☎ *0743 356043. Single bed and breakfast from £12.50.*
Grove Farm Preston Brockhurst, 8 miles north. ☎ *093928 223. Single bed and breakfast from £12.50.*
Youth Hostel

Shrewsbury Youth Hostel The Woodlands, Abbey Foregate, Shrewsbury. ☎ *0743 360179. Closed Christmas and January.*
Camp Site
Mill Farm Holiday Park Hughley, near Shrewsbury. ☎ *074636 208/255.*

EATING OUT
Good Life Wholefood Restaurant Barracks Passage, Wyle Cop. Eat here for less than £5; open during the day only.
Lion and Pheasant Hotel 49-50 Wyle Cop. ☎ *0734 236288. Meals for around £12, less for bar snacks.*
Poppy's Teashop Princess Street. ☎ *0743 232307. Light meals and snack for under £5; open until 4.30pm in winter, 7pm in summer.*

OUTINGS FROM SHREWSBURY

Walkers can follow many miles of footpaths in the Severn Valley, or take steeper routes on the

Stiperstones or Wrekin (both reachable by bus). The tourist office can supply walks leaflets. For leisurely strolls, a popular area is the Meres – a unique group of lake-like pools created in the last Ice Age. The largest is called The Mere, by the town of Ellesmere. You can walk beside the water, watch waterfowl, or take out a boat (45 minutes by Wayfarer, Wednesday only). Paths lead to other meres.

WROXETER AND ATTINGHAM PARK

Just outside Shrewsbury, Wroxeter was the site of the Roman town of Viriconium (20 minutes by Wayfarer bus). The most impressive part on show is the bath house remains, including steam and sauna baths and a gymnasium besides a swimming pool. You get a good idea of size of the place from the remains of one of the walls – it still stands over 20ft high. Closed on Monday from October to Easter.

Local flavour
Legends surround the jagged ridge of the Stiperstones. The novelist Mary Webb was drawn to the strange landscape, and described it in books such as *The Golden Arrow*. Today a large part of the hill is protected as a national nature reserve.

Moneysaver
The Wayfarer is a day trip service operated by various bus companies. Family tickets offer savings, and Wayfarer ticket holders may get reduced price admission to some places.

Attingham Park is a splendid mansion in a park landscaped by Humphry Repton (15 minutes by Wayfarer). It's splendid inside as well, with elaborate painted decorations and treasures of pictures and silver. The deer park and grounds offer walks, and there are picnic sites as well as a restaurant. The house is open from late March to September, Saturday to Wednesday afternoons, plus October weekends; the grounds are open all year.

SOUTH TO LUDLOW

Church Stretton became a market town in the 13th century, and then blossomed as a resort in the 19th. The great attraction is the surrounding scenery – there are pretty walks to take along Carding Mill Valley (a popular beauty spot), and tougher ones up the Long Mynd, a bleak, 10-mile ridge which gives huge views. With independent transport you could reach Acton Scott Working Farm Museum, three miles south, where most of the work is done by hand and horse power, and traditional farm breeds are kept. Open April to October. Church Stretton is 18 minutes by train from Shrewsbury.

Stokesay Castle has been gazing over its valley for 700 years, and it hasn't changed very much in that time. It's a fortified manor house rather than a castle, with a moat (dry), hall and towers. Run by English Heritage, it's open daily from early March to October (not Tuesday), otherwise at weekends only. It's a little under a mile from Craven Arms station (35 minutes).

The town of Ludlow climbs up a hill above the River Teme in a wonderful collection of mellow Georgian brick and earlier timber-framing (45 minutes by train). It was laid out as a market town in the 11th century, and is still one today: there are market stalls on Monday (also livestock), Wednesday (in summer), Friday and Saturday. Today people also visit for antiques, art galleries and bookshops, so Ludlow can be crowded. The town showpiece is the ornate, 17th-century Feathers Hotel.

Local flavour
The poem *A Shropshire Lad*, by A E Housman, gives one of the most evocative pictures of the Shropshire landscape. Housman is buried at Ludlow.

Ludlow Castle is open all year except December and January, and makes an open-air setting for performances of a Shakespeare play each summer during the Ludlow Festival (late June to early July, accommodation may be difficult to find then). Guided walks start outside at weekends from Easter to September, plus Wednesday and Thursday in the school holidays, and every day during the Ludlow Festival. There are plenty of places to eat and drink around the town, but De Greys café on Broad Street has an appealing period flavour.

MUCH WENLOCK AND THE EDGE

Much Wenlock is as quaint as its name, with a hotch potch of picturesque old buildings (40 minutes by bus). The stone Guildhall has a whipping post, complete with manacles. Wenlock Priory is the impressive ruin of a once-wealthy Cluniac house: closed Mondays from October to March. Drivers can take the B3478 along the spectacular escarpment of Wenlock Edge from here, with views across Ape Dale to the Long Mynd. The National Trust owns stretches of the 'Edge', and there are car parks along the way.

DOWN THE SEVERN

BUDGET FOR A DAY

Bus fare	2·00
Ironbridge Passport ticket	6·50
Lunch	3·00
Dinner	7·50
	£19·00

plus accommodation

Ironbridge takes its name from the world's first all-iron bridge, built across a gorge of the River Severn by Abraham Darby in 1779. It was intended to advertise skills of local ironmasters, and caused a sensation. There's no charge for walking across this piece of history, and the town of Ironbridge is a pretty place too, running along the side of the wooded gorge (about an hour by Wayfarer bus).

The bridge is now just the most famous of a group of other industrial sites and museums spread over six miles. A passport ticket to the whole lot costs about £6.50, and is valid until you've visited them all. They're linked in summer by a free minibus service, and are open from February to November. The largest is Blists Hill Open Air Museum, a re-created working Victorian township of the 1890s, incorporating blast furnaces, a mine and the Shropshire Canal, which were there already. The first building you come to is the bank, where money can be exchanged for special Ironbridge currency. After that, you could spend a few hours watching people practising their skills in the workshops. Buy beer at the New Inn or a bun from the bakery, and go home with a little bar of real wrought iron.

Other major sites include the Coalport China Museum, the Jackfield Tile Museum, the Museum of Iron and the Darby Furnace. Wayfarer buses offer various tour combinations.

Bridgnorth is further down the Severn, with High Town perched on a cliff above the river, and Low Town by its banks. They're linked by Britain's steepest cliff railway; another way down is via pretty, precipitous Railway Lane, and steps also run up and down the cliff face. In the High Town you can visit the ruined castle and explore old and picturieque streets.

The Severn Valley Railway is in Low Town, with steam-hauled trains along a 16-mile stretch of preserved line, mainly running May to September. There's a large collection of old rolling stock at Bridgnorth station: admission costs £1, refundable if you buy a train ticket. The full journey to Kidderminster costs around £7.50 (third class), which gives you a day's unlimited travel, during which you could stop at one of the restored old stations for a walk by the Severn. Hampton Loade has a rare, water-operated ferry. You can take shorter trips to the intermediate stations, which cost much less than the day ticket. Prices are higher for Gala weekends, four times a year. One Wayfarer bus serves the town; another runs direct to the railway.

The Midland Motor Museum is just south of the town (50 minutes by Wayfarer). Over 100 restored sports and racing cars and motor cycles are on display here, in the converted stables of Stanmore Hall. A nature trail goes through the grounds. Refreshments and picnic places available; admission £3.

STOKE-ON-TRENT

The city of Stoke-on-Trent, or the Potteries, is really six towns: Stoke, Fenton, Longton, Hanley, Burslem and Tunstall. The novelist Arnold Bennett made the Potteries famous as the 'Five Towns' in books such as *Clayhanger*, *The Old Wives' Tale* and *The Card*. It's said that he thought 'Five Towns' sounded better than 'Six Towns'. The great attraction is the pottery industry, past and present: this is the home of Wedgwood blue-and-white, Toby jugs, Staffordshire figures and a vast number of other china wares. The towns cover several miles and each has its own centre, so visiting isn't as straightforward as a trip to a compact town like Ludlow. It's useful to have the *Visitors' Map and Directory* – free from the tourist information centres in Hanley and Stoke. The China Service circular bus route goes round all six towns, with stops at factories, museums, shops and information centres on the way. An inexpensive ticket for a day's unlimited travel is available.

Local flavour
Staffordshire oatcakes are a local delicacy. They're a soft yeast pancake, cheap, easy to freeze and versatile. You can bake them in layers like lasagne or fry them to make tacos, but a popular way to have them is grilled with bacon, or with butter and jam.

The Potteries aren't picturesque – they're big, sprawling and busy – but they're full of life, atmosphere and local colour. It takes 1½ hours to get to Stoke by train, or two hours to reach Hanley by bus. Either would make a good starting point, and they're both on the China Service bus route.

Factories that offer tours include Minton

(telephone 0782 744766), Royal Doulton (telephone 0782 575454) and Spode (telephone 0782 744011). Tours should be booked ahead, and there may be a small charge. They're often in old and rambling buildings (interesting in themselves), so be prepared for stairs and walking. Over 30 pottery factory shops are spread through the six towns. They tend to sell perfect wares at the full retail price, but you may find bargains among the seconds and discontinued ranges. Factories in the Potteries close for the Midlands Fortnight (late June, early July), and the week of the bank holiday at the end of August.

The City Museum in Hanley has one of the biggest collections of English pottery and porcelain, especially Staffordshire wares; admission free. (The museum also has a Spitfire, because Hanley was the home of Reginald Mitchell, the Spitfire's inventor). The Wedgwood Visitor Centre includes an art gallery, demonstrations and a reconstruction of Josiah Wedgwood's original Etruria workshops (south of Stoke at Barlaston). The Gladstone Pottery Museum at Longton is a restored Victorian pottery, with demonstrations of traditional skills.

ALTON TOWERS

Moneysaver
Visit Alton Towers after 2.30pm for half-price ticket. Full-price tickets bought after 2.30pm are valid all the next day. The gardens can be visited for a much lower fee when the rides are closed (November to March).

Alton Towers is a few miles east of Stoke, but is best treated as a separate outing. It's accessible from distant corners of Britain on coach excursions, and you may be able to get a special excursion train, with a connecting bus from Stoke-on-Trent; ask tourist information centres.

This is Britain's oldest theme park, with well

Britain's best-known theme park has fun for all.

over 100 rides, including 'white knuckle' stomach-churners such as the Corkscrew, Thunder Looper and Black Hole. It's set around a ruined mock-Gothic mansion with 500-acre grounds, so you can also have a quiet time among the flowers and foliage of the extensive gardens. There's a wonderful view of the beautiful grounds from the sedate aerial tramway. Children are catered for by Kiddies Kingdom and Adventureland, and there's also a working farm, plus shops, a huge 3-D cinema, restaurants, parades and special seasonal events. The rides and attractions are open from late March to early November; closing time ranges from 5pm to 7pm. The £9.50 admission fee covers all the rides and attractions, as often as you like, all day.

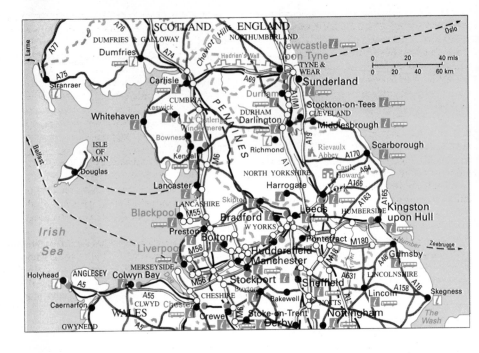

Northern England is a land of extremes, with some of Britain's biggest cities and its wildest, emptiest hills. Along the way there are five national parks protecting thousands of square miles of spectacular hill and mountain landscapes.

This is a great region for walking, but it's also a region of great character – or rather characters. One thing that seems consistent right across northern England is the openness of many of the people. When viewed beside their northern counterparts, some southerners seem a bit stuffy and reserved.

The suggested starting point is the splendid city of Chester, still centred on a site selected by the Romans nearly 2,000 years ago. It's also handy for Liverpool, where Beatles pilgrims can tour places associated with the 'fab four', and others can admire the sumptuous buildings remaining from the city's days of glory.

Buxton is a hilly spa town on the edge of the Peak District National Park. Pretty villages and towns, sheep-nibbled hills and deep river valleys are the order of the day, with high moorlands to the north.

Blackpool is the ultimate good-time seaside resort, with acres of amusements, donkey rides on the sand, pier theatres and plenty of entertainment all summer.

Windermere offers another change of scene: it is in the Lake District National Park, where lakes and mountains form postcard landscapes like a miniature Switzerland. Be sure to visit Skipton, well placed for the Yorkshire Dales National Park, and try to fit in a journey on the spectacular Settle and Carlisle Railway.

Local flavour

Artists have been attracted to the dramatic landscapes of northern England since the 18th century. J M W Turner made several tours in the late 1700s and early 1800s.

In York medieval streets are enclosed by medieval walls, and the whole city is surveyed by a splendid cathedral. The very stately home of Castle Howard and Rievaulx Abbey should not be missed. The North York Moors National Park extends to over 500 square miles of high land and dales.

Newcastle is easy to reach by train or bus; this is one of the north's big industrial cities, with busy streets, good shops, markets and lots of events. To the west is Hadrian's Wall, the cross-country barrier built by the Romans nearly 2,000 years ago. Beyond that, the Northumberland National Park has remote and little-visited hills, and the coast is beautiful.

When's the best time to visit? Crowds and traffic congestion build up quickly during the school summer holidays and holiday weekends, so if it's peace a seclusion you're after, it's worth avoiding the Lake District, Peak District and Yorkshire Dales at those times. Crowds tend to be concentrated in quite small areas though, and it's usually possible to find peaceful places if you're prepared to walk. If you want to see York, Liverpool and Newcastle in peace in the summer, look around early or late in the day. But crowds suit Blackpool, which feels a bit sad when it's empty.

Public transport from these main towns ranges from adequate to good, but is best in summer. A car might seem desirable for exploring the hills, but in summer isn't strictly necessary – it's possible to get about by bus or on minibus and coach tours.

Moneysaver
British Rail North Country Flexi Rovers give four days travel in any eight days, on seven scenic North Country routes, including the Settle and Carlisle line.

Neolithic people left mysterious monuments – two of the best are Castlerigg stone circle (near Keswick) and the strange ring of prone stones at Arbor Low in the Peak District. The most spectacular reminder of the Romans is Hadrian's Wall, but there are many others.

The region has castles and fortified houses, legacies of medieval border warfare. Northumberland is called the cradle of

A typical scene in the rural areas of the North.

Christianity in Britain – evocative reminders of Saxon Monasteries can still be found. Yorkshire has a group of exceptionally beautiful abbeys.

Industries are another integral part of this region. The industrial heritage goes back centuries – shipbuilding in Newcastle; Yorkshire towns were famed for wool; Lancashire towns for cotton, imported and exported through Liverpool.

Local flavour
The name 'scouse' for Liverpool people and the Liverpool accent probably comes from lobscouse – a sailor's stew.

Local flavour
Northumbrian pipes are similar to Scottish bagpipes but smaller, with a sweet and delicate sound.

For food the north is a great region for local specialities and traditional fare. Some dishes are familiar elsewhere – lamb stews outside Lancashire are known as Lancashire hotpot; roast beef all over Britain would seem incomplete without Yorkshire pudding. Grouse are shot on the high moors in summer, and pheasants appear in the shops later in the year. Northumberland rivers (north of Newcastle) are fished for salmon. It's the plainer fare that gives rise to regional pride, however: at the most basic level, northerners maintain that their chip shops fry a crisper, firmer chip than the soft southern variety. Cheeses include Cheshire, Lancashire and Wensleydale, available throughout Britain, but always better in their own localities.

The North Country also has some attractive local customs. Summer in the Peak District means well-dressing (see *Buxton*); rush-bearing takes place in the Peak and Lake Districts, and dates from the time when the rushes on church floors were renewed in an annual ceremony.

CHESTER

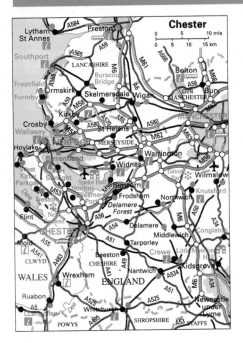

Council information kiosk, open every day at the Bus Exchange.

For accommodation, Chester has some reasonably priced hotels and bed and breakfast places, but beware – they get booked up.

From London, Chester is a little over four hours by coach, just under three hours by rail (London's Euston train station). Manchester International airport is less than an hour away by road, and has flights to the main business cities of Europe and North America, plus shuttle services from London. Liverpool airport is also in easy reach.

Chester's story begins with the Romans, who founded the fortress of Deva right where central Chester is today, and part-Roman, part-medieval walls still run round the city centre. The tourist information centre is at the Town Hall and guided walks start outside at 10.45am daily (not Sunday except in summer); in summer there's also a walk at 2.30pm each afternoon. Themed walks are also available.

Best of all are the Rows – covered shopping galleries above the street level stores, reached by steps. They go back to medieval times, although a lot of the black-and-white magnificence is due to Victorian rebuilding.

Chester should not be missed on a tour of England. It has wonderful old buildings, with streets and city walls going back to medieval and Roman times; and it's also very much a prosperous modern city – full of life, and a great place for shopping and window shopping.

Near by is the Wirral, the peninsula between the Dee and Mersey rivers. Places worth visiting range from the city of Liverpool to the vast grounds and stately mansion of Tatton Park and the higgledy-piggledy black-and-white manor house of Little Moreton Hall.

Buses and trains run from Chester to many of the surrounding places of interest: ask for the free guides to public transport at the County

Local flavour
Cheshire cheese is made on local farms and sold at Chester market. It goes well with apple pie – the saying is 'apple pie without the cheese is like a kiss without the squeeze'.

There are plenty of small specialist stores, and decorative signs on brackets add to the lively look of the streets. The covered market behind the Town Hall has stalls every day except Wednesday and Sunday. There are plenty of restaurants, coffee shops, and ancient pubs.

For a rooftop, backyard view of the city, walk along the top of the city walls. One place where you can climb up is by Eastgate, with its delightful Victorian iron-frame clock. Chester Cathedral, founded in the 10th century or before as St Werburgh's Abbey is impressive inside, with shadowy cloisters, intricate stone carving and a garden round a small fountain. You can get snacks and lunches in the old Refectory (not Sunday).

Follow Souters Lane for one of Chester's nicest places, the leafy Groves by the River Dee, with an Edwardian bandstand (band concerts on summer Sunday afternoons), ice cream kiosks, swans and boats. A Victorian suspension bridge crosses the river to parkland on the south bank.

Chester racecourse is just below the city walls on the land called the Roodee, where the Roman harbour used to be. River races take place on the Dee in March, with a regatta later in the year; in June the Cheshire Show is a big agricultural event. Visit in July for the music festival, or in late summer for the film festival.

Moneysaver
Ticket prices are low for the Gateway Theatre's Late Night Alternative shows and Studio Theatre. The main theatre offers reduced-price preview tickets.

The ornate Jubilee Clock adorns Chester's Eastgate, on the ancient town walls.

ORIENTATION IN CHESTER

INFORMATION
TOURIST OFFICE
Town Hall, Northgate Street.
☎ 0244 351609.
POST OFFICE
St John's Street.
PUBLIC LAVATORIES
Grosvenor Shopping Precinct; Princess Street.

TRANSPORT
BUSES
Bus Exchange, Princess Street (behind the Town Hall). There is an information kiosk here, or ☎ 0244 602666.

TRAINS
Chester station, off Hoole Road, a few minutes' walk northwest of the city centre. For information ☎ 0244 340170.
CAR HIRE
Adeva 3 Hartford Way, Sealand Industrial Estate.
☎ 0244 383111.
BICYCLE HIRE
Davis Brothers Cycles 6-8 Cuppin Street. ☎ 0244 319204.

ACCOMMODATION
HOTEL
Hamilton Court 5-7 Hamilton Street. ☎ 0244 345387. Single bed and breakfast from £15.

YOUTH HOSTEL
Chester Youth Hostel Hough Green House, 40 Hough Green. ☎ 0244 680056.
COLLEGE ACCOMMODATION
Chester College Holiday Office, Chester College, Cheyney Road, Chester CH1 4BJ
CAMP SITE
Chester Southerly Caravan Park Barlderton Lane, Martlston-Cum-Lache.
☎ 0829 270791.

EATING OUT
Chester Rows Restaurant 24 Watergate Street. ☎ 0244 316003. Fixed-price lunch £6.25. Two-course lunch from about £10.

OUTINGS FROM CHESTER

For cyclists the Cheshire Cycleway is a 135-mile route along quiet roads around the county. Tourist information centres should stock guides to this route and others, as well as details of coach trips.

THE WIRRAL PENINSULA

The Wirral Way is a 12-mile path and linear country park, running along a former railway line. Between Neston and West Kirkby it gives views over the Dee estuary – wonderful for bird-watching outside the breeding season, with thousands of ducks and wading birds.

Ness Gardens   Ness Gardens also give good views across the Dee estuary to Wales. These are the Botanic Gardens of the University of Liverpool, with 62 acres of lawns and plants. The gardens have a picnic area and a tearoom. Parkgate is a few minutes further along the estuary, and is another good place for bird-watching.

Local flavour
Traditionally made ice cream and locally caught shrimps are specialities of Parkgate.

Ellesmere Port   Ellesmere Port is on the north side of the Wirral, at the meeting point of the Shropshire Union and Manchester Ship Canals. The 19th-century docks and warehouses have been restored to form the Boat Museum – really a celebration of the canals, with workshops, boat rides and steam engines as well as over 50 canal boats.

Port Sunlight   Port Sunlight was built by William Hesketh Lever for workers at his soap factory (home of Sunlight Soap). It's a delightful village of gardens and cottages and Lutyens was among the architects who designed it. Lever became first Viscount Leverhulme, and opened the Lady Lever Art Gallery in the village in 1922. Pictures by Reynolds, Turner and Pre-Raphaelites can be seen here, together with china and antique sculpture.

MERSEYSIDE

Liverpool   Depending on your viewpoint, Liverpool means the Beatles, or football, or good art collections, or urban dereliction – it's a mixture of all those things, and well worth a visit if you don't mind a city that shows more wear and tear than usual.

The city prospered as a transatlantic port at the mouth of the River Mersey from the 16th century onwards, and it has some impressive 19th and 20th-century architecture, including two cathedrals.

Even locals get confused by the city centre one-way system, so if you want to drive into the city, you're advised to park and then walk or use buses to get around. There are plenty of buses, and most of the main 'sights' are within a square mile. For information on all bus, train and ferry travel on Merseyside, consult one of the Merseytravel shops, at Williamson Square or Clayton Square in the city centre, or at Pier Head. The city isn't ideal for cyclists.

A tour bus sets off from Clayton Square every day at 1pm for a one-hour trip round the main city landmarks. Guided walks start here every Thursday in summer, also there are also maritime walks on summer Saturdays. The Beatles Magical History Tour is a two-hour bus trip round sights such as Penny Lane and Strawberry Fields, starting at Clayton Square at 2.30pm daily.

Moneysaver
Merseywide is a free guide to places, transport and events of all sorts – from tourist offices.

The Walker Art Gallery has one of England's best art collections outside London – it's especially good for early Italian and Flemish paintings, and pre-Raphaelite pictures. There's also an award-winning sculpture gallery (free).

Next door is the Liverpool Museum, with artefacts from far afield: admission free, except for the Planetarium. There's no charge for the Natural History Centre on the second floor. The Museum of Labour History on the other side of the Walker is about Merseyside people; admission free.

Liverpool Cathedral is Britain's largest, an early 20th-century Gothic-style structure. Admission is free but donations are welcome, and you have to pay to climb the tower, for huge views. In contrast, the Metropolitan Cathedral has a very modern look – it was completed in 1967 and rises to a crown of tall pinnacles.

Pier Head is the departure point for ferries – and it's the best place to see the waterfront skyline formed by the Cunard Building, the Port of Liverpool Building and the Royal Liver Building, unmistakable with its 'Liver Birds' on the twin towers. The birds are mythical creatures, and are said to have given Liverpool its name. ('Liver' rhymes with 'diver'). Part of the ground floor is open to the public.

You can use the Mersey ferry to reach Wallasey and Birkenhead on the other side, or ask for a 'Stay Aboard Return'. The 'Ferry 'cross the Mersey' cruise is a 50-minute round trip. All boats have refreshments.

South of Pier Head around Albert Dock, is a huge quadrangle of restored warehouses. The Maritime Museum includes a reconstruction of an emigrants' ship, ship models and real boats, among other things. It also has events, and ticket holders qualify for a free boat ride. Some areas are closed from November to April. The

The Liver Building, as seen from across the Mersey.

other big museum is the Tate Gallery Liverpool, which puts on exhibitions from the national collection of modern art at the Tate in London (admission free). There are shops and eating places round the dock; also here is the Beatles Story, a 'sixties experience'. You're warned to beware of pickpockets at Albert Dock.

Moneysaver
Parking at the Maritime Museum car park costs £2, which covers museum admission for one adult. There's a large free car park on the other side of Albert Dock, from where minibuses run every 15 minutes to the city centre (fare 30p).

Entertainment needn't cost the earth – cheapest tickets for the Playhouse start at around £1 for a matinée performance, and the highest prices aren't very high. Other venues include the Empire for major touring productions, the Everyman, Bluecoat Arts Centre and Unity for innovative shows – and there are others, in and near the city. The Philharmonic Hall is the home of the Royal Liverpool Philharmonic Orchestra; the Royal Court has rock.

Speke Hall   Speke Hall is a half-timbered Elizabethan manor house, south of Liverpool beside the Mersey. Run by the National Trust, it's open from April to October (closed Monday except bank holidays). Public transport takes you only as far as the airport half a mile away: take the train to Garston (about 10 minutes from Liverpool Central train station on the Northern Line, and then the airport bus (short ride).

Southport and Coastal Nature Reserves
The National Trust runs 470 acres of dunes and pinewoods at Formby as a nature reserve. It's a pretty place to walk, and you'll almost certainly see red squirrels. Admission is free; there is a charge for parking. Its just under a mile from Freshfield train station – about half an hour from Liverpool Central station on the Northern Line.

Southport is a leafy resort to the north of Liverpool (40 minutes from Liverpool Central train station on the Northern Line). Lord Street in the middle of town, is wide and tree-lined with delicate wrought-iron canopies above the shops. The Atkinson Art Gallery is worth a leisurely visit (closed Sunday, admission free), as are the Botanic Gardens on the northern edge of town (admission free). Southport has lots of resort amusements, and miles of sandy beach – the sea is often invisible, but beware a fast-moving tide if you walk out in search of it. Bathing isn't recommended anyway.

Martin Mere is a Wildfowl and Wetland Trust centre, with wild birds from all over the world among pools, marshes and garden, plus thousands of migrant waterfowl in winter. A nature trail runs between bird-watching hides. The centre is 10 miles east of Southport: public transport is by train from Southport to Burscough Bridge and from there by bus.

TATTON PARK

Tatton Park is a splendid mansion with fine furniture and pictures, plus an orangery and gardens, and a huge deer park. Tatton Mere is a mile-long stretch of water for bird-watching, fishing and sailing; you can also hire bicycles, visit the much earlier Old Hall and see a 1930s-style farm. High-class antiques fairs, motor rallies, point-to-points and numerous other events are held. The house, hall and farm are open from April to October; the grounds and gardens are open all year. Run by the National Trust, but members pay for parking and for special events. The deer park is free to pedestrians. On summer Sundays bus X2 runs from Chester, otherwise catch the train to Knutsford, from where it's a two-mile walk.

MANCHESTER

Manchester is another big North Country city. It's the home of the Royal Exchange Theatre and many others, and Manchester music ranges from rock to the Hallé Orchestra. The Museum of Science and the Granada Studios are close together in the Castlefield area, close to Deansgate train station. The Museum of Science and Industry has steam engines and planes among its huge array of machines and displays, plus the Xperiment section with hands-on exhibits.

LITTLE MORETON HALL

Little Moreton Hall takes the art of timber-framing to extravagant lengths – the house is the most amazing moated cluster of gables, windows and carved woodwork. Run by the National Trust, it's open mid April to September afternoons, and at weekends in March and October. It really shouldn't be missed, though getting there by public transport is laborious: bus to Crewe, change for Congleton, and change again for Brownlow Heath, from where it's a mile walk.

BUXTON

Buxton sits among high hills at 1,000ft above sea level; a delightful little town, with steep streets, handsome stone buildings and warm water springs. It's a useful base for the Peak National Park, terrific walking country, with two distinct types of landscape – the south and central part is the White Peak, with limestone hills cut through by steep wooded dales and criss-crossed by dry-stone walls. The Dark Peak is much wilder, harsher country, mostly to the north, but reaching along the west and eastern edges as well. It rises to high, bleak moorland

and bog. Some find the Dark Peak too hostile, others love its remote emptiness, with no roads or houses for miles.

Buxton is in easy reach of good walking country, and of other attractions of the Peak – pretty villages, the wonderful stately home of Chatsworth, cable car rides at Matlock, caverns in the limestone rock and prehistoric sites. It used to be a lead-mining area, and there are industrial museums too. *Peakland Post* is a useful newspaper-style guide to places and events – free from information centres.

Local flavour
The Peak District custom of well-dressing probably has its roots in pre-Christian thanksgiving for water. The wells are decorated with pictures made of flower petals, and there may be a village festival at the same time.

A network of buses links the Peak villages and towns, with extra services on summer Sundays and bank holidays – but buses may be infrequent. Cycling is popular in the Peak, thanks to scenic cycle ways with gentle gradients along former railway lines.

This is a popular holiday area, with a lot of bed and breakfast accommodation, youth hostels, camping barns and camp sites. There's some self-catering too, mainly in cottages.

Buxton is 3½ hours from London by train (London's Euston station), change at Stockport; four hours 20 minutes by bus. From Liverpool it's two hours by train, change at Stockport; 2¼ hours by bus, change at Manchester.

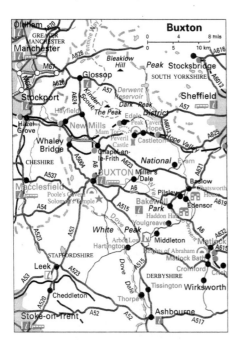

Manchester is just over an hour by train (Piccadilly station), and there is a shuttle bus which serves Manchester International airport.

The heart of the town is around the handsome 18th-century Crescent, part of which houses the tourist information centre. Guided walks start here twice a week, from June to September.

The former thermal baths at the Crescent are now a shopping arcade; the Pump Room is the Buxton Micrarium, where crystals and tiny living animals and plants can be viewed through microscopes; open late March to early November. The Pavilion and Opera House are close by, facing the pools and swans of the Pavilion Gardens.

Local flavour
The Roman spa baths at Buxton were called Aquae Arnemetiae. The spring water is pleasant to drink; you can buy it locally or fill a bottle free at St Anne's Well, by the Crescent.

The Broad Walk that runs along one side of the Pavilion Gardens is lined with hotels and bed and breakfast establishments. At the other end of town, the Peak Rail Steam Centre has a work-yard near the railway station, and you can see old rolling stock being restored (no charge).

A wide range of touring drama, dance and music is put on at the ornate Buxton Opera House. For three weeks in late July/early August, the it is the home of the Buxton Arts Festival. Details are available from the Buxton Festival Office, Hall Bank, Buxton, telephone 0298 70395.

Moneysaver
Ticket prices for the Opera House start low, and half-price tickets can be booked by the usual concession groups. The Arts Festival includes free and low-price events.

Buxton Country Park starts on the western edge of town, and includes Poole's Cavern, a natural limestone cave and a visitor centre. Best views of the town are from Solomon's Temple, a mock temple on the hill above. On the other side of Buxton, you can join the Monsal Trail, a former railway line over the White Peak to Bakewell. For most of the way it follows the River Wye, via Wyedale, Miller's Dale and Monsal Dale, which it crosses on a high viaduct.

ORIENTATION IN BUXTON

INFORMATION

TOURIST OFFICE
The Crescent, Buxton.
☎ 0298 25106.
Peak National Park Office
Baslow Road, Bakewell,
☎ 0629 814321. National park information also at Edale, Castleton, Bakewell, Fairholmes (Derwent Valley), Torside (Longdendale Valley), Hartington Old Signal Box.
POST OFFICE
9 The Quadrant.
PUBLIC LAVATORIES
Ashwood Park; Spring Gardens; Burbington Road; Cote Heath; Town Hall; Water Street.

TRANSPORT

BUSES
Most leave from the marketplace. For information contact Derbyshire County Council Busline, ☎ 0298 23098.
TRAINS
Buxton station, near the town centre. For information ☎ 061-832 8353.
CAR HIRE
G&T Self Drive 16-18 Bridge Street. ☎ 0298 22721/26554 (daytime), 0298 70205/22386.
BICYCLE HIRE
Peak Cycle Hire Centres
Details from information centres.
Cycle Hire Shipley Country Park Visitor Centre, Slack Lane, Heanor, Derbyshire. ☎ Langley Mill, 0773 719961.

ACCOMMODATION

GUESTHOUSES
Roseleigh Private Hotel 19 Broad Walk. ☎ 0298 24904. Single bed and breakfast from £15.

The Old Manse 6 Clifton Road, Silverlands. ☎ 0298 25638. Bed and breakfast from £12.

YOUTH HOSTEL

Buxton Youth Hostel
Harpur Hill Road. ☎ 0298 22287.
CAMP SITE
Thornheyes Farm Campsite
Longridge Lane, Peak Dale. ☎ 0298 26421.
CAMPING BARNS
Booking form from National Park Centre, Losehill Hall, Castleton, ☎ 0433 20373 to book.

EATING OUT

Chatters Café Bar Market Place. ☎ 0298 71516. Mexican-style specials, pizzas etc under £5.
Firenze Market Place. ☎ 0298 72203. Eat well for under £10.

OUTINGS FROM BUXTON

DOVEDALE

The River Dove takes a long, winding course through the White Peak, but its most famous stretch is Dovedale. On a bank holiday weekend Dovedale is more like an urban park than a remote valley. Drivers can park near Thorpe (no easy bus access). Paths by the river from Hartington may be quieter (45 minutes by bus).

An open air service every August at Eyam (say 'eem') recalls the one of the most poignant episodes in Peak District history. When the Great Plague of 1665-66 began claiming victims in Eyam, the villagers stayed in self-imposed quarantine to contain the disease, rather than escaping.

BAKEWELL, HADDON HALL AND CHATSWORTH

Bakewell lies in the heart of the White Peak, and it's another very popular spot (about 30 minutes by bus). There's a market on Mondays, and small shops in the town sell local produce. The

Old House is a folk museum, housed in a Tudor building which is interesting in itself. Allow time for the Old Original Bakewell Pudding Shop, where a delectable Bakewell pudding with coffee costs about £1.50.

Local flavour
Bakewell puddings are far nicer than the 'Bakewell tarts' sold elsewhere. The first pudding is said to have resulted from a misunderstanding, when a cook spread an egg mixture on top of a strawberry tart instead of putting in the pastry.

Haddon Hall lies a couple of miles southeast. It was started in the 12th century, evolved over the next 500 years, and was then left when its owners went to live elsewhere. Medieval kitchens, the painted chapel and furnishings from centuries ago give the house a Sleeping Beauty atmosphere. There are beautiful gardens. Open April to September, closed Sundays and Mondays in July and August, but open all bank holiday Sundays and Mondays.

Chatsworth House is the home of the Duke and Duchess of Devonshire, and it's one of England's most splendid houses. The approach gives a wonderful view of the house against a backdrop of steep woodland. Inside, Chatsworth is richly decorated and full of treasures. The showpieces of the gardens are the Cascade and the huge fountain (not always in operation); there are also paths across the parkland, a farmyard and an adventure playground (extra charge). Open late March to

Chatsworth is one of England's finest houses.

late October; admission is not cheap, and it costs £1 to park, but well worth the money.

Moneysaver
Chatsworth is well worth the admission fee, but you might come back to explore the estate villages and the parkland, for which there's no charge.

Buses run direct from Buxton to Chatsworth on summer Sundays and bank holidays (30 minutes). At other times, the only way is to catch the bus to Baslow, and then walk about two miles.

MATLOCK AND THE PEAKS TRAILS

BUDGET FOR A DAY	
Bus fare	2·95
Heights of Abraham	3·99
Bus to Crich	1·80
Tramway Museum	3·40
Lunch	2·50
Dinner	7·00
plus accommodation	£ 21·64

The Tissington Trail and the High Peak Trail are routes for cyclists and walkers along disused railway lines through some of the Peak's best scenery. See *Orientation in Buxton* for cycle hire. Buses run from Buxton to nearby Youlgreave on Saturdays, summer Sundays and bank holiday Mondays (15 to 45 minutes, £1.35 day return).

The High Peak Trail runs to Middleton Top, where the Middleton Engine can be visited on Sundays: it worked for 134 years, hauling wagons along the Middleton Incline (gradient 1 in 8).

Matlock Bath was a Victorian spa, in the deep gorge of the River Derwent just beyond Matlock (an hour by bus). Cable cars leave from near the train station, climbing over the river and high above the gorge to the Heights of Abraham, which includes a woodland park, Prospect Tower and two caverns. Or follow the path from the cable car starting point to High Tor Grounds, which also give views for a much lower admission charge.

Crich offers tram rides from the National Tramway Museum, which has retired trams from all over Britain and the USA, South Africa and Czechoslovakia. Some of the exhibits are static, and some offer rides along a mile of track. It's open from May to September (not Friday except in school holidays), plus weekends and bank holidays in April and October (30 minutes by bus from Matlock).

CASTLETON, EDALE AND THE DARK PEAK

Castleton's one through-road goes along the craggy green gorge of Winnat's Pass, a designated Site of Special Scientific Interest. If you're not driving, take the train to Hope, the next station east from Edale, change stations at New Mills. From Hope it's a five-minute bus journey or easy cycle ride along the Hope Valley. There are direct buses from Buxton on summer Sundays and bank holidays.

A steep walk up from the centre takes you to the ruins of Peveril Castle – the 12th-century keep is impressive, and you get fine views from up here. Run by English Heritage, admission is less than £1. Castleton also has spectacular limestone caverns with stalactites and stalagmites. Peak Cavern (once known as the Devil's Arse) is in the village, below the castle. The gaping cave entrance is Britain's largest;

inside, you can see rope-making machinery, which was in use until recently. Open from early April to late October. The other caverns are on the outskirts, below Winnat's Pass, and they're open all year. The 35-minute tour of Speedwell is a boat trip along an underground canal to the 'bottomless pit'; the others are Treak Cliff and Blue John, both of which have a series of extraordinary caves. Admission to the caves ranges from about £2 to £4.

Castleton celebrates 29 May with Garlanding Day, when the Garland King wearing a huge framework of flowers rides in procession on a white horse.

Local flavour
Shops in Castleton sell ornaments and jewellery made from locally mined blue john, a blueish purple stone which can only be extracted by hand.

The Dark Peak is crossed by the Pennine Way long-distance footpath. The southern starting point is at Edale, from where it climbs up immediately to the bleak moorland of Kinder Scout and then to the even more desolate Bleaklow. This is tough walking, and not to be undertaken lightly – serious walking gear, map, compass and rations are required. Always check weather conditions; at Edale details are supplied by the national park information centre.

The easiest way to get to Edale by public transport is by train to New Mills Newtown station (20 minutes), then walking to New Mills Central, from where it's about 15 minutes ride.

BLACKPOOL

Europe's biggest seaside resort is Blackpool, a kind of homely English version of Las Vegas, with lots of amusements and celebrity shows, seven miles of sandy beach, a promenade, donkey rides, and three piers (with amusements and shows), all overlooked by the Eiffel-lookalike of Blackpool Tower. Blackpool suits people of all ages, and it's best when it's busiest. It isn't the most sophisticated town in

England, but it is good fun.

Just north of Blackpool is the resort and fishing port of Fleetwood; just south is Lytham, with a much more sedate atmosphere. The stone-built county town of Lancaster could be reached on a day out, and there are many other Lancashire towns which are worth visiting on market days.

Blackpool stretches along the coast, but it's

easy to get from one end to the other, because trams run along the seafront. During the Illuminations you can become part of the show by taking an Illuminations tour on a vintage or spectacularly decorated tram.

Moneysaver
The best free show in Blackpool is the Illuminations, from the end of August to early November, when the whole of the promenade is decorated with lights and illuminated figures.

There are plenty of local buses and trains, but outings of any distance may involve changes. It's worth investigating coach excursions, which include markets and horse races as well as sightseeing. Trains don't run between Blackpool North and Blackpool South stations – they're both at the end of their own lines.

There's a huge amount of bed and breakfast accommodation in Blackpool. You may be able to find rooms even in the height of the summer,

Blackpool

but booking is advisable for weekends, bank holidays and school holiday weekends. The late October half-term break is busy because of the Illuminations. The north end of town is a good place to look for bed and breakfast a limited amount of self-catering apartments are available. The tourist information centre will supply details.

Local flavour
Blackpool has Britain's first and sole surviving electric public tram service.

The heart of Blackpool is the area around the 518ft Blackpool Tower, near which you'll find amusement arcades, waxworks, the Sea-Life Centre, fortune tellers, department stores, shopping arcades and the biggest venues for shows. The tower alone has several floors of entertainment, a ballroom, and rides to the top. Ticket prices range from about £3.50 to £5.

Behind the Tower are the Winter Gardens, which incorporate the Opera House – one of Europe's biggest theatres, with celebrity shows in summer. The other big theatre is the Grand, a painted and gilded Victorian setting for classy touring shows, including opera and ballet, plus band concerts and the Christmas pantomime.

Blackpool Pleasure Beach is a short tram ride south of the tower, and it offers another cluster of entertainments, with white-knuckle rides and ice skating, ice shows and cabaret; open Easter until early November, from 11am; admission is free, rides are charged individually; pay extra for shows. The main attraction of the nearby Sandcastle is the big under-cover pool, with waves, water chutes and the like, in an 84 degree Fahrenheit microclimate; but you'll also find amusements around the edge. If you just want to swim then the Lido is the best bet. Treat the sea water withg caution. Notices on the promenade give details of cleanliness tests.

Moneysaver
Swimming at the Sandcastle is cheaper after 4pm.

173

ORIENTATION IN BLACKPOOL

INFORMATION
Tourist Office
1 Clifton Street. ☎ 0253 21623.
Post Office
Abingdon Street.
Public Lavatories
Bus station; Church Street; Promenade; Central Drive car park.

TRANSPORT
Buses
Bus station, Deansgate (town centre). Various companies – information on all services in Lancashire from Transport Enquiry Line, ☎ Preston 0772 263333.
Trains
Blackpool North and Blackpool South stations, either side of town centre. For information ☎ 061-832 8353.
Car Hire
Century Self Drive 119-125 Buchanan Street. ☎ 0253 25212.
Bicycle Hire
Red Rose Cycles 1B/1C Charnley Road. ☎ 0253 20384. Bicycles at £5 day, £28 a week, plus £50 deposit (pushchairs and wheelchairs also available). Their recommended route for a local cycle ride includes the best ice cream stops.

ACCOMMODATION
Hotels
Cliff Head Hotel 174 Queens Promenade, Bispham. ☎ 0253 59086. Single bed and breakfast from £12.65.
Windsor Hotel 21 King Edward Avenue, Queens Promenade, Blackpool. ☎ 0253 53735.
Camp Site
Mariclough Hampsfield Camping Site Preston New Road, Peel Corner (on A583 half a mile south of M55 at junction 4). ☎ 0253 61034.

EATING OUT
White Tower Blackpool Pleasure Beach, Promenade/Balmoral Road. ☎ 0253 46710/41036 (Sunday lunch £7.25, evening meals £15.25).
Grandma Batty's Yorkshire Pudding Emporium North Shore. ☎ 0253 28923. Yorkshire pudding based main courses under £4.

OUTINGS FROM BLACKPOOL

COASTAL RESORTS

Lytham St Anne's is Blackpool's neighbour to the south, but it's more leafy and less brash (30 minutes by bus from Blackpool bus station). It has miles of sand and sand dunes, and four championship golf courses.

Local flavour
Lancashire has several folk dance and song clubs, and you may see clog dancing and other traditions in summer. Ask tourist information centres for the county council leaflet *Folk in Lancashire*.

Fleetwood is on the other side of Blackpool, and it's very different too, because it's a fishing port as well as a resort (40 minutes from Blackpool North Pier by tram). There are bowling greens and a promenade along the seafront, with the free show of ships heading for the docks. Fleetwood market is a popular outing from Blackpool, daily except Wednesday.

LANCASTER AND MORECAMBE

Lancaster has hilly streets of handsome stone buildings, overlooked by the medieval castle (1½ hours by bus). This isn't a prettily picturesque town, but it has character and a lively atmosphere. A literature festival is held here in October. There are outdoor markets on Wednesday and Saturday, and the covered market hall off King Street is daily except Wednesday and Sunday. Antique and bric-a-brac markets are held from Thursday to Saturday.

There are guided tours of the Shire Hall and old cells from Easter to September, and tours of the court and associated rooms at weekends and all through August. Signs direct you to St George's Quay, where the old Custom House is now part of the Maritime Museum.

Morecambe is on the coast close to Lancaster (1¾ hours from Blackpool). The best thing is the view over Morecambe Bay, a huge expanse of salt marshes and sands where thousands of wading birds feed in winter. Quicksands, estuaries and fast-moving tides make the bay notoriously hazardous for humans, but in summer there are guided walks from Arnside (12 miles from Morecambe by local train) to Kents Bank. Telephone 05395 32165 to book a place; free, but donations are invited.

THE LAKE DISTRICT

The Lake District is one of England's most beautiful and popular places, a combination of lakes and mountains that has attracted and enchanted visitors since the 1700s. The mountains aren't high by international standards, but they provide endless impressive views, especially when they're reflected in the waters of the long, narrow lakes.

The suggested base is Windermere which is well set up for visitors, with lots of accommodation and places to eat. The whole region is easily accessible from here, but if you want somewhere quieter to stay, there is plenty of choice throughout the Lake District. There's a lot of self-catering accommodation, in houses, cottages, apartments and caravans. There are also several camp sites and 27 youth hostels within the national park. Tourist information centres can supply an accommodation list. No season is really slack in the Lake District, so booking is always advisable.

Footpaths lead into the hills from Windermere, but the great attraction is Lake Windermere itself – a curving stretch of water some 10 miles long, with wooded banks and islands (see *Outings from Windermere*). A short walk from Windermere, the Steamboat Museum has a collection of working vintage craft on the water, and you can take a 40-minute cruise on steam launch *Osprey*.

Windermere is about two hours by train from Blackpool, nearly three hours by coach, change at Lancaster. It's between 3½ and five hours by train from London (Euston station), via Oxenholme station at Kendal; the coach trip from London takes about seven hours. Manchester International is the nearest airport, and has a shuttle air service from London Heathrow.

The region is a national park, and its biggest

A popular way to view Windermere is from the water.

175

landowner is the National Trust, so the scenery is carefully preserved. Walking is the most popular activity; the valleys and lower hills offer easy walks; fell walking (mountain walking) is a far tougher proposition, which requires proper equipment. Be prepared for rough, high terrain in conditions that are often cold and wet, whatever the weather lower down. Walkers should carry a map and compass, and should know how to use them.

There are plenty of opportunities for water sports, climbing, cycling and other pursuits. Or you could spend many days just tracking down places which have inspired or been the homes of writers, from Wordsworth to John Ruskin and Beatrix Potter. Whatever you do in the Lake District, be prepared for rain.

The Lake District can be very crowded. The M6 motorway along the eastern edge makes it easy to reach, and it's not unknown for the road system within the region to be completely blocked. Think twice before visiting during peak holiday times unless you're happy to be in a crowd.

A useful network of buses links the larger places, and coach tours are plentiful too. Minibus tours run to spectacular places that coaches can't reach – the tours will usually be more expensive than coach trips, but they may well be friendlier too. Mountain Goat offer a wide range of minibus tours almost daily in summer, and you can join them from several places around Windermere. Typical prices are £9 for a half-day tour, £16 for a day. Tourist information centres take bookings.

Local flavour

The poet William Wordsworth lived most of his life in the Lake District, and guests at the Wordsworth family home included Sir Walter Scott, Shelley, Keats, Emerson and Hawthorne.

ORIENTATION IN WINDERMERE AND BOWNESS

INFORMATION

TOURIST OFFICE
Victoria Street, Windermere.
☎ 09662 6499.
Lake District National Park
☎ 0539 724555 for
information.
POST OFFICE
Crescent Road, Windermere;
Ash Street, Bowness.
PUBLIC LAVATORIES
Ellerthwaite Square and New
Road, Windermere;
Promenade and The Glebe,
Bowness.

TRANSPORT

BUSES
Buses leave from the railway station. Ask the tourist information centre or main company, CMS, ☎ 0539 733221.

Minibus tours: Mountain Goat Tours, Victoria Street, Windermere, ☎ 09662 5161/2/3; Lakes Supertours, 1 High Street, Windermere, ☎ 09662 2751; Grass Routes, 145A Craig Walk, Bowness, ☎ 09662 6760. Browns (mainly coaches but also minibuses), Market Place, Ambleside, ☎ 05394 32205.

TRAINS
Windermere station, on north side of the town centre. For information ☎ 0524 32333.
CAR HIRE
Ansa International Belsfield Garage, Kendal Road, Bowness. ☎ 09662 5910/6089; evenings 09662 2474.
BICYCLE HIRE
Windermere Cycle Centre
South Terrace, Bowness,
☎ 09662 4479, also booking office at Victoria Street, Windermere,
☎ 09662 88308 .
Cycle Hire Shop Limefitt Park, Troutbeck,
☎ Ambleside 09662 34238.
Daisy Cycle Hire 135 Craig Walk, Bowness. ☎ 09662 2144.
Lakeland Leisure The Chalet, Station Precinct, Windermere. ☎ 09662 4786.

ACCOMMODATION

HOTELS AND GUESTHOUSES
Oldfield House Oldfield Road, Windermere.
☎ 09662 88445. Bed and breakfast from £13, includes use of small pool and sauna at local club.
Green Gables 37 Broad Street, Windermere.
☎ 09662 3886. Double bed and breakfast from £22.
YOUTH HOSTEL
Windermere Youth Hostel
High Close, Bridge Lane.

Troutbeck. ☎ *09662 3543.*
C*AMP* S*ITE*
Park Cliffe Farm Camping
and Caravan Estate *Birks*
Road, Tower Wood (4 miles

south). ☎ *05395 31344.*
Braithwaite Fold Caravan
Club Site *half a mile south of*
Bowness. ☎ *09662 2177.*

EATING OUT
Rogers *4 High Street,*
Windermere. ☎ *09662 4954.*
Main courses around £5 at
upstairs bistro.

OUTINGS AROUND THE LAKE DISTRICT

AROUND WINDERMERE

All kinds of boat trips are available on Windermere, but prices are not for the cost-conscious. However, if the temptation is too great, the options include a round-the-lake cruise from Bowness-on-Windermere, where you can also catch a boat to Ambleside (Waterhead) at the north end of the lake (1¼ hours), or to Lakeside at the south end. Steam-hauled trains run from Lakeside to Haverthwaite and a combined boat and train ticket is available. The sailing season is from Easter to October, with evening cruises from mid May to mid August. A ferry also goes straight across the lake. The cheapest cruise runs from Brockhole, although you will have to pay the admission charge first.

Brockhole is an Edwardian country house with grounds running down to Lake Windermere (seven minutes by bus). It's now a visitor centre run by the National Park Authority, with an exhibition, films, talks and other events, and trails through the grounds.

NORTH TO GRASMERE

Ambleside would be another good touring base for the southern part of the Lake District. It has a lot of accommodation, and much charm as well, with narrow streets of slate-built houses and good shops. You can get there by boat, or more quickly by bus: 15 minutes. The most curious sight is the tiny Bridge House, built as a summer house over a brook. A rush-bearing ceremony is held in July; the Ambleside Games are held in Rydal on the Thursday before the first Monday in August.

Just beyond Ambleside is Rydal, where

Wordsworth lived with his family at Rydal Mount from 1813 until his death in 1850 (25 minutes by bus). It's full of family possessions, and has a warm, lived-in atmosphere. The wonderful outlook over wooded hills is best enjoyed from the terraced 3½-acre garden which the poet designed; closed on Tuesdays from November to February.

Moneysaver
An Explorer ticket gives you a day's unlimited bus travel on CMS bus routes – buy the ticket on the first bus you board on the day. Four-day Explorer tickets must be bought in advance.

Dove Cottage in Grasmere was Wordsworth's home during his 'Golden Decade' – 1799 to 1808, when he wrote many of his most famous poems. The cottage has been open to visitors since 1891; there is a museum next door. Walkers can follow paths from both Grasmere and Rydal. (Grasmere is 35 minutes by bus).

Local flavour
Gingerbread has been a speciality of Grasmere for over a century.

WEST OF WINDERMERE

Hawkshead Narrow streets and squares make Hawkshead picturesque and popular. There's no through road, so visitors have to walk. A large car park is provided; by bus it's 20 minutes from Ambleside. Buses are infrequent, but they connect with services from Windermere. Wordsworth attended the Old Grammar School from 1779 to 1787 – it's open from Easter to October, and still has the desk where he carved his name (admission £1, 50p for children). There's no charge for 15th-century Hawkshead Courthouse, which can usually be visited from April to early November. Ask for the key at the National Trust shop in the village.

A gallery in Hawkshead shows the work of Beatrix Potter, who lived two miles south at Hill Top, Near Sawrey. She bought the cottage with income from *Peter Rabbit*, and wrote other favourites here. Run by the National Trust, open April to early November (not Thursday and Friday except Good Friday). No bus, but it's a natural destination for coach and minibus tours, or a two-mile walk from the ferry that crosses Windermere from Bowness.

Coniston Narrow Coniston Water stretches for some five miles, overlooked by the Old Man of Coniston (2,631ft). Paths lead into the mountains from Coniston village, which also has places to eat. It's on the same bus route as Hawkshead – half an an hour from Ambleside. Coniston Pier is about half a mile from the centre. You can rent a boat or windsurfing board here, or take a cruise. The National Trust's luxurious 1859 steam yacht *Gondola* departs four or five times a day, from April to early November. The 55-minute round trip costs around £4 (NT members are required to pay too), or a bit more if you break the journey.

On the east bank of Coniston Water woods rise up to Grizedale Forest and open moorland. There are several car parks and picnic sites; *Gondola* travellers can alight at Park-a-Moor. The *Gondola's* other halt is at Brantwood, an 'intellectual powerhouse' of the late 1800s, when it was the home of the critic and artist John Ruskin.

The Theatre in the Forest in Grizedale village is a 230-seat venue for plays, recitals, jazz, ballet, lectures and other events, open all year except January. The post offices at Coniston and Hawkshead sell tickets, as does Holdsworth's bookshop in Ambleside, and prices start low (there's no practical bus).

RAVENGLASS

Ravenglass on the west coast is the start of the Ravenglass and Eskdale Railway, a seven-mile narrow-gauge line between stern hills. The tiny trains stop at Muncaster where a watermill produces stoneground flour; other stations make good starting points for walks. Trains run several times daily (except Sunday) in summer, less frequently at other times. There's also a railway museum, open April to October.

To get to Ravenglass from Windermere, you have to go round or over the high mountains at the heart of the Lake District, including Scafell Pike (England's highest at 3,162ft). The Wrynose and Hardknott Passes provide a route through, but it's one of Britain's trickiest roads, with hairpin bends and 1 in 3 gradients (33%). The remains of a Roman bath house, granaries and other buildings survive in a spectacular setting at Hardknott Roman Fort.

Local flavour
The Biggest Liar in the World competition is held in November in Wasdale.

KENDAL

The 'auld grey town' of Kendal lies on the eastern side of the Lake District (half an hour by bus). It's a much bigger and busier place than the other towns described here. Visit on Wednesday or Saturday for the markets, which have been held in Kendal since 1189.

Local flavour
Kendal Mint Cake is a hard, mint-flavoured sugar bar, sold all over the Lake District as a compact emergency food for walkers (and as a souvenir).

The Kendal Museum dates from 1796 and includes dioramas of Lakeland habitats. Abbott Hall Art Gallery is a Georgian house with pictures by John Ruskin and George Romney; also here is the Museum of Lakeland Life and Industry. Best views of the town are from the ruins of Kendal Castle (no charge), which was the birthplace of Henry VIII's sixth and last wife, Katherine Parr. The Brewery Arts Centre is in a rambling 150-year-old building, and puts on a lively programme.

The Westmorland County Show is held in Kendal on the second Thursday in September, with prize livestock, traditional sports and other events.

Moneysaver
Kendal is the home of K Shoes, which has a factory shop selling seconds and discontinued lines at reduced prices. The shop is on the A65 to the south of the town.

Buses to Kendal go on to Levens Hall (15 minutes further). The hall is a stone-built Elizabethan mansion with a very mellow look, but the best bit is the garden, which has topiary in extraordinary shapes. The garden was laid out by a pupil of Le Nôtre who designed the gardens at Versailles. There's also a working steam collection here. Lunches and teas are available; open mid April to September, Sunday to Thursday. The garden stays open through October.

KESWICK

Keswick's setting is dramatic, with the mountains of Skiddaw and Blencathra rearing above, and Derwent Water lapping at its southern edge. It makes a popular base for the northern lakes of the Lake District National Park. (Say 'kezzick', not 'kes-wick'.)

Keswick is an hour from Windermere by bus. There's no train station, but buses run from Penrith, which is on the main railway line.

All roads to Keswick run through high, thinly populated country, but the little town itself is a hive of purposeful activity. It used to be a mining town but today the chief industry is

catering for walkers, climbers and other visitors. The Moot Hall in the town houses the information centre.

The world's first pencils were made in Keswick. The Cumberland Pencil Company's factory is here, with a museum next door. Videos reveal how pencils are put together, and exhibits include the world's longest pencil. There's a children's drawing corner.

Beside the lake, the Century Theatre puts on a summer programme of drama. In July Keswick's annual two-week religious convention fills the town. The Keswick Show takes place on the August Bank Holiday Monday – this is a big agricultural event, with traditional sports and livestock competitions. See also *Derwent Water* below.

Keswick Rambles are guided walks of about six hours, starting from the Moot Hall from Easter to October. They include mountain walks and you're expected to be suitably clothed and shod, but children from five upwards can join in. For other guided walks, see the national park's annual guide to events (free from information centres).

THE NORTH LAKES

Ullswater   Ullswater is the Lake District's second longest lake, with water sports and boats for hire. A path along the east bank gives fine views – one option is to take the reasonably priced steamer cruise from Glenridding to Howtown, and then walk the six miles back. The road on the other side leads past Gowbarrow Park, which includes the 70ft waterfall of Aira Force. There are coach tours but no practical bus service.

Derwent Water   The Keswick Launch company has rowing boats for hire on Derwent Water, a short walk from the town centre. They also offer 55-minute cruises round the lake in both directions, with stops at seven places on the way. Available from Easter to November, with evening cruises in summer.

Buttermere   The B5289 from Cockermouth is the gentle route to the stunning scenery of Buttermere. Approaching from Keswick means going over the winding Honister Pass (good for views). Buttermere village is a popular base for walks, from lakeside strolls to tougher climbs, but you can't get there by bus.

COCKERMOUTH AND WHITEHAVEN

Wordsworth was born in a large Georgian house in Cockermouth (35 minutes by bus). He wrote about the garden in his *Prelude*, and it's still delightful (National Trust, open April to early November, not Thursday). Buses go on to surprisingly large towns by the sea. Whitehaven is the home of Michael Moon's second-hand bookshop, which boasts a mile of shelves (an hour from Cockermouth).The September Crab Fair at Egremont near Whitehaven has been held since 1267. It starts with the parade of the apple cart, when apples are thrown to the crowd, and ends with the World Gurning Championships – the winner is the person who pulls the ugliest face.

SKIPTON

Skipton is attractive with its castle, cobbled streets and market, and is a good base for exploring the Yorkshire Dales National Park– a part of the Pennine where green, steep valleys ('dales') rise up to crags and high moors.

The dales are a real delight – crisscrossed by drystone walls which surround rich meadowland, and dotted with stone barns. In between, there's high moorland rising to over 2,000ft in places. Many parts can only be seen on foot, but most dales, including Wensleydale and Swaledale, have roads running through them.

Local flavour
The limestone geology of the Yorkshire Dales makes some dramatic features – white crags and cliffs, waterfalls and potholes, limestone pavements, and caves with stalactites and stalagmites.

You can choose from hundreds of miles of paths however, and the national park arranges guided walks. The Pennine Way long-distance footpath runs through the Yorkshire Dales on its challenging route through northern England. Malham, Horton (on the Settle–Carlisle railway line) and Hawes are all on the path. Walkers on the higher areas of the Yorkshire Dales should be prepared for rough mountain terrain. Boots, warm clothes, waterproofs and rations are advised, and you should know how to use a map and compass.

Apart from the natural spectaculars, the stone-built villages and small market towns scattered along the dales are often places of character, because they're centres for the surrounding sheep-farming country. The Yorkshire Dales also have their share of the county's extraordinary medieval abbeys (for others, see *York*). The abbeys are ruins now, but they're still remarkable. A few miles south of Skipton is the Brontë family home at Haworth, a hugely popular place to visit.

Most of the main centres around the Dales can be reached by bus from Skipton; services may be infrequent, but are better in summer, when the Dalesbus service supplements regular routes. Outside the summer, bus times depend mainly on the needs of school children and shoppers. Consult *Dales Connections*, a free guide to bus and train services available from tourist offices and national park centres. Using the railway is an outing in itself – Skipton is near the start of a spectacular 70-mile stretch between Settle and Carlisle. If you want to see the northern part of the Dales by public transport outside summer, you'll need to stay further north, perhaps at Richmond, Hawes or Leyburn.

The *Yorkshire Dales Visitor* is a newspaper-style guide to the national park's activities and facilities, available free from information centres.

Moneysaver
Bunkhouse barns are barns converted into basic hostels, with heating, showers and bunk beds. They cost from £2 to £5 per person per night.

There are several places offering bed and breakfast in Skipton, and some self-catering cottages, with a bigger choice in the surrounding villages. The Skipton tourist information centre can supply a list of all sorts of local places to stay, including a bunkhouse barn (see *Moneysaver*). Details of accommodation throughout the national park are available from national park centres or by post (send 45p) from Yorkshire Dales National Park, Colvend, Hebden Road, Grassington, Skipton, North Yorkshire BD23 5LB. Booking is advisable for the summer and weekends.

If your tour of the north leads you from Keswick to Skipton, 'Mountain Goat' run a direct service on certain days during the summer; otherwise there is no direct route. The most scenic way is to catch a bus to Carlisle (about 1½ hours) and then a train along the spectacular Carlisle–Settle route (about 2½ hours). No trains operate on winter Sundays. Another way is by bus to Lancaster (three hours) and then train (70 minutes). From London (King's Cross) it's 2½ hours to Leeds, where you change trains for a 45-minute run to Skipton.

Skipton is full of character, with narrow alleys leading off the main street and terraces of mill-workers' houses. There are small specialist shops and a market on Saturday, plus market stalls every day except Tuesday. The tourist information centre is in a small square off Sheep Street. Just behind that is the Leeds and Liverpool Canal, a cross-country highway for boat travellers, with cruises, boats for hire and a towpath to walk along.

Skipton Castle stands at the top of the town. The stronghold of the Clifford family from 1311 to 1676, this is one of the few medieval castles that's still intact and roofed.

ORIENTATION IN SKIPTON

INFORMATION
TOURIST OFFICE
8 Victoria Square. ☎ 0756 792809.
Yorkshire Dales National Park *Colvend, Hebden Road, Grassington, Skipton, North Yorkshire BD23 5LB. National park centres with full range of information at Grassington, Aysgarth Falls, Hawes, and Malham (Easter to October and some winter weekends); Clapham and Sedbergh (Easter to October); many other information points.*
PUBLIC LAVATORIES
High Street car park; Coach Street car park (off Gargrave Road).
POST OFFICE
Swadford Street.

TRANSPORT
BUSES
Leave from bus station, Keighley Road, south of centre. Operators are Keighley and District Travel Ltd, Central Buildings, Keighley Road, ☎ 0756 795331; Pennine Motors, Grouse Garage, Gargrave, ☎ 0756 749215.
TRAINS
Skipton station, short walk west of centre. For information ☎ 0274 733994.
CAR HIRE
Peter Watson *Otley Road. ☎ 0756 790533.*

BICYCLE HIRE
Mick Walker *Water Street.*
☎ *0756 794386. Cycles at*
£10 per day.
Dave Ferguson *1 Brook*
Street. ☎ *0756 795367.*
There are many other firms
hiring cycles in the national
park. Details of these, and
of the Yorkshire Dales
Cycle Route are available
from the National Park
Information Centre at
Colvend.

ACCOMMODATION
HOTELS
Both of these do evening
meals.
Craven House *56 Keighley*
Road. ☎ *0756 794657.*
Single bed and breakfast £14.
Highfield Hotel *58 Keighley*
Road. ☎ *0756 793182.*
Single bed and breakfast
from £17.

EATING OUT
Oats *Chapel Hill.* ☎ *0756*

798118. Lunches under £10,
dinner more expensive.
Red Lion Hotel *High Street.*
☎ *0756 790718. Bar lunches.*
YOUTH HOSTEL
The Old Rectory *Linton.*
☎ *0756 752400; this is the*
nearest, there are several
others in the national park.
CAMP SITE
Overdale Trailer Park
Harrogate Road. ☎ *0756*
693480 (half a mile from
centre).

OUTINGS FROM SKIPTON

EMBSAY AND BOLTON ABBEY

A few minutes bus ride takes you to the restored 1888 railway station at Embsay, just outside Skipton. Steam-hauled trains set off from here for an inexpensive 20-minute rural ride to Holywell Halt, which has a picnic area. Open on Sundays all year, and other days in summer.

Bolton Abbey village is 10 minutes further on at the southern end of Wharfedale. The 'abbey' was an Augustinian priory, founded in the 12th century, and now a graceful ruin in a leafy setting beside the River Wharfe. The nave is still used as the parish church.

WHARFEDALE

Grassington is the main village for Wharfedale. The quick bus route is via Linton (see below); the other way is along Wharfedale via Bolton Abbey, and takes about half an hour longer. This is an attractive stone village, with a cobbled market place and narrow streets and alleys. Today the village is a bustling touring centre, with lots of shops and a national park information centre.

Just across the river, Linton has stone houses around a green with a beck running through (20 minutes by bus). Buses stop outside Fountaine Hospital, a very imposing almshouse. Stepping stones, a packhorse bridge, a clapper bridge (made with stone slabs) and a road bridge cross the water.

MALHAM

The limestone of the Yorkshire Dales comes to the surface in spectacular style at Malham (40 minutes by bus). This is a natural destination for sightseers and field trips, and there's an information centre. You have to be prepared to walk to see the sights, even if you arrive by car, but there are signposted paths. The mighty cliff north of the village is Malham Cove: it rises 240ft high, and has a limestone pavement at the top. Malham Tarn is a mountain lake about 1½ miles further north, and is part of a nature reserve.

About the same distance northeast of the village, Gordale Scar is a limestone gorge between towering cliffs. One popular path leads by a waterfall called Janet's Foss. Many of the limestone pavements were scraped bare in the most recent Ice Age. Since then the rain has etched into the surface, creating crevices which may be full of flowers in summer.

CLAPHAM AND INGLEBOROUGH

Clapham is a pretty village on the south side of Ingleborough, another great area for limestone features (an hour by bus) and it has a national park information centre. A path leads about a mile north to Ingleborough Showcave, where a lighted footpath leads past stalactites, stalagmites and fossils: open March to October and winter weekends. There's another showcave at Ingleton, a few miles further on.

Moneysaver
Pennine Motors offers a special day ticket (around £5) which is valid on their routes, Embsay, Linton, Malham, Settle, Clapham and Ingleton. Buy the ticket on the first bus you board.

Ingleborough is also a potholer's paradise – one of its holes is the abyss called Gaping Gill, where Fell Beck plunges over 360ft into a cavern big enough hold York Minster's nave. For a few days in late May and late August, the Bradford and Craven potholing clubs set up a winch at the top, so that non-potholers can be lowered into this amazing place.

SETTLE AND THE RAILWAY

The best day to visit Settle is on Tuesday, when a big, lively market takes over the town centre

Ribblehead Viaduct on the Settle-Carlisle line.

(20 minutes by train). The railway from Settle to Carlisle runs for 70 miles through remote mountains and moorland with views of rivers and waterfalls. The most impressive features are the 24-arch Ribblehead viaduct and the Blea Moor tunnel.

WENSLEYDALE

Wensleydale cuts a broad green swathe through the middle of the national park. Hawes has a national park information centre and the Dales Countryside Museum, and attracts crowds of visitors in summer. It's still a centre for Dales farms however: after the summer, locally-reared sheep and cattle are sold in sales almost every day. There's a market on Tuesday all year.

Local flavour
Elijah Allen's grocery sells local cheeses and other specialities. Wensleydale cheese was first made from ewe's milk, probably by the monks of Jervaulx Abbey near by. The Wensleydale Creamery in Hawes uses cow's milk, but ewe's milk versions are also available.

A summer Dalesbus runs from Skipton to Hawes in about two hours. Garsdale train station is 50 minutes from Skipton. In summer a bus meets at least one train a day for the 10-minute ride to Hawes; there's also a less frequent winter service.

A short walk north takes you to Hardraw Force, where water plunges in a sheer fall of

nearly 100ft. Access is through the Green Dragon pub, which levies a small charge. A series of foaming waterfalls along the River Ure can be seen from well signposted paths and viewing points near Aysgarth, 10 minutes before Hawes on the Dalesbus from **Skipton**.

HAWORTH

Haworth, south of the Dales on the fringe of industrial West Yorkshire, was the home of the Brontë family and the bleak moors above helped inspire Emily Brontë's *Wuthering Heights*. You can reach it by catching the train to Keighley (15 minutes), and then changing platforms for the Keighley and Worth Valley railway – a preserved line with steam-hauled trains at weekends from March to October, daily in the Easter and Spring Bank Holiday weeks, and during July and August (15 minutes). The very steep main street leads up to the parsonage where the Brontë sisters lived their lonely lives and wrote their extraordinary novels.

YORK

Medieval streets, city walls, Viking connections and a soaring cathedral combine to attract millions of visitors to York each year. The city justifies all this attention, but it does get crowded; the best time to look round the old streets is in the late afternoon and evening when the biggest crowds have gone.

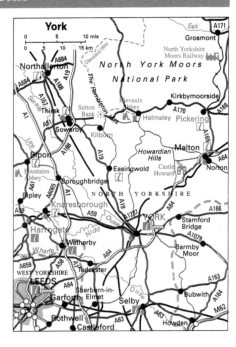

Moneysaver
The York Visitor Card costs 50p from tourist information centre, and gives a discount on admission to 12 popular places.

Local flavour
The name York comes from Jorvik, the 9th-century Viking town on this site. The Viking word for street survives as 'gate', and entrance gates are known as 'bars'.

York has theatres and a racecourse, good restaurants and lots of pubs. Out of the city, The North York Moors National Park rewards exploration, with extraordinary abbey ruins and another famous steam railway – in addition to the wonderful scenery.

Trains and tour buses will take you to all these places in summer, but you'll need independent transport for out-of-town sightseeing in winter. Within the city, cars are banned from several streets, and cycling is a popular way to get around. There is a park-and-ride scheme.

York is used to visitors and has a lot of bed and breakfast accommodation outside the city walls. Self catering in York itself is limited, but the tourist information centre can supply a list of places in the area. Booking is advisable for all types of accommodation: York is always busy, but especially so in summer and at weekends.

York is about 75 minutes from Skipton by train. It's two hours or less by train from London (King's Cross station), or four hours from London by coach. Leeds-Bradford airport is about 35 minutes by train: it has flights to other cities in Britain and mainland Europe, plus a summer flight to Toronto; Manchester International has more overseas flights (three hours by bus).

York today is a sizeable city, but the focus of interest is inside the medieval walls, still substantial and offering long stretches of high-level walking along their ramparts.

Volunteer guides lead free walking tours, starting at the tourist information centre at 10.15am and 2.15pm all year, and sometimes in the evenings too. There's also a guided Ghost Walk, starting at the Kings Arms Pub by the Ouse Bridge at 8pm each evening (charge).

Guide Friday/York Tour and City Tour both do open-topped bus rides round the city. Buses start every 15 minutes (less often in winter), and tickets are valid all day - prices from £3. The other way to see the city is from the River Ouse. There are paths beside it, and boat trips are available in summer.

York Minster is the biggest Gothic cathedral in northern Europe. If you want to savour the atmosphere of this huge church in peace, get there before 9am. It's worth taking binoculars for the fantastic stained glass and other finely detailed decorations. Admission is free, but a donation is suggested; there is a small admission charge for the Chapter House and you have to pay to visit the foundations in the cathedral, where Roman, Anglo-Saxon and Norman work can be seen alongside mighty 20th-century underpinning. It also costs extra to climb the tower, but the best city views are from here.

One luxurious way to start the day is to wander around the Minster while it's still empty, and then treat yourself to breakfast and the morning papers at Betty's elegant tearooms, another Yorkshire institution. Betty's also serves a fine tea and stays open until 9pm, but you may have to wait to get in.

A mesh of ancient streets in front of the Minster takes you to the Shambles, where the buildings haven't changed very much since the Middle Ages. It used to be the butchers' market, but antiques, gifts and fashion shops have tended to displace basic household suppliers around here.

In the 1970s Coppergate was the scene of an archaeological dig, which has been turned into the hugely popular Jorvik Viking Centre. In summer, be there early, or allow for a long wait. Also run by the York Archaeological Trust is the ARC, where you're invited to 'touch the past' by handling and studying archaeological finds (you're asked to book).

Other places to see in this area include Fairfax House, a Georgian mansion filled with fine furniture and clocks, and the wonderful Castle Museum, with a reconstructed Victorian street and rooms in period styles. All that's left of the castle itself is Clifford's Tower, which gives good views (English Heritage).

The 14th-century Merchant Adventurer's Hall is one of the best reminders of York's medieval merchants. It also has a chapel and housing for pensioners below (closed on Sunday in winter).

On the other side of the city, there's a botanical garden where medieval miracle plays are performed each summer, with the ruins of St Mary's Abbey as a backdrop. Also here is the Yorkshire Museum, which has a big collection of Roman and later finds, plus natural history and geology.

Just outside the walls by the station, old railway buildings house the National Railway Museum, with railway memorabilia from models and posters to steam locomotives and

The Minster, restored now after a freak fire in 1984.

royal coaches. This is as much a part of York as the Shambles – railways were big business here in the 19th century.

Local flavour
York is the home of Terry's and Rowntree confectionery firms.

York has over 70 pubs in or just outside the city walls, and can be very lively at night. Performances at the Grand Opera House and Theatre Royal range from touring opera to pantomime and pop; the arts centre has (sometimes wacky) music and drama; and the York Film Theatre offers alternatives to the city's chain cinemas.

Moneysaver
Free tours of the Grand Opera House start at 3pm on Thursday and last about 50 minutes. Sunday at the Arts Centre is usually Family Day, with live blues music and children's entertainment – admission free, breakfast available.

ORIENTATION IN YORK

INFORMATION
TOURIST OFFICE
De Grey Rooms, Exhibition Square. ☎ *0904 621756. Also in Rougier Street.*
POST OFFICE
22 Lendal.
PUBLIC LAVATORIES
Rougier Street; by tourist office; off Esplanade; St Sampson's Square (women); Parliament (men).

TRANSPORT
BUSES
Most leave from St Leonard's, outside the tourist office Buses for the sugested outings are Yorktour,

St Sampson's Square, ☎ *0904 645151.*
TRAINS
York station, west side of city centre. For information ☎ *0904 642155.*
CAR HIRE
Budget Rent-a-Car Old Station House, 15 Foss Islands Road (near Walmgate Bar). ☎ *0904 644919.*
BICYCLE HIRE
York Cycle Hire Fishergate Centre, Fishergate. ☎ *0904 626064 (or 0860 785839 mobile phone). Bicycles at £5.50 a day.*

ACCOMMODATION
HOTELS AND GUESTHOUSES
Arnot House 17 Grosvenor Terrance, Bootham. ☎ *0904 641966. Single bed and breakfast from £11.*
Alfreda 61 Heslington Lane, Fulford. ☎ *0904 631698. Double bed and breakfast from £25.*
YOUTH HOSTEL
York Youth Hostel Haverford, Water End, Clifton. ☎ *0904 653147.*
CAMP SITE
Rawcliffe Caravan Site Manor Lane, Shipton Road. ☎ *0904 624422.*

EATING OUT
Shapel's Bistro 2 Lendal. ☎ *0904 658227. Main courses around £5.*
Betty's Café Tea Rooms St Helen's Square. ☎ *0904 659142.*

OUTINGS FROM YORK

KNARESBOROUGH

Knaresborough has steep narrow streets and a castle high above the gorge of the River Nid (25 minutes by train). Across the river, Mother Shipton's Cave was the birthplace of a feared 16th-century character, said to have foreseen things such as telephones, aeroplanes and Australia. Next to the cave, the water from a limestone spring runs down and turns to stone the teddy bears and other objects hung here.

HARROGATE

Harrogate is a couple of stops along the line (35 minutes from York). It used to be a spa town, and the Royal Pump room still serves sulphurous water to the brave. Today the town thrives on conferences and trade fairs, but the parks and shops make a good day out for other sorts of visitors. Betty's Café Tea Rooms on Parliament Street was founded in 1919 - this is the parent of the Betty's in York, and tea here is a special experience.

THE MOORS

You should be able to reach the following places on the Yorktour Heritage bus, which runs in summer. Fares are around £4. Otherwise there's no easy public transport

Fountains Abbey   Cistercian monks founded Fountains Abbey in 1132. It's a ruin now, but a very extensive one, with high walls that look virtually complete. It is set in an 18th-century a landscape garden with a lake, mock temples and statues; beyond those is a deer park (National Trust). There is no charge for visiting just the deer park.

Castle Howard   A day out in itself, this vast stately home is filled with treasures and set among 1,000 acres of grounds, with a lake, fountains and rose gardens. This was the country-house setting for *Brideshead Revisited* on television, and it's still the home of the Howard family, who commissioned it in 1699. Open late March to early November.

Helmsley and Rievaulx   Helmsley is a pretty town of stone and red pantiles, with lots of shops and inns, a market on Fridays, and an information centre for the North York Moors National Park. The ruins and vast earthworks of Helmsley Castle are near the centre (English Heritage); so is Duncombe Park, which was designed by Vanbrugh and has an 18th-century landscaped garden. It's open Easter to September afternoons (not Monday or Tuesday).

From Helmsley, take a three-mile walk along the Cleveland Way long-distance footpath, or walk through the grounds of Duncombe Park and along the River Rye to Rievaulx Abbey, which rises tall and elegant in a deep, green, quiet valley. This was the first of the Cistercian abbeys in Yorkshire, and still gives a good idea of former glory (English Heritage). Paths lead on up to Rievaulx Terrace, a half-mile long lawn with enchanting views of the abbey and valley. The terrace was created for the Duncombe family in the mid 1700s and includes two mock temples, one of them richly painted inside. Run by the National Trust, it's open April to October.

Kilburn (near Helmsley) is the home of the Robert Thompson workshop, where furniture is handmade from English oak. Thompson died in 1955, but the workshop follows his custom of 'signing' each item with a carved mouse. The showroom can be visited.

Pickering Pickering is a busy market town, with steep streets and a market on Monday. It's also the start of the North Yorkshire Moors Railway, which offers steam-hauled rides along a scenic 18-mile route into the moors. Trains run mainly from April to October. A 'freedom of the rail' day ticket costs from around £6.

NEWCASTLE UPON TYNE

Local flavour
Newcastle and Northumberland used to be part of the kingdom of Northumbria. The lilting speech of this region comes from the Northumbrian dialect, and can be baffling to outsiders.

Newcastle is a big, lively city in the urban and industrial county of Tyne and Wear. The urban sprawl merges into seaside resorts on the coast, and it's also close to wild and open landscapes. This is border country, where the Romans built Hadrian's Wall right across Britain from east coast to west, to separate 'civilised' territory from the rest.

North of Newcastle is the county of Northumberland and the 400-square-mile Northumberland National Park. The coast is stunning, with long beaches and castles by the sea. South of the city the place not to miss is

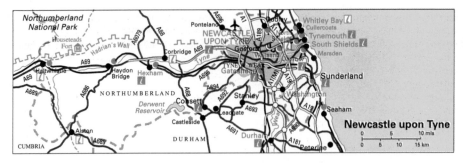

Durham, which has one of Britain's finest cathedrals.

For local travel, the Tyne and Wear Metro is a rapid transit system through the city and the surrounding urban area. Fares start very low. Details of all local public transport are available from the three Travelcentres in the city centre. For travel further afield, trains and buses serve surrounding towns, but transport to out-of-town places is not so good. Northumbria Car Tours do trips all year: they suggest an outline journey, but the details depend on what you want to see. Only seven can be carried, so this relaxed approach isn't too impractical. A combination of train and bicycle could work well.

There isn't a huge amount of budget accommodation, but it's supplemented in the summer and Easter vacations by students' rooms. Self-catering in the city itself is limited, but the surrounding area offers a much bigger choice: the tourist information centre can supply details.

Newcastle is an hour from York by rail, or

The famous Bridges across the Tyne are a sight to make any Geordie homesick!

2¼ hours by coach. If you're travelling from Keswick, there's a direct bus on Saturdays and Sundays (three hours). On other days, you have to go via Carlisle. Newcastle is three hours from London (King's Cross) by rail, 5½ hours from London by coach; two hours by rail from Edinburgh and 3½ hours by coach. Newcastle International airport is six miles north of the centre (frequent buses) for flights to cities in Britain and mainland Europe; Manchester International airport has more overseas flights and is five hours by bus.

Inexpensive guided city walks start at the Central Library from May to October, daily except Sunday, at 2pm. Summer Sunday walks start from the castle keep; there are also special theme walks and city coach tours.

Newcastle began as a fort on Hadrian's Wall, guarding a bridge across the River Tyne. The Normans founded the 'new castle' which still overlooks the river. Ships were built on the Tyne in the Middle Ages, and the 19th century saw a huge expansion of Tyneside shipbuilding and engineering but many yards have now closed. The oldest city buildings can be seen near the Swing Bridge, and the best city views are from the top of the castle keep (closed Mondays and bank holidays).

Local flavour

Newcastle people are 'Geordies', the name for all Tynesiders.

The city inland of the river was rebuilt in spacious style in the 19th century. Grey Street is an especially handsome curve of classical façades, leading up to the Theatre Royal and Grey's Monument. Central Arcade is worth a look for ornate decorations, and Grainger market for local flavour. One of the stalls has a Marks and Spencer Original Penny Bazaar sign overhead; another specialises in jaw-stopping toffee. It's open Monday to Saturday, as is the Green market off Clayton Street; the open-air Bigg market is on Tuesday, Thursday and Saturday.

This is a great shopping city – the Eldon Square complex looks a little like some vast space ship, but it does have a lot of stores, places to eat and a sports centre.

Newcastle also has several museums. The Laing Art Gallery is tucked away near the overhead motorway towards the east, and worth finding for paintings from the 18th century onwards, plus glass and ceramics (closed Mondays except bank holidays). Across the city, the Museum of Science and Engineering has working models and a section where children and others can try things out (closed Sunday and Monday.) The Museum of Antiquities at Newcastle University is the main museum for Hadrian's Wall (closed Sunday); there are Greek and natural history museums here too. Newcastle has two cathedrals as well

– St Nicholas is a fine medieval church; St Mary's was designed by Pugin.

Events include the Hoppings, Europe's biggest funfair, in late June on Town Moor.

> **Moneysaver**
> Admission to the museums mentioned here is free. The Museum of Science and Technology has free films on Saturday mornings; the Laing has free lunchtime talks.

Lots of restaurants (including a cluster in the small Chinese quarter), pubs, theatres and other venues combine to keep Newcastle humming at night. Famous names appear at the City Hall (for concerts) and the Theatre Royal; there are several other theatres and an arts centre; and pubs have live music. The Tyneside cinema offers alternatives to mainstream cinema; the Live Theatre just off the Quayside has seasons of Sunday lunchtime jazz. Newcastle has arts festivals and many other events; tourist information centres supply *Northern Events*, a free monthly guide to what's on.

ORIENTATION IN NEWCASTLE UPON TYNE

INFORMATION
Tourist Office
Central Library, Princess Square. ☎ 091-261 0691, ext 231 (city and surroundings); Central train station (city only).
Post Office
Eldon Square.
Public Lavatories
Tourist office; Eldon Square shopping centre; Eldon Gardens; Groat Market; by Swing Bridge.

TRANSPORT
Buses
Tyne and Wear area:

Information from Travelcentres at Haymarket Metro, Monument Metro and Central train station Metro, or ☎ PTE Travel-Line on 091-232 5325.
Northumberland: *Contact Northumbria Motor Services Ltd, Gallowgate, ☎ 091-232 4211.*
Minibus tours: *Northumbria Car Tours, 476 Oakfield Court, East Herrington, Sunderland, ☎ 091-520 1047.*
Metro
See above for Travelcentres and Travel-Line. National Express: Gallowgate, ☎ 091-261 6077.

Trains
Newcastle Central station, city centre. For information ☎ 091-232 6262.
Car Hire
Avis Rent-a-Car *7 George Street. ☎ 091-232 5283.*
Bicycle Hire
Centa Hire *217 Jesmond Road. ☎ 091-281 5376. Bicycles at £5 for the first day, £2 for each subsequent day, plus deposit.*

ACCOMMODATION
Hotels And Guesthouse
Chirton House Hotel *46 Clifton Road. ☎ 091-273 0407. Double bed and breakfast from £36.*
Clifton Cottage *Dunholme Road. ☎ 091-273 7347.*

Double bed and breakfast from £26.

COLLEGE ACCOMMODATION
Newcastle Polytechnic, Coach Lane Campus Halls of Residence Coach Lane. ☎ 091-232 6002. Summer vacation only, bed and breakfast from £11.
Newcastle Polytechnic,

Lavaine Hall c/o Business Services, Ellison Place. ☎ 091-232 6002. Easter and summer vacations, bed and breakfast from £9.
YOUTH HOSTEL
Newcastle Youth Hostel 107 Jesmond Road, Jesmond. ☎ 091-218 2570.

CAMP SITE
Caravan Club Site Gosforth Park Racecourse, High Gosforth Park, ☎ 091-236 3258 (summer only).

EATING OUT
King Neptune 34-6 Stowell Street, ☎ 091-261 6657/6660.

OUTINGS FROM NEWCASTLE

IN TYNE AND WEAR

The Coast   Cullercoats, Whitley Bay, Tynemouth and other seaside resorts can all be reached by Metro, and sandy beaches are the norm. A couple of miles from South Shields, Marsden has cliffs, caves and a huge rock which the sea has carved into an arch.

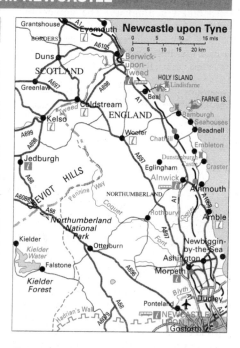

Local flavour
South Shields was the birthplace of Catherine Cookson, one of the bestselling authors ever. It's now promoted along with the rest of South Tyneside as 'Catherine Cookson Country'. Tourist information centres supply a free guide.

Jarrow   The ruined monastery in the middle of industrial scenery at Jarrow was a centre of learning in the 7th and 8th centuries (15 minutes by Metro from Central train station). This was the the home of the Venerable Bede (about AD672–735), who wrote around 80 books recording the knowledge of the time (his history of England is still consulted by historians today). The monastery church was founded in AD685, and has the oldest stained glass in Europe; also here is the Bede Monastery Museum (closed Mondays).

Washington   Washington is an ex-colliery town, and the former home of George Washington's family (20 minutes by bus from Eldon Square, Newcastle). His ancestors lived in the Old Hall in the 13th century, and the house belonged to the family until the 17th century. Run by the National Trust, it's open April to September (closed Friday except Good Friday).

DURHAM

Durham City grew up around the shrine of St Cuthbert, whose body was taken there by monks escaping Viking raids on Holy Island.

The heart of Durham is the steep-sided peninsula where the castle and cathedral rise high above the River Wear (20 minutes by train). It's a delightful city to walk in, as long as you're wearing the right shoes for cobbled and steep streets. The cathedral is stunning, very grand and very simple. It looks across Palace Green to the castle, which was founded in 1072: open for guided tours only, every afternoon in summer, but otherwise only Monday, Wednesday and Saturday. Like most of the buildings around here, it's now part of Durham University, the third oldest in England. The university's Oriental Museum just south of the centre is well worth a look; so allow time for just strolling around the streets, which date from Georgian times and earlier. Boats can be hired on the river.

ALONG HADRIAN'S WALL

BUDGET FOR A DAY

Explorer bus ticket	3·75
Hadrian's Wall Discount Ticket	5·00
Lunch	2·50
Dinner	7·50
	£ 18·75
plus accommodation	

The Emperor Hadrian had a wall built across Britain to stop raids from the unconquered land further north; work started in around AD122. The forts known as milecastles marked each Roman mile, with lookout turrets in between, and larger forts at every seventh mile.

The most impressive stretches of Hadrian's Wall are west of Hexham, in the windswept hills of the Northumberland National Park. In summer a special bus visits all the main sites on this central section; a day ticket costs around £3 and the bus sets off four times a day from Hexham (40 minutes by train). Drivers should follow the B6318.

There's no charge for seeing some of the best sections of Hadrian's Wall, or for several turrets and milecastles. Information centres supply leaflets with details of places to visit.

> **Moneysaver**
> The Hadrian's Wall discount pass saves money on entry to four out of six major sites. Some are free to English Heritage members and overseas holders of Heritage Cards.

Any visit should include at least one of the larger excavated forts and its associated museum. Housesteads fort is especially impressive – it occupies a high ridge on a spectacular stretch of the wall. The remains of a hospital, multi-seat latrine and other buildings can be seen, and there are good views and walks. Run by National Trust and English Heritage.

Hexham, as well as a convenient base for exploring the wall, is a sizeable and busy market town for the surrounding farming country. Market day is Tuesday

THE FAR NORTH

The Northumberland National Park The park runs north from Hadrian's Wall to the Scottish border, through remote, thinly populated hills. There is plenty of scope for walkers here, from rough but not desperately difficult paths along Hadrian's Wall, to the bleak Cheviot Hills in the far north. The national park authority arranges guided walks all year, including Explorer Tours with coach transport from Newcastle (about £5, excluding admission fees). Details from Armstrong Galley at 12 Haymarket, Newcastle. Walkers planning anything more than a short stroll should be properly prepared.

Kielder Forest in the west of Northumberland is the largest man-made forest in northern Europe, and includes its largest artificial lake. **Alnwick** Alnwick (say 'annick') is between the coast and the hills (1¼ hours by bus), an old stone-built town, with several pubs, a medieval costumed fair in June, a market on Saturdays, and some eccentric features – no one will move the dusty bottles in the window of the Old Cross Inn, because the man who put them there 150 or so years ago dropped dead. Alnwick Castle has been the home of the Percy family since 1309 and is sumptuous inside; open most afternoons from early May to late September.

Local flavour

Oak-smoked kippers are a speciality of Craster, on the coast near Alnwick, and can be bought in the village.

Farther north are Craster and Embleton for walks to Dunstanburgh Castle ruins; Seahouses, which is both a fishing port and the main resort, with boat trips to the Farne Islands bird sanctuary; and Bamburgh, where the mighty castle is inhabited, but can be visited.

Holy Island   Tides permitting, you can visit Holy Island (Lindisfarne), reached by a causeway from Beal. There's also a bus service, connecting with buses from Newcastle at least once a week – see the *Northumberland Public Transport Guide*. Holy Island is a popular spot but still has charm, and there are lots of wild flowers and birds. A fishing village is clustered in one corner, with the graceful ruins of Lindisfarne Priory near by (English Heritage, closed Monday in winter). Lindisfarne Castle is a 15th-century fort on a crag, transformed by Sir Edwin Lutyens in 1903 into a luxurious home. Run by the National Trust, it's open April to September (not Fridays except Good Friday) and some days in October.

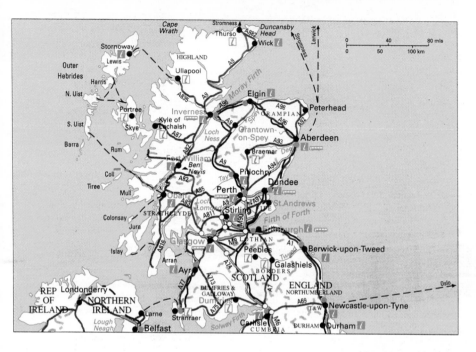

One of many nice things about Scotland is that the clichés turn out to be true. There really are magnficent mountains, and heather moorland which turns purple in summer for as far as you can see. There really are remote, romantic lochs, and deep glens with clear streams rushing through. A lot of Scottish people really do eat porridge for breakfast and haggis for supper. And golf really is a national game . Scotland has other things you might not expect – turreted castles like pictures in fairytale books, gardens full of sub-tropical plants, empty beaches of white sand, and summer daylight hours that virtually eliminate the night.

You might also be surprised by the differences between England and Scotland. Scottish banks issue their own banknotes, which are used alongside the usual Bank of England notes; most banks close for Scottish public holidays, but shops and other businesses often stay open, except for New Year's Day. Scotland has a public holiday on the first Monday in August (not the last, as in England). There are also local spring and autumn holidays. English

is the language spoken, but you might find the Glasgow dialect hard to understand, and you might find yourself impressed by a poetic turn of phrase in the Highlands.

Local flavour

Scotland has fewer restrictions on Sunday trading than England, and some stores are open on Sunday, especially in summer.

This chapter starts at Dumfries, in the southwest corner of Scotland. Dumfries is a base for exploring rugged hill country and a coast which is often overlooked by people rushing north to the Highlands. There are some exceptional gardens in this part of Scotland.

Next on the list is Glasgow, which has thrown off its old image of grime and depressed industry to reveal its parks, excellent museums and art collections, lively nightlife and exotic Victorian architecture. Glasgow was European

City of Culture 1990, and has become one of Britain's trendier cities. Besides the attractions of the centre, it's also in easy reach of Loch Lomond and the start of the Highlands.

Oban is a base for exploring a beautiful stretch of the west coast, and for sampling Scotland's islands. It's also within reach of the stunning Highlands scenery around Fort William. Inverness is next – a base for the strange, wild mountains in the north and a string of castles near the Moray Firth.

From Inverness we turn south again to Grantown-on-Spey, which has high mountains near by, castles and whisky distilleries to visit. Next is Pitlochry, which offers similar attractions in the Perthshire part of the Highlands.

South again into the rolling farmland of Fife is St Andrews, with ancient streets and Scotland's oldest university. For golfers the importance of St Andrews is that it's the home of the Royal and Ancient Golf Club.

Scotland's capital city of Edinburgh, overlooked by the castle on its crag, is a wonderful place just to walk around, with its higgledy-piggledy Old Town and elegant New Town – but it also has national art and museum collections, and the extraordinary attraction of the Edinburgh Festival, which offers three weeks of total immersion in the arts.

If you want to get round quickly, you'll need a car. Travellers from the south of England will almost certainly find the driving relaxing, despite the mountains, because there's so little other traffic.

The bagpipes are still an important element of any traditional gathering or event.

Moneysaver
You can save money with the Caledonian Express Tourist Trail Pass, and you can also get regional rail rovers.

It's possible to get around Scotland on buses, if you're prepared to take your time and be at the mercy of timetables (buses are often timed to suit school children and shoppers). In summer the most popular places are well served by coach tours.

Nearly every railway route in Scotland is worth travelling just for the views of lochs, sea and mountains. A combination of train and bicycle is popular in Scotland, although you have to make a reservation for certain routes.

There are some very grand hotels, but good inexpensive hotels exist too, and bed and breakfast places abound. The Scottish Youth Hostels Association (SYHA) has 80 hostels, and there are plenty of camp sites. Cottages and apartments for travellers are available too.

Scottish school summer holidays start at the end of June and finish about halfway through August. Demand for accommodation eases off a little until the English August Bank Holiday – except around Edinburgh, where demand during August is always heavy because of the Festival.

Moneysaver
High tea is a budget alternative to an evening dinner. There's usually a choice of main course, with an accompaniment of tea, bread, scones and cakes – a filling meal for well under £10.

Scotland's most famous dish must be haggis, which tastes much better than you might expect from reading list of ingredients (offal, suet and oatmeal, boiled in a stomach). The traditional accompaniment is potatoes and turnips ('neeps') – and a glass of whisky (try pouring a dash over the haggis). Salmon, trout and venison are all available fresh, and Aberdeen Angus cattle are a source of steaks. If you like takeaways (or carryouts, as they're called here), you'll enjoy Scottish fish and chip shops,

194

because they sell pizza, pasta, curry and other foods as well as fried fish.

Every Scottish town with tourists has shops selling tweeds, tartans and knitwear, which is often advertised as being at factory prices. Men often wear kilts for special occasions, but only rarely as everyday dress. You may find bargains, especially in light fashion knitwear, but the real advantage of buying in Scotland is the range.

The same goes for Scotch whisky – the advantage of being in Scotland is the choice rather than the bargains. The thing to look for is the pure malts, which can be hard to find elsewhere. Several distilleries offer free tours – see especially *Grantown-on-Spey* and *Pitlochry* in this chapter.

In summer, pubs and hotels often arrange ceilidhs (say 'kay-lees'), which are evenings of traditional music and dance for a low price, a good fun evening out. Towns which are popular with tourists may well have more lavish Scottish evenings too. Other events with a lot of local atmosphere are agricultural shows and

Highland games; these take place all over Scotland, not just in the Highlands. They're well worth attending, for local colour and a chance to see centuries-old heavyweight sports events, such as 'putting' the stone, throwing the hammer and tossing the caber. Tossing the caber is one of the most popular events in Highland games. The caber is a pine tree trunk, which the competitor endeavours to throw so that it curves over in a semicircle and falls in a straight line.

For advance information, write to the Scottish Tourist Board, PO Box 15, Edinburgh EH1 1UY.

Local flavour
Anything called Scotch whisky must by law have been made in Scotland. Distillers who produce whisky overseas and call it Scotch can be prosecuted. The word 'Scotch' is only used for whisky and a type of pie – otherwise, always use 'Scottish'.

DUMFRIES

Dumfries is Scotland's southern-most town, just across the border from England. From there you can explore Dumfries and Galloway, the lower left-hand corner of Scotland on the map; the scenery is beautiful – rugged hills and open moorland, with green pasture for sheep and cattle further down. Lochs are strung along the river valleys, with waterfalls in the higher, wilder places. There are also many miles of Forestry Commission plantations, which often

The 15th-century Devorgilla Bridge over the Nith.

have signed trails and other facilities for visitors. Along the coast you'll find some attractive little fishing ports, sandy beaches and dramatic cliffs. If you're relying on public transport, you might like to make a second base towards the west of the region, to explore its coast and gardens.

Quiet roads make for relaxing driving in this part of Scotland, and there's a scenic rail route up the west coast. Buses will get you to many interesting places, although Sunday services are patchy or non-existent. Bicycles can be rented in Dumfries.

There are several bed and breakfast places in Dumfries itself, and a huge choice of places to stay outside it.

Dumfries is 1½ hours by bus from Carlisle, so you could combine this region with the suggested tour of northern England. From Edinburgh it's two hours by bus; from Glasgow it's 1½ hours by rail.

Sir Walter Scott called Dumfries the Queen of the South. Today it's an imposing little town

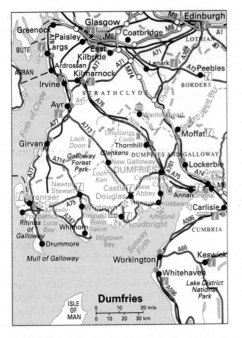

Dumfries

Bridge, built in the 15th century.

The tourist information centre is close to the river at the centre of town. The shopping streets that climb up from the river bank include market places (open on Sunday). There's a Burns monument at the end of the main street; also open to visitors are Burns House (where he lived for three years before his death in 1796) and the Robert Burns Centre. Keep the centre in mind for evening entertainment too – the audio-visual theatre reopens at night as a cinema, with tickets at a reasonable price.

> **Moneysaver**
>
> Dumfries museums are free or inexpensive, but you can make a small saving with a Museums Saver Ticket (around £1). The Burns Centre cinema does a reduced-price family ticket. Admission to Gracefield arts centre is free.

The Dumfries Museum is up the hill, and besides lots of displays on the area it has a camera obscura, which gives a view of the town and its surroundings. The Gracefield arts centre is just north of the centre.

of red sandstone, cut through by the wide River Nith. The two sides of the town are linked for pedestrians by the old but elegant Devorgilla

ORIENTATION IN DUMFRIES

INFORMATION
TOURIST OFFICE
Whitesands. ☎ *0387 53862*
POST OFFICE
Great King Street.
PUBLIC LAVATORIES
By tourist office, Whitesands; Dock Park; Munches Street.

TRANSPORT
BUSES
Whitesands. Information from the Bus Shop, Whitesands, or ☎ *0345 090510; or ask at the tourist office.*
TRAINS
Dumfries station, on north
side of town, a short walk from the centre. For information ☎ *0387 64105.*
CAR HIRE
Klic Cars St Mary's Industrial Estate. ☎ *0387 68777.*
BICYCLE HIRE
Grierson and Graham *Church Street.* ☎ *0387 53405. £10 a day for a mountain bike, or £4 for an older three-speed, plus deposit. They have folding bicycles too.* •

ACCOMMODATION
BED AND BREAKFAST
North Laurieknowe *3 North Laurieknowe Place.* ☎ *03870 5413. Prices here start at around £10 per person.*
Station Hotel *49 Lovers' walk.* ☎ *0387 50388. There are several other bed and breakfast places – the tourist information office can supply a list.*
CAMP SITE
Sandyhills Bay Leisure Park. ☎ *05577 267.*

EATING OUT
Several places in town do light lunches.
Sev's *on Whitesands do a quality, low price Scottish fry-up.*
Station Hotel *49 Lovers' Walk.* ☎ *0387 50388. Specialises in Scottish produce – they do a fixed-price lunch.*

196

OUTINGS FROM DUMFRIES

EAST TO GRETNA

Gretna Green is a little over an hour's bus ride away. The blacksmith's shop at Gretna Green used to be the first place across the border where runaway couples from England could get married without parental consent. This colourful past makes Gretna one of Scotland's most famous tourist spots.

Caerlaverock is 20 minutes south of Dumfries (buses run from Shakespeare Street). Caerlaverock Castle was built for the Maxwell family in the 13th century, and is still looks good with its towers, fine interior decoration and moat. There's no charge for the Caerlaverock nature reserve, a huge expanse of salt marsh and estuary mud and a wonderful place for bird-watching in winter. But parts of it are hazardous – contact the warden for advice before visiting, telephone 038 777 275.

New Abbey is a tiny place in wooded hills, half an hour from Dumfries. There's an 18th-century water mill, but the place to see is Sweetheart Abbey, a beautiful ruin of red sandstone, set off by a carpet of green lawn. Several walks can be taken from here – a board outside the abbey has a map with suggestions.

Local flavour
Sweetheart Abbey was founded by Devorgilla in 1273, to commemorate her husband, John Baliol. She also founded Balliol College, Oxford, in his memory.

Arbigland has historic connections with the United States – an 18th-century owner was William Craik, whose son James became George Washington's doctor and friend. Craik's gardener was father of Paul Jones who helped found the US Navy. He was born in a cottage near by. Spacious woodland and formal gardens, run down to a sandy beach; the gardens are open from May to September on Sunday, Tuesday and Thursday afternoons. Buses run to Kirkbean (half an hour from Dumfries).

SOUTHWEST – THREAVE AND KIRKCUDBRIGHT

Threave Gardens are run by the National Trust for Scotland, which has a gardening school here. There's a lot of variety – the recommended time to visit is summer, but the gardens are open all year and you'll almost always see something interesting. Threave Wildfowl Refuge has viewing points for watching wintering wildfowl on the River Dee. Threave Castle is a little further away: it's tower was built by Archibald the Grim, and you get there by boat (admission free, but small charge for ferry). About 45 minutes from Dumfries by bus to Castle Douglas – about a mile away

Kirkcudbright (say 'ker-koobree') is an elegant little port town on the River Dee, about an hour from Dumfries by bus). Sizeable fishing vessels can be seen in the harbour, and cruisers take passengers round the coast to Ayr on certain summer days. Reminders of Paul Jones can be seen in Stewartry Museum (open Easter to October but not Sundays). The handsome ruin right in the middle of town is MacLellan's Castle, which was a 16th-century mansion (closed on weekdays from October to March).

Local flavour
The Stewartry Museum in Kirkcudbright shows the work of artists who have been attracted to this region. So does Broughton House, which was the home of the painter E A Hornel (open in summer, but not Tuesday).

Tongland Power Station is a couple of miles north – it's one of a string of 1920s power stations in this part of Scotland. You can also see the enormous dam, which has a salmon ladder to allow fish to travel upstream. Tours are four times a day from May to August, and there's no charge. To book, telephone 0557 30114; there's free transport from Kirkcudbright.

WANLOCKHEAD

Wanlockhead is Scotland's highest village in the bleak windswept mountains north of Dumfries. Most of Scotland's lead came from here until quite recently, as did silver and gold. Today it's the home of the Museum of Scottish Lead Mining, with a walk-in mine, miners' cottages and even a well-stocked miners' library, founded in 1756. If driving you could also take in Drumlanrigg Castle, which is full of treasures; open Easter to mid October.

Moneysaver

There's no charge for tours of Bladnoch Distillery in Wigtown. This is Scotland's southern-most malt whisky distillery.

GALLOWAY

Just north of Newton Stewart is the Galloway Forest Park, with many miles of walking including the Southern Upland Way long-distance footpath. Southward are hills and a rocky coastline dotted with pretty fishing villages. This is an area with a long history. S Ninian founded a church at Whithorn in the 5th century, and today the town offers an archaeological dig, the ruins of the cathedral which houses St Ninian's shrine and early Christian sculpted stones.

Galloway House Gardens were created in the 18th century; Castle Kennedy is about 45 minutes away by bus and has masses of flowering shrubs; there are other gardens, but perhaps the most amazing is Port Logan, which has the sea on three sides – here you'll see tree ferns and palms, basking in a climate more like that of Cornwall than Scotland.

GLASGOW

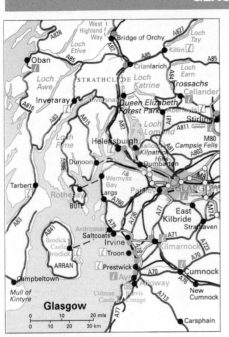

Glasgow

Glasgow was once considered to be a grimy ex-industrial place with social problems. Now the tables have turned. Glasgow has suddenly become trendy. The centre has been cleaned up to reveal wonderful Victorian architecture. There are coffee bars in place of dingy pubs, and a degree from Glasgow School of Art is a short cut to recognition in the art world. Glasgow's designation as European City of Culture 1990 epitomised the change of image, with a quite remarkable concentration of international art events.

That said, don't expect Glasgow to be all cappuccino and culture. And don't expect all Glaswegians to be thrilled by the city's renaissance – there's an argument that all the investment has gone into the centre, leaving some very run down suburbs. For visitors, it's definitely fun to visit, with plenty of things to see and a lively atmosphere. Glaswegians are noted for being outgoing and talkative.

You're never far from a view to the hills, and there are some beautiful places to visit near by. The coast is in easy reach for outings to the islands of Bute and Arran. Southwest of Glasgow, Ayr is a resort with plenty of character, and merges into Alloway, where Robert Burns was born. North of the city are Loch Lomond and the Trossach Hills.

Traffic can be very heavy, so drivers should park outside the city and catch a train in. Most suburban stations around Glasgow have free parking. Public transport is good, and a lot of places of interest are only a short walk from each other. Strathclyde Transport do a free *Visitor's Guide*, with a city map showing bus and train routes (ask the tourist information centre or Strathclyde Travel Centre). The Glasgow Underground runs round the centre, calling at 15 stations en route (it's known as the Clockwork Orange). There's a flat fare of about 50p for any length of journey. Trains and/or buses run to most of the places suggested for outings. The city isn't ideal for cyclists, but the Glasgow-Loch Lomond cycle way is well worth taking.

There are some bed and breakfast places near the city centre, and a much bigger choice further out. University halls of residence are open for bed and breakfast during the summer vacation (sometimes Easter as well).

Glasgow airport has flights from North America and mainland Europe as well as other parts of Britain. Scottish Citylink coaches run to Glasgow from London Heathrow and Gatwick airports (an eight or nine-hour journey). They have services from many other cities in England and Scotland as well.

The tourist information centre is in St Vincent Place. Guided walks start here from April to October. The nearest Underground is Buchanan Street.

For an instant taste of Glasgow's special architecture, stroll round the area called the Merchant City (by the tourist information centre). George Square is one of the city's showpieces. One side is filled by the City Chambers, built in Italian Renaissance style with a wonderful marble and alabaster staircase inside. No charge; guided tours are usually twice a day (not Thursday or weekends). The Stock Exchange in Nelson Mandela Square is another startling building. Walk up the High Street for Glasgow Cathedral, which was

Glasgow cathedral is one of the finest of its kind.

founded in the 6th century by St Mungo, Glasgow's patron saint.

Traffic-free Buchanan Street is the place for window shopping, especially at Princes Square, an ultra-snazzy, many-layered precinct. Argyle Arcade is lined with jewellers' shops, but it also has Sloan's bar, worth a look for its old-fashioned wood-panelled décor. The arcade leads into Argyle Street, where you'll find St Enoch's shopping centre. Besides being Europe's largest glass-covered mall, it also has an ice rink.

Sauchiehall Street is another popular traffic-free place to stroll. Along the way you pass the Willow Tearooms, with façade, furniture and fittings all designed by Charles Rennie Mackintosh. Just up the road is the Glasgow School of Art – perhaps the most amazing Mackintosh building. There are usually guided tours four times a day from Monday to Friday, and one on Saturday morning (times may change in term time).

Moneysaver
Admission to most of Glasgow's galleries and museums is free. There are commercial galleries too, which don't usually charge visitors.

The West End of town has a cluster of wonderful Victorian buildings. In Kelvingrove Park there's the wildly ornate Glasgow Art Gallery and Museum (free). Cross the park for Gothic-style Glasgow University, home of the Hunterian Museum and the Hunterian Art

Gallery (both free). You're close to the Botanic Gardens here, with the little River Kelvin and the enormous Kibble Palace glasshouse, where romantic statues are dotted among the foliage.

The Transport Museum in Kelvin Hall includes a reconstruction of a Glasgow street in 1938, besides lots of trams, trains and buses (free). The Tenement House in Buccleuch Street is in one of Glasgow's characteristic tenement blocks (National Trust for Scotland).

The East End (east of the city centre) has the People's Palace museum, which is for and about ordinary Glaswegians. It's on Glasgow Green, which runs along the River Clyde and has been a public park since 1662 (people used to dry their laundry on the grass).

Local flavour

The Barras (Barrows) open air street market is on Saturdays and Sundays in the East End, with over 1,000 stalls. You might find bargains; the stallholders' patter is an entertainment in itself, and there may be street musicians.

At Pollok Park, south of the River Clyde, a specially built gallery houses the Burrell Collection – all sorts of precious things amassed by Sir Wiliam Burrell, from medieval doorways to Degas paintings to fine lace. This is a special place, but don't forget Pollok House, in the same park, which has good collections too, or nearby Haggs Castle museum, purpose-designed for children. Admission to all three is free.

May is the time to visit for sheer concentration of arts events at the annual Mayfest arts festival; details from Mayfest Ltd, 18 Albion Street, Glasgow G1. You'll find something going on at all through the year though. Scottish Opera has its home at the Theatre Royal, which is also used by the Scottish Ballet and visiting productions; the Scottish National Orchestra is based at the Glasgow International Concert Hall, opened in 1990. Theatre ranges from the innovative productions at the Citizens' to family shows at the Pavilion – the Tron, the King's, the Tramway and many others all cater for a wide range of tastes, including a lot of experimental work. For rock music, nightclubs and the like, your best source of advice is *The List*. Theatre tickets are not expensive.

Moneysaver

Two Culture Bus routes go round Glasgow's sights. A day's unlimited travel on both routes costs around £4 ; the southern route costs around £2.50.

ORIENTATION IN GLASGOW

INFORMATION
TOURIST OFFICE
35 St Vincent Place.
☎ *041-204 4400.*
POST OFFICE
George Square.
PUBLIC LAVATORIES
Cathedral Square; St Vincent Place; Trongate.

TRANSPORT
CITY BUSES
Several operators, but for general information contact

Strathclyde Transport Travel Centre, St Enoch Square,
☎ *041-226 4826.*
LONG-DISTANCE BUSES/COACHES
Anderston bus station,
☎ *041-248 7432; Buchanan bus station,* ☎ *041-332 9191.*
TRAINS
Central and Queen Street stations. For information
☎ *041- 204 2844.*
CAR HIRE
Europcar 556 Pollokshawws Road. ☎ *041-423 5561*

ACCOMMODATION
HOTELS AND GUESTHOUSES

There are some bed and breakfast places in the city centre; more further out.
Rosemundy Guest House 50 Bentinck Street.
☎ *041-339 8220. Central, with family rooms as well as single and double.*
Kelvin Private Hotel 15 Buckingham Terrace, Hillhead. On the northwest edge of the city centre
YOUTH HOSTEL
Glasgow Youth Hostel 11 Woodlands Terrace.
☎ *031-332 3004.*

OUTINGS FROM GLASGOW

PAISLEY

Paisley merges into Glasgow, but it's a separate town with a character of its own. The big attraction is the collection of Paisley shawls at the museum (closed Sunday and public holidays; free). Coats sewing thread was first made in Paisley too, and one of the family founded the Coats Observatory. It has been watching the sky and the weather since the 1880s, and is open to visitors from Monday to Saturday in the afternoon (Saturday morning as well); no charge.

Local flavour
A Kashmiri motif was adapted in Paisley into what is still known as the 'Paisley' pattern. It was originally woven into fine silk shawls, which were fashionable for most of the 19th century.

ISLANDS

Waverley was the last of many paddle steamers to be built on the Clyde, and now offers day cruises from Glasgow to the Isle of Bute (Friday to Sunday in summer, from £11). Musicians on board are part of the Clyde steamer tradition, and there's a restaurant; or you can take a picnic. Tickets from the Glasgow tourist information centre, or from Waverley Excursions on Anderston Quay.

Moneysaver
Caledonian MacBrayne's family tickets cut the price of ferry day trips for two adults and two children. Day Saver ferry tickets are a special offer for a car and up to four people.

Catch the train from Glasgow Central railway station to Wemyss Bay for the ferry to Rothesay on the Isle of Bute. The whole journey takes about 1½ hours, and costs around £9 day return. The island is green and rolling rather than mountainous, with bicycles to hire, golf, pony trekking and beaches. Rothesay Castle is a stout medieval stronghold (closed on Fridays from October to March). On some summer days you can change ferries at Rothesay for a scenic cruise through the Kyles of Bute – about £2 extra.

For boat trips to the Scottish islands, the main company is Caledonian MacBrayne. Glasgow tourist information centre will have details. A trip to the Isle of Arran takes just over two hours and costs about £11 day return in total: catch the train from Glasgow Central railway station to Ardrossan for the ferry. Arran has spectacular mountain scenery and a beach near the ferry at Brodick. A bus meets some ferries for the two-mile journey to Brodick Castle, where sub-tropical plants flourish in the woodland and formal gardens. The castle is open from mid April to September (and some days in October); the gardens are open all year. There are restaurants at the castle and on the boat.

KILMARNOCK AND BURNS' COUNTRY

BUDGET FOR A DAY		
Day Tripper bus ticket		4·50
Dean Castle		1·00
Burns' Cottage and Museum		1·50
Johnny Walker Distillery	Free	
Culzean Castle		2·40
Lunch		3·00
Dinner		7·00
plus accommodation		£ 19·40

A grocer called Johnnie Walker started blending whisky in Kilmarnock in 1820 and his distillery is now the world's busiest. Guided tours are twice a day from Monday to Friday, and last about two hours (no children under 14).

Moneysaver

There's no charge for tours of Johnnie Walker's whisky distillery. Children (and locals) get into Dean Castle free; Dean Castle Country Park is free for everyone.

Robert Burns published his first collection of poems in Kilmarnock in 1786. He wanted the money to emigrate to Jamaica – he had had an affair with a local girl, and her father was threatening to prosecute. The poems were so successful, though, that Burns decided to stay. He has a very grand monument in Kay Park (good views from here), and you can see some of his manuscripts at Dean Castle, on the edge of town. The castle also houses renowned collections of armour, tapestries and musical instruments.

Robert Burns was born in Alloway, which is just on the edge of Ayr, a sizeable resort with shopping streets, lots of seaside amusements, a long beach, parks and the River Ayr Walk, which runs through the town. If you want to 'do' the Burns sights, start at Burns' Cottage in Alloway, the place where he was born in 1759 (closed Sundays from November to March). The ticket also lets you visit the museum next door and the Burns Monument. Alloway and Ayr are full of places which appear in Burns' poems – Ayr and Glasgow tourist information centres have details. You can rent a bicycle for local sightseeing from AMG cycles in Dalblair road (from £6 a day plus deposit, telephone 0292 287580).

Local flavour

Robert Burns is still a genuinely popular figure and his birthday on 25 January is a national celebration.

Culzean Castle (say 'cullane') is the most visited National Trust for Scotland property – 12 miles or half an hour by bus from Ayr. There's an old tower at the core of the castle, but it's really a splendid 18th-century house, designed by Robert Adam and set on a cliff: open from April to October. The grounds are a country park, with many acres of garden, deer, walks, an adventure playground and a stretch of coastline. The park is open all year, and free, though you pay around £4 to park.

LOCH LOMOND AND THE TROSSACHS

Loch Lomond is Scotland's biggest loch in area, and it's reckoned one of the most beautiful, dotted with wooded islands and set among hills which merge into mountains. This is a good area for water sports and fishing . It takes 40 minutes by train to reach Balloch, at the southern end of the loch. There are lochside and woodland walks at Balloch Castle Country Park; and the *Countess Fiona* offers a meandering cruise to Inversnaid and back. Inversnaid has a waterfall, and a stretch of the West Highland Way long-distance footpath takes you to the cave of the outlaw Rob Roy MacGregor.

Just east of Inversnaid is the area of lochs and hills known as the Trossachs. A popular beauty spot is Loch Katrine, which also provides Glasgow's water. The steamer *Sir Walter Scott* does a round trip from Trossachs Pier four times a day in summer (twice a day at weekends). The pier has a huge car park, and an ice cream vendor who has been seen driving home in a Porsche – if you want solitude, you must come here in the evening or out of season.

Callander has an information centre for the Trossachs and several walks start in the town. It's an easy day trip from Glasgow for drivers (36 miles). From May to September, bus travellers can take a daily Scottish Citylink coach from Glasgow's Buchanan bus station (just over an hour's journey), but would have to stay overnight.

Local flavour

The Trossachs were the haunt of Rob Roy Macgregor, a real-life folk hero and outlaw of the 18th century. Sir Walter Scott made him and the area famous with his novels *Rob Roy* and *The Lady of the Lake*.

OBAN

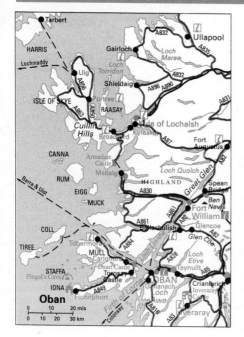

Oban

Whichever way you go to Oban, by road or rail, it's a journey through remote and beautiful mountain scenery. The town takes you by surprise with its crowds and bustle, and it's a delightful place .

Oban is on the complicated west coast of Scotland, with mountains behind and sea lochs running deep inland. It has been a resort since Victorian times, and is well supplied with things for visitors to do. The great attraction is the islands that lie just off this coast. Kerrera is the closest; the biggest is Mull, which you can easily reach on a day's outing. Just off Mull is Iona, a small island of huge significance in the early days of Christianity; just north of Iona is Staffa, with the spectacular Fingal's Cave.

The remote, pretty town of Inverary is a few miles inland; Glen Coe is in reach for walks in a stunning mountain landscapes. Fort William is about two hours away: make a second base here if you want to walk up Ben Nevis, the highest mountain in Britain.

You can take a car to Mull, but there's plenty to see without one, and coaches will take you to ferries for Iona and Staffa. You do need independent transport for Inverary and Glen Coe from Oban, though the latter can be visited from Fort William instead.

Bed and breakfast prices start below £10. There are also cottages and apartments to rent from below £100. The tourist information centre can supply a list.

Oban is three hours from Glasgow by rail or by Scottish Citylink coach. From Inverness it's four hours by bus (change at Fort William).

Moneysaver

There's no charge for visiting the Oban works of Caithness Glass. Glass-making is from 9am to 5pm, and paperweights are a speciality.

Oban has lots of shops (which may be closed on Thursday afternoons) selling knitwear, tartans and craft type goods; for serious outdoor wear and equipment, try Nancy Black in Argyll Square. The best town views are from McCraig's tower, which is the vast, Colosseum-like structure above the town, built in the 1890s, and now the town's number one sight. For beaches you need to go two miles out of town to Ganavan sands.

The Argyllshire Highland Gathering is held in Oban in August, and includes traditional

McCaig's Tower was an early job-creation scheme.

sports, music and dance. There's a Highlands Music and Dance Festival in spring, and you'll usually find ceilidhs and other Scottish music .

Don't be put off by the unglamorous exterior of McTavish's Kitchen – this is an ideal place to try haggis with neeps and tatties (turnips and potatoes). They do other dishes too, and the restaurant upstairs offers Scottish music and dancing. There are several other restaurants in the town.

ORIENTATION IN OBAN

INFORMATION
TOURIST OFFICE
Argyll Square. ☎ 0631 63122.

TRANSPORT
BUSES
Buses leave from the railway station. For information ask the tourist information centre. For long-distance buses and coaches contact Scottish Citylink, ☎ 041-332 9191.

TRAINS
Oban station, by the harbour. For information ☎ 0631 63083.
CAR HIRE
Foss Self Drive West Highland Crofters and Farmers, Oban. ☎ 0631 63565.
BICYCLE HIRE
Grahams Cycles 9-15 Combie Street. ☎ 0631 62069. Three-speed bicycles from £5 a day or £30 a week, mountain bikes from £10 a day or £30 a week, plus deposit.

ACCOMMODATION
BED AND BREAKFAST
Ardblair Dalriach Road. ☎ 0631 62668. Bed and breakfast prices start at £12 single, and there are good views.
YOUTH HOSTEL
Oban Youth Hostel Esplanade. ☎ 0631 62025. Closed in winter

EATING OUT
McTavish's Kitchen George Street. ☎ 0631 63064. You can eat very well for under £5 in the self-service section.

OUTINGS FROM OBAN

ISLANDS

The main ferry company for the islands is Caledonian MacBrayne, which does crossings for cars as well as foot passengers from the Railway Pier. Smaller operations advertise along the seafront in summer.

Kerrera is an island for walks and picnics. Boats leave from Gallanach, about two miles from Oban, for the five-minute crossing.

Mull has mountains, woods, lochs and 300 miles of coastline, with sandy beaches and lots of scope for walking and bird-watching. The nearest landing point is Craignure (40 minutes); It takes about an hour longer to reach Tobermory, the picturesque little main town.

You can take a boat direct to Duart Castle, home of the Chief of Clan MacLean since the 13th century (open May to September). Boats also go direct to Torosay Castle, where the great attraction is the 12-acre garden. The house is open from April to September, the garden is open all year. The other way to reach Torosay is by Mull Rail's miniature railway. The diesel or steam-hauled trains meet Caledonian MacBrayne ferries at Craignure in summer.

Caledonian MacBrayne do a daily tour to Staffa and Iona from May to September, leaving Oban at 10am and returning at 7.40pm (sometimes earlier). Not cheap, but these are two exceptional places, and you get to them via a beautiful drive across Mull.

Moneysaver
Bicycles go free on the Mull ferry.

St Columba came to Iona from Ireland in AD563, and founded an abbey from which Christianity spread through Britain. The present abbey building dates from the 13th century – it's the home of the Iona Community, but can be

204

visited. The Riellig Oran is the burial place of Scottish kings and Iona has several carved Celtic crosses. Six miles from Iona is Staffa, a block of basalt formed into densely packed hexagonal pillars jutting out of the sea. Fingal's Cave has been carved out of the rock by the waves and is over 200ft long, nearly 70ft high. Weather permitting, the thrill is to walk inside and feel the resonance of the sea. Weatherproof clothing and sensible shoes are advised.

Local flavour
Fingal the giant is said to have built a road between Staffa and Ireland, where it emerges as the Giant's Causeway. Both are part of the same rock formation.

BEN NEVIS AND GLEN COE

Fort William is two hours away by bus. It's popular as a base for tours, with lots of shops selling outdoor gear and gifts, but it doesn't have the same charm as Oban. Ben Nevis towers above, however, and if you want to tackle Britain's tallest mountain (4,406ft), this is the place to start. One side has spectacular precipices, and is strictly for mountaineers; the other side has a path which you can reach from the town. It takes from three to five hours to walk up the mountain, and another 2½ hours to walk down, so you need rations, sensible shoes and clothes for all weathers. The views from the top are wonderful on a clear day.

The surrounding landscape of mountains and lochs offers all sorts of outdoor activities. Off Beat Bikes rents mountain bikes and supplies you with a rucksack, trail map and helmet if necessary. They're at 4 Inverlochy Place, telephone 0397 2663. Nevis Range is a ski area, four miles north of Fort William; in summer you can ride the cable cars to a 2,300ft viewpoint.

Glen Coe is an overpowering landscape, with steep, bare mountains rising on either side. The events of the Glen Coe massacre in February 1692 compound the haunting atmosphere. Troops who had been billeted on Clan Macdonald families suddenly turned on their hosts and murdered more than 40 men, women and children. The reason was that the Macdonalds had been slow to swear allegiance to King William III. It's beautiful in a solumn way, and offers walks of various levels of difficulty. A large part of Glen Coe is owned by the National Trust for Scotland, which has a visitor centre where you can buy maps and guides. This isn't landscape to tackle lightly, so they arrange guided walks as well.

There's a folk museum with a traditional heather-thatched roof in Glencoe village, and a notice board suggests walks to take. Glencoe Mountain Bike Hire is opposite the post office (telephone 08552 685).

Catch the train to Taynuilt (20 minutes) for cruises on Loch Etive (April to mid October). The 20-mile loch is frequented by seals, and stretches from the coast to the mountains of Glen Coe. A little further along the line, Falls of Cruachan is the stop for a tour of the spectacular Cruachan hydro-electric power station. This is a popular outing, so get there early to be sure of a place on a tour – there is a charge for tours, but admission to the visitor centre is free. Open late March to late October.

Watch for golden eagles and peregrine falcons; in forests look out for red squirrels, red deer and roe deer. Red deer can sometimes be seen grazing on open mountain sides.

INVERARAY

MacDougalls Tours do excursions from Oban to Inverary in summer; otherwise you'll need independent transport. It's a very neat, white town on the shores of Loch Fyne – it looks like a stage set and was in fact built as a complete town in the 18th century. The Duke of Argyll had the old Inverary knocked down when he rebuilt his castle in the mid 1700s, and constructed this new town instead. There are lots of tearooms, tartan and woollen-wear shops, and the old town jail has been restored as a 'living history' experience with lots of gruesome scenes.

Inverary Castle is the home of the Duke of Argyll, head of Clan Campbell. (It was a

Campbell who led the Glen Coe massacre, and there's still bitterness about that today.) The castle is a romantic, mock-Gothic affair, with treasures collected by generations of the family on view inside. It's open from early April to early October (not Fridays, except in July and August).

> **Local flavour**
> The Loch Fyne Oyster Bar at Cairndow serves fresh seafood, prepared in simple but delectable ways – telephone 0499 6264.

SKYE

Skye gets so much praise that a lot of people go there half expecting to be disappointed. But the island almost always lives up to expectations, and more. It really is beautiful, with endless wonderful views. Nowhere is far the sea, and the coastline winds and wriggles for hundreds of miles. Mainland tourist information centres will have details; there's also a summer tourist information centre at Broadford on Skye, telephone 04712 361.

Ferries from Mallaig take 30 minutes to reach Armadale on Skye. Between May and around mid October, these are car ferries, with connecting trains for non-drivers along a spectacular route from Fort William (80 minutes). There's also a five-minute ferry crossing between Kyleakin (on Skye) and Kyle of Lochalsh, which has trains to Inverness.

> **Moneysaver**
> The Early Bird Saver to Skye is a day return for a car and up to four passengers (summer only). You have to travel on the first and last ferry of the day.

The Clan Donald Centre is at Armadale Castle, which has woodland gardens: open mid March to October.

If you're not driving and want to spend a while on Skye, the best option might be a Caledonian Express coach to Broadford or Portree, Skye's capital, with whitewashed houses round a harbour. Coaches go on as far as Uig, for ferries to Harris and Uist in the Western Isles. The full journey from Fort William to Uig takes about four hours.

INVERNESS

Inverness is called the capital of the Highlands – it's a sophisticated town near the far north of Scotland, and is a base for exploring some very remote places. Mountains and lochs are close by, empty beaches of white sand are commonplace around the northwest coast, and there are some spectacular cliff coastlines. South of Inverness is Loch Ness, the reputed home of a monster, spotted at intervals over several centuries. East is the Moray Firth coastline, with castles, pretty seaside resorts and fishing villages.

Inverness has good national transport links, and local transport is supplemented by coach tours in summer. You may decide that a car is essential for exploring, but train journeys from Inverness are recommended because they go through beautiful scenery to places worth seeing. You can carry bicycles on most trains,

Urquhart Castle overlooks Loch Ness.

but booking is essential in summer.

There are a lot of bed and breakfast places in the town, and prices start below £12. There are also some very cheap hostels for backpackers on minimal budgets.

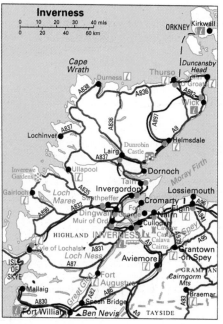

Inverness

museum and art gallery, whose pictures include a portrait of Bonnie Prince Charlie in jowly middle age (closed Sundays except July and August; no charge).

The Castle isn't very old, but it stands on a site where there has been a castle for about 1,000 years. The Drum Tower can be visited in summer. The earliest known owner of a castle at Inverness was the Macbeth of Shakespeare's play. Bonnie Prince Charlie had an earlier version of the castle blown up in 1746. The man who lit the fuse died in the explosion, but his dog was blasted across the river and only lost its tail.

Local flavour

Fish and fishing have always been important in this part of the world. Trout and salmon frequent the lochs and rivers. For information on angling, ask the tourist information centre.

Buses from Oban take about four hours (change at Fort William). Inverness airport has flights from London Heathrow and Gatwick, as well as Scottish cities.

Inverness is a handsome town, with spacious main streets and the River Ness running through – there's a riverside walk, and footbridges take you to the Ness islands. If you're looking for local specialities, James Pringle makes kilts and knitwear in cashmere and lambswool. The Clan Tartan Centre can be contacted on 0463 223311. At Strathaird Salmon (telephone 0463 225959), curing and slicing can be seen.

Guided walks start from the Town House

Moneysaver

Free or low-priced music should be easy to find in summer. A piper (bagpipes) plays on Castle Hill every evening except Sunday during the summer, and pubs, clubs and hotels often stage Scottish music, jazz, rock or discos.

Visit at Easter for the folk festival; visit in July for the Inverness Highland Games day. The cathedral has Sunday concerts in summer, and Eden Court Theatre has a very wide range of shows all year.

ORIENTATION IN INVERNESS

INFORMATION
Tourist Office
23 Church Street. ☎ 0463 234353.
Post Office
Post Office Avenue.

Public Lavatories
Bus station; Bank Street; Castle Wynd.

TRANSPORT
Buses
Bus station, off Strothers Lane near the town centre. Various companies: ask at

the tourist office.
Trains
Inverness station, Station Square. For information ☎ 0463 238924.
Car Hire
Budget Rent-a-Car Railway Terrace. ☎ 0463 239877.
Bicycle Hire
Sharps Cycle Hire 1st Floor,

Highland Rail House, Station Square, Academy Street. ☎ 0463 236684.

ACCOMMODATION
Old Rectory 9 Southside Road. ☎ 0463 220969.
St Anne's Hotel 37 Harrowden Road. ☎ 0463 236157.
YOUTH HOSTEL
Inverness Youth Hostel 1 Old Edinburgh Road. ☎ 0463 231771. Closed for one month in winter.
CAMP SITE
Bunchrew Caravan Park ☎ 0463 237802.

EATING OUT
Glen Mhor Hotel 10 Ness Bank. ☎ 0463 234308. Has a restaurant and bistro.
Haydens Café Bar 37 Queensgate. ☎ 0463 236969. Open all day, serving main courses such as lasagne for under £5.

OUTINGS FROM INVERNESS

Some of these places can't be reached by public transport, but you'll almost certainly find a summer coach excursion from Inverness.

WEST TO THE COAST

Routes west of Inverness go through some of the most magnificent mountain scenery in Scotland, sometimes on single-track main roads.

The train route to the west coast is one of the most scenic journeys in Britain, and ends at Kyle of Lochalsh, which has ferries to Skye (see *Outings from Oban*). The whole route takes two hours. Ullapool on the west coast is an hour by bus. After a long journey through seemingly empty landscapes, it takes you by surprise – a pretty ferry (to the Isle of Lewis) and fishing port-resort. In summer you can take boat outings to see seals and wild birds.

Summer days are very long at this latitude, especially this far west; the drawback is the short hours of daylight in winter.

Inverewe Gardens are north of Gairloch on the west coast, and are one of the showpieces of the Highlands. Plants from South America and the south Pacific grow alongside native Scottish heather, thanks to the Gulf Stream. The gardens are open all year until sunset..

LOCH NESS

Loch Ness is a 20-mile stretch of dark, peaty and very deep water, starting just south of Inverness. Loch cruises start on the Caledonian Canal,

about 20 minutes' walk from the town centre (about £4 for 2½ hours). The scenery is more oppressive than beautiful, but the point is to look out for the Loch Ness Monster, recorded in legend and even on camera, but never actually proved to exist. A good vantage point is Urquhart Castle, the ruin of what was Scotland's biggest castle (infrequent bus to Drumnadrochit). The east side is the most picturesque.

EAST TO NAIRN

There is a string of interesting places between Nairn and Inverness (no practical buses though). Culloden Moor, five miles from Inverness, is where Bonnie Prince Charlie's Jacobite army was crushed on 16 April 1746. The battle only lasted 40 minutes, but more than 1,000 of the prince's army were killed and there followed repressive measures against Highlanders, incuding the outlawing of bagpipes. The battlefield is always accessible; admission to the National Trust for Scotland visitor centre costs about £1.

A mile from Culloden are the Clava Cairns, a group of burial cairns and standing stones, placed here perhaps 3,000 years ago.

> **Moneysaver**
> There's no charge for visiting Clava Cairns, in an area rich in ancient sites.

Fort George is a huge artillery fortification,

built after the Battle of Culloden to keep the Highlands under control.

Local flavour
Traditional Highland cheeses are made at Highland Fine Cheeses in Tain (an hour from Inverness by train).

Cawdor Castle (five miles from Nairn) is indelibly linked with Shakespeare's Macbeth, who was Thane of Cawdor, and it's now one of Scotland's most popular outings. The oldest part is a 14th-century tower, built round a tree; the castle also has turrets, a drawbridge and beautiful gardens, with nature trails; open May to September.

Nearby Kilravock Castle is equally ancient. Guided tours of the house are on Wednesday; the grounds are open every day except Sunday, from May to September.

THE RAILWAY NORTH – JOHN O'GROATS

The railway line north from Inverness winds beside rivers, coast, mountains and moorland. The whole journey to Wick or Thurso takes about three hours from Inverness, and you may well see red deer roaming empty northern stretches. In summer you can alight at Dunrobin for Dunrobin Castle, which began as a square fort in the 13th century, and is now a palatial mansion, open June to mid September. The sea is close by, and there are formal gardens open all year, and free when the castle is closed (half a mile from Golspie trainstation).

Infrequent buses run from Wick and Thurso to John O'Groats, the most northerly village on mainland Britain. The highest cliffs in Britain are at Clo Mor, near the wild heights of Cape Wrath, reached by ferry and minibus from near Durness. There's no easy way to get there by public transport from Inverness.

GRANTOWN-ON-SPEY

The Spey is one of Britain's premier fishing rivers.

Grantown-on-Spey is in easy reach of all the things you might expect of the Highlands of Scotland – spectacular scenery, romantic castles, whisky distilleries and salmon rivers, besides the inevitable golf. It stands on the River Spey, and has been popular with visitors since the 19th century.

There are some beautiful walks or you can go pony trekking, and there are water sports on the lochs that feed the River Spey. In winters,

Grantown becomes a base for skiers visiting the slopes at nearby Aviemore.

The Queen and her family spend part of the summer hunting and fishing at Balmoral, on the other side of the Cairngorm mountains. The river here is the Dee, and 'Royal Deeside' has fine scenery too.

Public transport in the area is best in summer, when it's supplemented by coach tours. If you want to get about and do a lot of sightseeing, then you'll need a car.

Moneysaver
Travel with the mail from Grantown on a three-hour Land Rover post bus around the surrounding landscape. The post office has a timetable.

There is a lot of accommodation in and around Grantown, including hostels. Bed and breakfast prices start below £10, and there are also houses, chalets, and caravans to rent. The tourist office can supply a list.

Grantown-on-Spey is just over an hour from Inverness by bus. The nearest train station is Aviemore (half an hour by bus), which is on the main north-south line through Scotland.

Grantown is stately little stone town, not very different from when it was first built in the late 1700s. It was the creation of Sir James Grant, who meant it to be a textile town, but Grantown became a resort instead. The Spey is a celebrated angling river, with salmon fishing best in spring and late summer, sea trout in June and July.

Grantown-on-Spey

Local flavour

Walker's butter shortbread, made at Aberlour-on-Spey, is hard to beat, and the company has a shop on the main street in Grantown.

Weekly ceilidhs are held in Grantown in summer, and several hotels have entertainment. Highland Games are held in June, followed by the annual show of the Strathspey Farmers' Society – this event goes back over 200 years, and includes a funfair and dance.

ORIENTATION IN GRANTOWN-ON-SPEY

INFORMATION
TOURIST OFFICE
High Street. (personal callers only).
Aviemore and Spey Valley Tourist Board, Grampian Road, Aviemore, Inverness-shire PH22 1PP (for correspondence).
☎ 0479 810363.
POST OFFICE
High Street.

TRANSPORT
BUSES
Highland Omnibuses and Citylink. ☎ 0479 810658.
TRAINS
The nearest station is Aviemore. ☎ 0479 810221.
CAR HIRE
Grants of Aviemore Ltd
Grants Service Station, 62 Grampian Road. ☎ 0479 810205.
BICYCLE HIRE
Logans Bike Hire
Crann-Tara Guest House, High Street. ☎ 0479 2197.

ACCOMMODATION
GUESTHOUSES
Culdearn House
Woodlands Terrace.
☎ 0479 2106. Offers considerable luxury, and is run on 'house party' lines: single bed and breakfast from £19.95.
Dar-Il-Hena Grant Road.
☎ 0479 2929. A comfortable house with a garden – single bed and breakfast from £12; a week with dinner from £195.

EATING OUT
Ben Mhor 57 High Street.
☎ 0479 2056. Bar lunches available.
There are a number of other hotels which offer meals to non-residents.

OUTINGS FROM GRANTOWN-ON-SPEY

AVIEMORE AND LOCH GARTEN

Aviemore has mushroomed as a resort since the 1960s – it's best known for skiing, but has sports facilities and nightlife all year (40 minutes by bus). It's also the starting point of the Strathspey Railway, a preserved line with steam-hauled trains in summer. The 20-minute ride gives fine views of the Cairngorms before descending into Boat of Garten.

Loch Garten is an 4,000-acre Royal Society for the Protection of Birds (RSPB) reserve, including part of the ancient Caledonian forest as well as the loch. You might see eagles, ravens and rare butterflies here, but the real stars are the ospreys. They migrate 3,500 miles from Gambia to nest at the loch each spring. Access to this part of the reserve is restricted, but from around April to August you can watch ospreys on the nest from an observation hide.

THE WHISKY TRAIL

The Malt Whisky Trail is a signed road route to eight distilleries, including Glenfiddich, Glen Grant and The Glenlivet. Some of them can be reached on the Heatherhopper and Speyside Rambler summer bus routes. The whole route is about 70 miles: ask the tourist information centre for details. There's no charge for visiting the distilleries on the Malt Whisky Trail. The vast copper stills, mashing tuns and arrays of casks are an impressive sight, and you're usually offered a complimentary dram. Young children may not be allowed to all areas.

Local flavour

Baxters began selling homemade jam over 120 years ago. They now sell a variety of quality foods in over 60 countries. The factory is a mile west of Fochabers, with free guided tours, woodland walks, a restaurant, picnic area and shops.

SCOTTISH CASTLES

There are several castles in reasonable driving distance of Grantown; most can't be reached by public transport but coach tours may be available. The Castle Trail is a signed road route to nine castles and mansions, from Corgarff in the west to spectacular Fyvie and Castle Fraser in the east. The whole route is about 150 miles.

Corgarff is by the Lecht Pass (A939), with huge views across the Cairngorms. The castle is a tall tower house, converted into a garrison and set in a neat star-shaped wall. Kildrummy is a ruined 13th-century castle – it was demolished after the 1715 Jacobite uprising, but you can still identify the different rooms and towers. The mansion of Leith Hall has grown around a 17th-century tower and has Jacobite relics (open May to September in the afternoons. The grounds and gardens are open all year, with walks and a picnic area (donation requested). Huntly and Balvenie are romantic and substantial ruins (Balvenie is closed from October to March).

Craigievar is best described as a fairytale castle – a tall cluster of conical roofed turrets, hardly changed since it was completed in 1626. The castle is open from May to September in the afternoons; the grounds are open all year, with a picnic area and woodland walks.

ROYAL DEESIDE

BUDGET FOR A DAY	
Day tripper bus ticket	3·50
Balmoral Castle and Grounds	1·20
Braemar Castle	·60
Royal Lochnagar Distillery	Free
Lunch	3·00
High tea	6·00
plus accommodation	£ 14·30

Balmoral Castle is a royal family holiday home

beside the River Dee (just under two hours by bus from Grantown). In May, June and July the ballroom and grounds are open to visitors (not Sunday). In August the royal family arrives, and Balmoral becomes strictly private once more.

Balmoral is in between Braemar and Ballater, both of which are attractive places with plenty of places to stay, should you wish to make a base on Royal Deeside. They have tourist information centres, but for advance details write to Kincardine and Deeside Tourist Board, 45 Station Road, Banchory AB3 3XX, telephone 03302 2066.

> **Moneysaver**
> The best free thing along Royal Deeside is the walking among wonderful mountain views. There's no charge for visiting Royal Lochnagar Distillery near Balmoral.

Accommodation in both gets booked up in summer; Braemar Highland Gathering in early September attracts thousands of spectators, including members of the royal family. Booking for tickets opens in early February. Braemar Castle is a handsome turreted stronghold with a prison pit below, which has been turned into a family home: open May to early October.

Ballater is yet another neat, stone-built planned town of the 18th century – it was designed as a resort for people taking the spa waters at nearby Pannanich Wells (still available).

The Cairngorms should be treated with respect by walkers. The higher areas may have snow well after summer has started elsewhere. Proper walking gear is essential.

Banchory (45 minutes by bus) is another base for walks, including one to the salmon leap at Bridge of Feugh. Three miles east of Banchory is Crathes Castle (no bus), a romantic place with turrets and rare painted ceilings, 18th-century formal gardens and grounds. The house is open from May to September, and weekends in April and October; the gardens and grounds are open all year. Crathes Craft Studios and Pottery are just by the entrance.

ABERDEEN

The River Dee meets the sea at Aberdeen, where it's spanned by a medieval bridge (1½ hours by bus). Aberdeen is a handsome granite city which has become the main base for the North Sea oil industry, but it is still a major fishing port too. The auctioning of the catch each weekday morning between 7am and 8am is one of the sights of the city. It also has several parks, a cathedral, a long-established university, and an art gallery and museum.

PITLOCHRY

Pitlochry is a base for Perthshire, a landscape of wooded hills, rushing rivers and deep glens with heather moorland mountains rising to either side. It's a magical part of the Highlands, where everyday concerns seem to vanish. It's a great area for field sports, water sports, climbing, golf (there's a championship course) and especially walking. The ski slopes of Glen Shee aren't very far away, so Pitlochry is also a winter resort.

If it feels too quiet, then the 'Fair City' of Perth is in easy reach. The landscape switches quite abruptly around here, from mountains into the rich farmland of raspberries and other fruit, with fishing ports of great character on the coast.

You'll need a car if you want to do a lot of

Queen's View looks out over Loch Tummel.

sightseeing. Pitlochry has reasonable buses, including post buses, supplemented in summer

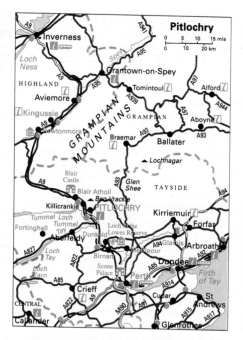

Pitlochry

0 5 10 15 mls
0   10   20 km

place for outdoor pursuits rather than sightseeing, but it does have two popular places to visit. One is the Pitlochry Festival Theatre, its season from April to October, and the range of productions is very wide. Another sight is the hydro-electric power station on the River Tummel, where you can watch salmon travelling up river in a specially built fish ladder that bypasses the dam. You can also have a look at the turbine hall. No charge, except for a minimal fee to an exhibition area, open from late March to late October.

Blair Atholl distillery is on the south side of town, with guided tours (and free dram), from Monday to Saturday all year, and on Sunday as well in summer. (Despite the name it's in Pitlochry rather than Blair Atholl village.) The tiny Edradour distillery is a couple of miles east in a very pretty setting. Open every day for guided tours.

Riverside walks start in the town; places to walk near by Loch Faskally (the reservoir for the dam), Ben Vrackie and the Pass of Killiecrankie.

Nearby Blair Castle, tall and white, with turrets and battlements, is Scotland's 'most visited private home'. It's the home of the Duke of Atholl, the Chief of Clan Murray. The Atholl Highlanders are the duke's private army, the only one in Europe. Armour, china and other collections can be seen inside; outside there are parklands with peacocks, walks and pony trekking, open April to late October, telephone 079681 207.

The Atholl Country Collection in Blair Atholl is a folk museum with displays on local crafts such as flax making, open on summer afternoons and all day in July and August. There's also a working 17th-century watermill in the village, open April to October.

by coach tours. It's on the railway to Perth, from where roads radiate in all directions.

There are a lot of hotels and other places to stay in and around Pitlochry, with bed and breakfast prices starting below £10. Self catering in chalets, cottages and caravans is also possible. The tourist information centre can supply a list.

The easiest way to get to Pitlochry by public transport from Grantown-on-Spey is via Aviemore, from where it's 1½ hours by train, two hours by bus. It's two hours from Edinburgh by train.

Pitlochry is in a deep wooded valley, with mountains all round and lochs near by. It's a

---

ORIENTATION IN PITLOCHRY

INFORMATION
Tourist Office
22 Atholl Road. ☎ 0796 2215/2751.
Post Office
Atholl Road

Public Lavatories
West End car park; Burnside Road (Atholl Road).

TRANSPORT
Buses
Various operators, ask at the tourist information centre.

Trains
Pitlochry station, ☎ 0738 37117.
Car Hire
Pitlochry Self Drive Mr I Hendry, Four Season, Higher Oakfield. ☎ 0796 2080.
Bicycle Hire
Atholl Activity Cycles Folk

Museum Park, Tilt Bridge, Blair Atholl (mid May to mid October)
James Stewart *Allt na Fearn, Killiecrankie.* ☎ *0796 3553. Mountain bikes at £10 per day, £6 for half a day, plus deposit.*

ACCOMMODATION
GUESTHOUSES
Fasganeoin *Perth Road.* ☎ *0796 2387. A traditional family-run concern that does teas and Scottish evening meals: single bed and breakfast from £17, or from £115 for a week. There are also several bed and breakfast places which have rooms for around £12.*
YOUTH HOSTEL
Pitlochry Youth Hostel *Breaknowe, Knockard Road.* ☎ *0796 2308.*
CAMP SITE

Faskally Home Farm ☎ *0796 2007.*

EATING OUT
Craigtower Hotel *134-36 Atholl Road, in the town centre.* ☎ *0796 2590. Two restaurants for lunch, high tea (around £7) or dinner (under £15). Several other hotels do food, and there's a coffee bar/restaurant at the theatre.*

OUTINGS FROM PITLOCHRY

THE TRAIN NORTH

The train north from Pitlochry takes one of Britain's most scenic rail routes. It climbs to 1,484ft, with mountains twice that height in view. Stop at Newtonmore for the Clan Macpherson museum (May to September, free), with various clan treasures. The clan has a rally at the Newtonmore Highland Games, which are held in August (an hour by train). Kingussie is five minutes down the line: alight here for the open air Highland Folk Museum, with reconstructed traditional houses.

Local flavour
Shinty is a game 'like hockey, but bigger', found in northern Britain and in North America.

DUNKELD AND BIRNAM

South of Pitlochry, Dunkeld is very picturesque, with several buildings preserved by the National Trust for Scotland (not open, but nice to look at). Dunkeld Cathedral was rebuilt in the 12th century on a much earlier site, and has a beautiful setting by the River Tay. Paths lead by the river and round the village via the Birnam Oak – last remnant of the Birnam Wood in Shakespeare's *Macbeth*. West of Dunkeld, Fortingall has a 3,000-year-old yew tree which is said to be Europe's oldest living thing. Southeast of Dunkeld, Meikleour has the world's tallest beech hedge, planted in 1746.

Two miles east of Dunkeld is the Loch of the Lowes nature reserve, which has a visitor centre and hide equipped with binoculars (no charge, donation invited). You could see ospreys here.

PERTH

Perth has a lot of attractions: good shops in the Georgian streets, and a leisure pool with jacuzzis and bubble beds, flumes and an arch through which you swim from inside to outside. There's a straightforward 25-metre swimmers' pool too. The city museum and art gallery (free) is close to the Fair Maid's House, made famous by Sir Walter Scott in *The Fair Maid of Perth*. It now has crafts on show (free).

Along the street is St John's Kirk, where in 1559 John Knox ignited the Reformation in Scotland; across the River Tay is the Branklyn Garden; small, but special for its alpine and peat-loving plants (National Trust for Scotland). Bell's Cherrybank Gardens are a pretty place to visit (free), around the headquarters of the distilling company Arthur Bell. The museum of the Black Watch regiment is at Balhousie Castle (free) on North Inch.

The Lower City Mills in central Perth is a

Victorian watermill which produces flour and oatmeal. There are craft workshops here too.

Moneysaver
There's no charge for guided tours of Dewar's scotch whisky bottling plant at Inveralmond, a mile north of Perth. Caithness Glass factory at Inveralmond.

Scone Palace is two miles north of Perth (15 minutes by bus). On the outside, the house dates back to the early 1800s, but its origins are far older. Scone was the coronation place of Scottish kings until the 17th century, and the coronation Stone of Scone stood on the Moot Hill here. (It was stolen by the English in 1296, and taken to Westminster Abbey in London.) Open from Easter to mid October.

Fairways Heavy Horse Centre is two miles east of Perth. Clydesdale horses are bred here,

and the foals make an enchanting sight in summer. There's also a blacksmith. Open April to September.

GLAMIS

Glamis village is a pretty little place, where the National Trust for Scotland runs a row of cottages as the Angus Folk Museum (open at Easter and from May to September). Glamis Castle is the vast mansion house of the Bowes-Lyon family, and was the childhood home of Elizabeth Bowes-Lyon, now the Queen Mother. The house dates mostly from the 17th century, but it has a far older core – there's a legend that Shakespeare's Macbeth murdered Duncan here. Guided tours go round the house, and you can also explore the gardens and grounds, which have picnic area (there's also a restaurant). Open May to September afternoons (not Saturday). No direct public transport from Pitlochry.

ST ANDREWS

St Andrews is about equally famous as 'the home of golf' and as Scotland's oldest university town. Even without those credentials, its old streets would be pleasant to stroll around, and it's on the coast.

The town is a natural base for exploring northeast Fife, the block of land between the Firth of Forth and the Firth of Tay. The scenery is mostly low-lying farmland, with some historic houses and castles, and the enchanting East Neuk fishing villages along the coast.

Moneysaver
Most of the main sights charge an admission fee, but the old town centre is a sight in itself – and free, as are the Lammas Fair (August) and the Kate Kennedy pageant (April).

Buses run to all the places suggested for outings, and there's also a railway across the area, with a bus link to St Andrews. This is easy cycling country, and you can rent bicycles here. Bed and breakfast prices start at around £10 in the town, £9 in the East Neuk fishing villages. St Andrews is two hours from Edinburgh by coach; there's also a train to Leuchars, where there's a connecting bus.

Before the 1600s, the cathedral was probably the most important thing about St Andrews: it housed the shrine of St Andrew, Scotland's patron saint. Today the cathedral is in ruins, but well worth seeing. The main streets run roughly parallel towards it, and in between those are narrow lanes and alleys, which sometimes join two streets and sometimes stop at a dead end. Guided walks start at the tourist office twice a day except for Monday, with evening walks as well in August.

The university was founded in 1410 and the first college buildings are not much later. You can only visit on guided tours, which are led by students in the summer vacation, from Monday to Saturday (small charge).

The 18th hole of the famous Old Course is overlooked by the Royal & Ancient Clubhouse.

Local flavour
It's traditional for St Andrews students to walk along the pier on Sunday morning wearing their red academic gowns.

Running round the cathedral is the 16th-century precinct wall which leads to the little harbour and pier (built of stone looted from the cathedral). There's a real sense of the past at the Pends, where the street runs through the arches of the original main gatehouse. Some huge fragments of the cathedral are left, including the landmark of twin conical turrets. There's also a museum, covered in the cathedral admission price.

The castle stands right by the sea near the cathedral (it used to be the main residence of the bishops). It's now a ruin, with a history of bloodshed, a bottle-shaped dungeon, and 'secret passages' – some dug by attackers to undermine the walls, some dug by defenders to intercept them.

Go to the other end of town for golf. This is where the Royal and Ancient Golf Club House overlooks the Old Course, revered scene of open championships. There's a ballot for visitors who want to play on the Old Course – any golfer can enter, so long as they have a letter of introduction or handicap certificate (no play on Sunday). It's easier to get access to the other courses – the New, Jubilee and Eden. Clubs can be hired.

Golfers have played on the links at St Andrews since the 15th century, when King James II banned golf, because it was distracting people from archery practice. The Royal and Ancient Golf Club was founded in 1754, and is the world authority on rules.

The British Golf Museum is opposite the Royal and Ancient Club House: lots of clubs, balls and other memorabilia, and touch-activated screen information. The Sea Life Centre, a spectacular aquarium, is close by. The best bargain, though, is the botanic garden, which tends to be eclipsed by the more famous sights. In summer it stays open to 7pm, and admission is only 50p.

St Andrews is a great place for shopping and window shopping, especially in the North Street/South Street area. .

Local flavour
The butcher John Scott and Son in Market Street makes high quality haggis and black pudding.

St Andrews has an arts festival, or visit in August for the Lammas Fair, which began as a medieval market and is now a colourful affair with numerous stalls and sideshows. For year-round entertainment the main venue is the Byre Theatre (it really was a byre once), which puts on a wide range of shows all year. The Crawford Arts Centre has exhibitions and a lot of children's events; in term time, you may find concerts and other events at the university.

ORIENTATION IN ST ANDREWS

INFORMATION
TOURIST OFFICE
78 South Street. ☎ 0334 720021.
POST OFFICE
South Street.
PUBLIC LAVATORIES
South Street (by West Port); Church Street; harbour; Bruce Embankment Putting Green.

TRANSPORT
BUSES
Outings suggested are by Fife Scottish, bus station, City Road,
☎ 0334 74238.
TRAINS
Leuchars station.
CAR HIRE
Bennetts 66 Largo Road.
☎ 0334 72101.
BICYCLE HIRE
Christies Market Street.
☎ 0334 72122.
Three-speed bicycles cost about £4 a day.

ACCOMMODATION
Albany 56 North Street.
☎ 0334 77737. Central and comfortable. Single bed and breakfast starts at £15, double at £28. A week's full board costs from £130 to £210.

EATING OUT
McGregors Market Street. Lunchtime self-serve salads for under £5.
Russell Hotel 26 The Scores.
☎ 0334 73447.
Scores Hotel 76 The Scores.
☎ 0334 72451.

OUTINGS FROM ST ANDREWS

LEUCHARS

The village of Leuchars is five miles northwest, with a Royal Air Force base and a church worth seeing for fine 12th-century work. Half a mile off is Earlshall Castle, still lived in by the descendants of Sir William Bruce who built it in the 16th century. There are topiary chess pieces in the garden. Open at Easter and from June to mid September, in the afternoons (not Tuesday).

The best free things near Leuchars are Tentsmuir Forest and Tentsmuir Beach, for swimming, walks and bird-watching. They're about three miles from the village (no buses).

Craigtoun Country Park is two miles southwest of Leuchars (20 minutes by bus), and it's popular with families. There are gardens, a lake and amusements such as trampolines, putting and crazy golf. The Rangers at Craigtoun Country Park lead free guided walks in summer; themes of the walks range from bird-watching to myths and legends. Open from April to September.

EAST NEUK VILLAGES

Narrow streets or 'wynds', golden stone and whitewash, red pantiled roofs and stepped gables are all features of the East Neuk fishing villages. The gables are probably a legacy of old trading links with the Netherlands.
Crail   Crail is the closest to St Andrews (30 minutes by bus), and has the most beautiful cluster of old streets. Among them are craft shops (including a pottery selling terracotta ware), and a town museum (small charge).

Moneysaver
Crabs and lobsters are a good buy at Crail harbour. Fish are fresh from the boat at Pittenweem fish market.

Anstruther and Cellardyke   These twin villages used to form one of Scotland's busiest ports, but visitors have replaced working boats at the pretty harbour today. The Scottish Fisheries Museum is in an old ships' chandler's building: open all year.

For a small charge you can visit the North Carr lightship, now floating in the harbour (open Easter to September, and weekends in October). In summer boat trips go the Isle of May, which has seals and wild birds (trips cost about £7).

Pittenweem This is a deep cave in the rock near the centre of the village which is said to have been St Fillan's retreat back in the 6th century. It is still used regularly for services. Three miles inland is tall, turreted Kellie Castle (no buses): open May to October afternoons, and weekend afternoons in April. The idyllic walled garden is open all year; National Trust for Scotland.

St Monans and Elie The last of the villages on our tour of East Neuk are St Monans, with its higgledy piggledy streets, fishing boats and ancient church beside the sea; and Elie, a popular seaside resort. The windsurfing off the sandy beach is said to be good. (Elie is an hour by bus from St Andrews.)

FALKLAND

Well inland, Falkland Palace stands right on the main street of this neat and pretty little village . The palace was a royal hunting lodge, used by Mary Queen of Scots among others. Behind it is a garden, where the Royal Tennis Court was installed in 1539. Run by the National Trust for Scotland, it's open April to October. Looming over the village are the Lomond Hills, with paths for walkers.

LOCH LEVEN

The whole of Loch Leven is a nature reserve with restricted access, but Kinross has a lochside park with picnic tables (an hour by bus from St Andrews). Ferries set off from here for the island castle where Mary Queen of Scots was imprisoned. (the admission price includes the fare). The garden of Kinross House can also be visited. There's an observation post for bird-watchers at Vane Farm (off the B9097 – no buses).

EDINBURGH

Edinburgh is dominated by its castle, venue of the annual Edinburgh Military Tattoo.

Edinburgh has been called a lot of things in its time, from the 'Athens of the North' in the 18th century, to 'Auld Reekie' not so very long ago (it used to be notoriously smoky). Edinburgh is quite unique and even has its own way of talking and doing things.

The main landmark is Edinburgh Castle, rising high above the city on Castle Rock.

Stretching away from the castle is the Old Town, an extraordinary clutter of ancient streets and courts clinging to the central spine of the Royal Mile. Contrasting with this is the New Town, a series of elegant Georgian streets and squares. Edinburgh has some rather grand Victorian suburbs too.

For three weeks each summer, the city is transformed by the Edinburgh Festival and Fringe (the Fringe is an adjunct of the main festival, with avant garde and experimental art). The streets teem with performers and their audiences, and this is a wonderful time to visit if you want theatre, music and other arts, with some world-famous names on the bill. Details from Edinburgh Festival Society, 21 Market Street, Edinburgh EH1 1BW (for the Festival); and Fringe Office, 180 High Street, Edinburgh EH1 1QS. In the evenings the Edinburgh Military Tattoo takes over the castle Esplanade. If you want to stay in or near Edinburgh during the Edinburgh Festival, you must book accommodation well ahead.

The Pentland Hills and others offer bracing walks close to the city. Enchanting Culross is not far over the Forth, and there are seaside resorts in easy reach. On a longer day out you could reach the Borders country to the south or visit Glasgow, St Andrews and Perth (described under *Pitlochry*); you could see all the really famous Scottish places on day trips by coach.

Edinburgh has a lot of bed and breakfast accommodation. The tourist information centre can supply details of houses and apartments to rent for a week or so.

Edinburgh airport has flights from international destinations as well as from London Heathrow, Gatwick and Stansted. The journey from London to Edinburgh takes about five hours by train, eight hours by coach. From St Andrews, it's two hours by coach.

The tourist information centre is on Princes Street, which runs through the middle of the city This is also the place to find out about the many guided walks available. Guide Friday tour buses run every 15 minutes, daily, and Lothian Regional Transport also run open-topped buses round the city: about £3 for a day ticket.

Princes Street is the main shopping street of the city, with a mixture of high-class stores and high street chains overlooking Princes Street Gardens. The main railway line and Waverley train station are down here too.

Moneysaver

A day ticket on the Lothian Regional Transport costs about £1.50. Flat-rate tickets are also available for longer periods.

Local flavour

A true story: an elderly resident was heard to remark 'Edinburgh, aye, a fine city, but 'tis a pity they built the castle so close to the railway station'.

Edinburgh Old Town teemed with intellectual talent in the 18th century. Daniel Defoe, the philosopher David Hume, and the economist Adam Smith all lived there; Robert Burns stayed near Lady Stair's House and was fêted in the town.

The main route through the Old Town is known as the Royal Mile, and a walk along it is a must. (allow time for several detours down 'wynds' and into courts and alleys). Plaques along the way tell about events and residents.

Near the castle end of the Royal Mile, the Outlook Tower gives all-round city views, and has a camera obscura for an alternative view of the city; Gladstone's Land is a 17th-century, six-storey tenement – you can visit the lower floors, which are furnished in period style. Open April to October, it's run by the National Trust for Scotland. Other places open include the Museum of Childhood, the city museum in Huntly House (1570), and John Knox's House, which is one of the oldest Old Town houses. The People's Story in Canongate Tolbooth is about the unsung 'ordinary people' of Edinburgh; Acheson House is the Scottish Craft Centre, with select craft work on display.

The two major landmarks at each end of the

Edinburgh

Royal Mile are Edinburgh Castle and the Palace of Holyroodhouse. The oldest part of the castle is the Chapel of St Margaret, who died here in 1093; the rest of it has been shaped by centuries of sieges and warfare.

Mary Queen of Scots held court at the Palace of Holyroodhouse. She married her second husband Lord Darnley there, and the place where her secretary Rizzio was murdered is marked. It's usually open and has some splendid interiors, but is still a royal residence – closed for three weeks in May, and again in late June/early July.

Greyfriars Kirk below the Royal Mile has witnessed some momentous events in Scottish history, and all sorts of famous Scots are buried in the kirkyard (guided tours in summer). You can see the resplendent George Heriot School from here too. Greyfriars Bobby was a Skye terrier who watched over his master's grave for 14 years, breaking his vigil only for meals at a nearby restaurant. He has his own statue near the kirk.

The City Art Centre has Edinburgh's own art collection; the National Gallery of Scotland has a good collection of pictures by Raphael, Titian, Van Gogh and other notables, including Scottish artists. The Royal Museum of Scotland is equivalent to London's British Museum, V&A, Science Museum and a few others, all compressed and combined into one rather beautiful old glass and cast iron construction on Chambers Street. Across town in Queen Street, you can see the Scottish sections of the Royal Museum, with the National Portrait Gallery in the same building. For 20th-century pictures, head west to Belford Road for the Scottish National Gallery of Modern Art.

Georgian House on Charlotte Square has been restored to look as it would have done in around 1800 (open from April to October, National Trust for Scotland). If you keep going north you'll reach the Royal Botanic Gardens.

Local flavour
The wealthy philanthropist Andrew Carnegie was born in Dunfermline, just across the Firth of Forth from Edinburgh. His humble first home is now a museum.

For year-round entertainment there are the Scottish National Orchestra at Usher Hall, Scottish Chamber Orchestra and others, supplemented by visiting artists; the Playhouse, King's Theatre, Bedlam Theatre and others put on a wide range of productions, and the Filmhouse offers alternatives to the mainstream cinemas.

Moneysaver
You should be able to find an enormous number of low-priced shows during the Edinburgh Festival, and free shows outside in the streets and parks. Unsold tickets for some productions are sold at half price on the day.

ORIENTATION IN EDINBURGH

INFORMATION
TOURIST OFFICE
Waverley Market,
3 Princes Street. ☎ *031-557 1700.*
POST OFFICE
4 Waterloo Place.
PUBLIC LAVATORIES
Canongate (foot of Royal Mile); Castle Terrace car park; The Mound (Princes Street); Princes Street Gardens; Haymarket; Waverley Market (Princes Street).

TRANSPORT
BUSES
Lothian Regional Transport, ☎ *031- 220 4111; or contact the Busline public transport information service,* ☎ *031-225 3858.*

TRAINS
Waverley station, ☎ *031-556 2451.*

ACCOMMODATION
GUESTHOUSES
Dorstan Private Hotel *7 Priestfield Road.* ☎ *031-667 6721. Exceptional quality for its price range; evening meals available.*
Ellesmere House *11 Glengyle Terrace, by the*

Meadows park. ☎ 031-229 4823.

YOUTH HOSTEL
Edinburgh Youth Hostel (Bruntsfield) 7 Bruntsfield Crescent. ☎ 031-447 2994.
Edinburgh Youth Hostel (Eglinton) 18 Eglinton Crescent. ☎ 031-337 1120.

CAMP SITE
Mortonhall Caravan Park 38 Mortonhall Gate. ☎ 031-664 1533.

EATING OUT
The Rose Street area is lively in the evenings, and it's packed with restaurants; the Royal Mile also has places which don't cost the earth.
North Sea Village Restaurant 18 Elm Row, Leith. ☎ 031-556 9476. Tasty Chinese seafood.
Shamiana 14 Brougham Street. ☎ 031-228 2265. North Indian cuisine.

OUTINGS FROM EDINBURGH

LINLITHGOW

Mary Queen of Scots was born at Linlithgow Palace, and it's still impressive even though it was gutted by fire in 1746. On the south side of town, you can take cruises on the Union Canal. A few miles northeast is Blackness Castle, built in the 15th century and still strategically important in the 18th; also in this direction is the House of the Binns, a 17th-century mansion built by General Tam Dalyell (say 'dee-yell'). Open May to September (not Friday). Cairnpapple Hill is south of Linlithgow: here you can see an ancient sanctuary and burial place dating back to around 2000BC. It's set in the Bathgate Hills, and you get huge views from the site. Open all year, except Fridays, from October to March.

NEWTONGRANGE AND PRESTONGRANGE

Mining isn't usually associated with Edinburgh, but it lies in the middle of a coal belt. The Lady Victoria Colliery at Newtongrange is now part of the Scottish Mining Museum – they don't offer underground tours, but you get an extensive guided tour of the surface workings (hard hat provided, and there's a tearoom). The Prestongrange part of the museum is at Prestonpans, east of Edinburgh, with an exhibition in the old canteen, and a colliery power house to tour. There's a picnic site here, with extensive views across the Firth of Forth towards Fife.

NORTH BERWICK AND HADDINGTON

At the seaside resort of North Berwick you can take boat trips out round Bass Rock to look at sea birds, or walk inland up North Berwick Law. Dunbar is another resort, facing out to the North Sea and a little further from the city.

Haddington is a delightful town for strolling about, with numerous interesting old buildings (nearly 300 have been declared of special historic or architectural interest). The gardens of Haddington House are known as St Mary's Pleasance – they've been restored in 17th-century style, and can be visited.

THE BORDER COUNTRY

You won't find craggy mountains in the borders, but the contrast of rounded heather-covered hills and deep, green valleys has its own beauty.

Driving is the easiest way to explore this kind of rural landscape, but bus travel is reasonable in the Borders too. Cyclists can test themselves on the hills or just potter along the river valleys. There are places that hire bicycles in Peebles, an hour from Edinburgh by bus.

Peebles Peebles stands on the green banks of the River Tweed, and it's the sort of town where you always feel close to open country. The tourist information centre is in the rather grand Chambers Institute. There's also a picture gallery (no charge). Don't miss the mosaic war memorial in the courtyard.

The Museum of Ornamental Plasterwork is

just what it says, and you can have a go yourself (they lend you an apron and wellies). An ancient cobbled stair leads down to the banks of the River Tweed, reputed to be one of the best salmon fishing rivers, where townsfolk still have a right to dry their laundry.

There are paths along the river Tweed and a trail in Glentress Forest, on the edge of town. Neidpath Castle stands above the River Tweed a mile west of Peebles. You can see a prison pit inside, and there are good views from the parapets; open Easter to September

Kailzie and Traquair   Kailzie Gardens is less than three miles from Peebles, with a formal walled garden, ornamental ducks and 15 acres of wild garden set among trees. There's a restaurant and a gallery here. Open on some early weekends in the year, then from April to October.

Traquair House is Scotland's oldest inhabited house. William the Lion (1143-1214) held court here, and Mary Queen of Scots visited in 1566. The Bear Gates haven't been opened since Bonnie Prince Charlie left through them in 1745. The grounds offer walks beside the River Tweed and a picnic area; there are also craft workshops and a restaurant. Open at Easter, weekends in May and then from late May to September in the afternoons (morning as well in July and August).

Local flavour

Traquair House has a brewery, which originally made ale for the workforce. Today ale is brewed once more, in a 200-gallon copper first installed in the 18th century. It's on sale by the bottle.

Innerleithen   Innerleithen is a textiles town, but it also became a spa in the 19th century, when the spring was made famous by Sir Walter Scott's novel, *St Ronan's Well*. Five minutes further on is Walkerburn, with the Scottish Museum of Woollen Textiles (free). It's on a mill premises, with a shop.

Selkirk and Bowhill   The Royal Burgh of Selkirk climbs up a hill above the Yarrow valley, with fine views and textile mills below. At the top of town the Selkirk Bannock Shop sells the local speciality – a sweet fruit bread. Halliwells House is the town museum; free guided walks in summer.

Three miles from Selkirk is Bowhill, the Georgian mansion of the Dukes of Buccleuch, open in July and exceptional for its art collection. The huge grounds are open April to late August for walks, pony trekking and mountain biking (telephone 0721 22934).

Moneysaver

Galashiels, Selkirk and other Borders towns have numerous mill shops.

Abbotsford   Abbotsford near Galashiels was transformed by Sir Walter Scott from a farmhouse into a romantic Gothic-style mansion. Open March to October. Bus travellers must alight at the Abbotsford roundabout and walk half a mile along the B6360.

The Abbeys   The abbeys at Jedburgh, Melrose, Kelso and Dryburgh were founded by King David I (1124-53). All of them were repeatedly ransacked by the English during centuries of border warfare.

Melrose Abbey is a beautiful ruin of pink-gold stone in Melrose town. The heart of King Robert the Bruce is buried here. By the abbey, Priorwood Gardens specialises in flowers for drying, and has an orchard with old varieties of apple. Open April to December, closed on Sunday except May to October (National Trust for Scotland, free).

Jedburgh's abbey is the most complete of the Borders abbeys, with delicate window tracery. Dryburgh Abbey, perhaps the most beautiful of the Borders abbeys in its peaceful setting by River Tweed southeast of Melrose, is the burial place of Sir Walter Scott.

Kelso has another of the Borders abbeys, and is also a pretty town with a wide central square. Sales of horses, ponies and rams are held here, and the Border Union Show is a big summer event. On the edge of town is Floors Castle, the vast palace of the Dukes of Roxburghe: open from Easter to late September, not Friday or Saturday except in July and August.

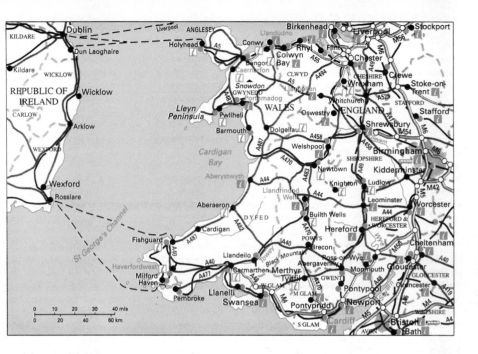

Wales is a place of contrast and variety. Its landscapes range from desolate, remote moorland to lush valleys and rugged coastal cliffs. Its communities include the urban and industrial and the remote rural. Here you will hear a confusing collection of accents, both in English and in Welsh, which is widely spoken in the west and north of the country.

Local flavour

Welsh is believed to be one of Europe's oldest languages. Don't be frightened by the unique 'll' sound which turns up in so many place names. It's pronounced by placing the edge of the tongue against the upper teeth and blowing.

This chapter starts at the capital of Wales, Cardiff, a city which grew around the shipping industry, carrying coal from the Rhondda mines to countries all over the world. It makes a good base for trips to the south and west and most

major Welsh centres are fairly easy to reach from the city.

Haverfordwest is the next stop, a market town which gives access to the beautiful Pembrokeshire coast and the Preseli Hills, then twist and turn with the dramatic western coastline to Aberystwyth, a university town and seaside resort well placed for visits to mid Wales and its barren, windswept mountains. Along the coast is Porthmadog, a cheerful town at the base of the Llyn (Lleyn) Peninsula, where

The emblem of the Welsh Dragon.

you could spend days exploring the coastline and village; Caernarfon, whose castle recalls an era of conflict and conquest; and the unforgettable rugged landscape of Snowdonia National Park.

Llandudno takes you firmly into the traditional seaside world. This is a large, busy beach resort with a funfair atmosphere in summer and plenty of family appeal. From here you can sample some of the legend and history of North Wales: on the wooded island of Anglesey, where druids once practised mysterious religious rites. Llangollen is a focus for international song and dance set in the lovely Vale of Llangollen on the River Dee.

Around Brecon, on the edge of the Brecon Beacons National Park, the wide sweep of mountains, dividing south and mid Wales, takes in desolate moorland, eerie lakes and green, wooded valleys: a perfect illustration of the vast range of experiences offered by this small nation.

The easiest way to see Wales is by car. Any travel by public transport, particularly from south to north Wales, needs a good deal of planning and checking. Buses are the answer when the railway line runs out, and these are usually more frequent during the week (some services peter out altogether on Sundays and bank holidays). There are several different bus operators in Wales. Some areas are covered by private firms such as Silcox or Richard Brothers (in the west) and Crosville (in the north). Then there are the county-run buses, such as Bws Gwynedd or Clwyd, and the buses which come under the umbrella of South Wales Transport.

Most operators have a selection of discount tickets. For instance, you can get unlimited travel for a day or a week on several South Wales routes with the Roverbus tickets: get day tickets

on the bus, weekly tickets from National Welsh, Red and White or South Wales Transport offices or agents. Crosville buses have a day ticket for travel on their services (except service 700), and an economy ticket giving a week's travel between two named points, as well as weekly and monthly rovers.

Moneysaver
Several tourist information centres offer free booking services. Staff will advise you on accommodation and reserve your room for a small deposit, which is taken off the bill at the end of your stay.

If you plan to combine rail and bus travel it's worth looking at the North and Mid Wales Rover, giving unlimited travel on trains within the area bounded by Aberystwyth, Shrewsbury, Crewe and Holyhead, along with travel on the narrow-gauge Ffestiniog Railway Link and on all Crosville (except 7XX) and Bws Gwynedd buses. A Freedom of Wales Rover offers unlimited travel on trains in Wales, plus travel on the Ffestiniog Railway.

Some of the old industrial or passenger rail links have now benefited from their curiosity value, and there are no fewer than 10 narrow-gauge railways in Wales, known collectively as the 'Great Little Trains of Wales'. Wanderer Tickets are available at the following stations: Bala Lake; Brecon Mountain; Ffestiniog; Llanberis Lake; Talyllyn; Vale of Rheidol (Aberystwyth); Welshpool and Llanfair, and Welsh Highland Railway (Porthmadog) or from Great Little Trains of Wales, Pant Station, Merthyr Tydfil, Mid Glamorgan, telephone 0685 4854. Prices depend on the number of days/trips covered.

CARDIFF

Cardiff is a city which has found new life in the past 10 years or so. This is Europe's youngest capital – it gained its status only in 1956 – but until recently it seemed destined to slide into shabbiness and faded grandeur. All that has

changed: elegant Victorian and Edwardian buildings have been spruced up, the docklands which first brought the city wealth have been given a facelift, and new ventures in the arts, in leisure and in shopping facilities have made

Cardiff a cosmopolitan centre, without causing it to lose its unique character.

Reaching Cardiff is fairly easy. There are frequent rail links from London Paddington and the journey takes about two hours. Railair coaches from Heathrow and hourly trains from Gatwick run to Reading, where you can pick up an Intercity service to Cardiff. Intercity services also run from Newcastle and Leeds, via Sheffield, Birmingham and Derby.

Coaches to Cardiff run from London (Victoria); National Express coaches run to the city from most major centres in Britain. Cardiff airport, west of the city, takes summer charter flights from New York and Toronto.

There are good motorway links with the Midlands, Scotland and with southeast England. From London the M4 takes you directly to Cardiff via the Severn Bridge (toll).

Cardiff is the biggest urban centre in Wales, set on the southeastern coast, in the most Anglicised and industrialised part of the nation. It was 'black gold' – coal – which brought Cardiff, and much of the rest of South Wales, into being. While the Rhondda Valley towns north of the city sprouted up around the mines themselves, Cardiff made its money from the docks, built by the Second Marquess of Bute in 1839, and became the world's biggest coal-shipping port. The Butes were a powerful family here, and many of the city's sights are legacies of their reign. New offices and museums are now found in the docklands, where families from all over the world once formed a lively and close community. 'Fun with science' is offered at Techniquest, at the bottom of Bute Street, where hands-on displays are a great hit with children. Across the road is the

Cardiff Castle is largely a Victorian creation.

Welsh Industrial and Maritime Museum, which has working models to explain the dizzying pace of industrial development in the area over two centuries. Open daily except Monday, but open on bank holiday Mondays).

No visitor to Cardiff should miss a tour of Cardiff Castle, which is set right in the middle of the city centre. It was originally a Roman fort, but the present building is mainly the creation of Victorian architect William Burges and the Third Marquess of Bute, who brought their romantic medieval fantasies to life in rooms such as the great banqueting hall, the Chaucer room and the Arab room. The guided tour is well worth the extra cost. Open daily; tours May to September, from 10am.

The National Museum is housed in one of the impressive white civic buildings in Cathays Park. Silver and porcelain displays here date from the Middle Ages, and there is a good art exhibition, featuring Welsh and European artists and including work by Poussin and Renoir. Fees vary for temporary exhibitions.

You could easily spend the best part of a day at St Fagans Welsh Folk Museum on the western

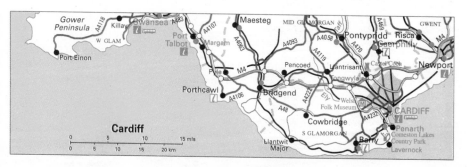

edge of the city. Set in the grounds of Fagans Castle are cottages, workhouses, a woollen mill, 19th-century school and other buildings, brought from all over Wales to illustrate life through the centuries. In the castle are examples of Welsh crafts, costumes and toys.

Local flavour
The National Museum's staff conduct annual guided walks in mid and south Wales. Afternoon walks are about four miles, evening walks about two; bring sturdy shoes and rainwear.

Llandaff Cathedral is easily reached by bus or on foot (about a half-hour walk) from the city centre and is worth visiting for its magnificent Epstein sculpture, *Christ in Majesty*. Alternatively you can walk there through Llandaff Fields, a stretch of parkland reached from Cathedral Road.

Spectacular arrangements of rhododendrons, azaleas and other exotic plants can be seen in season at Cefn Onn Gardens, in Lisvane on the city's northern outskirts. Admission is free and the park is open daily till dusk

Cardiff's main shopping centre is compact and pleasant, but for the real bargains and the real character go to the splendid Victorian indoor market, a crowded hotchpotch of stalls selling anything you care to think of.

Moneysaver
For second-hand bargains visit Jacob's Market, on West Wharf at the bottom of St Mary Street, open on Thursdays and Saturdays.

There's no shortage of entertainment in the city centre: the New Theatre, in Park Place, is the home of the Welsh National Opera (half-price standby seats are available 24 hours before performances). The much younger Sherman, on Senghennydd Road (a five-minute walk from Queen Street) shows Welsh and English language drama; and there are cinemas, galleries and workshops in the Chapter Arts Centre in Canton (buses from the station or Castle Street). St David's Hall hosts the annual Welsh Proms, a series of concerts (tickets from £2.50; book early) and the Cardiff Festival of Music (September to October). Free craft stalls and exhibitions are set up in St David's Hall, where you can also enjoy a coffee in the main lounge.A free gallery shows locally and internationally designed jewellery and textiles at Oriel, in The Friary (off Queen Street).

One of the best areas for reasonable accommodation close to the city centre is Cathedral Road, which runs from Castle Street.

ORIENTATION IN CARDIFF

INFORMATION
TOURIST OFFICE
8-14 Bridge Street. ☎ 0222 227281.
POST OFFICE
The Hayes, Hill Street. ☎ 0222 227363.
PUBLIC LAVATORIES
Hayes Island; St David's Centre; Kingsway; High Street; Bus station; Dumfries Place car park; Mary Ann Street car park; Greyfriars Road.

TRANSPORT
BUSES
National Welsh coaches, 33 West Canal Wharf, ☎ 0222 371331. Cardiff Bus, Wood Street, ☎ 0222 822722.
TRAINS
Central station, ☎ 0222 228000. Local services to Penarth, Barry and the Rhondda Valleys run from Queen Street station.
CAR HIRE
Avis **Rent-a-Car** 4 Saunders Road, Station Approach. ☎ 0222 342111.

Hertz Rent-a-Car 9 Central Square. ☎ 0222 224548.
Crwys Auto Service 59 Crwys Road. ☎ 0222 225789.

ACCOMMODATION
HOTELS AND GUESTHOUSES
Balkan Hotel 144 Newport Road. ☎ 0222 463673. Bed and breakfast from £15.
Clare Court Hotel 46/48 Clare Road, Grangetown. ☎ 0222 344839. Bed and breakfast from £14.
Ferrier's (Alva) Hotel 130/132 Cathedral Road.

☎ *0222 383413. Bed and breakfast from £21.*
***Princes** 10 Princes Street, Roath.* ☎ *0222 491732. Bed and breakfast from £11.*
Y*OUTH* H*OSTEL*
***Cardiff Youth Hostel** Wedal Road, Roath Park.* ☎ *0222 462303.*

EATING OUT
***Campanile Hotel** Caxton Place, Pentwyn.* ☎ *0222 549044. Dinner £7 – £9.*
***Holiday Inn** Mill Lane.* ☎ *0222 399944. Dinner from £13 plus à la carte.*
***Riverside** 44 Tudor Street.* ☎ *0222 372163. Cantonese*

cooking. Dinner from £11 plus à la carte.
***Armless Dragon** 97 Wyeverne Road, Cathays.* ☎ *0222 382357). Dinner from £12.*
***Blas ar Gymru** 48 Crwys Road.* ☎ *0222 382132. Medieval and traditional Welsh food; dinner from £15.*

OUTINGS FROM CARDIFF

CASTELL COCH AND CAERFFILI CASTLE

Castell Coch (Red Castle), was created by the architects of Cardiff Castle. Its fairytale towers peer incongruously over beech woods above the A470 dual carriageway at Tongwynlais, and its rooms are crammed with murals and carvings of medieval romance. Get to Tongwynlais by bus and then walk up the steep hill for about a mile. From Castell Coch, take an hour's trip on the bus on from Tongwynlais to the stark contrast: Caerffili Castle, where one of the (genuinely) medieval towers leans over at an alarming angle. You can get to Caerffili from Cardiff by train or by bus.

Moneysaver
Ask at the Cardiff Bus office about summer open-top bus tours, in and around Cardiff. A family ticket can be good value.

PENARTH

Penarth's genteel seafront and pier are only a few miles west of the city centre and can be reached by bus, or by train. Nineteenth-century Turner House, on Plymouth Road at the top of The Dingle, shows changing exhibitions (free), and you can walk through Alexandra Gardens or Windsor Gardens down to the seaside

esplanade and pier (free). Just beyond Penarth, on Lavernock Road (B4267) is Cosmeston Lakes Country Park (open all year; free) where there are woods, parklands and a lake. In the next-door Medieval Village a reconstructed 14th-century community has an exhibition and craftsmen at work (no charge for the museum; a tour of the village costs £1; children/senior citizens 50p).

SWANSEA

It's an easy trip from Cardiff to Swansea (frequent trains or non stop shuttle coach), and from this busy city with its new marina development you can travel out to see the wild cliffs and open beaches of the Gower coast.

On the way to or from Swansea, spend part of the day at Margam Park near Port Talbot. There is usually children's entertainment on summer afternoons, and the grounds include ornamental gardens and the ruins of a 12th-century abbey. Cardiff Bus run day trips (about £6) to the Gower two or three times each summer; telephone 0792 396521 to check.

Local flavour
Don't be put off by the idea of eating seaweed: that's what laverbread is, and it sells like hot cakes at Swansea market. It's cooked with oatmeal and bacon, looks something like spinach, and tastes great.

HAVERFORDWEST

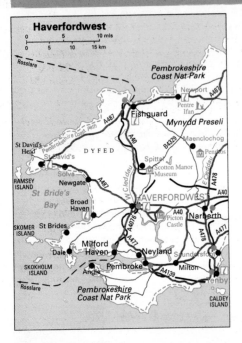

Haverfordwest

This busy market town is a handy base for visits to the county which used to be Pembrokeshire and is now part of Dyfed. The Preseli Hills provided the bluestones of Stonehenge; St David's is Britain's smallest city; and the beautiful Pembrokeshire coast is part of Britain's smallest national park.

From Cardiff, you can reach Haverfordwest on the A40, by rail, or by coach. A few direct trains run there: otherwise, change at Carmarthen, Llanelli or Swansea. Coaches run from Cardiff bus station once daily at 4pm. Be sure to book a seat in advance (about £1 extra).

Haverfordwest is dominated by its medieval castle, one of a line of defences built by the Normans. There's a museum and art gallery there now. Local art is shown in the gallery, and the museum traces the history of the town, which was once a county in its own right.

The main focus of town is High Street, on a hill lined with graceful three-storey shops. At the top is St Mary's Church, where the

graveyard once doubled as a market square (markets are now held in St Thomas's Green, on Saturdays from May to September; and at Riverside market, daily except Sundays).

Beside the River Cleddau, which flows through the town, are the ruins of a supposedly haunted 13th-century priory and more modern attractions too. Buildings on the quay have been converted into interesting shops and restaurants, and more are planned in the new Riverside Quay Shopping Centre.

Some of the attractions within a few miles of Haverfordwest are easy to reach by car but virtually impossible by public transport. The Scolton Manor Museum at Spittal is only five miles north of town on the B4329. A manor house, stable block and exhibition hall tell the story of Pembrokeshire life from two points of view – the labourer's and the gentry's. The museum costs 50p (children free) and the grounds have picnic sites and a nature trail (open Tuesday to Sunday all year). Picton Castle, four miles east of Haverfordwest on the A40, shows a collection of Graham Sutherland paintings and gives tours on Thursday and Saturday afternoons from July to September, and on bank holidays at the end of May and the end of August. Open from April to September (adults £2, children £1).

At Penrhos, near Maenclochog, there's an example of the 'overnight house' (Ty un nos), with its original furniture and remains of outbuildings. Cottages built between sunset and dawn on common land entitled the owner to the freehold and all the land within a stone's throw. The roof had to be on and the chimney smoking by the time the sun came up.

At the Coffee Tavern, a first floor café in High Street, a window seat gives a great view of the shoppers below. Wilton House, in Quay Street, is in an ex-saddlery with sober wood décor: you can buy lunch here for about £3. Two doors down, the Copper Kettle sells snacks and hot meals, and there's a wholemeal restaurant over the road. Food and bar snacks are on sale in the old Bristol Trader Inn on quay, next door to the Granary Restaurant.

For good value bed and breakfast, look round

the St Thomas's Green area, at the top of town. There are quiet places further out from the centre, but they're best reached by car (see *Orientation*, below).

ORIENTATION IN HAVERFORDWEST

INFORMATION
Tourist Office High Street. ☎ 0437 763110/766141.
National Park Information Centre: 40 High Street. ☎ 0437 66141.
Post Office Quay Street. ☎ 0437 763242.
Public Lavatories Castle Lake car park; Riverside market; St Thomas's Green; Museum

TRANSPORT
Buses
Bus and coach station: Bridgend Square. ☎ 0437 763284.
Trains
Train station, Cartlett Road. ☎ 0437 762293.
Car Hire
Dragon Drive near the railway station. ☎ 0437 765357.
Wellhill (Hertz) Merlin's Bridge. ☎ 0437 766748.
Bicycle Hire
Adventure Days Twr-y-Felin Outdoor Centre. ☎ 0437 720391. Mountain bikes about £6 per half day.

ACCOMMODATION
Hotels
Broadhaven Hotel Broad Haven, seven miles west of Haverfordwest. ☎ 0437 781366. From about £18 per person per night.
Pembroke House Hotel Spring Gardens. ☎ 0437 3652 and 5511. From £24 per night.
Youth Hostel
Broad Haven Youth Hostel Broad Haven, Haverfordwest. ☎ 0437 781688.

EATING OUT
Hotel Mariners Mariners Square. ☎ 0437 763353. Dinner from £9 plus à la carte.
Pembroke House Spring Gardens. ☎ 0437 3652 and 5511. Dinner from £9 plus à la carte.

OUTINGS FROM HAVERFORDWEST

Using Haverfordwest as a base, you can find any number of attractive villages and impressive views in Pembrokeshire. Try Newport, with its castle overlooking Market Street and the megalithic Pentre Ifan Cromlech, three miles southeast; or the charming fishing village of Solfach (Solva). The Pembrokeshire Coastal Walk is a bracing way to enjoy views of sea and windswept cliffs. Guided walks are run by the National Park Authority.

Moneysaver
Pick up a free copy of the National Park Authority's *Coast to Coast* newspaper at the tourist information centre, for news of events, craft workshops and a diary of talks and walks.

The picturesque harbour at Tenby.

TENBY AND SAUNDERSFOOT

You'll find the sea, sandy beaches and little medieval streets at Tenby, 10 miles east of Pembroke on the A478 (buses run by Expresswest and South Wales Transport. The trip takes nearly an hour by bus, but it's much cheaper than the train.

If you're going by car, take advantage of the park-and-ride scheme, which buses visitors free from the Salterns car park, near the railway viaduct, to South Parade, in the centre of town.

Most people come to Tenby to sit on the beach, but there are plenty of other attractions. There is no charge for watching potters at work in Tenby Pottery in Upper Frog Street (Monday to Friday and Saturday morning); or you could take a 20-minute boat trip to Caldey Island, 2½ miles out to sea, where monks make scent from the flowers (frequent boat service).

It's only three miles from Tenby to Saundersfoot, a busy little harbour with lots of places to eat and stay. The trip takes 15 minutes on the bus from Tenby; or you can travel direct from Haverfordwest on the Cleddau Mini (three a day).

ST DAVIDS

The Welsh Patron Saint is enshrined in Britain's smallest cathedral city, St David's (frequent buses, 40 to 55 minutes). The cathedral is open daily (no cost, but donations are appreciated), and worth visiting for its carved choir stalls, sloping nave and Irish oak roof. A Bach Festival is held here each spring. Ruins of the Bishop's Palace can be seen across the River Alun.

> **Local flavour**
> The inhabitants of the Gwaun Valley still celebrate New Year on January 13th, having steadfastly refused to acknowledge the introduction of the Julian Calendar in 1752.

From St David's you can take a boat trip in the summer to Ramsey Island, to see bird life, seals and deer. Boats leave from St Justinian's lifeboat station (cost: about £5; £3 to land on the island).

ABERYSTWYTH

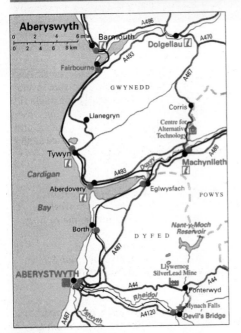

You can expect to find more than the average seaside town at Aberystwyth. This is the home of the first modern Welsh university (student population 3,000), set right in the middle of Cardigan Bay, on the west coast of Wales. For such a centrally placed town, Aber (as it's locally known) can be fairly awkward to reach. There's no direct rail link between Haverfordwest and Aberystwyth, and the very indirect route, via Llanelli and Shrewsbury, demands time, patience and money (a single costs about £41). Richard Bros run four buses a day in the week (not on Sundays, nor on bank holiday Mondays); change at Synod Inn and possibly Cardigan too, depending on the service. The journey takes about four hours; use a Day Rover ticket, about £3.

Down at sea level, Aberystwyth takes on the character of a Victorian seaside resort, with a wide promenade, pebbly beach and pier. There's always some entertainment going on here in summer, much of it free: Punch and Judy shows, brass band concerts, a free children's paddling pool on the promenade; or you can pay for boat rides round the bay or donkey rides on the beach. At the end of the seafront is the original university building, a rambling neo-Gothic landmark. In fact the University College (part of the University of Wales) is now at Penglais Campus, on a hill overlooking Cardigan Bay. It's a steep trek to the campus (buses from the train station) – but here you'll find the National Library of Wales (free), which has a copy of every book published in Britain, as well as the oldest complete Welsh manuscript, *Llyfr Du Caerfyrddin (The Black Book of Camarthen)*. The University Arts Centre has a free gallery.

Theatr y Werin (The People's Theatre) is based at the Arts Centre. Tickets for events start at about £3.25, with concessions, and you can ask here for details of the Annual Aberystwyth Music Festival (end July/beginning August).

Moneysaver

A coffee or a meal at the University Arts Centre is excellent value: you can get a pizza or meat dish for £1.50 to £2.50, and the café has wide windows looking out over the sea.

From 430 ft Constitution Hill, at the northern end of the promenade, there are fine views. You can make the journey to the top by foot, or take the electric train (cost: £1 return; open daily Easter to October). At the top an extra 50p takes you into the camera obscura, where there's a huge, circular view of the town and its surroundings.

The town centre spreads uphill from the seafront and sprawls out along the Rheidol valley. There are plenty of shops, cafés and free exhibitions. The Ceredigion Museum in the tourist information centre on Ffordd y Môr (Terrace Road), tells the story of the district and ancient princedom of Ceredigion. Aberystwyth Yesterday uses furniture, toys and clothes to take a nostalgic look at the town (free; Rhodfa'r Gorllewin/ Western Parade). And a free display on food and farming has been set up on Pier Street by the National Farmers' Union.

Budget shopping is easy to find in Aberystwyth. Look around the side streets for bargain antiques and clothes. Peacocks, next to the tourist information centre, sells budget family clothes, and you can buy anything and everything at 'Cheap Charlie's', Charlie's Stores, on Lon Cambria (Cambrian Place) off Terrace Road.

Cafés and restaurants are dotted all around town. Get a flavour of the Welsh seaside at Ernie's Fish and Chip Restaurant on Portland Road, off Terrace Road, where cod and chips and tea cost about £2.50. The National Milk Bar, on the Corporation Street/Terrace Road corner, is a mid-Wales institution selling inexpensive snacks and meals; and Y Graig is a wholefood licensed restaurant/café serving vegan and other meals for under £4 and advertising local events on its notice boards.

Aberystwyth is full of bed and breakfasts, small hotels and guesthouses. There are several on the seafront, but in term-time these might fill up quickly with students. Try wandering closer to the centre, along Rhodfa'r Gogledd (North Parade) and Queen's Road, for converted family homes offering accommodation.

ORIENTATION IN ABERYSTWYTH

INFORMATION
TOURIST OFFICE
Lisburne House, Ffordd y Mor (Terrace Road).
☎ *0970 612125.*
POST OFFICE
Great Darkgate Street.
PUBLIC LAVATORIES
St Michael's Place; South Marine Terrace (by harbour); Glyndwr Road; near Crown Buildings; Norton Terraced.

TRANSPORT
TRAINS
Train station, Alexandra Street. ☎ *0970 612377.*
BUSES
Crosville Buses: Bus Depot, opposite Gateway supermarket,
☎ *0970 617951. Most buses leave from Western Parade, outside the railway station.*
CAR HIRE
Europcar Cambrian Street.
☎ *0970 611050.*

ACCOMMODATION
Glyn-Garth South Road.
☎ *0970 615050. From £12*

per night.
Llety Gwyn Hotel
Llanbadarn Fawr. ☎ 0970
623965. From £15.50 per
night.
Shangri-La 36 Portland
Street. ☎ 0970 617659.
About £10 per night.
Windsor Private Hotel 41
Queens Road. ☎ 0970

612134. From £12.50 per
night.

EATING OUT
Belle Vue Royal Marine
Terrace. ☎ 0970 617558.
Dinner from £9.50 plus à la
carte.
Cambrian Alexandra Road.
☎ 0970 612446. Dinner

from £8.50 plus à la carte.
Court Royale Eastgate.
☎ 0970 611722. Dinner
from £5.
Groves 42-46 North Parade.
☎ 0970 617623. Dinner
from £8.50.
Queensbridge Promenade,
Victorian Terrace. ☎ 0970
612343/615025. Dinner £9.

OUTINGS FROM ABERYSTWYTH

DEVIL'S BRIDGE

The little steam train which runs from
Aberystwyth to Devil's Bridge is the remnant of
a busy commercial line. These days it carries
tourists from the station on Alexandra Road to
the gorge, where three bridges, each higher than
the last, span the Mynach Falls, and a
treacherous flight of steps, Jacob's Ladder, leads
to the bottom. There are nature trails from all
stops along the line (ask for details at the station)
and the train journey itself, a stiff 700ft climb,
takes about an hour (cost: about £8 – one child
free with each adult, other children £4). A
cheaper option is to get there by bus; Evans
Buses of Tregaron run a school service there for
about £1.60 return.

One of the 'Great Little Trains of Wales' carries
passengers on the Vale of Rheidol Light Railway.

LLYWERNOG SILVER-LEAD MINE

At the Llywernog Silver-Lead Mine, 11 miles
east of Aberystwyth (off the A44), one of the
countless mining ventures of the area has been
re-created. Prospecting started here in the 18th
century, but the bare Cambrian mountains have
attracted miners since prehistoric times for their
impure lead – that impurity being silver. A
Miner's Trail, laid out in the windswept hills
near Ponterwyd, links a museum, working water
wheels and machinery (cost: £2.25;
students/senior citizens £1.75; children 95p.
Open Easter to October). Crosville buses run
there: £2.30 return.

CENTRE FOR ALTERNATIVE TECHNOLOGY

At Panperthog (Crosville bus), is the Centre for
Alternative Technology, which has been
waiting for the world to catch up with its
energy-saving policies for 15 years. Workers on
site live by solar, wind and water-produced
energy, and hands-on displays show how. You'll
need an afternoon at least to make the most of
your visit and explore the 'political maze',
garden and Green house. A wholefood café
serves healthy lunches for little more than £1.
Open daily all year.

Local flavour
Home-cooked wholefood is sold at the
Centre's Quarry Shop in Machynlleth.

232

PORTHMADOG

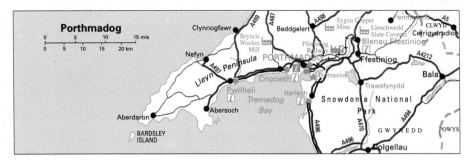

Porthmadog was created by MP William Madocks, who hoped to attract travellers on their way to Ireland, and reclaimed 7,000 acres of land from the sea across Glaslyn Estuary. His plan failed when the tourist traffic was diverted to Anglesey, and it was the slate industry that brought money into the town. Nowadays this is a resort with a real seaside flavour, even though the sea is actually a short bus ride away.

The journey from Aberystwyth to Porthmadog is a tour in itself – especially by train. It's well worth setting aside extra time to explore places on the Cambrian Coast Line: the beach resorts of Fairbourne and Barmouth, and Harlech, with its imposing 13th-century castle. A Cambrian Coast Day Ranger ticket gives unlimited travel between Aberystwyth, Machynlleth and Pwllheli, Monday to Friday only). Adults pay about £8.50, up to four children can accompany an adult for £1.50 each.

TrawsCambria coaches run from Aberystwyth to Porthmadog and Bws Gwynedd has about five daily services making the two-hour journey Monday to Saturday. Cheapest fare is a Crosville £3 rover ticket.

You're not likely to forget how near the sea is to Porthmadog. There are glorious views of mountainous coastline from its streets, and miles of sand dunes and coves to explore at nearby Black Rock Sands and Borth y Gest. (Swimmers should stay away from the southeast end of Black Rock Sands and stay near the shore at Borth y Gest.) The harbour is a focus of town life, and its Maritime Museum traces a history of seafaring and slate-shipping.

There's marvellous inland countryside, too. Perhaps the best way to see it is on the Ffestiniog Railway (see *Outings*, below); but you can also take the 30-minute trip to Pen y Mount on the narrow-gauge steam Welsh Highland Railway (departure point opposite British Rail station).

In Porthmadog itself you pay only 25p (children free) to see and work in the Porthmadog Pottery, easy to spot with its giant mural at the bottom of Snowdon Street. It doesn't matter how disastrous your pot-throwing is – you can take it home with you afterwards! Next door is the Madog Motor Museum, where there's a fast-growing display of vintage cars and motorbikes.

A 10-minute bus ride from town (three a day) takes you straight to the Italian coast. Portmeirion is an Italianate village whose domes, columns and carvings are crowded on to a wooded peninsula off the A487. This is another one-man fantasy made real by architect Sir Clough Williams-Ellis. You can stay at its cottages or hotel (some of the rooms are built into the cliff), but a day's visit is easier on the budget. Portmeirion's flowery pottery is well known and you might pick up some bargains at the seconds shop.

Three and a half miles from Porthmadog off the A487, the working Bryncir Woollen Mill gives a free look at its production methods; its fine tweeds, flannels and tapestries are on sale at the mill shop. Penmachno Woollen Mill is also free (Easter-mid November) and has a riverbank walk and waterfall near by. It's on the B4406, two miles from town.

Portmerion is a little piece of Italy in Wales.

Wyddfa (Snowdon Street), Oriel Rob Piercy is a free art gallery with a smart tea shop selling cakes and snacks. For a seaside flavour, buy your fish and chips (to take out only) at J&Js, near the Porthmadog Pottery. For a fresh seafood meal try the Harbour Restaurant on High Street.

Moneysaver

The Craft Centre, next to the tourist office, has good quality woollens with prices to match, but the end-of-line reductions are worth looking for.

Inexpensive shops and cafés are a speciality of Porthmadog. Owen's Commercial Bakery, opposite Woolworth on High Street, has a small café at the back serving breakfast, snacks and afternoon teas; you can buy Welsh cakes and bara brith in the shop. Around the corner on Heol yr

Accommodation is not hard to find. Try wandering down the streets which lead off High Street and Snowdon Street: you'll find plenty of family houses offering bed and breakfast.

ORIENTATION IN PORTHMADOG

INFORMATION
TOURIST OFFICE
High Street. ☎ 0766 512981.
PUBLIC LAVATORIES
Heol y Parc, near
Information Centre; High
Street, near Midland Bank;
Avenue Road, opposite
Coliseum.

TRANSPORT
BUSES
National Express coaches
and some Gwynedd services
leave from the park in High
Street; others go from the
Australia pub down the road.
TRAINS
British Rail Porthmadog
station, High Street. For

information ☎ Chester 0244
340170 or Llandudno
Junction 0492 585151, or
0766 512340.
Ffestiniog Railway near the
harbour. ☎ 076613402.
Welsh Highland Railway
High Street. ☎ 0766 513402
or 051 6032696.
CAR HIRE
Glyn Williams Glanaber
Garage, Borth-y-Gest.
☎ Borth-y-Gest 2364.

ACCOMMODATION
HOTELS AND GUESTHOUSES
Oakleys The Harbour.
☎ 0766 512482. from £12
per night.
Owen's Hotel High Street.
From £14 per night.
FARMHOUSE
Cefn Uchaf Country Guest

House Garndolbenmaen,
about five miles north.
☎ 076675 239. Vegetarian
meals a speciality, from £12
per night.
CAMP SITES
Black Rock Camping Park
Black Rock Sands, Morfa
Bychan. ☎ 0766 513919
summer; 075881 3223
winter. From £5 per pitch per
night.
Garreg Goch Caravan Park
Black Rock Sands. ☎ 0766
512210. From £3.10 per night.

EATING OUT
Harbour Restaurant High
Street. ☎ 0766 512471.
Dinner from £6.50.
Hotel Portmeirion
Penrhyndeudraeth. ☎ 0766
770457. Dinner from £15.

OUTINGS FROM PORTHMADOG

THE FFESTINIOG RAILWAY

The narrow-gauge Ffestiniog Railway runs

along the Cob, past the estuary, and out to the Snowdonia National Park. It once carried slate from the quarries of Blaenau Ffestiniog; now it takes passengers on the 13-mile trip. It's not cheap, but this is a unique experience: after the rugged beauty of Snowdonia, you can experience the grim legacy of Blaenau Ffestiniog's industrial past as a slate centre.

Local flavour
If you don't mind setting out on the 8.30am train, you can make a considerable saving on the Ffestiniog Railway's Earlybird ticket.

BUDGET FOR A DAY	
Bus fare	·90
Castle	1·50
Beach	Free
Lunch	2·00
Dinner	7·00
Tea	1·40
plus accommodation	£ 12·80

When you get to Blaenau, take a bus or walk to the Llechwedd Slate Caverns or the world's biggest slate mines at Gloddfa Ganol (open Easter to September). Here you can get a real taste of the quarrymen's world, from displays and trips into the dripping, half-lit caverns. Wear warm clothes and sturdy shoes: the mines are cold. If you prefer to travel by bus from Porthmadog to Blaenau, there is a Bws Gwynedd service (£10.40 day return).

BEDDGELERT

Northeast of Porthmadog on the A498 is the little village of Beddgelert (three Crosville bus services daily, 30 minutes). The beauty of the soaring mountain landscape is the main pleasure of this trip, but you might be moved by the Grave of Gelert (the meaning of the village name), commemorating the faithful hound of Prince Llywelyn. Don't shed too many tears: both grave and hound are probably 19th-century inventions designed to pull in tourists.

Near Beddgelert is the 19th-century Sygun Copper Mine (open mid March to October and most winter weekends). On the outskirts of the village is Cae Du, a 300-acre working farm which has a lake, Shetland ponies and a spectacular setting.

CRICCIETH

At Criccieth, a 20-minute bus ride to the west, a 13th-century castle ruin stands high on its own outcrop, looking over the town. Built by Llywelyn the Great, it now has exhibitions on the Welsh castles and Geraldus Cambrensis (Gerald of Wales), a 12th-century monk-cum-travel writer who did the rounds of Wales trying to whip up recruits for the Crusades).

CAERNARFON

The medieval town of Caernarfon has 13th-century walls weaving through the busy streets, and the turrets of the handsome castle can be seen above the trees. A look inside the castle is essential (open all year). It was built by Edward I to mark his conquest of Llywelyn the Last.

On Victoria Dock, the Maritime Museum features a 1937 steam dredger, Seiont II; and on Llanbeblig Road a museum shows finds from the excavated Roman fort of Segontium, which lies behind it (voluntary donation suggested).

LLANBERIS

Moneysaver
There are discounts on the 9am train on the Snowdon Mountain Railway.

Llanberis is an excellent base for visits to the Snowdonia mountain range. The steam-powered Snowdon Mountain Railway starts here on its journey up Snowdon, but it's not cheap: return fare £8.50, £5.50 for children;

single £6, £3 for children. There's a daily service from March to November, but it depends on the weather and number of passengers. If you prefer to walk, take an OS map, compass, good boots, warm clothes, first-aid, food, a torch and a whistle, and tell the National Park Information Centre which route you're taking. The easiest trail is the well-marked Llanberis Path, a five-mile climb. The Llyn Padarn Country Park at Llanberis has a slate museum, and the Llanberis Lake Railway makes 40-minute trips along Lake Padarn shore.

LLANDUDNO

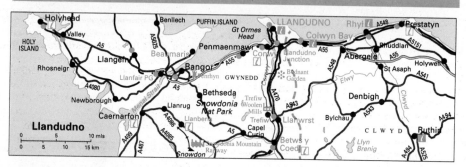

As soon as you reach Llandudno you will know that this is a no-nonsense, bucket-and-spade, fish-and-chips seaside town in the old tradition. Apart from sea and sand, Llandudno has a choice setting, between the bays of Conwy and Colwyn; its two headlands are Little Orme and a huge rocky outcrop, known as Great Orme's Head, which dominates the town.

Since 1902 visitors have travelled up Great Orme on the only cable-hauled tramway in Britain. Fares from Victoria train station are about £2 to the 679ft summit, but cheaper if you alight at the halfway stage and walk the rest of the way. At the top, as well as tremendous views and good hill walks, there's a visitor centre and adventure playground, and remnants of earlier times include a Bronze Age burial chamber (cromlech) near the Half Way Station, and St Tudno's Church, originally built in the 6th century and still in use today. A cable car also runs from the exotic gardens of Happy Valley; or you can get there by coach. Grwp Aberconwy run a range of coach tours in and around Llandudno, starting in Prince Edward Square.

Llandudno is proud of its connections with Charles Dodgson, better known as Lewis Carroll, author of *Alice in Wonderland*.

Dodgson based the character of Alice on Alice Liddell, whose family had a summer home in the town; a White Rabbit statue on the West Shore commemorates the association. In the Rabbit Hole, on Trinity Square, you can walk through animated scenes from the book, with narration provided on a tape recording.

Mostyn and Lloyd Streets are the main shopping areas – long, wide and crowded, with old-fashioned covered walkways. Cafés are not hard to find. At Bathers Bakery, Mostyn Street you can have a filling 'all-day breakfast'; and Tribells fish and chip restaurant on Lloyd Street serves meals at reasonable prices. For Welsh teas or snack lunches for about £2, try the

The White Rabbit Statue is on the West Shore.

pleasant Gegin Gefn (Back Kitchen), behind a gift shop on Mostyn Street.

The busy centre, around and on Lloyd Street, is a useful place to start looking for bed and breakfast places – try Deganwy Avenue, or Chapel Street, where there are several hotels and guesthouses in large, smartly painted Victorian terrace houses.

Moneysaver
If you want to sample Welsh entertainment at no great price, look out for male voice or ladies' choirs performing at the local chapels. Concerts usually cost about £1.50.

ORIENTATION IN LLANDUDNO

INFORMATION
Tourist Office
Chapel Street. ☎ 0492 76413.
Post Office
14 Vaughan Street. ☎ 0492 75571.
Public Lavatories
West Parade; North Parade; George Street; Craig y Don Promenade.

TRANSPORT
Buses
Crosville Wales Ltd, Glan y Mor Road, Llandudno Junction. ☎ 0492 592111/81226.
Trains
Augusta Street. ☎ 0492

85151.
Car Hire
Aberconwy Builder Street West. ☎ 0492 874669.
Godfrey Davis Europcar Mostyn Broadway. ☎ 0492 78608.

ACCOMMODATION
Hotels And Guesthouses
Brannock Private Hotel 36 St Davids Road. ☎ 0492 77483. From £10 .
Brigstock Private Hotel 1 St David's Close. ☎ 0492 76416. From £11.50.
Cranberry House 12 Abbey Road. ☎ 0492 79760. From £10 .
Minion Private Hotel 21-23 Carmen Sylva Road. ☎ 0492 77740. From £9 .
Montclare Hotel North

Parade. ☎ 0492 77061. From £12 per night.
Youth Hostel
Colwyn Bay Youth Hostel Foxhill, Nant-y-Glyn, Colwyn Bay, Clwyd. ☎ 0492 530627.

EATING OUT
Belle Vue 26 North Parade. ☎ 0492 79547. Dinner from £8.
Dunoon Gloddaeth Street. ☎ 0492 860787. Dinner £8.50-£9.50 plus à la carte.
Gwesty Leamore 40 Lloyd Street. ☎ 0492 75552. Dinner £8-£12.
Risboro Clement Avenue. ☎ 0492 76343. Dinner £9-£11.50 plus à la carte.

OUTINGS FROM LLANDUDNO

ANGLESEY

Anglesey has been inhabited since the Bronze Age and is dotted with ancient sites, as well as places of interest from the more recent past. Beaumaris Castle is on the southeastern coast (small extra charge to see medieval entertainment on Sunday evenings in August). In Beaumaris jail (1829) you can visit cells and an enormous wooden treadmill, and take the grim walk to the scaffold door.

Other possibilities in the area include a trip along the toll road to the island's eastern tip to view the sea birds and lighthouse on Ynys Seiriol (Puffin Island). You can also visit the place with the longest name in Britain: Llanfairpwllgwyngyllgogerychwyrndrobwll-llandysilioggogogoch – fortunately known by locals as Llanfair PG; or nearby Plas Newydd, an 18th-century mansion which houses Rex Whistler's biggest wall painting, and relics from the battle of Waterloo.

BODNANT

There are several regular bus services to

Bodnant, two miles to the south on the A470, where 70 acres of gardens are laid out in a stunning setting. Floral displays include azaleas, magnolias, rhododendrons and camellias. It's open from early March to the end of October and is on a regular bus route.

TREFRIW WOOLEN MILLS

Near the market town of Llanrwst, on the B5106 (30 minutes' drive), Trefriw Woollen Mills still produce bedspreads and tweeds using traditional processes and 19th-century manufacturing methods. On summer Sundays, Tuesdays, Wednesdays and Thursdays a handspinner gives demonstrations (admission free). Bws Gwynedd run buses frequently from Mostyn Street to Trefriw all week; it takes about an hour.

BETWS-Y-COED

The A470 follows the River Conwy down to the popular beauty spot of Betws-y-coed, a little town in the wooded Vale of Conwy. Walks in Fairy Glen, just down the road, and nature and forest trails lead from Betws, and the famous Swallow Falls are near by. The bridge at the eastern entrance to town commemorates the Battle of Waterloo, and the Ty Hyll (Ugly House), made of massive boulders, is beside the A5 heading west.

RHYL

Rivalling Llandudno in seaside popularity is the resort of Rhyl, with its funfair and inventive leisure attractions: the Skytower on West Promenade reaches 200ft into the air, or you can travel through ancient Wales at the Knights Caverns on West Parade; or find guaranteed good weather at the Suncentre on East Parade.

Buses to Rhyl run from the Marks and Spencer store on Mostyn Street every 20 minutes and the trip takes an hour.

CONWY

A 15-minute bus journey takes you from Llandudno to Conwy, whose massive castle was built out of the rock on the estuary. Three-quarters of a mile of well-preserved town walls extend from the castle gates, with no fewer than 22 towers. Canoe trips round the Conwy Estuary are organised by Kevin Coleman (book in advance: telephone 0492 596457). You need casual clothes, soft-soled shoes and picnic lunch, and you must be able to swim; Mr Coleman supplies the rest (cost: from £10 per person per half day).

LLANGOLLEN

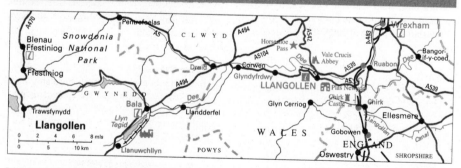

Llangollen is not what you might expect from a centre for international culture. Nevertheless, this small, pretty town on the River Dee plays host once a year to dancers, singers and

238

instrumentalists from all over the world for the International Musical Eisteddfod, a combination of festival, competition and fair. If you plan to be there for the spectacle, in the first week of July, you'll need to book well ahead; but it's worth braving the crowds for the colour and the bustle and, above all, the excellent music (for the Eisteddfod Headquarters see *Orientation*, below).

Despite its international links, Llangollen is not the easiest place to reach. There's no British rail link, so to get there from Llandudno you need to take the train to Chester, where you change for Ruabon to Llangollen, five miles away.

The Pont Cysyllte aquaduct on the Llangollen Canal carries narrowboats across the valley.

Llangollen's bridge is a handsome arched structure dating back to the 14th century. Beyond it is the terminus of the Llangollen steam railway runs three miles to Dee, where you can walk to Horse Shoe Falls, or along the canal back to town. Trips to Berwyn cost about £2m return; to Deeside Halt (22 minutes), about £3.

Parallel to the River Dee is Llangollen Canal, where you can take horse-drawn barge trips; boats leave about every half hour between 11am and 5pm in summer, and the trips take 45 minutes. On the Wharf there is a Canal Exhibition.

Don't miss seeing Plas Newydd, the elegant black-and-white half-timbered house which was the home of two 18th-century celebrities, the Ladies of Llangollen Lady Eleanor Butler and Miss Sarah Ponsonby. The Ladies and their maid are buried in St Collen's Church, by the river bank, worth a visit for its impressive carved roof.

For less than £1 you can watch weavers working on hand or machine looms and see a Victorian classroom at the Woollen Mill near the river.

open daily from the end of March to the end of October; rest of year, poen Monday to Saturday and Sunday afternoons. Buses run to Valle Crucis on Tuesdays and Fridays; some on school days only. High above Llangollen, though accessible by a steep climb from Wharf Hill, is dramatic Castell Dinas Bre, on the site of an Iron Age hill fort.

Other places to visit include the European Centre for Traditional and Regional Cultures (ECTARC), on Castle Street, and its study and administrative centre around the corner on Parade Street, both of which have free exhibitions; and the Llangollen Motor Museum, at Pentrefelin, on the river towards Horse Shoe Pass. It's open daily Easter-October, Monday to Friday in winter.

Celtic Woollens on Castle Street sell love spoons as well as good quality Welsh wool products. Do not miss the shop called YsiopfachgardiauwrthybontdrosyrafonDyfrd − wyynLlangollen, whose address is in the title: the little card shop by the bridge over the River Dee in Llangollen.

> **Local flavour**
> Brethyn Cartref, a fine Welsh tweed, is still used for shawls, scarves and other clothes, and is on sale in several shops.

> **Local flavour**
> Bara brith is a widely available Welsh speciality, but the recipe varies according to preference. Some add a hint of spice; some use treacle; some let the mixture soak overnight in tea.

There are two evocative medieval ruins near the town. Two miles away are the remains of the 13th-century Cistercian abbey Valle Crucis,

Sample a Welsh afternoon tea at the Cottage Tea Rooms, Castle Street, where you can also have a three-course lunch for around £6. At the Bensons hotel/pub on Bridge Street a meal of steak, chips and peas costs less than £5, and there's a choice of inexpensive snacks.

Places to stay are easy to find, both in the centre and further afield.

ORIENTATION IN LLANGOLLEN

INFORMATION
Tourist Office
Town Hall, Castle Street.
☎ 0978 860828.
International Eisteddfod Headquarters: Berwyn Street 0978 860236.
Public Lavatories
Heol y Farchnad (Market Street) car park.

TRANSPORT
Buses
Most buses stop opposite car park on Heol y Farchnad

(Market Street).
Trains
Llangollen railway, ☎ 0978 860979.
Bicycle Hire
Llangollen Wharf. ☎ 0978 860702. Prices start at £8 a day; tandem £12 a day.

ACCOMMODATION
Hotels And Guesthouses
Abbey Grange Hotel Abbey Road. ☎ 0978 860753. From £14 per night.
Britannia Inn Horse Shoe Pass. ☎ 0978 860144. From £16 per night.
Rhydonnen Ucha Rhewl,

beyond Glyndyfrdwy. ☎ 0978 860153. From £12.50.
Farmhouses
Pen Lan Farm. ☎ 0978 860745. From £9.50 .
Youth Hostel
Tyndwr Hall Tyndwr Road. ☎ 0978 860330.
Camp Site
Ty-Ucha Farm Maesmawr Road, one mile east of Llangollen. ☎ 0978 860677.

EATING OUT
Ty'n y Wern Shrewsbury Road, one mile east on A5. ☎ 0978 860252. Dinner for under £10.

OUTINGS FROM LLANGOLLEN

CHIRK CASTLE

Chirk Castle, lived in by the Myddleton family since the 1590s, shows the changing styles of 400 years. This very stately home sits in the little village of Chirk, near the English border on the A5. Look out for the magnificent wrought-iron gates; open afternoons April to September, Tuesday to Friday and Sunday; October to early November on weekends. Bryn Melyn and Bws Clwyd buses have frequent services making the 20-minute trip in the week.

BALA

Bala, in the heart of Welsh-speaking Wales is surrounded by mountains and set on the tip of Llyn Tegid (Bala Lake). Bala was once a Methodist centre but now attracts worshippers of watersports, who come to canoe, fish and sail on the longest natural stretch of water in Wales.

The Bala Lake Railway travels along the shore to Llanuwchllyn on the old narrow-gauge track (return fare about £3.50; family tickets available. Bws Gwynedd travels there seven times a day Monday to Saturday and twice on Sunday in the high season.

Local flavour
The Gwyniad, a white member of the salmon family, is only found in the waters of Llyn Tegid.

WREXHAM

Wrexham's famous landmark is the 136ft tower of the 15th-century St Giles' Church, the burial place of Elihu Yale, who founded Yale University. Erddig, a 17th-century mansion south of Wrexham, re-creates the life of the past 200 years with original furniture and utensils, a museum, smithy and bakehouse. Open daily except Thursday and

Friday April to June and September to early October; daily except Friday from July to the end August. Wright's buses run from Market Street to Wrexham Monday to Saturday; Crosville run seven buses each Sunday. The trip takes under an hour.

BRECON

BUDGET FOR A DAY	
Cathedral	Free
Brecknock Museum	Free
Barracks	·50
Canal trip	2·50
Brecon Mountain Railway	3·00
Lunch	2·00
Dinner	8·00
plus accommodation	£16·00

In summer Brecon is packed to the brim with hikers, who use it as a base for exploring the dramatic scenery of the Brecon Beacons National Park. Its rural setting, its narrow streets and old buildings and its modern attractions and facilities all contribute to Brecon's down-to-earth charm.

Local flavour
Lovespoons were traditional Welsh betrothal gifts from the 17th to the 19th centuries, and became elaborate works of art, using symbols such as padlocks and hearts in the designs.

Travelling around the 519-square-mile national park, is easiest by car. If you do use public transport, be prepared: there's no British Rail link, and bus information is hard to find. The travel agency on the central square might be able to provide timetables – but virtually the only way to find out the fares is by asking the drivers. Most buses run Monday to Friday and leave from the Bulwark, opposite St Mary's Church.

Brecon's homely cathedral, the Priory of St John the Evangelist, has stood on its hill above the River Honddu for about 700 years, and is well worth a browse.

In the centre of town, you can sample the crafts and history of the area for no charge at the Brecknock Museum in the Old County Hall, Glamorgan Street. The collection of love spoons is the highlight here, each one beautifully carved out of a single piece of wood.

Walk down the Watton, a street lined with pubs and guesthouses, to the Barracks with its impressive crenellated tower. In a house next door is the South Wales Borderers Museum (admission 50p), packed with memorabilia of the famous regiment.

The vintage Brecon Mountain Railway is open daily end May to end September, plus Easter weekend and May Day weekend, and for Santa Specials in December. It is well signposted and travels into the national park, with stops for picnics or walks along the Taf Fechan Reservoir. There's also a museum and workshop showing how the locomotives are repaired (The fare is about £3 return and includes admission to locomotive workshop).

If you're in Brecon on a Tuesday or Friday, take advantage of the busy market. The Brecon Crafts Fair is set up on High Street on the third Saturday of the month; and the permanent Corporation Market has clothes, fruit and a saddlery in its stone hall.

The Watton is lined with small hotels and guesthouses such as the family-run Grange, and is convenient for the centre.

ORIENTATION IN BRECON

INFORMATION

TOURIST OFFICE
Cattle Market car park. ☎ 0874 2485/5692.
National Park Information Centre: Watton Mount, ☎ 0874 4437.
Brecon Beacons Mountain Centre, near Libanus. ☎ 0874 3366.
POST OFFICE
St Mary Street.
PUBLIC LAVATORIES
Castle Street; off Struet; Lion Yard; off Watergate; near Usk Boathouse.

TRANSPORT

BUSES
Catch buses from The Bulwark, opposite St Mary's Church. For information on National Welsh and Silverline buses contact the British Rail Travel Agency, The Travel Centre, 99 The Street, ☎ 0874 4948/5054.
CAR HIRE
County Garage The Watton, Brecon. ☎ 0874 2266.
David Taylor Brecon Castles Service Station, Esso Garage, Llansaes. ☎ 0874 3905.
BICYCLE HIRE
Talybont-on-Usk Venture Centre ☎ 087487 458.
Cambrian Cruisers Marina Pencelli. ☎ 087486 315.
PONY TREKKING
Upper Cantref Pony Trekking Centre Llanfrynach. ☎ 087486 223.
BOAT HIRE
Royal Oak Inn Pencelli. ☎ in advance: 087486 621.
Water Folk Craft Ltd (canal trips) ☎ 087486 382.

ACCOMMODATION

HOTELS AND GUESTHOUSES
Beacons Guest House 16 Bridge Street. ☎ 0874 3339. From £11.
The Coach Orchard Street, Llanfaes. ☎ 0874 3803. From £16 per night.
The Grange The Watton. ☎ 0874 4038.

EATING OUT

Beacons Guest House 16 Bridge Street. ☎ 0874 3339. Dinner £5-£8.
Castle of Brecon Castle Square. ☎ 0874 4611. Dinner from £9.50.
Wellington The Bulwark. ☎ 0874 5225. Dinner £7.50-£10.50 plus à la carte.
Griffin Inn Llyswen, along the A470 to the northeast. ☎ 0874 85241. Dinner from £12.

OUTINGS FROM BRECON

THE BRECON BEACONS NATIONAL PARK

The Brecon Beacons National Park stretches from the border with England to the county of Dyfed in the west. It takes in a radically varying landscape: from the soft outlines of the Black Mountains in the east to the confusingly named Black Mountain, remote and empty, in the west. There are popular long-distance routes and countless walks to take, but it is vital, when venturing into the hills, to be properly prepared. That means being able to use a compass and map; taking waterproofs and extra warm clothes; a whistle, first-aid kit and food and hot drink. Good shoes are essential – and *never* trust fine weather; mountain conditions change with alarming speed.

The Brecon Beacons National Park Mountain Centre is west of Libanus off the A470, 1,100ft up, with panoramic views and generally safe walking, as well as all the information you need, a small exhibition and café. The centre is free but parking costs 50p.

CARREG CENNEN CASTLE

Towering over the beautiful Cennen Valley,

about 35 miles west of Brecon, this 13th-century fortress was eventually reduced to ruins by a few hundred men, who knocked it down in the mid 15th-century to prevent its use as a shelter for bandits. A prehistoric cave can be reached through a long cliff tunnel in the castle ruins (open daily all year).

Local flavour
Carreg Cennen's ancient cave is said to harbour a sleeping Welsh army, waiting for its call to rid the nation of the Saxons.

Llanthony Priory's evocative remains stand in a remote valley on the edge of the Brecon Beacons.

LLANTHONY PRIORY

Llanthony Priory, in the Black Mountains about 30 miles from Brecon, is worth a visit for those who have a car. Built in the 12th century on the site of a 6th-century hermitage, the priory has been home to a colonel and a poet, as well as the Augustinian priors; the chief attraction of its ruins, which now incorporate the tiny Abbey Hotel bar, is their setting in the glorious Ewyas Valley.

THE TAWE VALLEY

Halfway between Brecon and Swansea, on the A4067, the Dan-yr-Ogof show caves present a fairy grotto of stalagmites and stalactites in weird and wonderful formations. There's also a caving museum, and, in the nearby Dinosaur Park, you can see full-size models of prehistoric animals. Bring warm clothes for the cave tours, which are chilly even on fine days. Admission is about £3.50; open April to the end of October). Silver Line buses run three times a day (except Sunday) to Dan-yr-Ogof. The caves are near Penscynor Wildlife Park, which is worth seeing as part of the same trip, as are the Aberdulais Falls (National Trust).

M

Y